EARLY INTERVENTION FOR READING DIFFICULTIES

Early Intervention for Reading Difficulties

The Interactive Strategies Approach

SECOND EDITION

Donna M. Scanlon
Kimberly L. Anderson
Joan M. Sweeney

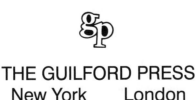

THE GUILFORD PRESS
New York   London

Library of Congress Cataloging-in-Publication Data

Names: Scanlon, Donna M., author. | Anderson, Kimberly L., author. | Sweeney,
   Joan M., author.
Title: Early intervention for reading difficulties : the interactive
   strategies approach / Donna M. Scanlon, Kimberly L. Anderson, Joan M.
   Sweeney.
Description: New York : Guilford Press, [2017] | Includes bibliographical
   references and index.
Identifiers: LCCN 2016040934| ISBN 9781462528097 (pbk. : alk. paper) | ISBN
   9781462528103 (hardcover : alk. paper)
Subjects: LCSH: Reading--Remedial teaching.
Classification: LCC LB1050.5 .S228 2017 | DDC 372.43--dc23
LC record available at *https://lccn.loc.gov/2016040934*

About the Authors

Donna M. Scanlon, PhD, is Professor in the Department of Literacy Teaching and Learning at the University at Albany, State University of New York. Dr. Scanlon has spent most of her career studying children's reading difficulties. Her studies have focused on the relationships between instructional characteristics and success in learning to read and on developing and evaluating approaches to preventing and remediating reading difficulties. Findings from studies that she and her colleagues conducted contributed to the emergence of response to intervention as a process for preventing reading difficulties and avoiding inappropriate and inaccurate learning disability classifications. Most recently, Dr. Scanlon's work has focused on the development of teacher knowledge and teaching skill among both preservice and inservice teachers for the purpose of helping teachers to prevent reading difficulties in young children and remediate reading difficulties among older children.

Kimberly L. Anderson, PhD, is Assistant Professor in the Department of Literacy Studies, English Education, and History Education at East Carolina University in Greenville, North Carolina, where she teaches K–2 literacy methods courses. Her current research focuses on improving small-group, supported literacy instruction in the kindergarten classroom and the relationships among teacher knowledge, teacher practice, and student outcomes with regard to the foundations of reading development. Dr. Anderson worked for several years as a research associate at the Child Research and Study Center, University at Albany, and has contributed to the research on the interactive strategies approach (ISA) by serving as an intervention teacher in an early study; by providing professional development for teachers learning to implement the ISA in the early primary grades in both classroom and intervention settings; and by collaborating with preservice educators from institutions across New York State on enhancing preservice teacher knowledge related to early literacy development and instruction.

Joan M. Sweeney, MSEd, is a Reading/Literacy Specialist in the North Colonie Central School District in Latham, New York. Previously, she was a research associate in the Child Research and Study Center, University at Albany, where she provided intervention for struggling readers, supervised intervention teachers, and coached classroom teachers utilizing the ISA to support children's literacy development.

Preface

This second edition of *Early Intervention for Reading Difficulties* is intended to help teachers develop and refine their knowledge and skills related to early literacy development so as to enable them to effectively teach beginning and struggling readers. Like the first edition, this edition describes the interactive strategies approach (ISA; Vellutino & Scanlon, 2002), an instructional approach developed and tested in a series of large-scale studies that investigated ways to prevent and remediate early reading difficulties. These studies revealed that teachers utilizing the ISA in classroom, small-group, and/or one-to-one settings were able to substantially reduce the number of children who demonstrated early reading difficulties. These studies also contributed to the body of research that ultimately became the rationale for the response-to-intervention (RTI) approach to preventing reading difficulties and determining whether a child should be deemed eligible for special education services.

Given that it has been several years since the last of the studies focused at the primary level were completed, one might wonder why we elected to develop a second edition of the book. When Craig Thomas, Senior Editor at The Guilford Press, originally suggested a second edition, we were reluctant to agree. However, upon further consideration, we identified four major reasons for writing a second edition, which we list below, along with a description of what is new in this edition.

First, with the emergence of the Common Core State Standards (CCSS; National Governors Association Center for Best Practices & Council of Chief State

School Officers [NGA & CCSSO], 2010), which, at least initially, were widely adopted, it seemed important to illustrate the ways in which the instruction based on the ISA aligns with the Standards. To that end, throughout the text, we offer connections to the CCSS and, on occasion, offer our views on the appropriateness of some aspects of the Standards.

Second, over the years, we have had multiple inquiries from teachers and schools about the extent to which use of the ISA was appropriate for use with children who were learning English as an additional language. While the studies that demonstrated the efficacy of the ISA did not include many children who were first learning to speak English, we have subsequently provided ISA professional development for teachers in schools that serve large numbers of English learners (ELs), and they reported very positive outcomes. Work with these schools led us to peruse the research literature on early literacy learning among ELs so as to provide guidance to help enhance teachers' ability to implement the ISA in a way that was sensitive to the unique characteristics of children who were simultaneously learning spoken English. In the second edition, we include the guidance that we developed in this context. While we do not claim expertise with regard to the literacy and language development of ELs, the early feedback we have had on this guidance has been positive.

The third rationale for a second edition has to do with the teacher educators, teacher leaders, teachers, and preservice teachers who have used the book and provided feedback. While people were generally positive about the content and presentation of the material in the first edition, many offered useful suggestions for improvement. A number of the suggestions called for more examples of explicit instructional language, such as the sample instructional scripts that were included in the first edition. Several have been added. We also had multiple inquiries related to the order in which certain phonological and alphabetic skills should be taught. This led to the development and inclusion of a decision tree to inform decision making related to which alphabetic skills children were ready to learn. It also led to the rearrangement of sections of Part II, "Learning the Alphabetic Code." In addition, although automaticity with word identification and other foundational skills and the role of fluent reading in enabling comprehension were addressed in the first edition, we received requests for a more specific focus on fluency, so we have added a new chapter on this topic.

Finally, developing a second edition gave us the opportunity to update the text with regard to the research foundations upon which we build. Much has been learned about early literacy development and literacy learning difficulties in the years since the first edition was originally submitted for publication, and we have updated the research reviewed in many of the chapters throughout the book accordingly. In addition, the publication of the second edition has provided the opportunity for purchasers of the book to access numerous downloadable resources that can be used to support instruction based on the approach to instruction described.

Structure of the Book

Like the first edition, the second edition is largely structured around a set of instructional goals for early literacy learners, particularly students who struggle with literacy acquisition. In Part I, "A Comprehensive Approach to Early Intervention," Chapter 1 describes the ISA in general terms and gives an overview of the studies that demonstrate its effectiveness in preventing early reading difficulties. It discusses the ways in which the ISA differs from other approaches to early literacy instruction and how the ISA might be implemented in an RTI context. Finally, the chapter explicates the need for comprehensive literacy instruction, briefly notes the factors that place children at risk for literacy learning difficulties, and lists instructional goals around which the ISA is organized.

Chapter 2 discusses how both the instructional goals and the general instructional premises of the ISA may be incorporated into language arts instruction at the classroom level. A major theme of this chapter is that instruction should be responsive to the broad spectrum of students in a typical classroom. To this end, we suggest that language arts instruction include a combination of whole-class, small-group, and one-to-one instruction. Whereas small, ability-based groupings are at the heart of responsive instruction at the classroom level, we argue that a diversity of learners must be considered in all aspects of language arts instruction.

Chapter 3 addresses motivation, the first of the ISA's instructional goals. In our work with teachers relative to the ISA, we have always identified motivation to read and write as the first and most important goal of early literacy instruction, particularly for children who begin their schooling with comparatively limited early literacy skills. We discuss the need to be attentive to motivational factors that impact reading development because these factors have a powerful influence on success (or lack thereof). Attention to motivational issues, particularly the development of intrinsic motivation and a sense of competence relative to literacy, should pervade interactions with early literacy learners.

Parts II through IV are also organized around instructional goals to encourage teachers to view instruction in a goal-oriented way. Chapters in these parts feature checklists of goals and subgoals, skills, strategies, and attitudes or approaches to literacy learning with which teachers can track the performance of their students and plan instruction. The use of the checklists (which we call *snapshots*) is based on the premise that virtually every instructional interaction gives teachers the opportunity to evaluate and document children's learning and, thereby, to guide their planning of future instruction.

Part II, "Learning the Alphabetic Code," focuses on the development of alphabetic knowledge and the understanding of how printed language relates to spoken language. Chapters 4 through 11 detail instruction related to the development of print conventions, letter-name knowledge, letter-sound knowledge, skill with the alphabetic code (both early and later phases of development), skill with using phonograms to puzzle through words in word families that feature those phonograms, and knowledge of morphology and how to approach the decoding of multisyllabic words. The development of accuracy and automaticity with these foundational skills allows the developing reader to effectively identify (read) unfamiliar printed words.

Part III, "Word Learning," focuses on the development of sight vocabulary (i.e., words that can be identified automatically) through explicit teaching of high-frequency words and through the application of word-learning strategies that enable the reader to effectively identify unfamiliar words and, ultimately, to learn them to the point where they become part of the reader's sight vocabulary. We emphasize teaching children to use both the letters in the unknown words and the semantic and syntactic context in which words occur in the process of word solving. In Chapter 12, extensive discussion is devoted to providing explicit instruction in the use of a specific set of word identification strategies to facilitate word solving in context that, in turn, leads to word learning. We stress helping children to become independent word solvers so that their reading skills improve each time they read to the point where they will ultimately be able to devote most or all of their cognitive resources to understanding the meaning of the text rather than to the process of word solving. Chapter 13 discusses ways to build skill with high-frequency words.

Part IV, "Meaning Construction," focuses on the purpose of reading: meaning making or making sense of what is read. Comprehension requires the ability to devote most of one's cognitive resources to meaning construction; we have included a chapter on fluency (Chapter 14) in this section, since being able to read fluently frees up the cognitive resources needed for comprehension. In addition, comprehension also depends on the reader's language skills and general (background) knowledge, both of which are major topics in this part. Chapter 15 describes instruction that supports the development of language skills, especially knowledge of word meanings. Chapter 16 discusses methods of fostering the development of knowledge and active engagement with the meaning of text.

Last, Part V, "Integration of the Goals," changes the lens from a focus on the individual goals of instruction to how these goals can "hang together." Chapter 17 addresses how the goals might be addressed in the context of small-group and one-to-one instruction within and beyond the classroom. We emphasize the need to provide more intensive instruction for children who experience the greatest difficulties and encourage teachers to coordinate instruction across instructional settings so that children who receive instruction beyond the classroom are not being asked to learn more than their classroom peers. We detail the lesson structure used in the ISA and the thinking, planning, instruction, record keeping, and reflection components of small-group and one-to-one lessons. This chapter includes sample lessons and lesson plan structures for small-group and one-to-one instruction.

In the final chapter, Chapter 18, we revisit the content and conclude the book. Especially important is the model presented in Figure 18.1 on page 416, which represents our vision of the complexity of the reading process and the multiple elements to which teachers of early literacy learners must attend.

Throughout the text, we also draw readers' attention to the book's companion website (*www.guilford.com/scanlon-materials*), which provides access to various reproducible forms included in the text, as well as instructional resources, which are discussed but not presented in the text.

Acknowledgments

This text has evolved over the course of nearly 30 years of research focused on preventing reading difficulties among young children. Major work on the text occurred in the context of research supported by grants from the National Institute of Child Health and Human Development (Grant No. R01 HD42350) and the Institute of Education Sciences at the United States Department of Education (Grant No. R305W060024). The opinions expressed in this book do not necessarily represent those of the funding agencies

The number of people who should be recognized for their contributions to the research and thinking reflected in this text is immense. We are especially indebted to the children and teachers who participated in the research and allowed us to study their learning and development, and to the school administrators and administrative support staff who facilitated our work.

Our thanks also go to our colleagues and friends who sharpened our thinking about early literacy development and helped us to figure out how to share our thinking with preservice and inservice teachers. The following people played particularly prominent roles: Frank Vellutino, Lynn Gelzheiser, Laura Hallgren-Flynn, Peter Johnston, and Virginia Goatley. We also wish to thank Peggy Connors, Andrea Daley, Deb Rutnik, Danielle Snyder, and Laura Jackson for serving as "model" ISA teachers. Several of the descriptions of instructional interactions are derived from videos of their teaching.

With respect to the conduct of the research, we wish to thank Diane Fanuele for so ably managing the copious amounts of data the studies generated. Finally, we express our sincere gratitude to Sheila Small, a longtime (now retired) research coordinator at the Child Research and Study Center at the University at Albany. Her dedication to ensuring high-quality and timely data collection, and her incredible ability to build and maintain strong relationships with participating schools, contributed immeasurably to the research on early literacy development, which is the foundation for the instructional practices described in this book.

Special thanks are also due to Molly Jaffe Douglas and Melissa Anderson, who contributed most of the artwork—both in the book and in the resources provided on the book's website.

DONNA M. SCANLON
KIMBERLY L. ANDERSON
JOAN M. SWEENEY

Contents

PART I

A Comprehensive Approach to Early Intervention

CHAPTER 1

The Interactive Strategies Approach

Children vary considerably in the ease with which they learn to read. Some learn with fairly little instructional guidance, whereas others find it to be a nearly impossible undertaking given the instruction typically offered in schools. A substantial body of research has accumulated in recent years that indicates that most early reading difficulties can be prevented through the implementation of appropriately targeted and intensified instructional interventions (e.g., Brown, Denton, Kelly, Outhred, & McNaught, 1999; Center, Wheldall, Freeman, Outhred, & McNaught, 1995; Coyne et al., 2013; Mathes et al., 2005; Gomez-Bellenge, Rogers, & Fullerton, 2003; O'Connor, 2000; O'Connor, Harty, & Fulmer, 2005; Scanlon, Vellutino, Small, Fanuele, & Sweeney, 2005; Scanlon, Gelzheiser, Vellutino, Schatschneider, & Sweeney, 2008; Torgesen et al., 2001; Vaughn, Linan-Thompson, & Hickman, 2003; Vellutino et al., 1996; Wanzek & Vaughn, 2008). Recently, the types, intensity, and responsiveness of interventions have drawn researchers' attention as efforts are made to optimize efforts to reduce the incidence of early reading difficulties. This more recent research suggests that, especially for the children who experience the greatest difficulties learning to read, responsive instruction is critical (Coyne et al., 2013; Simmons, 2015).

This book describes one approach to early literacy instruction and intervention—the interactive strategies approach (ISA; Vellutino & Scanlon, 2002)—which was developed and tested over the course of three major longitudinal studies that focused on reducing the number of children who experienced serious

3

reading difficulties in the early primary grades. These studies demonstrated that instruction based on the ISA has a positive impact on student achievement when implemented by classroom teachers and when implemented in small-group and one-to-one intervention settings beyond the classroom. Before describing those studies, we provide a brief introduction to the ISA.

Research-Based Instruction

At a time when schools are called upon to implement research-based instructional practices, it is important to consider the distinction between "research-based" approaches and "research-tested" approaches. Many instructional approaches that are identified as research-based are simply that—based on research. The *research-based* label can be attached to a product or program if the developers have simply familiarized themselves with the research and then based their program on what was learned in that research. The What Works Clearinghouse (WWC), which is sponsored by the Institute of Education Sciences at the U.S. Department of Education (*ies.ed.gov/ncee/wwc*), reviews the scientific evidence on education programs, including beginning reading programs, to evaluate their effectiveness and serves as an unbiased source of information relative to research-tested educational products. Although there are many programs and approaches that have not been evaluated by the WWC (including the ISA), this website offers a valuable resource for schools as they contemplate investments in instructional materials and programs. In addition, for educators who want to do their own investigation of the research support for particular instructional programs or approaches, Duke and Martin (2011) provide useful guidance on interpreting research.

Characteristics of the ISA

The ISA is an *approach* to early literacy instruction, not a program. It is not tied to particular instructional materials, nor does it provide highly scripted instructional interactions. Rather, the ISA offers a way to conceptualize early literacy development and to support children as they learn to read and write. We view teachers as professionals who use their knowledge of their students' skills and abilities, in combination with knowledge of their curricula and the process of literacy development more generally, to plan and deliver effective literacy instruction. Although we do make some suggestions for instructional materials that are illustrative of the types of materials we encourage teachers to use, we also offer ideas for how teachers might evaluate and utilize the materials they have to more effectively meet the needs of their students—particularly those who find it challenging to learn to read. Our primary goal in this book is to help teachers more thoroughly understand early literacy development and to effectively respond to, plan for, and teach the children who find reading acquisition challenging.

The ISA places particular emphasis on meeting the needs of children who struggle at the early stages of learning to read through careful analysis of their literacy skills and provision of instruction that is responsive to their current capabilities. In order to provide such responsive instruction, teachers need to become highly knowledgeable about early literacy, how it develops, and how to respond to literacy learning difficulties. Therefore, the development of teacher knowledge related to early literacy development is a major focus of the ISA and thus a major focus of this book.

The name of the approach conveys the importance placed on helping children become strategic in their reading and writing endeavors. From our perspective, the goal of instruction should be to teach foundational skills and strategies that children will learn to use independently, flexibly, and interactively while reading and writing. Through this active and thoughtful engagement, children will grow as readers and writers. An important goal of instruction is to help children develop a *self-teaching mechanism* (Share, 1995, 2008) that will enable them to learn more about written language through engagement in the processes of reading and writing. To facilitate self-teaching, instruction should provide children with guided practice in reading and writing in contexts that are motivating and rewarding and using materials that are interesting, personally meaningful, and manageable (meaning not too difficult).

The logic behind the ISA stems from what we know about the development of certain reading-related skills and the young child's ability to comprehend written text—which is, after all, the only reason for reading. For children in the primary grades, the ability to comprehend written material is largely dependent upon their ability to accurately and quickly identify the words in the text. This is true partly because many of the materials that early primary-grade children read are not very challenging conceptually. Of course, when children do encounter reading materials that are conceptually challenging, fast and accurate identification of the majority of words in the text is still an important determinant of comprehension. However, the child's general world knowledge, language skills, engagement, and active thinking about the meaning of the text are also important determinants of comprehension.

In order to facilitate teachers' thinking about and planning for the needs of their literacy learners, much of this book is organized around a set of instructional goals that can be addressed in a variety of settings (e.g., whole class, small group, one to one) and instructional contexts (e.g., read-aloud, shared reading, writing). The purpose of organizing instruction around a goal structure is to encourage teachers to be mindful of what they are trying to accomplish with their students in each instructional context and thus to avoid engaging children in instructional activities that do not move them forward relative to their literacy learning goals.

In given primary classrooms, there is likely to be considerable diversity in the literacy skills and abilities of the children. Classroom teachers using the ISA are encouraged to be mindful of this diversity as they plan and deliver whole-class and small-group literacy instruction. To address the needs of the children who struggle the most with literacy acquisition, classroom teachers are encouraged to provide small-group reading instruction on a daily basis, with lessons planned to specifically meet the needs of the children in the group. For children who qualify for intervention beyond the classroom, intervention teachers are similarly encouraged to provide instruction that is responsive to the children's current capabilities. Further, instruction in these settings should be supportive of the children's classroom language arts program as well, so that the children are better prepared to profit from classroom instruction (Simmons, 2015; Wonder-McDowell, Reutzel, & Smith, 2011).

What's Different about the ISA?

In discussing the ISA, we are often asked to indicate how it differs from other approaches to early literacy instruction and intervention. If teachers experienced in using the ISA were asked this question, they would, most likely, talk about the approach to helping young children learn how to effectively puzzle through unfamiliar words encountered while reading. In the ISA, children are explicitly taught word-solving strategies and are coached in their use. The goal is for the children to become so effective and independent in word solving that they essentially have a self-teaching mechanism (Share, 1995) that enables them to learn to read the huge number of words that proficient readers ultimately know.

If we were asked the same question, we would agree with the teachers that the approach to teaching word-solving strategies is the most obvious difference between the ISA and other comprehensive approaches. However, we would add that the approach to teaching about the alphabetic code for the purpose of facilitating word learning is more thorough than many other approaches and more attentive to the need for children to learn to be flexible in their decoding attempts due to the irregular nature of English spellings. We would also argue that the attention given to enhancing children's vocabulary and word knowledge and to the impact of these knowledge sources on both oral reading and comprehension distinguishes the ISA from many other approaches to early literacy instruction. Finally, we would add that, unlike many other approaches to early literacy instruction, the foundational principles upon which the ISA is built are applicable across both classroom and intervention settings and, in fact, the ISA has been researched and found to be effective in whole-class, small-group, and one-to-one instructional settings.

Studies of the ISA

In the first study of the ISA (Vellutino et al., 1996), an early version of the approach was developed and implemented in the context of one-to-one tutoring for struggling first-grade readers. Participating children were randomly assigned to receive ISA-based tutoring or the instruction and intervention normally offered in their schools. Children who participated in the ISA tutoring were substantially less likely to experience long-term reading difficulties than were children in the comparison group.

The second study (Scanlon et al., 2005) was undertaken to address two concerns: that intensive one-to-one intervention was too costly for schools to sustain on a large scale and that, even when children were provided with intensive one-to-one intervention in first grade, some continued to experience significant reading difficulties. To address these concerns, we attempted to reduce the number of children who would qualify for intensive intervention in first grade by identifying children who were at risk for literacy learning difficulties at kindergarten entry and instituting intervention in a small-group context during the kindergarten year. The logic was that beginning intervention in kindergarten would prevent early limitations in literacy skills from growing and becoming debilitating. It was anticipated that this intervention would reduce the number of children who qualified for more intensive intervention in first grade and would reduce the severity of difficulties among children who continued to struggle despite kindergarten intervention. Random assignment to treatment conditions was, once again, utilized. The results indicated that participating in the ISA kindergarten intervention substantially reduced the number of children who qualified as poor readers in first grade. Further, for children who did qualify as poor readers in first grade, those who had participated in the ISA-based kindergarten intervention were less likely to demonstrate severe reading difficulties at the end of first grade than were children who had not participated in the ISA-based intervention in kindergarten. Thus the effects of kindergarten intervention were evident a full year after the children had left kindergarten, and this was true regardless of the type of intervention they received in first grade. It is also important to note that, in one combination of conditions, more than half of the children who qualified for intervention at the beginning of first grade (by scoring below the 15th percentile on a standardized measure of early literacy skills) made strong gains during first grade and scored above the 50th percentile at the end of the year. Thus, for children who did not respond well to an initial attempt to intervene, a second round of intervention that was more intensive and more specifically targeted to meeting their individual needs was effective in accelerating their reading growth.

The third major study of the ISA (Scanlon et al., 2008; Scanlon, Anderson, & Gelzheiser, 2010) involved implementing the ISA in one of three ways at both the kindergarten and first-grade levels. One approach involved providing small-group and one-to-one interventions for children, much like what was done in the Scanlon et al. (2005) study. The second approach involved providing ISA-based professional development for classroom teachers that entailed engaging the teachers in a summer workshop that paralleled the professional development provided for intervention teachers and thereafter providing in-school consultation and coaching on the implementation of the approach. The third type of implementation involved both direct interventions for children and professional development for their classroom teachers. All three approaches were effective in reducing the incidence of reading difficulties by the end of both kindergarten and first grade. However, the anticipated benefit of the condition in which both intervention and professional development were provided did not materialize. School personnel, upon hearing of this surprising outcome, suggested that it may have been the result of classroom teachers feeling that they did not need to attend to the needs of the students in ISA-based intervention because their needs were being met in instructional contexts beyond the classroom. This, of course, is not the purpose of intervention programs, and we have no way to evaluate this possibility. However, it does give us reason to strongly caution schools that are implementing interventions on behalf of struggling readers to be certain that the interventions are an add-on to, rather than a replacement for, the instruction that would normally be available in the classroom.

The ISA and Response to Intervention

As a result of the extensive research on the effectiveness of instructional enhancements in preventing long-term reading difficulties, including research on the ISA, in the past decade or so, there has been a major conceptual shift in thinking about how schools and teachers should respond to children who demonstrate reading difficulties. Whereas, in the past, children who were judged to be otherwise "normal" but who lagged seriously behind their peers in the development of reading and other literacy skills were often identified as learning disabled, it is now widely recognized that an individual's ability to become literate is the result of a complex interaction between the underlying characteristics of the child and his or her prior experiences and the amount, type, and quality of the instruction that he or she receives. Although it is certainly acknowledged that some children need more instructional guidance to learn to read and write and that some, in fact, need very intensive and individualized support, we now recognize that nearly all children who are not hampered by severe intellectual, perceptual, or emotional limitations can develop reading and writing skill. As a result of this shift in thinking, a process for determining whether a child should be identified as learning disabled has been made available to schools through federal legislation passed in 2004. The Individuals with Disabilities Education Improvement Act (IDEIA) encourages schools to identify children who are at risk of experiencing learning difficulties early in their schooling and to begin interventions in an effort to ameliorate those difficulties. Further, information about the child's response to instruction is used in determining whether he or she should ultimately be identified as learning disabled. This process is widely referred to as *response to intervention* (RTI; National Association of State Directors of Special Education, 2005). An important advantage of an RTI process is that it has the potential to prevent children from experiencing long-term learning difficulties because efforts to intervene are instituted before learning gaps have a chance to grow and become disabling. As a result, the process has the potential to reduce the number of children who may be inaccurately id/ learning disabled due to inadequate instructional experiences.

At this time, the most widely recognized model of RTI utilizes a tiere... to implementation. This approach (as described by Fuchs & Fuchs, 2006) entails (1) universal screening of all children, (2) identification of children who appear to be at risk of not meeting grade-level expectations and closely monitoring their progress, and (3) gradually increasing the amount and/or intensity of instructional support offered to children who do not show the gains needed to meet grade-level expectations. While there appear to be as many models of RTI implementation as there are research groups exploring the RTI process (Scanlon, 2011), most models involve three or four tiers of intervention, with Tier 1 encompassing instruction and intervention provided by the classroom teacher, Tier 2 involving more intensive and expert intervention provided beyond the classroom, and Tiers 3 and 4 providing even more intensive intervention and/or special education services, depending on the model.

Since passage of the IDEIA legislation in 2004 and the issuance of the accompanying regulations (Yell, Shriner, & Katsiyannis, 2006), much has been written about the RTI process (Gersten et al., 2008; Fuchs & Vaughn, 2012). Most of the practitioner-oriented literature has focused on the broad frameworks for RTI approaches and on the demands of the record keeping needed to document interventions and progress. Remarkably little has been written about the instruction that is offered to children who are at risk of experiencing long-term difficulties. In fact, especially in the early years of RTI, instructional recommendations were often limited to advice to adopt research-based programs and to implement them with fidelity (e.g., Brown-Chidsey & Steege, 2005; Mellard & Johnson, 2008). However, research on instructional effectiveness suggests that it is what the teacher does rather than the program she or he uses that is the most important determinant of children's achievement (Duffy & Hoffman, 1999; Konstantopolous & Sun, 2012; Nye, Konstantopolous, & Hedges, 2004; Scanlon et al., 2008; Tivnan & Hemphill, 2005). Consistent with this research, some of the most recent studies of the effectiveness of RTI indicate that child outcomes are improved when the interventions they receive are more responsive to what they know and are able to do (Al Otaiba et al., 2014; Coyne et al., 2013; Simmons, 2015) rather than being highly scripted and delivered with fidelity.

From early on, in work on the development of the ISA, as noted earlier, we focused on the development of teacher knowledge related to early literacy development and instruction so as to enable teachers to provide effective early literacy instruction across instructional contexts and curricula. We argue that the nature and quality of instruction are the most important determinants of a child's response to instruction and intervention. Further, we argue that, to be optimally effective, the instruction offered across instructional settings and contexts (i.e., the different tiers of intervention) should be responsive to the children's needs and be coherent and mutually reinforcing. This position is based on both empirical and logical grounds. Empirically, it has been found that a greater degree of curricular congruence across instructional settings is associated with stronger reading outcomes in the primary grades (Borman, Wong, Hedges, & D'Agostino, 2001; Wonder-McDowell et al., 2011). On logical grounds, if our goal is to enable children to benefit from and succeed in the classroom language arts program, it seems that alignment of instruction across classroom and intervention settings would be the most prudent approach. Of course, if the classroom language arts program is weak and/or inappropriate for the children who qualify for intervention, modifications to the classroom program would be an important (first) step in enhancing the quality of instruction that is offered.

The ISA and the Common Core State Standards for English Language Arts

Research on the ISA predates the development and adoption of the Common Core State Standards (CCSS; National Governors Association Center for Best Practices & Council of Chief State School Officers [NGA & CCSSO], 2010). However, the logic and emphases of the ISA are well aligned with some of the major shifts that are called for by the Standards. The three key shifts are:

1. Regular practice with *complex texts* and their academic language.
2. Reading, writing, and speaking *grounded in evidence from texts,* both literary and informational.
3. *Building knowledge* through content-rich nonfiction.
   (*www.corestandards.org/other-resources/key-shifts-in-english-language-arts*)

Essentially, as these three key shifts suggest, the CCSS are built on the premise that knowledge development and reading development are closely linked (Cervetti & Hiebert, 2015). To help students meet the standards, we need to be addressing knowledge development from early on. And, although the ISA is intended for students in the primary grades, who probably are not ready to be reading the complex texts referenced in the standards on their own, these students are certainly able to engage with, learn from, and discuss information-rich texts that are read to them. Such engagement will help to prepare them for the expectations that they will face as they progress through the grades.

The CCSS also provide a good deal of guidance related to foundational skill development—the aspects of reading development that have traditionally been the major focus of primary-grade reading instruction. Here again, the ISA aligns well with the standards and provides teachers with effective practices to help children, even those who struggle with foundational skills, to attain those standards. Understanding how the writing system works and developing skill with reading printed words enables children to comprehend progressively more complex written texts.

The ISA and English Learners

In the past few decades, there has been a dramatic increase in the number of students in U.S. schools who are classified as English learners (ELs). The current estimate is that ELs constitute approximately 9% of the student population (Kena et al., 2014). While this increase in the number of children who need to rely on school to help them learn the English language has generated some research on methods for doing so, the research has not led to a widely accepted consensus on best practices. However, there is a developing consensus that suggests that, for children who speak very little English, schooling should initially focus on developing their skill with oral English and, whenever possible, developing written language skills in the language of the home (August, McCardle, & Shanahan, 2014). The theory behind this is that, under these circumstances, children will develop some foundational knowledge about how written language works and will be able to generalize at least some of this knowledge (depending on the similarities and differences between the languages) when they have sufficient skill with spoken English to allow them to begin to understand instruction about written English. In fact, in a review by Garcia (2000), it was found that, among children in grades K–2, reading in the home language was a better predictor of reading in English than was the student's oral English skills.

In our research on the ISA, because of the locale in which the research was done and the populations served by the schools that agreed to participate, we have not had the opportunity to explicitly evaluate the effects of the ISA on ELs. However, our reading of the research on how to help ELs develop oral as well as written language skill in English suggests that the instructional practices that we advocate are aligned with what the research suggests, albeit sometimes with some modifications that are responsive to the children's first language. We discuss these modifications in the appropriate chapters.

Reading Is a Complicated Process
That Requires Comprehensive Instruction

Reading is a complex process that requires the analysis, coordination, and interpretation of a variety of sources of information. In order to effectively meet the needs of literacy learners, especially those who struggle, instruction needs to take account of this complexity. Consider, for example, what is involved in reading and understanding the simple text below:

Matt was going to Sara's party. Sara likes kites. Matt can bring her a kite.

To understand this text, the reader obviously needs to be able to (1) read the words, (2) retrieve the words' meanings, (3) put the words together to form meaningful ideas, and (4) assemble a larger model of what the text is about (Kintsch, 1998). Because difficulties with any of these processes can result in reading difficulties, all of these important processes need to be considered when designing instruction to help children learn to read.

Because teachers are proficient readers and perform many, if not all, of these processes effortlessly, they are sometimes surprised by, and insensitive to, the complexity of the processes. By becoming more attuned to these complexities, teachers can become better able to provide instruction and guidance to students who are learning to read. To help teachers gain these insights, we begin with an (incomplete) analysis of what a reader might do while reading the text about Sara's party.

Read the Words

All of the words in this text are known to proficient readers. They can identify them automatically with little or no conscious thought. As a result, readers can devote most, if not all, of their thinking to making sense of the text. For beginning or struggling readers, however, some of the words will be somewhat or very unfamiliar, and they *will* have to devote thought to figuring out the words. Their success in doing so will depend on several things, including what they understand about how the alphabetic code works (i.e., how the printed letters represent the sounds in spoken words) and their ability to make use of other sources of information, such as the context in which the words occur. For example, if students attempted to "sound out" the word *was*, it would rhyme with *pass* rather than with *fuzz*! Using the context of the sentence in combination with the information provided by the letters in the word, beginning readers would be more likely to figure out the word.

Retrieve the Words' Meaning(s)

The meanings of words are usually accessed quite automatically while reading *if* the words are in the reader's vocabulary. So, for example, readers who know what a kite is will activate that knowledge when reading the word *kites*. In fact, having knowledge of kites will allow readers to confirm that the printed word is, in fact, pronounced as *kites* rather than as *kit-es* or *kite-es*. For a word such as *can,* which has more than one common meaning (the container vs. the ability to do something), proficient readers generally become aware of only the meaning of the word that is signaled by the context.

Assemble Words to Form Idea Units

As noted, the context in which a word occurs helps readers identify the word and, for words with more than one meaning, helps readers to identify the intended meaning of the word. One of the ways that context operates is through read-ers' knowledge of spoken language and the implicit rules regarding which words can follow one another. For example, the verb meaning of *can* is selected in the sentence *Matt can bring her a kite,* partly because, within a sentence in English, a noun is more often followed by a verb than by another noun. Moreover, if in this sentence the proper noun *Matt* were to be followed by another proper noun (such as *Jack*), there would be a comma between the two proper nouns—another signal to which proficient readers attend unconsciously. Even when none of the words has multiple meanings, a hallmark of proficient reading (and listening) is that readers/listeners process the words in meaningful units or phrases. A mean-ingful unit might be a sentence, if it is short enough, or it might be only a part of a sentence—but the part would comprise a unit of meaning. For example, the sen-tence *Sara likes kites* might be processed as one meaningful unit because it is only three words long and presents a fairly simple idea. However, the longer sentence *Matt was going to Sara's party* might be processed as two meaningful units (e.g., *Matt was going [somewhere]* and *to Sara's party*). Exactly how a sentence would be processed would depend on a variety of factors, including how familiar readers/listeners are with the general topic, how easily they can access the meanings of the individual words, how easily they can identify the individual words, and so on.

Assemble a Larger Model of the Text

By this point, readers of this chapter are likely to be growing weary of thinking about all of the things that proficient readers do while reading just three fairly sim-ple sentences. However, so far the discussion has hardly touched upon the major purpose of reading and what is, perhaps, the most complicated part of the process: to understand, interpret, and/or react to what is stated in the text. In order to fulfill this purpose, readers must relate the idea units to one another to form a conceptual understanding of the text that spans the sentences and taps readers' knowledge in ways that facilitate comprehension (Kintsch, 1998; Perfetti, Landi, & Oakhill, 2005). That is, while reading a text, readers "read" more than what is actually on the page; how they understand the text depends on what they already know about the topic. So, for example, if they know something about birthday parties, readers may infer that Sara's party is a birthday party because that is the kind of party to which one might bring a toy for a present. Readers are also likely to make some inference about Sara's age, because it is less likely that one would bring a kite to a very young child or to an elderly adult. A discussion of the extent of thinking and inferring that might go on relative to this little bit of text could be quite extensive. Many readers, for example, construct a visual image of the two characters, includ-ing what they are wearing, what color hair they have, and so forth. The print on the page stimulates readers to think and visualize. For fully engaged and proficient readers, the thinking generally goes far beyond what is literally stated on the page.

The previous discussion is not intended to make teachers feel overwhelmed by what needs to be taught (although this would be a reasonable reaction). Rather, the purpose is to help teachers more fully appreciate the complexity of the processes involved in reading and to develop insights into aspects of the process that may need explicit instructional attention.

In what follows, we present information on how to support children's development as they are learning to read. Early in reading development, learning to read the words is a major hurdle, and so we focus a good deal of the discussion on this critical aspect. However, as the preceding analysis emphasizes, reading the words is only a part of the process. Early literacy instruction needs to attend to all aspects of the process. Teachers need to provide instruction that helps children develop knowledge of word meanings and the background knowledge that will enable them to do the kind of inferencing and reading between the lines that proficient readers do quite effortlessly. Teachers of beginning readers also need to ensure that the children understand that the purpose of print is to communicate, because only when readers understand that there is a message in the print will they engage in thinking beyond the initially challenging step of figuring out the words.

Children Who Struggle with Literacy Acquisition

We have known for many years that children who lag behind their peers in early reading development are at high risk of experiencing prolonged reading difficulties (Francis, Shaywitz, & Steubing, 1996; Juel, 1988; Phillips, Norris, Osmond, & Maynard, 2002; Prochnow, Tunmer, & Chapman, 2013; Rayner, Foorman, Perfetti, Pesetsky, & Seidenberg, 2002) and, ultimately, of being identified as learning (or reading) disabled. Research comparing children who struggle with reading and those who learn to read with comparative ease has identified critical areas that differentiate the two groups. Much of that research was comprehensively summarized in the book *Preventing Reading Difficulties in Young Children* (Snow, Burns, & Griffin, 1998) and in an article by Vellutino, Fletcher, Snowling, and Scanlon (2004). Similar findings emerged in the National Early Literacy Panel report (2008). Based on this body of research, there is a fairly strong consensus about the areas of difficulty that affect struggling readers and about the role of instruction in preventing reading difficulties. We briefly summarize this research below and periodically revisit it in relevant sections of this text.

Phonological Processing Difficulties

The research indicates that the most common area of difficulty among children who are identified as struggling readers at the early stages of learning to read is phonological processing (Snow et al., 1998). Because there is also strong evidence that the phonological processing skills of struggling readers can be improved through instruction and practice (e.g., Ball & Blachman, 1991; Blachman, 1991; Scanlon et al., 2005; Tangel & Blachman, 1992, 1995; Vellutino et al., 1996), we devote a substantial portion of this book to ways to promote the development of phonological processing skills, including the ability to attend to and manipulate the individual sounds in spoken words and to use the relationships between letters and their sounds to figure out the pronunciation of printed words. However, this focus should not be interpreted as suggesting that *all* early literacy instruction should emphasize phonological components. Indeed, many children appear to become proficient in the phonological domain with relatively little explicit guidance. Instruction that is too heavily focused on phonological skills may do little to further the development of these children.

Limitations in Language and General Knowledge

Research has demonstrated that vocabulary knowledge influences comprehension (Perfetti & Stafura, 2014) and that, when measured at the preschool and/or primary level, it is one of the best predictors of reading comprehension in late elementary grades and throughout schooling (Scarborough, 2001; Storch & Whitehurst, 2002). That is, in general, children who know the meanings of fewer words when they are young are likely to have greater difficulty comprehending the things they read when they are older (Cain & Oakhill, 2011; Cunningham & Stanovich, 1997; Quinn, Wagner, Petscher, & Lopez, 2015). There is also evidence that classroom instruction can influence vocabulary knowledge. For example, Dickinson (2001) reports that, in preschool settings, the amount and quality of the language used by the children's teachers, the kinds of verbal interactions that occur in the classroom, and, more specifically, the types of interchanges that occur during read-alouds influence the development of oral language and vocabulary. In other words, early childhood teachers, in their instructional interactions with children, have the potential to positively influence language skills that are *critical* to future success in the comprehension of text. Whitehurst and Lonigan (1998) have provided similar findings with regard to book interactions between parents and their young children.

As discussed above in relation to the CCSS, reading comprehension is also influenced by the general knowledge possessed by readers. That is, what one already knows about a topic influences the acquisition of new information about that topic (Bransford & Johnson, 1972; Cain, Oakhill, Barnes, & Bryant, 2001; Neuman, 2006). Children who have had limited opportunities to develop the knowledge base that is expected in school are at a serious learning disadvantage as they progress through the elementary grades because they are expected to build on a knowledge base that is shaky or even nonexistent. ISA teachers are encouraged to use information-rich children's books—both books that are read to children and books that the children read themselves—as a major resource for the development of language and general knowledge. We contend that early literacy instruction for all children, but particularly for children who demonstrate difficulties, needs to lead children to expect that the texts they listen to and read will make sense (Perfetti et al., 2005). Without this expectation, we are allowing children to become passive comprehenders—that is, children who do not take an active role in making sense of the texts they read. To this end, we urge teachers to model and foster children's engagement with text meaning during interactive read-alouds from the very beginning.

Instructional Goals in the ISA

Taking into account the multiple factors that influence an individual's ability to comprehend written texts, the ISA is organized around a set of instructional goals. Teachers are encouraged to view instruction as a goal-oriented activity wherein they work to help children achieve identified goals, using a variety of instructional formats and materials. The goals range from the relatively simple and straightforward (e.g., developing letter-name knowledge) to those that are quite complex and involved (e.g., helping children become strategic and active readers). Subsequent chapters in this book are devoted to discussing each of the goals in detail. As we discuss each goal, we highlight the importance of being able to view literacy and literacy-related skills from the perspective of a young child who is a relative novice when it comes to understanding the intricacies of written language and how it relates to spoken language. Often, in our formal and informal observations of teachers working with young children and in our own work with young children who are struggling to learn about written language, we are struck by how difficult it is for highly literate people to take a step back and understand the complexity of reading and writing processes from the perspective of a child who is just beginning to experience print. This is a theme to which we return frequently in discussing the ISA goals, because one of our major purposes in this book is to help teachers develop greater expertise in identifying and responding to the difficulties experienced by struggling readers. Understanding the source of a child's confusion is an important step in responding to that confusion.

In the goal chapters, we review the relevant research for each goal and discuss how the goal relates to reading and writing processes more generally. We also discuss and provide sample instructional activities that can be used to help children achieve the goal, and, where relevant, we discuss more and less challenging aspects of particular activities—often presenting a sequence of objectives within given goals. We discuss informal assessment tools for many of the goals and the need to use assessment to guide grouping decisions and instructional planning. Each of the goals is briefly described below.

Motivation to Read and Write

> The child will develop the belief that reading and writing are enjoyable and informative activities that are not beyond his or her capabilities.

In discussing this goal, we focus on a variety of factors that contribute to motivation, such as ensuring that children face an appropriate level of challenge in literacy tasks, expressing enthusiasm for reading and writing activities, actively engaging children in thinking about and responding to texts, making read-alouds an important and interactive part of the day, and construing reading and writing as privileges rather than as jobs (e.g., "You *get* to finish your book before recess" rather than "You *have* to finish your book before recess").

Alphabetics

> The child will understand the relationships between printed and spoken language and will be able to use these relationships in reading and writing.

This overarching goal includes several individual goals related to the development of skill in using the alphabetic code. Each of the alphabetics goals is identified and described briefly below.

Purposes, Concepts, and Conventions of Print

> The child will understand that the purpose of print is to communicate. The child will also understand the basic print conventions, such as the left-to-right and top-to-bottom sequencing of print, where to begin reading, the concepts of letter and word, and so forth.

Children who have had little exposure to written language are apt to be unaware that print is actually a form of language and that it is possible to translate print into spoken language and spoken language into print. In addressing this goal, we discuss the need to be explicit about the relationship between spoken and written language and the multiple ways in which print is used to communicate.

Understanding these foundational concepts is critical if children are going to make progress with literacy development. For children who do not yet have these concepts established, instruction needs to be explicit and should introduce one new concept at a time. Previously taught concepts should be revisited until they are well understood.

Phonological Awareness

> The child will have a conceptual grasp of the fact that words are made up of somewhat separable sound segments. Further, the child will be able to say individual sounds in words spoken by the teacher and blend separate sounds to form whole words.

In addressing this goal, we attempt to attune teachers to the phonemes in spoken language. Many highly literate adults are confused about how to segment words in which there are more letters than sounds (e.g., *mouse*) or more sounds than letters (e.g., *box*). We discuss various approaches to developing phonemic awareness, with a particular emphasis on blending and segmenting. We also discuss the relative difficulty of analyzing words into different units (onsets and rimes vs. individual phonemes) and discuss the features of phonemes that make them more and less challenging for children to attend to and/or manipulate.

Letter Naming

The child will be able to name, rapidly and accurately, all 26 letters of the alphabet, both upper- and lower-case versions.

In discussing this goal, we begin to address fluency with foundational skills as an important contributor to reading comprehension. We stress that automaticity (speed) with letter identification is important in order to free up cognitive resources for higher-level skills. To promote fluency with letter identification, we stress the importance of having children say the letter names frequently during the course of the various activities used to promote letter-name knowledge.

We also discuss young children's tendency to rely on the names of the letters as an aid to remembering their sounds. For example, the sound for the letter *b* is the first phoneme in its name (/b/).[1] Thus, for many letters, if children know the name of the letter, it will be easier for them to remember the sound for the letter.

Letter–Sound Association

The child will be able to associate the most common sounds of individual letters with their printed representations.

For this goal we continue to focus on the relationship between letter names and letter sounds, how to take advantage of that relationship, and how to address the confusions that arise with letters for which the relationship does not hold. We discuss the utility of using key words to help children remember letter–sound correspondences, of using the same key words across instructional settings and grade levels, and of explicitly teaching children how to use the key words when reading and writing.

The Alphabetic Principle and the Alphabetic Code—Early Development

The child will understand that the letters in printed words represent the sounds in spoken words and will understand how to use the beginning and ending letters in words in attempts to read and spell words.

---

[1]To denote the sound of a letter, we follow the convention of enclosing the letter in slashes.

In the chapter devoted to this goal, we describe instruction designed to help children acquire a conceptual understanding of the alphabetic principle; that is, the fact that the letters in printed words represent the sounds in spoken words.

Phonograms and Word Families

> The child will develop the ability to use frequently occurring phonograms (e.g., *ay, ell, op*) to read and spell words.

Word families are built around phonograms. For example, from the *ay* phonogram the words *day, may, say, way, play, stay, tray,* and many others can be formed. The goal is to help children learn common phonograms and how to use them to effectively puzzle through printed words that contain those phonograms and to support conventional spelling of those words as well.

The Alphabetic Principle and the Alphabetic Code—Later Development

> The child will understand how to use all of the letters in printed words as an assist in determining the pronunciation of the word. Similarly, the child will learn to represent all of the sounds in a spoken word with an acceptable letter when writing.

In discussing this goal, we address ways to increase skill with decoding and encoding by teaching children about consonant digraphs, consonant blends, short and long vowels, and vowel digraphs. We stress the benefits of guiding children to be strategic as they apply their developing knowledge of the alphabetic code in authentic reading and writing situations.

Morphological Units and Multisyllabic Words

> The child will understand that words are often composed of more than one unit of meaning (e.g., root words plus prefixes and/or suffixes) and will learn how to break longer words into meaningful units and/or syllables as an assist to reading and spelling them.

It is important for children to attend to all of the letters in written words when attempting to identify unfamiliar words, in order to store thorough representations of those words in memory. However, ultimately, children need to learn to process larger orthographic units rather than puzzling through words in a letter-by-letter fashion, as this will help them to develop fluency. Explicit instruction in how to make use of these larger units can help learners to make progress toward proficient reading and writing.

In discussing this goal, we focus on instruction around frequently occurring inflectional suffixes and derivational prefixes and suffixes. Learning how to interpret and use these affixes can simplify aspects of word solving and help to expand children's knowledge of word meanings. In this same chapter, we also discuss ways to help children learn about clues to syllable boundaries and how to apply this knowledge when puzzling through longer unfamiliar words.

Word Learning

| The child will learn to effortlessly identify a large number of written words.

This major goal is addressed via two subgoals, each of which focuses on a different vehicle for word learning. Although the term *sight vocabulary* is sometimes used to refer to high-frequency words or irregular words, we use the term to refer to all words that can be identified effortlessly "at sight."

Strategic Word Learning

| The child will develop flexibility and independence in applying code-based and meaning-based strategies to identify and learn unfamiliar words encountered in text.

Strategic word learning is a central goal of the ISA, as having the ability to puzzle through and accurately identify unfamiliar words provides children with a powerful mechanism by which to expand their sight vocabulary and thereby their ability to read. We emphasize the need for children to use both code-based and meaning-based strategies in interactive and confirmatory ways.

High-Frequency Words

| The child will be able to read the most frequently occurring words accurately and quickly.

Although many of the words that become part of a child's sight vocabulary are learned during the course of strategic reading, some words warrant special instructional attention. These are words that occur frequently in print and are somewhat more difficult to learn due to their irregular spellings and/or abstract nature. Teachers are encouraged to explicitly teach and provide practice with such words. We discuss game-like drill activities that motivate children to practice the high-frequency words and texts that provide additional practice.

Meaning Construction

| The child will have the language skills and knowledge base needed to enable him or her to derive and construct the meaning of the texts that are read.

Comprehension is the goal of reading. Because children who are identified as struggling readers in the early primary grades are generally labeled thusly on the basis of their difficulties with the alphabetic coding and word-learning aspects of reading, the importance of attending to meaning construction is sometimes overlooked, but it should not be. Instruction specifically focused on enhancing comprehension is addressed through discussion of three goals: fluency, vocabulary and language development, and comprehension and knowledge.

Fluency

> The child will be able to read grade-appropriate text accurately with appropriate speed and with phrasing and intonation that conveys the intended meaning of the sentence.

Fluency is included under the overarching goal of meaning construction because, in order to construct meaning while reading, readers need to devote the majority of their cognitive resources to meaning construction rather than to word solving. Fluent reading is also a signal that the reader is comprehending—at least at the sentence level—because, without comprehension, it would be difficult for the reader to apply the appropriate intonation. Being able to read fluently does not, of course, guarantee comprehension of the larger text, but it increases the likelihood that the reader will comprehend.

Vocabulary and Oral Language Development

> The child will learn the meanings of new words encountered in instructional interactions and will be able to use the words conversationally. Further, the child's ability to understand and use complex grammatical structures will improve.

Reading is a language skill. Children need to develop the vocabulary and other language skills upon which reading comprehension depends. Teachers are encouraged to be alert to vocabulary and syntactic challenges throughout their instructional interactions. The opportunities for the development of vocabulary and syntactic knowledge provided by interactive read-alouds are a major focus relative to this goal. However, teachers are also alerted to the fact that children frequently encounter unfamiliar words in their own reading and that word identification difficulties are sometimes caused by not knowing the meaning of printed words. When this happens, the reader cannot decide (or confirm) whether a word has been accurately decoded.

Comprehension and General Knowledge

> The child will develop the foundational knowledge and comprehension skills and strategies that will enhance his or her ability to construct the meaning of, and learn from, texts heard or read.

For children in the early primary grades, the development of active engagement in meaning construction is discussed in the context of read-alouds and supported reading. We encourage teachers to model comprehension strategies and to engage children in conversations that require the use of those strategies (e.g., "I think he's going to get a puppy for his birthday. What do you think he's going to get? Why?").

To help build the critical knowledge base upon which comprehension depends, we encourage teachers to read informational books to the children as often as possible. As children begin to read texts on their own, teachers are urged to engage children in discussions of what they are reading so as to avoid allowing children to develop the belief that reading is about saying the words right (and quickly) and not about meaning construction.

General Principles for Preventing Reading Difficulties

One of the main purposes of early intervention efforts is to prevent early differences in literacy skills from growing and becoming disabling. Although the specific content of what is taught is an important factor in the success of interventions, there are equally important general principles of instruction that can help maximize the impact of the instruction offered.

Teach Children to Be Effective and Independent Problem Solvers

Vygotsky (1978) was a developmental theorist who believed that much of what children learn as they grow and develop is the result of extended interactions with adults or more expert "others." Vygotsky argued that the skills that children acquire reflect the internalization of problem solving that they have initially done in collaboration with adults, who have provided *careful verbal guidance to direct and guide children's thinking.* The theory is that children internalize the verbal guidance initially provided by their teachers in such a way that it becomes a form of inner speech that influences their thinking when they encounter similar problems.

If we assume that adults' speech (and, through it, adults' thinking) is, on some level, internalized by children, then it becomes important to carefully consider our instructional language and to try to take the perspective of the children relative to our language. Do we use terms or expressions that may not hold the same meaning for the children? It is all too easy to inadvertently use terminology that carries no meaning or a different meaning for children who struggle with literacy acquisition. For example, for some beginning kindergartners, a *letter* is something that comes in the mail, not a little squiggle that is associated with a sound. It is remarkably easy to wrongly assume that children know or understand things; as a result, an instructional episode may be quite confusing to them. Virtually every teacher has had this experience.

It is also important to give children the opportunity to see how to use the problem-solving processes we teach. Because problem solving is a thinking process, the only way the children can "see" the process is if we think out loud so that they can vicariously experience the process. The instructional jargon for this approach to instruction is called *think-aloud,* and it is an important component of instruction designed to develop strategic thinking. When we think out loud for the children, we are essentially guiding the development of their thinking.

Vygotsky (1978) also argued that the most effective instruction focuses on skills and abilities that are somewhat challenging for a child to handle independently but that are easy enough for the child to handle when assistance is offered at key points. The disparity between what children are able to do with and without assistance is referred to as the *zone of proximal development*. From a Vygotskian perspective, the role of a teacher is that of a skilled collaborator. In this role, teachers must be:

- Adept at evaluating children's current level of competence and deciding what they are ready to learn next.
- Facile at modifying the demands of the task so that it suits the needs of each child.

Based on Vygotsky's theory, Wood, Bruner, and Ross (1976) developed the concept of *scaffolding* as an analogy for the role that skilled collaborators play in supporting a child's learning. Scaffolding involves the provision of various types of support that allow children to successfully accomplish a task that is too challenging for them to accomplish on their own. The scaffolding technique also involves the gradual *reduction* of support as a student demonstrates the ability to regulate his or her own thinking and problem solving. In order to do the types of assessment, modification, and scaffolding suggested here, it is necessary for teachers to have a firm grasp of the developmental progression of the skills they are helping students develop.

Ensure That Students Are Actively Engaged in Learning

The more reading and writing children do, and the more they practice the underlying skills that are foundational for reading and writing, the more quickly they become proficient. This is true when children actually engage in the cognitive processes required to read and write. Unfortunately, children sometimes find ways of avoiding the thinking parts of instructional activities. For example, in a choral reading situation, when the entire class or group is engaged in reading the same text, some of the children may not be looking at the words and thinking about them. Rather, they may be simply gazing in the right direction and saying the words just slightly after their friends say them. These children may look engaged, but they are not. They need the opportunity to read text to the teacher or to a friend in order to fully engage in the necessary thinking processes.

Similar types of disengagement can arise when a teacher calls on one child *before* asking a question. For example, if the teacher is engaging the children in a shared writing activity and wants to know what letter to use at the beginning of the word *dog,* she might call on one child, saying, "Jake, what letter do I need at the beginning of the word *dog*?" As soon as the teacher says Jake's name, some of the children in the group may disengage, knowing that they will not be expected to answer. If, on the other hand, the teacher asks the question without immediately calling on an individual, more of the children are likely to engage in the thinking. Better still, if the children all have dry-erase boards on which to write, they could all engage in the task. The teacher might say, "Write down the letter you think I need at the beginning of the word *dog*." This allows every student to respond; as a result, they are *all* likely to benefit from the instructional interaction. We strongly encourage teachers to incorporate opportunities for every student to respond during the course of instruction.

KEEP IN MIND   In developing instructional activities, an important question to ask is "What are the children likely to be thinking about/focusing on during the activity?" If the conclusion is that they are unlikely to be focused on the skill or concept (the goal) that the activity was designed to support, the activity should be redesigned.

Another consideration relative to the relationship between engagement and learning is the fact that children sometimes become overly involved in the hands-on (e.g., cutting, gluing, coloring) aspects of instructional activities and are not really thinking about the skill or concept that the task was designed to support. It is important to make clear to the children why they are doing specific things and what they can do during the hands-on aspects of the activity to support their learning. For example, if children are learning the sound of the letter *m* and gluing macaroni to a cut-out of an *M,* while they are doing this, they might be encouraged to think of other words that have the /mmm/ sound that is heard at the beginning of the word *macaroni* and to share their ideas with other children at the table. If children are not provided with guidance in how to think about the instructional activity, at least some are apt to devote most of their thinking to the gluing and fine-motor activity or, in this instance, to thinking about the food they are manipulating. Similarly, if children are practicing their spelling words by writing them several times, it would be helpful for them to say each letter as they write it and then say the word each time it is completed. It would also help if they tried to write the word from memory each time and then checked it against a model. Otherwise, the spelling practice may become nothing more than an unengaged copying task.

The general point with regard to engagement is that teachers need to guide how children think about instructional activities so that the activities actually move the children forward in literacy acquisition.

Set High Expectations for All Children

At various points in the history of education, people have believed that some children were just destined to have great difficulty learning to read and/or write and that there was little to be done to help them overcome their difficulties. Research has demonstrated that students tend to live up to the expectations we have for them (Smith, Jussim, & Eccles, 1999). Thus a belief that a child is unlikely to make progress has the clear potential to slow the progress made by that child. Conversely, the expectation that a child will succeed academically increases the likelihood that she or he will do so. In fact, research conducted in "beat-the-odds" schools, in which children succeed at much higher levels than might be expected given their socioeconomic circumstances, indicates that a common characteristic of such schools was that school staff held high expectations for all of the children (Taylor, Pearson, Clark, & Walpole, 2000).

What Does "Ready to Learn" Mean?

For many years there was a commonly held belief that children needed to be developmentally ready to learn to read. Exactly what people meant by "being ready" varied, but it was certainly tied to the child's age and, in some cases, physical development. For example, some thought that children should not be taught to read until they had lost their first tooth!

What we mean when we use the phrase *ready to learn* is that the child has the prerequisite conceptual understandings and skills to allow him or her to benefit from instruction in a certain area. Every child is ready to learn something. Our job as educators is to figure out *what* the child is ready to learn, not *whether* the child is ready to learn.

The research on the success of early literacy interventions makes it easier to hold high expectations for children who initially demonstrate limited literacy skills. Every child is expected to do well in reading and writing development, and, if the child is not progressing, we are more inclined to examine the instruction than to examine the child to determine what has gone wrong. In other words, instruction is now considered to be a much more powerful influence on a child's reading and writing development than it once was. Children do learn what we teach them, as long as we teach them what they are ready to learn. The challenge, of course, is that the children in any given classroom generally are not all ready to learn the same things. Nevertheless, they are all expected to attain the same grade-level standards. This is why different amounts and intensities of instruction and intervention are so important to promoting literacy success. In a classroom setting, working with small, flexible, skills-based groups for a substantial portion of the language arts block offers the greatest opportunity for the teacher to meet this challenge. Similarly focused small-group and one-to-one instructional contexts enable intervention teachers to respond to the needs of the children who are more challenging to teach.

Integrate Support Services with the Classroom Program

For children who are receiving intervention services beyond the classroom, it is important that the instruction in all settings works toward mutually supportive ends (Allington & Johnston, 1989; Mosenthal, Lipson, Torncello, Russ, & Mekkelsen, 2004; Wonder-McDowell et al., 2011). To the greatest extent possible, intervention teachers should support and reinforce the content of the classroom program. For example, at the kindergarten level, if instruction about the alphabet is sequenced in a particular way, it makes sense to sequence alphabet instruction in intervention settings to parallel the classroom sequence. Similarly, if key words are used in the classroom to support the learning of letter sounds, supplementary instruction should use the same key words. Likewise, it is helpful to determine which high-frequency words children are expected to know by the end of a given grade level and to make these words a priority for instruction. Additionally, some of the reading materials used in intervention settings should come from the classroom program. Such a purposeful selection gives the children the opportunity to interact with these materials in a way that they may not experience in the larger classroom context. Many more opportunities to build congruence could be suggested. By increasing the congruence between classroom and supplementary instruction, we hope to increase the impact of both the classroom instruction and the intervention support. The children who struggle in the classroom program will be better prepared for subsequent instruction in the classroom if they have reviewed some of the material in another context.

Plan for Success

In all instructional interactions, teachers should make every effort to structure the activities so that the children experience success and the rewarding feelings that go along with it. Teachers should help students recognize that their successes are due to their efforts. Conversely, teachers should avoid making negative and discouraging comments. Although a teacher may sometimes feel frustrated that he or she has yet to find a way to help a particular child accomplish a particular objective, communicating this frustration will only serve to make the child feel that the situation may be hopeless. If the child is not progressing in a certain area, it is important to try to determine the source of the problem. Perhaps the level of difficulty needs to be reduced. Perhaps the child is misconstruing the task. Perhaps the teacher is using terminology for certain concepts that is different from the terminology to which the child is accustomed. It is particularly important for teachers who are providing supplementary instruction to be aware of the terminology used in the children's classrooms. For example, whereas adults and most older children readily recognize the equivalence of terms such as *upper-case* and *capital,* young children often do not. Attending to potential stumbling blocks such as task difficulty or confusion regarding terminology before they occur will help to ensure that children experience success and continually move forward in their literacy development.

Track Student Progress

Because knowing what children are already able to do is so essential to knowing what they are ready to learn next, it is important for teachers to keep records of their students' skills and strategies. To this end, for most aspects of literacy development that are discussed in this book, we provide skill and strategy checklists to facilitate record keeping and, most importantly, to support teachers as they reflect on their students' current abilities and plan instruction.

Because teachers usually use such record-keeping devices in the context of working with small groups of children, each checklist provides space for teachers to record information on up to five children. We refer to these checklists as "snapshots" because they allow teachers to get a quick look at the skills, strategies, and attitudes/beliefs of children in a particular group to inform their instructional planning. Each snapshot is discussed in some detail in the relevant chapters of the book.

> *Note.* The companion website includes downloadable copies of the group snapshots as well as versions that can be used to track individual students' development across time.

Many of the snapshots call for the teacher to rate children's skills and strategies using a 3-point scale: *beginning, developing,* and *proficient.* Such ratings are appropriate for what Paris (2005) refers to as *constrained skills*—skills that are learned over a relatively short time span and that are mastered by most students. These ratings are also appropriate for evaluating strategy usage. As illustrated below, to make the record keeping as efficient as possible, teachers are encouraged to use slashes to denote their judgment of individual children's standing relative to particular skills and strategies. However, some teachers prefer to use the letter codes.

- ◻ *B—Beginning* indicates that instruction has addressed the objective but that the child has only a preliminary understanding or capability with regard to that particular objective.
- ◻ *D—Developing* indicates that the child has some understanding of the objective but does not reliably demonstrate that understanding or capability or is not yet automatic (fluent) with the skill.
- ◻ *P—Proficient* indicates that the child reliably and automatically demonstrates the understanding or capability.

In other instances, the snapshots call for teachers to indicate whether individual children's capabilities in given areas are *well developed, appropriately developed,* or *need development.* Essentially, this rating reflects the teacher's judgment as to whether or not this is an aspect of literacy development that requires greater instructional emphasis.

Organization of the Book

The remainder of this book is largely organized around the instructional goals for young children detailed earlier and the instructional methods for helping children to achieve those goals. However, first we devote Chapter 2 to describing what a typical week and a typical day of language arts instruction might look like in a kindergarten or first-grade classroom, our purpose being to provide a framework for considering how the goals would be addressed in the context of language arts instruction. Next, Chapter 3 discusses academic motivation as it relates to literacy learning and particularly for those who struggle with literacy acquisition. Thereafter, we devote Part II to the development of skill with the alphabetic code, which covers everything from developing an understanding of the purposes and conventions of print to learning to process larger orthographic units such as morphemes and syllables in multisyllabic words. Next, Part III is devoted to word learning, with separate chapters discussing the different ways in which sight vocabulary is developed—through strategic word solving while reading and via explicit instruction and practice with high-frequency words. In Part IV, on meaning construction, we discuss the language, background knowledge, engagement, and fluency factors that influence readers' ability to comprehend the things they read, and we suggest ways of supporting the development of these important contributors to comprehension. Finally, Part V covers implementing intensified ISA-based instruction in an RTI context and summarizes the discussions across the text.

Throughout the goals chapters, we provide commentary on the relationship between each goal and the standards from the CCSS to which it pertains. In addition, we provide instructional considerations pertinent to addressing the needs of EL children.

CHAPTER 2

Responsive Instruction

Within an RTI process, effective and differentiated classroom instruction is a crucial component of efforts to address the needs of children who appear to be at risk of experiencing literacy learning difficulties. In the RTI model that we propose, classroom instruction takes account of the diversity of student skills during the course of whole-class, small-group, and one-to-one instruction. Further, to better address the specific needs of the children who are identified as at risk, classroom teachers plan small-group instruction such that they have the opportunity to teach the children who are at greatest risk more intensively than the children who are not identified as being at risk. Intensification can be accomplished in a number of ways. For example, teachers might arrange their weekly schedules so that they can meet with the at-risk group(s) on a daily basis, while working with the children who are not at risk somewhat less frequently. In addition, group size would, ideally, be smaller for the at-risk children than for the children who are not at risk. Children with the most extreme needs—that is, those who make limited progress when provided with intensified classroom instruction—would receive additional intervention beyond the classroom either in the context of small-group (Tier 2) or

---

What Is the Relationship between RTI and the CCSS?

While the goal of RTI is to ensure that all children have the instructional support they need to meet grade-level expectations, the CCSS serve to standardize, across states, what those expectations should be.

---

one-to-one (Tier 3) instruction. These more intensive forms of intervention are discussed later in the chapter. We first focus on instruction provided by the classroom teacher for the full spectrum of students.

Classroom Instruction in an RTI Context

In a typical primary-grade classroom, children will have a variety of skills and be at different performance levels with regard to reading and writing. In fact, estimates suggest that in a typical classroom, the reading levels of the children can range across three grade levels or more (Chorzempa & Graham, 2006). Instructional plans need to consider the current literacy status of all the children in the class. Once this information is established, a teacher with a clear understanding of the instructional goals will be better able to address students' literacy development via instructional formats that include whole-class, small-group, and one-to-one instruction. Although it is not possible to specify the ideal mix of formats, it is clear that a mix is ideal. Several research groups have provided evidence that children, particularly those who struggle, make better progress in classroom programs and intervention settings in which they are grouped by reading level for supported reading lessons and are given the opportunity to read texts that provide some, but not too much, challenge (e.g., Ehri, Dreyer, Flugman, & Gross, 2007; National Early Literacy Panel, 2008; Scanlon et al., 2008; Taylor et al., 2000; Wanzek, Roberts, Al Otaiba, & Kent, 2014; see also Pressley & Allington, 2015).

Whole-Class Instruction

Instruction offered to the entire class is appropriate for many components of language arts instruction, including read-alouds, shared reading, shared writing, and oral language activities. Whole-class instruction provides the opportunity to involve all of the children in activities that (1) foster active engagement with the meanings of texts, (2) illustrate the use of word identification strategies, (3) build foundational skills such as knowledge of how the alphabet works, and (4) help to build oral language and general knowledge. However, even during whole-class instruction, teachers need to be mindful of, and to plan for, the variety of skill levels in the class. For example, during a shared writing activity, when the teacher writes in collaboration with the students, a first-grade teacher might:

- Engage all of the children in the composition of the message.
- Model and engage the children in stretching and segmenting some of the words to meet the needs of children who have yet to become fully phonemically aware.
- Encourage the children to refer to the class word wall for the spelling of recently taught high-frequency words.

- Explicitly discuss and model the formation of a few of the letters as she writes them.
- Discuss spelling and print conventions for children who are at different points along the developmental continuum (perhaps directing attention to the key-word chart for the spelling of the short-*a* sound for the children at an earlier point of development and discussing the -*tion* spelling unit for children who are further along).

The point is, in whole-class instruction, the teacher should plan to provide multilevel instruction that keeps all children engaged and moving forward.

Small-Group Instruction

Small-group configurations generally involve grouping children by instructional level, by the need for instruction on particular skills or strategies, and/or by interest (e.g., a group interested in a particular topic or book). All of these approaches to grouping may occur in any given classroom. For purposes of primary reading instruction, however, it is important that the children receive their supported reading lessons in small groups formed on the basis of their current reading levels and skills.

Supported Reading

We use the term *supported reading* rather than *guided reading* in order to distinguish small-group reading instruction provided in the ISA from guided reading as described by Fountas and Pinnell (1996), as the two approaches differ in several important ways. For example, the ISA places heavier emphasis on explicit and systematic instruction related to the alphabetic code, and, in most lessons, new decoding elements are taught and practiced in preparation for reading a book in which words that include that decoding element will be encountered. In guided reading, the decoding skills that are taught are drawn from the text, based on the challenges the children encounter while reading, and become the focus of instruction after the children have read the text. Further, in the ISA, children are taught a small number of specific word-solving strategies and are explicitly taught how to utilize them in interactive and confirmatory ways upon encountering unfamiliar words in context. Independence in the use of these strategies is an important instructional objective. In guided reading, teacher prompting is used to guide children's word-solving attempts, but the children are not given a specific list of strategies.

Small-group formats are more effective in accelerating children's progress because they allow the teacher to differentiate instruction such that the texts that the children read provide an appropriate level of challenge and the focus of skill and strategy instruction is targeted so as to bring the children just a bit further along relative to what they are currently able to do. Further, small-group instruction allows the teacher to more effectively monitor what the children understand about reading and writing and to determine what they are ready to learn next. The group snapshots provided in the upcoming chapters are intended to help teachers keep abreast of the skills and strategies of the children who have been grouped together and to allow teachers to consider whether children who are in a given group are appropriately placed by examining similarities and differences in profiles within and across groups.

One-to-One Instruction

Virtually every classroom teacher in the primary grades offers some one-to-one instruction (sometimes referred to as *side-by-side instruction*). Such instruction is provided in contexts in which the teacher confers with individual children about their reading, writing, and other academic work. In the context of both whole-class and small-group instruction, teachers often provide children with the opportunity to work independently for periods of time. For example, children might be asked to discuss with a partner how they think a particular book will end or to write a journal entry relating to the same question. During such activities, the teacher can be attentive to individual children to make sure that they are engaged in productive ways and can be alert for opportunities to guide their thinking relative to the instructional activity in which they are involved. The problem-solving skills and strategies that teachers address in these one-to-one interactions will vary considerably from child to child.

Developing a Language Arts Program for Readers at Multiple Levels

Language arts instruction at the primary level typically comprises several fairly distinct components that together address the instructional goals discussed in Chapters 3 through 16. Table 2.1 lists the goals and the components of instruction during which the goals might be addressed. The checkmarks in the table indicate which goals might be addressed within the various components of language arts instruction. The purpose of this table is to demonstrate that multiple goals can and should be addressed in each component of language arts instruction, a notion consistent with the CCSS claim that "several standards can be addressed by a single rich task" (NGA & CCSSO, 2010, p. 5).

In a typical classroom, a substantial proportion of the language arts program is delivered to the whole class at once. To plan for the full spectrum of students who will participate and to engage all of them productively, teachers need to be

TABLE 2.1. Intersection of the Goals of Instruction and the Components of Language Arts Instruction

Language arts components	Instructional groupings	Motivation	Alphabetics			Word learning		Meaning construction		
			Print concepts	Phonological analysis	Alphabetic coding skills (letter names, sounds, alphabetic principle, etc.)	Strategic word identification	High-frequency sight words	Fluency	Language and vocabulary development	Knowledge and comprehension
Read-aloud	WC, SG, and I	✓		✓	✓	✓		✓	✓	✓
Shared reading	WC, SG, and I	✓	✓	✓	✓	✓	✓	✓	✓	✓
Independent and buddy reading	WC, SG, and I	✓	✓	✓	✓	✓	✓	✓	✓	✓
Writing/composition	WC, SG, and I	✓	✓	✓	✓	✓	✓		✓	✓
Oral language	WC, SG, and I	✓		✓	✓	✓		✓	✓	✓
Foundational skills	WC, SG, and I	✓	✓	✓	✓	✓	✓	✓	✓	✓
Supported reading group	SG and I	✓	✓	✓	✓	✓	✓	✓	✓	✓

Note. WC, whole class; SG, small group; I, individual. Adapted from Scanlon and Anderson (2010). Copyright by the International Literacy Association. Adapted by permission.

knowledgeable about the abilities and understandings of all of the children and to rely on this information as they interact instructionally with individual students within the larger context. For example, at the beginning of first grade, students are likely to be at very different places in terms of their literacy development. For purposes of discussion, we describe four different "types" of students that might be in a single early primary class. However, before doing so, it is important to emphasize that literacy development is a fluid and multidimensional process and that children do not necessarily fit neatly into a given type. Of the many different dimensions along which a literacy learner might be described and considered, for current purposes we focus primarily on the dimensions related to the development of the ability to read the words in connected text. In doing so, we do not wish to diminish the importance of general language and vocabulary knowledge nor the importance of background knowledge in contributing to children's ability to comprehend the texts they read. However, because at early stages of development the latter characteristics are often unrelated to the child's abilities to read the words in the text (see Paris & Paris, 2007) and because most of the research on reading difficulties suggests that most early reading difficulties are due to difficulties with figuring out how to read printed words, we develop our characterization around those early, foundational skills. Our characterization draws heavily on, but is not totally consistent with, the work of Ehri (2005).

Emergent Readers

Emergent readers have very limited understanding of the role played by print in the reading process. Emergent readers may know the names of few, if any, letters and have limited understanding of the most basic print conventions. When they attempt to read emergent-level books, they rely primarily on the pictures and their memory of the text if it has been read to them previously. They may or may not understand many other aspects of reading, such as that books tell stories and/or are sources of useful and interesting information.

Developing Readers

Developing readers have begun to learn something about the alphabet and the alphabetic principle. They may know the names of most of the letters and the sounds of many of them. When attempting to identify printed words, developing readers tend to rely on a combination of the alphabetic code and the context in which the word occurs, with the relative weight placed on one source of information, changing gradually from heavy reliance on context to greater reliance on the code. Developing readers may be able to identify many of the most frequently occurring words with relatively little effort.

Maturing Readers

Maturing readers are effective word learners who use both code-based and meaning-based strategies fairly efficiently to puzzle through unfamiliar words. However, their need to word-solve is still apparent, as evidenced by either multiple attempts at the pronunciation of the occasional word (during oral reading) or by hesitation over a word followed by accurate identification. Because maturing readers are effective word solvers, their sight vocabulary grows rapidly (when they engage in reading, of course). Further, when reading texts that do not contain too many unfamiliar words, they tend to sound quite fluent as they read.

Proficient Readers

Proficient readers are able to quickly analyze and identify unfamiliar words, even those that are composed of multiple syllables. Part of their efficiency is due to the fact that they have stored many larger orthographic units (e.g., *-tion, re-, -ly, -ing*) in memory. Thus, although they do not necessarily know all of the words, they figure them out so quickly that they sound fluent. Proficient readers are able to devote virtually all of their thinking to interpreting and responding to the texts as they read.

In the primary grades a classroom might be composed of all four types of readers—as well as readers at all the intermediate points between the types described. However, at each grade level and at different points in the year, the mix of children is likely to be different. Thus, early in kindergarten most children are likely to be emerging or developing readers, whereas at the beginning of first grade most are likely to be developing readers, a few might be described as maturing, and a very few as either emergent or proficient. By the beginning of second grade we would expect the balance to shift again, with a few being described as developing readers, most looking like maturing readers, and several likely to be proficient. Regardless of the distribution of students along the continuum, the classroom teacher is responsible for providing instruction that moves all students forward.

Although small-group instruction is one of the most effective ways of addressing the diversity of skill levels found in typical primary-grade classrooms, many instructional needs of the children in a class can be addressed through whole-class instruction. Because whole-class instruction influences the development of all children, it could be argued that, for some goals, it is a more efficient form of instruction.

A Weekly and a Daily Schedule in First Grade

In this section we discuss the balancing act that teachers face in planning and delivering language arts instruction for a classroom full of students who differ substantially in their literacy skills. We illustrate how small-group instruction might fit into the context of the broader language arts program and into the context of the instructional day. As an example we provide a possible first-grade weekly schedule and discuss each component of the day. The schedule itself is outlined in Figure 2.1. All of the components on the schedule involve literacy skills (broadly defined as reading, writing, listening, speaking, and representing/illustrating).

Attendance, Lunch Count, Book Browsing, and Writing

The day begins with a 10- to 15-minute period during which the children have time to put their belongings away, socialize a bit, sign in for attendance and lunch purposes, and do a little reading or writing if time permits. They may read one or more books that were read previously, browse through a book previously read by the teacher, explore the classroom library, and so forth. Many teachers also offer the children the opportunity to do some writing during this segment of the day. They might write notes or letters to friends, write in their journals, or document observations related to an ongoing science project, for example. During this

	Monday	Tuesday	Wednesday	Thursday	Friday
8:15–8:30	Attendance, lunch count, book browsing, and writing	Attendance, lunch count, book browsing, and writing	Attendance, lunch count, book browsing, and writing	Attendance, lunch count, book browsing, and writing	Attendance, lunch count, book browsing, and writing
8:30–8:40	Morning meeting	Morning meeting	Morning meeting	Morning meeting	Morning meeting
8:40–8:55	Shared reading	Shared reading	Shared reading	Shared reading	Shared reading
8:55–9:10	Introduction of center activities	Introduction of center activities	Introduction of center activities	Introduction of center activities	Introduction of center activities
9:10–9:35	Group 1	Group 4	Group 3	Group 1	Group 2
9:40–10:05	Group 2	Group 1	Group 4	Group 2	Group 1
10:10–10:35	Group 3	Group 2	Group 1	Group 3	Group 4
10:35–10:50	Snack and discussion	Snack and discussion	Snack and discussion	Snack and discussion	Snack and discussion
10:50–11:20	Read-aloud	Read-aloud	Read-aloud	Read-aloud	Read-aloud
11:20–11:50	Writing and composition	Writing and composition	Writing and composition	Writing and composition	Writing and composition
11:50–12:35	Lunch and recess	Lunch and recess	Lunch and recess	Lunch and recess	Lunch and recess
12:35–1:15	Special	Special	Special	Special	Special
1:20–2:05	Math	Math	Math	Math	Math
2:05–2:20	Wrap-up and reflection	Wrap-up and reflection	Wrap-up and reflection	Wrap-up and reflection	Wrap-up and reflection

FIGURE 2.1. Sample daily schedule for first grade. Although it is not explicitly blocked out on the schedule, it is understood that a focus on science and social studies content is a critical aspect of primary-grade instruction. We strongly encourage teachers to integrate content-area subject matter into the various instructional components described above, particularly shared reading, center activities, read-aloud, and writing/composition. When necessary, teachers might opt to use one of the writing/composition or math blocks for introducing a new unit or theme, then continue with the remainder of the schedule as usual.

period, the teacher has time to attend to necessary paperwork, including notes from parents, and to greet individual children and make them feel welcome.

Morning Meeting

Many teachers have a brief morning meeting in which they bring the whole class together and outline the day. Teachers use this period in many different ways to address literacy and other academic goals. For example, some teachers focus the children's attention on a large calendar to help the children learn to read numbers, or the names of the days of the week, or the letters in the name of the month. They might also use it to teach and reinforce certain science concepts by, for example, engaging the children in observing and recording characteristics of the weather and placing symbols for rainy, sunny, snowy, or cloudy on the calendar each day.

Shared Reading

During shared reading, the teacher and the class read a text in which the print is large enough for all of the children to see comfortably, and the teacher explicitly directs their attention to the print by pointing to the words as she reads. Shared reading often occurs immediately after the morning meeting and may, in fact, blend in with the morning meeting. For example, one of the texts used for shared reading may be a teacher-prepared passage on chart paper that describes the schedule for the day (e.g., what the special [art, music, library] is, whose birthday it is, plans for a field trip) for the class to read together. Alternatively, the teacher may use a big book or poem for shared reading. Often teachers use such a text to introduce, review, and/or practice high-frequency words and/or specific decoding elements.

Many of the big books used for shared reading are at a level of challenge that would make them accessible to most children following a few experiences with shared reading of the book. Thus shared reading can provide an opportunity to expose all children to grade-level texts in alignment with the expectations of the CCSS. Many publishers provide instructional materials that include a big book and accompanying child-size versions of the text.

Teachers implementing the ISA use shared reading as an opportunity to model and engage children in the use of word-solving strategies. Periodically, while sharing the reading, the teacher stops at a word that lends itself to being identified by using particular strategies. Modeling and discussing with the class how to puzzle through the word, the teacher notes the usefulness of the strategies once the word is identified. Teachers often post a large-print version of the strategies list (see Chapter 12 and Figure 12.1) so that it can be seen by all of the children. Many teachers leave the materials used during shared reading available for the children to use during center time or as a free-choice activity. Young children often delight in playing teacher and will enthusiastically gather together some friends to serve as students as they take on the role.

As teachers plan and deliver a whole-class shared reading lesson, they need to think about the full spectrum of students who will participate in the lesson and attempt to engage all students productively. This, of course, requires that the teacher do different things for different students in the class. In Table 2.2 we describe how a shared reading lesson might vary for children at different points along the developmental continuum. The table presents each of the instructional goals that teachers might address in the lesson and provides a brief glimpse of what teachers might do (or plan to do) for children at different points along the continuum. Typically, of course, the students in a given class will not be distributed evenly along the continuum. Therefore, teachers should distribute their time and focus in accord with the composition of their class. That is, if most of the children are emergent readers, the instructional interaction would focus on basic print concepts and the identity of individual letters that the children are learning, as well as the meaning of the text being read. If, on the other hand, most of the children are developing readers, most of the instructional interaction related to alphabetics would focus on engaging the children in puzzling through single-syllable words. As noted in Table 2.2, instructional interactions during shared reading can and should attend to multiple aspects of the reading process.

Introduction of Center Activities

Centers are intended to provide the opportunity for children to work productively toward academic goals when the teacher is working with other children in a small-group context. While it may not be necessary to set aside time to introduce center activities every day, it is important to be sure that there is time in the schedule to do so if necessary. Several suggestions for literacy-focused center activities are described later in this book. In addition, centers focused on math, science, social studies, and art—all of which involve literacy to some degree—should be included. In considering the daily schedule, notice that there is a permeable (dashed) line between the "shared reading" segment and the "introduction of center activities" segment in Figure 2.1. As it is often necessary to allocate more time to introduce more complicated centers and projects, this permeable line suggests this need for flexibility. For example, in preparing children to learn in a center that is cross-curricular (e.g., involves science and/or math and reading and writing), such as studying the life cycle of a plant, the teacher might utilize the entire 30-minute block to familiarize the children with center activities and expectations.

Small Literacy Groups

Small-group literacy instruction provides the classroom teacher with the greatest opportunity to differentiate instruction and to better meet the needs of children who are at different points in development (Lou, Abrami, & Spence, 2000; McCoach, O'Connell, & Levitt, 2006; Valiandes, 2015). This format is a critical component of language arts instruction and requires careful planning and organization to realize its full potential. In order to discuss small-group instruction in detail while not "breaking the flow" of our description of the daily schedule, we have postponed a full discussion to a later segment of this chapter.

(text resumes on page 42)

TABLE 2.2. Teacher Thinking before and during Shared Reading, Related to the Goals and to Children at Various Points in Development

Goal	Emergent	Developing	Maturing	Proficient
Motivation	Encourage enjoyment and engagement with text.			
Alphabetics				
Purposes and conventions of print	Model and discuss print conventions, such as the right-to-left and top-to-bottom directionality of print.	Model and discuss print conventions such as the use of spaces to demarcate words and some of the most frequent punctuation (capitalize the first word, use of periods and question marks).	Model and discuss more advanced print conventions, such as print size, exclamation points, and quotation marks. Discuss text features for informational text (e.g., table of contents, glossary, labels).	Model and discuss commas, colons, semicolons, etc. Discuss text features for informational text (e.g., table of contents, glossary, labels).
Phonological awareness	Occasionally select texts characterized by rhyme and alliteration to help heighten children's sensitivity to sounds.	Occasionally select texts characterized by rhyme and alliteration to help heighten children's sensitivity to sounds.	Goal accomplished.	Goal accomplished.
Letter names	Draw children's attention to the letters they are learning the names of, invite them to find letters that have recently been introduced (recognition) or to name letters that they are expected to know (identification).	Build fluency with letter identification by occasionally inviting children to name all of the letters in particular words.	Goal accomplished.	Goal accomplished.
Letter sounds	Not a focus at this time.	Emphasize the sounds of some letters as words are articulated or ask children to provide the sound for a particular letter encountered in the text ("This word starts with *S*; what sound will this word start with?"). Occasionally model use of the key-word chart when discussing letter sounds.	Encourage children to participate in puzzling through words to enhance fluency with letter sounds.	Goal accomplished.

(continued)

39

TABLE 2.2. (continued)

Goal	Emergent	Developing	Maturing	Proficient
Early development of skill with the alphabetic code	Not a focus at this time.	Occasionally draw children's attention to the beginning letters in words as they are reading. As readers grow, draw attention to ending letters as well.	Goal accomplished.	Goal accomplished.
Phonograms and word families	Not a focus at this time.	Draw children's attention to examples of words that include phonograms that have been taught. Model use of the phonogram chart.	Provide opportunities for children to attempt to solve words in word families that have been taught.	Goal accomplished.
Later development of skill with the alphabetic code	Not a focus at this time.	Not a focus at this time.	Draw attention to all of the letters in one-syllable words—particularly in regularly spelled words.	Goal accomplished.
Morphological units and multisyllabic words	Not a focus at this time.	Discuss pronunciation and meaning changes with inflectional endings.	Model and engage students in approaches to puzzling through words with multiple syllables and/or multiple inflectional affixes.	Engage students in solving words with a variety of derivational and inflectional prefixes and suffixes and/or multiple syllables.
Word learning				
Strategic word learning	Model the use of picture cues when reading highly predictable text.	Guide word solving by occasionally modeling the use of context in combination with partial alphabetic information—beginning letters and, later, final letters. Revisit some of the	Occasionally draw children's attention to more detailed alphabetic information and to larger orthographic units and illustrate how to use that information in combination	Occasionally draw children's attention to larger orthographic units (word families, prefixes, suffixes, and other recurrent spelling patterns) and illustrate how these units can be used

	word-learning strategies that were used while reading, after reading, and discussing the entire text.	with context in order to solve unfamiliar words.	in combination with context to facilitate identification of and deduce the meanings of unfamiliar words.	Goal accomplished.
High-frequency words	Point out any high-frequency words that are being taught and provide the opportunity to do a word hunt after the text has been read and discussed.	Point out the high-frequency words that the children have been learning. After the entire text has been read and discussed, occasionally give children the opportunity to do a word hunt for words they know or are learning.	Occasionally fade voice while leading the choral reading so that children have the opportunity to retrieve learned high-frequency words from memory.	

Meaning construction

Fluency	Read the text multiple times to enable the children to chime in on second and subsequent readings.	Read the text multiple times. Encourage the children to chime in on second and subsequent readings. On occasion draw attention to the voice changes signaled by common sentence-ending punctuation marks and how those changes influence interpretation of the meaning of the text.	Model fluent and disfluent reading of the text and engage the students in discussion of the characteristics of fluent reading. On occasion, draw attention to the role of punctuation marks such as quotation marks and commas and their influence on phrasing and intonation.	Goal accomplished.
Vocabulary and oral language	Explain the meanings of unfamiliar words and syntactic structures as they come up in the text. Encourage the children to ask about the meanings of words or phrases they do not understand. Teach or revisit meanings of a few words in follow-up activities.			
Comprehension and world knowledge	Engage children in actively thinking about the meaning of the text before, during, and after reading it with them. Facilitate the process of making connections between what the children already know and what they encounter in the text. Encourage the children to ask questions when they do not understand what is happening in the text. Across the year, and as more informational texts become available in big book formats, teachers are encouraged to include a balance of information-rich and literary texts and texts that are representative of a variety of cultures and genres.			

Snack and Discussion

Snack time can be used to support the development of children's language skills by incorporating activities such as *describe and guess,* which is a bit like *show and tell* but which requires the use of more sophisticated language (see Chapter 15). This is also a time for the teacher to model and encourage social but unstructured conversations among children. If the teacher explicitly models conversations by joining different groups of children, over time the children are likely to begin to emulate the conversational conventions that the teacher demonstrates.

Read-Aloud

A read-aloud involves the teacher reading a book or other text without the expectation that the children will attend to the print. Reading aloud to children and engaging them in discussion of the text before, during, and after it is read provides a powerful vehicle for:

- Expanding their vocabulary and syntactic skills.
- Developing knowledge and vocabulary related to the science and social studies content, particularly if several books on the same or related themes are read.
- Modeling and engaging the children in active processing of the text.
- Increasing motivation for and interest in reading.

Further, in the early primary grades, books used for read-aloud can help to promote the development of phonological awareness if they contain rhyme or alliteration. And alphabet books help develop knowledge of letter names and letter sounds because, in most such books, the letter that is the focus of each page is large enough for children to see even when the rest of the words are not.

Many times the books teachers select for reading aloud are related to a classroom theme (e.g., seasons, oceans, early settlers). Reading several books related to a common theme helps children to develop more thorough knowledge and vocabulary related to that theme and enables the teacher to integrate science and social studies content areas into the language arts curriculum.

Teachers might also organize book selection around author or genre studies. Reading and discussing several books by the same author helps children learn about the authors' craft and contributes to their writing development by highlighting characteristics and tactics of different authors. Genre studies (biography, fairy tales, memoirs, etc.) help children develop schemas for the different genres. When children understand the characteristics of a particular genre, they are likely to use that knowledge to guide their interpretation of texts. For example, knowledge that a folk tale generally is intended to teach a lesson puts the reader on the alert to look for the lesson the tale is trying to teach. Thus the genre itself gives the reader a purpose for reading. Moreover, engaging children in noticing characteristics of various genres and writing styles provides them with models that they may want to emulate in their own writing.

As for other components of instruction offered in a whole-class format, it is important to try to engage the entire class and to give some forethought to how a particular text might be used to support progress toward the various instructional goals. Moreover, particularly for children who have been identified as being at risk, those who have limited experience with being read to, and/or those who find it difficult to attend to text in the context of whole-class instruction, it is also productive to read aloud in small-group or one-to-one situations. Classroom volunteers can be particularly helpful in providing additional opportunities for children to listen and respond to books. Of course, volunteers may need guidance in how to effectively engage children in read-alouds, as some well-intentioned adults believe that children should be silent while being read to.

It should be noted that although the packed daily schedule presented in Figure 2.1 could suggest that there is no time allocated to science and social studies, this is not the case. When the class is focusing on particular themes or topics in science or social studies, books related to those themes should be selected for shared reading and/or read aloud; those themes could also be carried forward in the writing/ composition block. Further, as noted previously, one or more of the centers offered during small-group time could be devoted to providing the children with additional opportunities to engage with that content.

Writing and Composition

Different formats for writing activities should routinely be part of the instructional day for primary-level readers, including emergent and beginning readers. In one, the teacher does the writing with assistance from the child(ren). In another, the children do the writing with guidance from the teacher. In addition, children should explore writing independently in the context of open-ended writing opportunities in the classroom (e.g., journal writing, observation logs).

In the sample schedule, writing and composition immediately follows read-aloud largely because teachers sometimes want their students to incorporate, in their own writing, elements of what was discussed during the read-aloud. So, for example, early in first grade, the teacher might ask the children to draw a picture of the portion of a text that interested them the most (or surprised or bothered them the most) and to write a caption for the picture. As children progress as readers and writers, they might engage in a variety of writing types. For example, the children might be asked to:

- Collaborate in developing a class book that tells further adventures of a character they learned about during a read-aloud.
- Write a letter to an author inquiring about reasons for certain decisions that he or she made in writing the text.

- Write a new ending for a story that was read.
- Keep a journal telling what they have learned related to a particular theme they have been pursuing through read-alouds.
- Model their writing after a particular genre or author's style.
- Write a letter to a friend telling the friend why he or she would probably like a particular book.

Whether the writing is focused on reacting to a specific text or is of a more creative nature, the writing/composition portion of the day often begins with a mini-lesson in which the teacher models and discusses certain aspects of the writing process. In the early primary grades, teachers often focus on both the mechanics of writing (letter formation, spacing between words, punctuation, sound spelling, conventional spelling, etc.) and on the construction of meaning (formulating the intended message, considering wording, revising for clarity, etc.). Mini-lessons often take the form of shared writing during which the children have the opportunity to observe as the teacher writes, modeling her thinking and engaging the children in as much of the problem solving as they are able to do (e.g., thinking about how to word a statement, stretching the words to analyze the sounds, thinking of the letters needed to represent the sounds).

Once the children begin to write, the teacher circulates for a period of time, providing guidance and encouragement in the form of mini-conferences. Alternatively, teachers sometimes choose to create temporary groups to teach specific writing conventions and strategies during writing time. Thus the teacher might meet with one group of children one day and a different group of children the next. While the teacher is meeting with groups, the remaining children continue to work on their own compositions and/or engage in conferences with their peers. Some time is set aside at least a couple of times each week for individual children to share their writing with classmates.

In planning and delivering writing instruction, teachers engage in the same sort of thinking about the instructional goals and the competencies of their students as was detailed in Table 2.2.

Small-Group Literacy Instruction

In order to be able to work fairly productively with children at various points in the development of language arts skills, teachers need to plan and organize instruction carefully. As noted above, providing small-group instruction is particularly important for primary reading instruction and, therefore, should be a daily occurrence once the school year gets under way. Initially, however, in preparation for small-group instruction, teachers need to (1) identify which children will be grouped for instruction, and (2) prepare children to work productively when they are not directly engaged with the teacher.

Grouping for Supported Small-Group Literacy Instruction

The process by which teachers might form groups for supported small-group instruction varies considerably depending upon the children's grade level, the instructional program in use, and the point in the school year. For example, early in the school year in kindergarten, groups may be formed on the basis of the children's phonological skills and understanding of the writing system. Children who demonstrate similar levels of skill would be grouped together. As the school year progresses, however, the teacher might regroup children based on ongoing observations of what the children know and are able to do, perhaps using checklists such as the snapshots described in subsequent chapters.

As the children advance, their ability to read leveled texts or their ability to read texts in the core reading series may serve as the basis for forming instructional groups. Young children who are learning to read in a particular curriculum are likely to learn the things that are emphasized in that curriculum, so assessment should certainly evaluate the extent to which children have learned what has been taught (e.g., specific decoding principles, high-frequency words, specific strategies for word solving). As children progress as readers and as they read more and more texts, their abilities will broaden and likely be progressively less dependent on the particular curriculum. At this point, assessment for the purpose of forming instructional groups (and informing instruction) can use more general (less curriculum-specific) measures of reading.

KEEP IN MIND Regardless of the approach used to forming instructional groups, it is important to consider the groups to be temporary and flexible. Children's reading progress typically does not proceed at a fixed rate, particularly when efforts to intervene are in place.

As an alternative, instructional groups might be formed on the basis of periodic administrations of more formal assessments that can be used for the purpose of documenting progress. However, depending on the assessment used, multiple administrations can be time-consuming and may add little to inform grouping decisions or instructional planning. It is the child's performance on a day-to-day basis that is particularly important rather than the child's performance at a single point in time. This last point should not, of course, be taken as a rationale for doing away altogether with systematic data collection; such data are needed for the purpose of documenting growth. Rather, the point is that teachers who are well informed about early literacy development, who are working closely and thoughtfully with children in small-group settings, and who are systematically documenting children's performance during ongoing instructional interactions will likely know more about the students' abilities than can be learned from more formal assessments.

Preparing Children to Work without the Teacher during Small-Group Time

Ideally, the children in a supported small-group literacy context should receive the undivided attention of the teacher. However, because teachers are generally responsible for the entire class, they need to prepare the children to work effectively and independently when they are involved with their small groups. To accomplish this, many teachers, particularly in the primary grades, report that during the first week or two of school, they do not actually work with small groups but rather invest time in teaching children the routines and procedures that will eventually govern their independent work once they begin to meet with groups. Teachers typically develop a number of centers or stations in the classroom where individuals or groups of children engage in practice and reinforcement activities for particular academic skills and/or in activities that provide the opportunity for new learning/knowledge building. For example, a teacher might develop a listening center where the children listen to recordings of information books or a computer center where the children watch videos relating to the science or social studies content about which the class is learning.

Planning, Planning, Planning

The activities in which the children engage should be so well planned and so well described to them that little or no teacher support is required once the children have learned what to do at each center. All of the necessary materials should be readily available and accessible to the children. For centers that focus on the development of early literacy skills, such as knowledge of high-frequency words or the development of skill with the alphabetic code, the activities should lend themselves to some degree of differentiation. Thus each child might have a folder at the center that contains items that are matched to his or her current skill level.

Another aspect of planning is deciding which children will be placed together at each center. In our opinion, centers work best when children at various points of development interact. This way the children who are a bit further along can assist children who are less so, and both are likely to benefit from the interaction.

Setting Reasonable Expectations

It is unlikely that young children will be able to sustain productive engagement with the same activity for prolonged periods of time. Therefore, the activities designed for each center should generally require no more than 15–20 minutes to complete, and at least some of the centers should encourage the children to talk with their friends as they engage in learning activities. This conversational aspect will help to promote language development and to deepen the children's learning by providing them with the opportunity to gain other children's perspectives. For example, in the listening center, the book to which the children listen might be marked with sticky notes that signal them to stop and discuss (1) their predictions, (2) how what happened in the story/text compared to their predictions, (3) what they are wondering about, (4) how they would feel in a similar situation, and/or (5) what they learned.

To ensure quiet, productive activity as transition times approach, it is important to have appealing but simple activities for the children to engage in once they have completed the major center activity. For example, there might be options such as playing games with high-frequency words or decoding elements or book browsing and independent or buddy reading.

Teaching for Self-Regulation

In order to provide the teacher with the focused time needed to provide instruction in small-group contexts, children need to learn to work productively and independently when they are not directly engaged with the teacher. This independence requires them to regulate their own behaviors and to solve small problems without seeking assistance. Self-regulation develops more readily when it is guided by the teacher—that is, when the means of self-regulation are directly taught (explained and modeled) and when attempts at self-regulation are explicitly noticed and publicly valued.

To establish the desired self-regulation, the teacher might spend the first week or two of school demonstrating what to do in the centers, discussing what to do if problems arise, monitoring and guiding the children's problem-solving skills while engaged in the centers, and explicitly acknowledging evidence of self-regulation and engagement (e.g., "Alex already found his folder and got busy with writing and checking his spelling words right away"; "I see that Kayla and Olivia are already very interested in their book in the listening center!"). As the children begin to show some independence in utilizing the centers, the teacher should begin to work with the small groups, initially for relatively short periods of time, working up to the full amount of time planned by the end of the third or fourth week or so of school.

"Eyes in the Front of Her Head"

Although effective primary-grade teachers are often described as "having eyes in the backs of their heads" because they seem to know what's going on in all parts of their classrooms at all times, it is more likely that their "with-it-ness" is due to careful planning and positioning: They anticipate potential difficulties in the classroom and try to prevent them. Moreover, when they organize for small-group instruction, they position themselves so that they can see the entire classroom and monitor the children who are not in the group with which they are working.

Assistants in the Classroom

The foregoing discussion has assumed that the classroom teacher is the lone adult in the room. However, if additional adult resources are available, instruction has the potential to be even more productive. For example, if a classroom aide is available during the period in which the teacher is providing small-group instruction, the aide can monitor and support the children who are engaged in center activities. If more than one additional adult is available, those adults can be pressed into service in providing guided practice opportunities for the children. For example, they might listen to individual children reread and discuss books that were previously read with the teacher, or they might do small-group interactive read-alouds. To be optimally effective in either of these roles, the assistants/volunteers will typically benefit from some orientation and guidance concerning the goals of these activities and how they might support children in achieving those goals.

Teaching Small Groups

In the schedule presented in Figure 2.1, it is assumed that the teacher has four different groups of children with whom she or he works during the course of a week. Group 1 is at the earliest point in development and would consist largely or exclusively of children who have been identified as being at risk; the schedule allows the teacher to work with these children 5 days a week. Group 2 comprises children who are somewhat more advanced in terms of their early literacy skills but are not yet at grade level. Some of these children may have been identified as at risk but may be showing sufficient growth such that they do not need the level of intensity provided for the children in Group 1. The schedule allows the teacher to meet with students in Group 2 on 4 days of the week. Groups 3 and 4 consist of children who are at grade level and somewhat above grade level, respectively. Because these children are predicted to readily meet or exceed grade-level expectations by the end of the year, the teacher needs to meet with them less frequently and/or less intensively to support their development. In the schedule there is time for the teacher to meet

---

Note

Although it might seem a bit unfair to provide children who are at or above grade level with less instruction, it is important to note that there is a growing body of research which indicates that such children tend to make greater progress when provided with more opportunity to work independently (Connor, Morrison, & Katch, 2004; Connor et al., 2011). The reason may be that, for children who have the necessary foundational skills and the ability to effectively puzzle through unfamiliar words encountered while reading, more independent work time provides more time to read and, thus, to grow as readers.

with each of these groups three times per week. An alternative for Groups 3 and 4 might be to meet with them 5 days per week but for abbreviated lessons on 2 of the days. Thus, in the schedule depicted in Figure 2.1, the teacher might opt to meet with Group 3 and Group 4 students on both Thursday and Friday, with the time set aside for that block divided between the two groups.

As depicted in the sample schedule, the teacher meets with different groups in different time slots each day. The rationale for this is twofold. First, because children are likely to move back and forth between and among groups as their literacy skills develop, having the groups meet in a different order on each day may help to avoid having the children develop a strong sense of which group is the "top" and "bottom" reading group. Given that identifying oneself as being in the bottom reading group can have a serious negative impact on one's sense of efficacy, it is clearly desirable for the children to perceive the groups as fluid (and for the groups to *be* fluid, of course). Second, having the groups meet at a different time each day will help to ensure that the students in each group have the opportunity to receive some of their small-group literacy instruction when they are relatively fresh.

The instruction provided during small-group time should be guided by the skills and performance levels of the children in the group. Children who are performing at levels substantially below grade level (Group 1 in the current scenario) are obviously ready to learn very different things than children who are performing substantially above grade level. For example, the children in Group 1 may be limited in their phonemic awareness, knowledge of the alphabet, and understanding of print conventions. Thus these skills will need to be explicitly addressed in the small-group context, at least early in the year (and these children should be provided with additional support services from the beginning of the school year). Children in Groups 3 and 4, on the other hand, probably have these skills fairly well established, and, as a result, most of their small-group time can focus on engaging them in learning more advanced skills and strategies and in reading and responding to books and other texts.

In the ISA, the typical components of a small-group lesson include the following:

- Rereading a book or books from previous lesson(s).
- Alphabetics, including isolated phonological analysis instruction for children with very limited skill, and instruction on decoding and encoding skills.
- Reading a new book or books.
- Writing.
- Practicing high-frequency words.

Table 2.3 on pp. 51–53 provides an outline of what small-group lessons might look like at the beginning of first grade for children in the four groups described above. For purposes of illustration, Group 1 is assumed to be at an emergent level, and Groups 2, 3, and 4 are considered to be at various points along the continuum that might be considered "developing." If there are maturing or proficient readers in the class, the teacher might need to consider adding a group and/or arranging for these children to join a second-grade group taught by another teacher. (Please note that the group designations in Table 2.3 are different from the *emergent, developing, maturing,* and *proficient* designations illustrated in Table 2.2). At the beginning of first grade, it is unlikely that many children would have the skills of a mature or proficient reader. However, the range of skills within the "developing" designation is likely to be broad enough to warrant separating children into groups for reading instruction.

Prior to meeting with the groups, the teacher selects the new book(s) for each group to read. Because the groups are at different points in development, each group will read different books—books that provide them with some challenge but not so much challenge as to create frustration. The teacher plans the alphabetics portion of the lesson with an eye toward helping the children to meet the challenge(s) that the book will present.

In reviewing Table 2.3, note that, when specific instructional activities are named (e.g., onset–rime blending, singing the alphabet), these are meant as examples only. Different activities (e.g., sorting pictures by ending sound, filling in missing letters on an alphabet strip), based on students' developing skills, would be selected on different days.

Interventions beyond the Classroom

Where Does Time for Intervention Fit In?

For at-risk children who are deemed to be in need of additional support services, it can be more than a bit of a challenge to find time in the day to provide *additional* intervention services. However, if it is determined that a child needs more instructional support than what can be provided within the classroom program, that support needs to be provided *in addition* to the supported small-group reading provided in the classroom. Only then can intensification of instructional experiences be achieved. In the sample schedule provided in Figure 2.1, the ideal time for additional intervention would be during the times when the classroom teacher is engaged in providing small-group instruction to children in groups other than the one to which the child belongs. Because children would probably benefit from a bit of a break between their small-group classroom instruction and their intervention lesson, it may be ideal to allow them 15–25 minutes of center time between the two lessons. If the intervention teachers cannot accommodate to the rotating schedule suggested, of course, the time slots for individual groups would need to be stabilized.

(text resumes on page 54)

TABLE 2.3. Small-Group Lesson: Four Different Groups in One Classroom at the Beginning of First Grade

Lesson components		Group 1 (lowest)	Group 2	Group 3	Group 4 (highest)
Rereading	All groups	Each child individually reads one or two books from prior small-group sessions. Children are allowed to choose their books from a selection provided by the teacher. The teacher listens in and provides guidance to individual children.			
	Separate groups	Teacher attends to print concepts and conventions.	Teacher attends to voice–print match, use of initial letter cue, and context.	Teacher attends to confirmatory use of print (including single letters and larger orthographic units) and context for word solving.	
Phonological analysis	Separate groups	Teacher engages children in onset–rime blending.	Teacher engages children in phoneme segmentation using sound boxes.	Not needed.	Not needed.
Decoding and encoding	All groups	Teacher plans to teach a specific decoding skill that can be applied in the new book that the children will read.			
	Separate groups	Sing whole alphabet song a few times while pointing to letters. Then focus on learning the names of one or two letters that occur frequently in the new book for the day.	Focus on letter–sound correspondence for consonants that occur frequently in the new book for the day and/or on a new word family that will appear multiple times in the book. For word families, practice incorporates one or more previously taught word families.	Depending on the characteristics of the book to be read, the teacher may teach and/or review word families or other decoding elements that will enable children to successfully puzzle through unfamiliar words that will appear in the day's new book(s).	

(continued)

TABLE 2.3. (continued)

Lesson components		Group 1 (lowest)	Group 2	Group 3	Group 4 (highest)
Reading new books	All groups	Teacher prepares the children to successfully read the book selected for the group. Part of the preparation occurs in the alphabet knowledge segment of the lesson (see above). Additional preparation may include: (1) teaching a new word identification strategy that can be applied in the new book and/or reviewing strategies that have already been taught; (2) teaching one or more high-frequency words that will occur in the text and which the children are unlikely to be able to identify, given their current decoding skills and the contextual support for word identification provided by the text; and/or (3) providing a book introduction that is sufficiently detailed as to allow the children to be successful in the text but not so detailed as to limit the children's opportunities to be strategic. Each child will have the opportunity to read the entire book at least once during the small-group session. The teacher provides the level of support that is appropriate. There should be a focus on the meaning of the text before, during, and after reading the new book. If time allows, two books may be read during this segment of the lesson.			
	Separate groups	Text selection: Use texts in which there is a reliable and repetitive language pattern and a close correspondence between the pictures and the text. Texts that support the development of letter recognition and identification are preferred.	Text selection: Use texts that make some use of repetitive language and provide the opportunity for the children to effectively use initial letters in combination with context to puzzle through unfamiliar words. Texts specifically designed to promote the development of high-frequency sight vocabulary might also be used.	Text selection: Dependent on the instructional materials in use.	
High-frequency words	Separate groups	Children rely on nonalphabetic features for word learning until they learn about the alphabet. Word learning is very idiosyncratic. Only words in which the children can identify all of the letters should be taught. Words should be initially taught in preparation for a book that the children will read.	To begin to learn high-frequency words, children need to attend to the letters in the words. Texts in which the high-frequency words occur in slightly different contexts will facilitate this learning; so too will having opportunities to write and name the words in word-learning games (see Chapter 13) and in the writing portion of the lesson.	The introduction of high-frequency words before reading a text should become more selective. Teachers should explicitly introduce high-frequency words from upcoming texts only if, in his or her judgment, the children do not have the skills and strategies to successfully identify them on their own. (The ability to do so will, of course, depend in part on the contextual support for word solving.)	

	All groups	High-frequency words serve as an important anchor for children in puzzling through texts at their level. Helping children to become automatic in identifying words they have encountered in text will allow them to be more effectively strategic in puzzling through less familiar words. A variety of game-like activities, such as sticky-note bingo (see Chapter 13), can be used to support the development of fluency with high-frequency words.		
Writing	All groups	Shared writing conducted in whole-class contexts provides the teacher with the opportunity to demonstrate various aspects of the writing process. In small groups, children should be involved in both shared and supported writing, with the teacher specifically focusing on what the children are ready to learn. In small-group and intervention lessons, writing may occur following the reading of a book and typically (but not always) involves writing a response to the book that was read. To maximize the use of the time available to write, the teacher often provides a fairly specific writing prompt.		
	Separate groups	Teachers need to focus on print concepts and the formation of individual letters. They may serve as scribes in the composition process. Teachers often model, and engage children in analyzing, the phonological components of words to be written.	Teachers model and engage children in composing messages and analyzing the phonemes in individual words. Particular emphasis is placed on analyzing and spelling the beginning sounds in words. Children are encouraged to use the key word chart to remind them of letter–sound relationships and to refer to the "Words I Know" chart for the spellings of known high-frequency words.	Teachers model and engage children in more thorough sound analysis and spelling of words. Children are encouraged to refer to available resources to support their spelling, including the book they are responding to and the key word, "Words I Know," and phonogram charts.

What Do/Should Intervention Lessons Look Like?

Early research on the ISA focused solely on providing interventions beyond the classroom (Vellutino et al., 1996; Scanlon et al., 2005). The classroom application of the approach was based on the success of the interventions and the belief that classroom teachers would benefit from having the knowledge and insights into literacy development that we had been developing with the intervention teachers with whom we worked. Therefore, from our perspective, Tier 2 and Tier 3 interventions should look very much like high-quality, supported, small-group literacy lessons that would be provided in the classroom. Ideally, however, the group size in intervention settings beyond the classroom would be smaller than the group sizes that are possible or necessary at the classroom level. This smaller size would allow the intervention teacher to individualize instruction a bit more than the classroom teacher is typically able to do. As we stress at several points throughout this book, in order to maximize the effectiveness of literacy instruction for children in intervention, it is important to ensure that the instruction offered in the classroom and instruction offered in intervention settings are mutually supportive. We address this topic in several ways in upcoming chapters that focus on the instructional goals of the ISA. We feel that when classroom and intervention teachers share a common set of instructional goals and continually reflect on ways to address those goals, the instruction they offer is more likely to be effective in supporting children's literacy development.

CHAPTER 3

Motivation to Read and Write

MOTIVATION GOAL

The child will develop the belief that reading and writing are enjoyable and informative activities that are not beyond his or her capabilities.

Motivation is what gets one going, keeps one engaged, and moves one forward in any task that requires effort. Attention to children's motivation for reading and writing is especially important in discussions of RTI because it is widely recognized that individuals who find learning challenging are apt to try to avoid those learning situations (Morgan, Fuchs, Compton, Cordray, & Fuchs, 2008; Stanovich, 1986; Taylor & Adelman, 1999). Children who are involved in an RTI process related to literacy are, by definition, experiencing difficulty with literacy acquisition.

If students are not motivated to learn to read and write, instruction will have limited impact. Most young children begin school eager to learn to read and write and fully expect that they will successfully learn to do so (McKenna, Kear, & Ellsworth, 1995). Unfortunately, this initial motivation begins to wane by as early as second grade (Marinak, Malloy, Gambrell, & Mazzoni, 2015). When children encounter difficulties with learning, their enthusiasm is likely to dissipate, their beliefs about themselves as learners are likely to change, and they may come to view literate activities as work rather than as enjoyable and informative undertakings. Indeed, children who struggle with becoming literate often try to avoid reading and writing; as a result, they do less of it and make less progress. The challenge for teachers, then, is to try to avoid this downward spiral.

Motivation and the CCSS

The CCSS call for students to achieve at higher levels than they have in the past with the goal of ensuring that all students are college and career ready by the time they leave high school (NGA & CCSSO, 2010). Remarkably, although there is a wealth of research demonstrating strong relationships between motivation and academic achievement, with the work of Guthrie and his colleagues being especially prominent (e.g., Guthrie & Wigfield, 2000), the CCSS do not address motivation nor take account of the guidance that such research provides. In fact, if anything, the emphasis in the CCSS on increasing the complexity of the texts that students are required to read, increasing performance expectations more generally, and using approaches to assessment that communicate to a large number of students, their families, and teachers that they are failing has the clear potential to reduce students' academic motivation and, thereby, their achievement. Thus the CCSS have the potential to produce the exact opposite effect from the one the Standards were intended to achieve.

Research clearly demonstrates that, on average, achievement motivation is enhanced when students encounter moderate rather than extreme levels of challenge in their academic endeavors and when their attention is turned to their effort rather than to achievement or ability levels (Dweck, Walton, & Cohen, 2014). Although the CCSS may have many potentially positive influences, the lack of attention to the social/emotional aspects of student learning is likely a disservice to students and the cause more generally.

Motivation and ELs

Depending on their degree of proficiency with English, young children who are simultaneously learning the spoken and written forms of a second or additional language are apt to experience substantial challenges. Numerous aspects of the additional language are likely to be confusing and challenging to them in its spoken form, including the words for common objects, concepts, and actions, the sentence structures, the way intonation is used to signal meaning, and the phonemes that are used (or not used). Learning the written form adds additional challenges and potential points of confusion. For example, in comparison with the first language, the additional language may differ in the level of information provided by the symbols that make up the printed language (e.g., phonemes in English, entire words in Chinese) and how the print is oriented (e.g., words are read from left to right in English, from right to left in Arabic, and from top to bottom in Chinese).

All of these challenges have the potential to overwhelm a young child. To help children build and maintain enthusiasm for learning to speak, read, and write in the additional language, teachers need to be sensitive to the types of challenges the child faces given his or her particular home/first language so as to help the child meet those challenges. In subsequent chapters, as we discuss specific aspects of the reading process, we offer some examples of how teachers can be responsive to various types of language differences. In this chapter on motivation, we simply highlight the need for sensitivity to these differences. Virtually everything we discuss in this chapter related to motivation applies to all young children—those who are learning English as an additional language and those for whom English is their first language.

Teaching to Promote Motivation to Learn

In this chapter we discuss things that teachers can do that may maintain and enhance children's initial enthusiasm and help them to adopt belief systems that promote active and joyful engagement in literate activities. The topics to be discussed include:

- The importance of engaging children in reading and listening to interesting texts and reacting to them.
- The importance of providing children with some choice in what they read and write.
- Helping children develop a sense of competence and confidence in their literacy skills by:
  o Ensuring that the texts they encounter, particularly those they read and write, are not too challenging.
  o Helping them to develop effective approaches to solving problems they encounter with both word reading and comprehension.
  o Scaffolding their reading—providing just enough support to allow them to succeed but not so much support that they do not learn how to engage independently.
- Helping the children to value literacy for its own sake rather than viewing it as "work" for which they should be rewarded.
- Helping children to notice their successes and to attribute their success to things that are under their control—such as the amount of effort they expend and the strategic problem solving they do—rather than to factors that are beyond their control.

Promoting Interest in Books

Teachers often identify "developing a love of reading" as one of their major instructional goals (Nolen, 2001). Clearly, children are more likely to love reading if they love the books that they read or hear and if they enjoy the interactions that occur around these books. In the early primary grades (and before), reading aloud to children provides an important context for developing this love. Children who have had a lot of positive experiences with being read to are likely to already love being read to and will continue to enjoy it and profit from it during the primary-grade years (and beyond). However, many children who struggle at the early stages of literacy development have not had the hundreds (or thousands) of hours of book experience we would like them to have. Therefore, they may not yet know about the pleasure that books can provide. It will be especially helpful to engage these children in listening and reacting to books that are of particular interest to them. Thus a teacher might make a point of choosing to read a book on certain cultural traditions, certain animals, certain family dynamics, and so forth, because she or he knows that those topics will be of particular interest to one or more of the students. Letting children know that a book was selected for them because of their particular interests will help them to understand that books can be special to them as individuals—a very motivating thought!

Web Resources

There are several websites that can assist teachers (and parents) as they endeavor to identify books that may appeal to the varied interests of young children. *Titlewave.com*, for example, allows searches based on major topics (e.g., animals, holidays, science, people) and subtopics within those topics (e.g., polar bears, Cinco de Mayo, habitats, U.S. presidents). Further, particular interest levels can be designated (e.g., kindergarten through third, fourth through sixth), as can book levels as indicated by grade and month in school (e.g., a book at level 1.8 would be a book that an average child in the eighth month of first grade should be able to read fairly independently).[1] Other useful websites for searching for books by interest level include *Amazon.com*, *Kansas.bookconnect.com*, and *Scholastic.com*.

Lastly, the website for the Collaborative in Equity Literacy Learning (CELL; *http://cell.msmc.edu/literature/*) provides access to annotated bibliographies on more than 150 multicultural books, organized by grade bands, that can be used to diversify the elementary section of Appendix B of the CCSS.

Interactive Read-Alouds

We discuss the value of interactive read-alouds in several of the upcoming chapters because they are valuable in many ways. In this chapter we focus on the role of interactive read-alouds in promoting motivation to read and write. Books read during interactive read-alouds are often more challenging than books that the children would be able to read on their own, and the reader generally does not direct

---

[1] It is important to note that there are a number of ways in which books are "leveled" for readability and that the leveling systems generally do not totally agree with one another. We are not necessarily endorsing the leveling system utilized by any of the websites we cite.

Interactive Read-Alouds
from a Motivational Perspective

Be enthusiastic. The teacher should show enthusiasm for and interest in the reading materials in use.

Collaborate—don't test. Interactions concerning a text should have a collaborative rather than a test-like tone. The teacher should avoid asking questions to which she or he clearly already knows the answer. There is no reason to ask such questions other than to "test" the children's understanding. Rather, teachers should offer their own thinking about the text and invite children to share theirs. Both the teacher and the children should ask genuine questions, analyze, interpret, and react to the text. Teachers should avoid the use of evaluative language. For example, rather than asking whether a prediction was right or wrong, the teacher might ask whether the children's prediction *matched the author's thinking.*

Discuss the illustrations. The teacher should occasionally provide opportunities for the children to enjoy and discuss the illustrations and to use the illustrations to inform their understanding of the text. For example, children might use an illustration to determine how a character was feeling (by considering the character's facial expression) or to infer what time of year the story takes place (by noticing what the characters are wearing or what the environment looks like). In an informational text, the children can be encouraged to attend to the illustrations to better understand the sequence of steps in a process or to assist in comparing and contrasting characteristics. Such attention to illustration also supports the related informational text standard in the CCSS (RI.1.7: Use the illustrations and details in a text to describe its key ideas).

Encourage personal reactions to the text. Encourage the children to discuss how they might have reacted and/or felt in a situation similar to that depicted in the story and/or what they found surprising or interesting about the information in the text. The teacher should also share her or his personal reactions (but should not dominate the conversation).

Edit or modify the text. Occasionally rewrite a portion of the text in a way that the children suggest. For example, in the book *The Velveteen Rabbit* (Williams, 1922) the children might like to add a page or two telling how the boy got a new rabbit. Or, in an informational text about the life cycle of butterflies, the children might be assisted in finding additional illustrations or explanations of points in the metamorphosis.

Act out portions of the story. It is often fun for children to act out some or all aspects of a story they have heard. Such activities engage the children in (sometimes passionate) discussions of the sequence of story events, which has many benefits for their language development and supports many of the Reading Standards for Literature of the CCSS. Providing a few props (e.g., items of clothing befitting the main characters) can be particularly motivating. Also, providing a copy of the text for children to refer to as they plan their reenactment will help them to view books as valuable resources (Welsch, 2008).

the children's attention to the print very much, if at all. When reading books with pictures, the reader does, of course, encourage the children to attend to the pictures to enhance both their understanding of the text and their aesthetic experience. What makes an interactive read-aloud *interactive* is that the children and the reader engage in conversation about the book and that the conversation is not entirely controlled or initiated by the reader. Thus, ideally, in an interactive read-aloud the children are free to offer their observations, ask and answer questions, make predictions, and generally react to the text fairly freely. The reader also shares her or his thinking and draws children's attention to various aspects of the text, depending on the purposes for reading a particular text.

At the most obvious level, reading aloud to children helps to build motivation to read, because listening to books that capture their imagination or offer information that interests them is just plain enjoyable for them. They get "hooked" and are apt to want to listen to more books on the same or similar topics and/or by the same author. Reading aloud to children can also promote children's interest in composing their own texts, particularly when children are helped to notice and appreciate what authors and illustrators do in creating books. For example, while children often readily become involved in the storyline of a fictional book, they are often surprised when, on occasion, the reader steps back a bit to help them think about the author's and illustrator's craft. For instance, the reader might point out how the author makes the audience feel particular ways by the words he or she chooses or how the illustrator conveys information that is not made explicit by the author.

While a teacher may, and typically should, have multiple reasons for selecting a particular book to use for an interactive read-aloud, developing a love of reading and writing should always be an important purpose. Thus, *the first encounter with a book should always be focused on stimulating enjoyment and comprehension of the text.* In the box entitled "Interactive Read-Alouds from a Motivational Perspective," we provide some suggestions for making interactive read-alouds fun and motivating experiences.

Supported, Buddy, and/or Independent Reading

When the children are doing the reading themselves, either with teacher guidance (supported reading), with a friend (buddy reading), or independently, attention to the motivational features of the experiences is extremely important, as it is during these experiences that children develop their sense of themselves as readers. With regard to promoting interest in books, children, especially those with limited early exposure to books, need to be introduced to the wide variety of books currently available to be read by beginning readers and, once introduced, need to be encouraged to notice which topics/authors/genres they find appealing. With the emergence of the CCSS, there has been much greater emphasis on the inclusion of informational texts in children's reading diet, and with that emphasis has come an increase in the number of nonfiction texts written to be read by young children.

Motivationally, this shift may prove to be particularly beneficial for young boys, as research suggests that they have a stronger preference for reading informational texts than fictional offerings.

Providing Choice in What Is Read

Providing children with choices about which books they read has been shown to have a large benefit in improving reading comprehension (Guthrie & Humenick, 2004). As children's familiarity with various topics/authors/genres increases, they are likely to develop individual preferences, which, essentially, is part of developing an identity as a reader (Johnston, 2004). Although it is certainly not possible to offer children complete choice, especially in the context of small-group reading instruction, for which the teacher needs to plan book introductions and skill instruction that will prepare the children to read the books to be read during lessons, there can be many opportunities for children to choose their reading materials at other points in the day.

Developing a Sense of Confidence and Competence

Several factors can influence the development of confidence and a sense of competence for beginning and struggling readers. We discuss three particularly important factors in this section: keeping the challenge at a moderate level, helping children develop effective approaches to problem solving, and providing just enough support in problem-solving situations.

Moderate Degree of Challenge

As Schultheiss and Brunstein (2005) report, successful experiences lead to hopefulness and an inclination to seek further opportunities to solve similar problems, whereas repeated experiences with failure lead to expectations of further failure and therefore lead one away from engagement. This is one of the reasons that RTI has the potential to be so powerful: In comparison to pre-RTI days, it encourages schools to organize instruction to meet students' needs sooner and in smaller instructional groupings. This, in turn, allows for greater individualization with regard to instruction, and such individualization is likely to lead to greater gains on the part of children.

When children are frequently asked to read texts that are too difficult for them, as texts for struggling readers often are, they are likely to try to find ways to avoid the whole enterprise. They might, for example, try to engage the teacher and/or peers in conversation, or they might find multiple excuses to move around the classroom (to use the rest room, to sharpen a pencil, to get a drink of water, etc.) or indicate that they are tired and put their heads down on the table.

When the teacher sees behaviors, such as those described in the previous paragraph, an important question to consider is "Am I asking this child to do something that, from the child's perspective, is too challenging?" If the answer is yes, or possibly yes, the teacher should consider ways to reduce the level of challenge, at least temporarily, in order to begin to build the child's confidence. In the context of reading, this might mean offering easier texts or making the texts more accessible, as described in Chapter 12 at the "More Support" end of the continuum described on pp. 261–262. In upcoming chapters we revisit the issue of literacy-related challenges in various ways. For now, the "take-away message" is that the level of challenge that children encounter in literacy activities affects their sense of competence and their literacy motivation more generally.

Easy Reading

In my (JMS) reading room, in addition to books that are at an appropriate level for supported reading groups and that allow students the right amount of successful problem solving, I also have books available for my first graders that they are able to read independently. They enjoy going back to these books and reading them again and again. (It does not have to eat up a lot of time.) I think it's important for them to have these experiences with books in which students feel complete competence. They beam. Videotaping them and showing them the videos also provides them feedback, which builds their confidence and helps them to see themselves as readers. I think one of the benefits of this practice is that my struggling readers see peers in their classrooms who are reading without consciously employing strategies, and they recognize them as "good" readers. When the children who struggle read texts without the need for conscious word solving, they, too, feel like "good" readers.

Developing Effective Approaches to Problem Solving

Instruction that focuses on the development of word identification strategies has the potential to contribute to children's sense of competence[2] as readers because it gives them the tools to figure out unfamiliar words that they encounter in text—one of the most challenging parts of the reading process for many beginning and struggling readers. Here we address aspects of instructional and interpersonal interactions around word solving that can influence the child's willingness to engage in the process. This willingness (or motivation) is important because, if readers believe that they will be able to figure out the unfamiliar words they encounter, they are much more likely to expend the effort that it might take to do so.

For most individuals, a sense of competence develops through successful experiences with a particular activity and recognition of that success. With regard to

---

[2] A sense of competence is sometimes referred to as *self-efficacy,* which Bandura (1997) defines as learners' perceived capabilities for learning or performing actions at designated levels.

word solving, we have found it useful to explicitly teach several word identification strategies (as discussed in Chapter 12) and to provide the children with guidance and practice in using the strategies in interactive and confirmatory ways, ultimately helping them to become spontaneous and independent in the use of their problem-solving skills and to recognize their own ability. For example, the teacher might say, "I saw you make that first sound and then read past that puzzling word to get a better idea of what word would make sense. You are really thinking like a reader!" or "I see you checking your key word chart to help you remember the sound of that letter! That's what readers do when they need to!" Both of these comments focus on the problem-solving process, provide the reader with a vote of confidence in her or his word-solving skills, and, therefore, help the reader build a sense of competence.

In addition to explicit discussion of word-solving strategies, the way in which teachers and peers talk about and react to successes and difficulties with word solving can be very influential in shaping how learners think about the process and their own ability to engage in that process. For example, when a child encounters an unknown word in text and the teacher says "Oh, that's a hard [tricky, challenging] word," it might lead some children to give up on solving the word. As an alternative, the teacher might use the word *puzzling* to describe the unknown word because it more clearly conveys the need to think about what the word might be and to use various sources of information to solve it.

The reactions of peers (and others, such as parents and older siblings) to children's word-solving efforts can also influence their motivation and sense of competence. For example, when someone loses patience with a child's attempts at puzzling through a word and does something that reflects that impatience, it is likely to diminish the child's sense of competence. Reactions that might undermine a child's confidence include providing the word (with an impatient tone of voice) or saying things like "You know that word!" or "You just read that word on the other page!" So too are comments such as "Who can help Alex?", which conveys that, although Alex can't solve a particular word, the teacher fully expects that other children can.

We encourage teachers to put word solving in a positive light by talking about how figuring out a new word is a bit like doing a puzzle: You may need to think about several different things (e.g., the shape of the piece, the color of the piece, the larger picture into which the piece must fit) in order to figure out which piece fits just right. By emphasizing the pleasure of figuring something out, we can put word solving in an entirely different light both for children who may become impatient while waiting for a peer to figure things out and for those who may need a bit more time to puzzle through a word. We do not, of course, wish to suggest that word-solving assistance should never be provided. Indeed, providing thoughtful in-the-moment assistance with word solving is an important aspect of literacy instruction. However, the assistance offered should have the goal of enhancing children's word-solving strategies and their sense that they have the ability to puzzle through unfamiliar words successfully.

Scaffolding Children's Reading

Building a sense of competence for carrying out a complex process such as reading occurs over a protracted period of time and, for some children, requires a substantial amount of teacher guidance. The way in which the teacher provides guidance and the kind of guidance provided can make a difference. A teacher who is too directive may prevent the child from engaging in the kind of problem-solving efforts that will build his or her ability to problem-solve independently and thereby interfere with the development of a sense of competence. On the other hand, a teacher who offers too little guidance may put children in the position of being overwhelmed and frustrated in their attempts to read; this too will interfere with their development of a sense of competence. Thus an early literacy teacher needs to do a bit of a balancing act to try to ensure that the support that she or he offers is "just right."

To do so, teachers must have insight into how children approach a task so that they can recognize the children's sources of confusion and help to effectively clear them up. For example, when a child misidentifies a word encountered while reading, the teacher is likely to recognize the error immediately—because the teacher already knows the word. The child, on the other hand, obviously does not already know the word and therefore may not realize that an error has occurred until he or she gets further along in the sentence or paragraph. The teacher's response to the child in this situation will influence the child's sense of competence and hence his or her motivation to persist. If the teacher jumps right in to correct the child before the context has clued the child in to the problem, the child's sense of competence can be undermined. If, however, the teacher provides the child with the time to notice and potentially correct the error, the child's sense of competence is likely to be enhanced. Tables 3.1 and 3.2 provide some examples to illustrate this point. We discuss the issue of trying to offer just the right amount of support in several places throughout this book. The point here is that appropriate scaffolding makes an important contribution to children's sense of competence.

TABLE 3.1. Sample Interactions Following a Word Identification Error That *Will* Promote a Sense of Competence in Reading

Teacher response	Child's possible interpretation
Waits until the child has read far enough along to realize that an error has occurred.	"I'm not sure about that word—but maybe I'll figure it out if I read a little further."
Notices when the child notices a word identification error (e.g., "I hear you slowing down there—are you thinking that something is not quite right?").	"It's OK to slow down and think a bit when something doesn't seem right."
Notices when the child spontaneously corrects a word identification error and encourages the child to reflect on this success (e.g., "I noticed that you went back and changed that word. How did you know that that word was . . . ?").	"I know how to figure out words."

TABLE 3.2. Sample Interactions Following a Word Identification Error That *Will Not* Promote a Sense of Competence in Reading

Teacher response	Child's possible interpretation
Too much support: Identifies the error *before* the child has read far enough to realize that an error has occurred.	"I can't do this on my own" or "I need someone to tell me the words I don't know."
Too little support: Allows the child to keep reading, despite error(s).	"Guessing at the words seems to be OK with my teacher" or "All I have to do is say something and keep going—I'm not sure what I'm supposed to be doing here!"

Attributions for Success

Motivation researchers have identified two general types of beliefs that students may hold with regard to their academic/intellectual abilities: fixed versus malleable (Dweck & Molden, 2005). That is, some students believe that their abilities are fixed or unchangeable—for example, believing "I'm not good at reading and I will never be." Students who hold this belief may see little reason to expend the effort it might take to improve. Other students appear to believe that academic abilities are malleable (they can be changed). Such students believe that their current status, whatever it may be, is temporary. Children who hold this belief are more likely to maintain motivation in the face of difficulty (Niiya, Crocker, & Bartmess, 2004).

Early research relating to children's motivation to read indicated that children in the early primary grades tended to think of their abilities as changeable and under their control. They tended to believe that, if they put in enough effort, they could do just about anything (Chapman & Tunmer, 1995; Nicholls, 1978, 1990). Children attribute their learning successes to their efforts rather than to innate abilities. Older students, on the other hand, particularly those who struggle with academics, tended to think of their abilities as being unchangeable and not within their control. They did not see their efforts as being an important determinant of their progress. Needless to say, once struggling learners come to believe that there is little they can do to improve their reading ability, their motivation to engage in reading is likely to be substantially diminished. Unfortunately, because of the systems in place both at the time this research was done and currently, schools contribute to this belief system by identifying the children who make the least progress as *learning disabled* or, in some settings, *dyslexic,* which has the clear potential to diminish motivation and create a sense of helplessness both in the child and in those responsible for teaching him or her.

Although we found no recent research that directly addresses young children's attributions for success and failure in literacy acquisition, informal polls of teachers we know who are working with young children suggest that things have changed. Several indicate that by January of their kindergarten year some children have already developed a fixed mind-set. We speculate that this may be due to the incredible increases in the amount of assessment they experience these days as compared with the time of the original research. When children are frequently asked to do things that are too challenging for them, which is what happens on assessments for children who are performing below grade-level expectations, it seems only logical that they would come to believe that they will forever be less able than their peers. This is something that educators need to work against, as well as working against the extensive amount of testing in general.

Thus an important goal of early intervention for struggling learners is to keep children from adopting beliefs about their abilities that are counterproductive. One way of doing this is to help children become stronger readers—which is the focus of much of this book. However, there are other ways to try to keep children from adopting a fixed view of their abilities. To do this, we encourage teachers to explain the roles of practice and effort and to help children reflect on their successes.

The Role of Practice and Effort

In general, the more reading a child does, the easier reading becomes. Although teachers clearly understand this, some children do not. Children who struggle, particularly those who are frequently asked to read texts that are too challenging for them, can come to believe that reading will always be difficult for them—because it always has been. This is a very logical but unfortunate conclusion.

Several of the teachers with whom we have worked have found it useful to explain the practice–progress relationship through the use of analogies that illustrate how effort can serve to make a task that seems very challenging eventually manageable and, ultimately, nearly effortless. For example, for a child who already knows how to ride a bike, a teacher might talk about how hard and frustrating it was to learn and how easy it is now. Alternatively, for children who have younger

---

An Anecdote

I (DMS) once observed a little boy who was receiving daily one-to-one tutoring in reading and making very little progress. After observing a lesson and finding nothing clearly amiss in its focus and pace, I had a little chat with the child. I explained to him that Mrs. D (the tutor) really knew how to teach children to read and that if he really tried to do the things that Mrs. D asked, it would be much easier to learn to read.

"Really?!?" he said with a note of both disbelief and surprise and eyes opened wide.

"Really!" I said with conviction.

From that point forward, the child made much more rapid progress. The tutor was astounded, and so was I. The child's sudden increase in rate of progress might certainly have occurred without this little chat. However, in light of the research discussed in this section (which, at the time, I had not yet read), it seems possible that his enhanced growth may have been due to a newfound belief that he *could* learn to read.

siblings, the teacher might talk about how difficult it is initially to learn to walk and/or talk and how easy it is for (most) children in kindergarten and first grade to do those things.

Attending to and Reflecting on Success

Although we certainly want children to be willing to expend the effort it will take to grow as readers, simply telling them to try harder is not likely to accomplish this goal. It has long been recognized that one of the most effective ways to elicit desired behaviors from children is to attend to desired behaviors. For example, when a group of kindergartners becomes too noisy during a read-aloud, one of the most effective ways to quiet them down is to notice the children who are engaged in the story in appropriate ways: "Mike and Michaela are listening and thinking . . . ."

A similar tactic can be used in supporting individuals concerning word solving or comprehension monitoring: "You went back and reread that when it wasn't making sense to you. That worked, didn't it?" Particularly when children are first learning to be strategic readers, noticing and naming children's productive attempts at problem solving reinforces those strategies. Further, children can be encouraged to attend to and reflect on their own successes initially by asking them to explain how they solved particular problems ("How did you know that word was . . . ?") and later by asking them to identify and reflect on instances when they were effective problem solvers.

Goal Orientation: Intrinsic versus Extrinsic Motivation

A child who is intrinsically motivated wants to do/learn/participate in something because it is interesting and valuable to her or him. On the other hand, a child who is extrinsically motivated engages in activities for the sake of earning social rewards, such as praise or recognition, or physical rewards, such as stickers or some form of token that can be traded for a desired commodity (free time, reduction in homework, etc.). In a very simplified form, a summary of the research on extrinsic versus intrinsic motivation suggests that children who are intrinsically motivated to learn are more likely to succeed at challenging academic tasks (see Schunk, Pintrich, & Meece, 2008), whereas students who need to be extrinsically motivated in order to engage in academically challenging tasks tend to have poorer academic outcomes.

Although students can be both intrinsically and extrinsically motivated, schools tend to be organized around extrinsic motivation systems—grades, rewards, and praise—so many students tend to focus on the external reward. Because research suggests that intrinsic motivation leads to greater long-term learning, the motivational systems that characterize schools need to be carefully considered. McKenna et al. (1995) documented a general decline in motivation for reading among children as they progressed through the elementary years. This decline may well be related to the extrinsic motivational systems that characterize many schools.

Many of the suggestions made earlier in this chapter will help to promote the development of intrinsic motivation. In addition, we encourage teachers to do the following:

- *Treat reading and writing as a privilege (not as work).* When teachers treat reading and writing as jobs that must be accomplished or completed in order to gain access to more preferred activities (e.g., recess or free-choice time in the classroom), children, especially those who struggle with literacy acquisition, are likely to view reading and writing as work. If, on the other hand, teachers convey the idea that reading and writing are pleasurable activities that are valuable in their own right, children are more apt to adopt such a perspective. Think, for a moment, about what we convey to children when we say, "Let's get our (reading or writing) work done so that we can have free time." One translation of this is, "Let's get this unpleasant (reading or writing) work done so that we can have the reward of not having to read or write anymore!" Such a message is clearly not intended. Minor changes in wording can dramatically alter the interpretation of a statement or request. Table 3.3 provides some suggestions for rephrasing to send very different motivational messages.

- *Avoid social comparisons and encourage personal comparisons.* Because children begin their school careers at very different places in development, progress and achievement for each child need to be evaluated using different metrics. For example, a child who begins kindergarten knowing the names of all of the letters of the alphabet is not necessarily a better student than one who knows few letters at the beginning of the school year but learns several during the first few weeks or months of school. However, it is not unusual to find classrooms in which student achievement, even on such foundational skills, is publicly posted, apparently with the intention of motivating more students to attain the same level of skill. In such a classroom, children who begin school with very limited early literacy skills are apt to begin to view themselves as inadequate early on. This self-perception of inadequacy can, ultimately, lead children to adopt identities in which they perceive themselves unable to perform at a level commensurate with their peers. Such a perception is likely to limit the children's willingness to exert the effort needed to grow and develop in literacy. On the other hand, if the same children were given the opportunity to evaluate their performance relative to their previous levels, there is a greater likelihood that they would experience the motivating feelings that come with advancing skills and accomplishments.

- *Use feedback judiciously to encourage intrinsic motivation and a mastery orientation.* What teachers say to children matters tremendously and can have significant impact on how children view themselves as learners. Teachers can convey that academic engagement and performance are primarily for the purpose of

TABLE 3.3. Unmotivating and Motivating Messages Teachers Might Send

Unmotivating messages	Motivating messages
"We need to read this book today before recess."	"We get to read this book today before recess."
"For homework, you need to practice these letters you don't know."	"For homework, you need to practice these letters you don't know *yet*."
"I want to see what you are going to write next. You need to finish your journal entry before you go to the block area."	"I can't wait to see what you are going to write next. I hope you *get* to finish your journal entry before you go to the block area."
"Let's see how many of these letters you know."	"Let's see how many of these letters you *already* know."
"Each of you will do a report on dinosaurs."	"You will each have a chance to do a report on a dinosaur that you are especially interested in."
"That's a hard word."	"That's a puzzling word."

pleasing the teacher ("What a good job" or "I like the way you . . .") or gaining social recognition ("You're so smart!")—both of which are, essentially, forms of extrinsic motivation. On the other hand, teachers can convey that learning and performance are rewarding in their own right ("What an interesting thought!" or "I bet it felt great to figure that out!"). Such responses to student thinking help to promote the development of intrinsic motivation.

Changes in Teachers' Language

In our work with both beginning and experienced teachers, we have often been surprised by how challenging it is for some of them to change their language in the ways suggested above (including in Table 3.3), but we certainly understand why such change is challenging. We are, essentially, encouraging teachers to change highly practiced ways of interacting. That said, most teachers who make the suggested changes report that they do see the impact on children's motivation. For example, with the simple addition of the word *already* when a teacher sits with a child to do an assessment (e.g., "I want to see how many of these words you *already* know") changes the situation from one in which the child, particularly one who is not meeting grade-level expectations, may feel that the focus is on what he or she can't do to one in which the child gets to show off what he or she *already* knows. As another example, the inclusion of the word *yet* (e.g., "We haven't learned how to do this *yet*") contributes to motivation by conveying the teacher's belief that the children will learn and communicates that children's abilities are malleable. Teachers report that recording themselves teaching and listening to those recordings helps them to attend to their language choices and work toward making the recommended changes.

Parents and Caregivers and Motivation

Parents and caregivers play an important role in children's literacy development, and their role with regard to motivation can be especially prominent. Although a thorough discussion of their roles in children's literacy development is beyond the scope of this book, we want to share a free (downloadable) resource that we and our colleagues developed to inform parents'/caregivers' efforts to support children's literacy learning and development. The resource is a booklet entitled *Helping Your Child Become a Reader* (Scanlon, Anderson, Morse, & Yurkewecz, 2012) that is made up of 20 questions that are frequently asked by those attempting to support the literacy development of beginning and struggling readers and answers to those questions. The answers are research-based and intended to be parent/caregiver-friendly. The booklet can be accessed at the following websites:

> *www.albany.edu/eltl/donna_scanlon.php*
> *www.albany.edu/crsc/parentbooklet.shtml*
> *www.isaprofessionaldevelopment.org*

It can be printed in its entirety or by individual questions—an option that was recommended by teachers who felt that parents might not read the entire booklet but would read individual questions, particularly if they were responsive to the individual parent's questions or a teacher's concern about a child's reading experiences at home.

Documenting Literacy Motivation

To help teachers be mindful of their students' motivational status, we provide a list of motivational characteristics that can be used to periodically document students' status on a variety of dimensions of motivation (see Figure 3.1). This tool, like the snapshots that are provided in most of the subsequent chapters, is intended to allow teachers to document the characteristics of children who are assigned to the same small group for literacy instruction. The teacher would list the names of children in the group at the top of each column and then rate each child on each characteristic on the basis of informal observations made during instruction. As depicted in the key for Figure 3.1, we suggest using a 3-point rating scale ranging from a "not at all" rating to an "absolutely" rating for a child. The purpose of these ratings is *not* to provide an overall score for motivation but to give a snapshot of the motivational status of the children in an instructional group. This enables the teacher to reflect on what may need to be done instructionally when students are observed to lack motivation and/or to hold beliefs that are associated with limitations in motivation.

The online supplement to this book (see the box at the end of the table of contents) provides similar snapshots that can be used to document the status of individual students across time as a means of documenting growth and change.

Group Snapshot—Motivation					
Student names					
Interest and engagement in read-alouds					
Child is enthusiastic about fictional read-alouds.					
Child is enthusiastic about informational read-alouds.					
Child demonstrates active engagement when being read to.					
Enthusiasm for reading and writing					
Child is enthusiastic about reading.					
Child is enthusiastic about writing.					
Self-perceptions					
Child perceives him- or herself as a capable reader.					
Child perceives him- or herself as a capable writer.					
When encountering difficulty while reading, child appears to believe that he or she has strategies to be successful.					
Interests					
Child has developed interests in particular genre/series of books.					
Understanding of the connection between practice and progress					
Child believes that his or her status as a reader is dependent on his or her effort.					
Child understands that reading practice will lead to reading growth.					

Key:
N = Not at all   S = Somewhat   A = Absolutely

FIGURE 3.1. Group snapshot for motivation.

PART II

Learning the Alphabetic Code

Introduction

The ability to accurately and automatically read the words in printed text enables readers to devote most of their cognitive resources to the process of meaning construction. There are tens of thousands of words that proficient readers of English can read automatically. Most of these words are not explicitly taught but, instead, are learned by effectively puzzling through unfamiliar words encountered while reading. Especially for beginning and struggling readers, multiple accurate identifications of previously unfamiliar words are required in order for the word to become part of the reader's sight vocabulary. Skill with the alphabetic code is an important (but certainly not the sole) contributor to the ability to puzzle through and identify unfamiliar written words and is an aspect of literacy development that frequently lags behind for students who experience literacy learning difficulties (Snow et al., 1998; National Reading Panel [NRP], 2000; Vellutino et al., 2004).

In Part II, we discuss some of the critical understandings that individuals need to develop in order to learn to read in an alphabetic writing system such as English. First, they must understand that the *purpose of print* is to communicate, and they must understand the basic *conventions of print*, such as that we read from left to right and, generally, from the top to the bottom of the page. They must also recognize that spoken words are composed of somewhat separable sounds that are strung together, and they must be able to manipulate those sounds (separate or segment the sounds in spoken words in attempting to write them and blend sounds when attempting to pronounce unfamiliar words encountered in printed

73

text). Someone who can analyze and manipulate the individual sounds in spoken words is said to have achieved *phonemic awareness*. Readers also need to understand that the letters in printed words represent the sounds in spoken words. This association is often referred to as the *alphabetic principle*; understanding the alphabetic principle enables children to learn to use the *alphabetic code* (or what many people refer to as *phonics*). Clearly, to understand the alphabetic principle and how to make use of the alphabetic code, one must know something about *letter names* and must be familiar with the most common sounds associated with the letters (*letter–sound association*). As readers gain skill and experience with an alphabetic language, they learn to process *larger orthographic units* such as phonograms (e.g., *ook, ight*), prefixes, and suffixes, and they learn to automatically identify other, larger orthographic units such as *tion*. Being able to process these larger units allows readers to be more efficient in identifying unfamiliar words.[1]

Figure II.1 provides a schematic representation of the progression from earlier to later phases of the development of skill with the alphabetic code. All phases are supported by and facilitate engagement in reading and writing, as depicted by the banner running across the bottom of the figure. On the far left, phonemic awareness and letter identification (letter-name knowledge) are identified as starting points for the developmental sequence. Instructionally, these two skill areas might be addressed separately until the student develops some familiarity with each. As depicted by the two-headed arrows, engagement in reading and writing (in this case, shared reading and writing activities) may help children become phonemically aware, learn the names of printed letters, and simultaneously learn about the purposes and conventions of print. Reciprocally, learning about letter names and becoming attuned to the sounds in spoken words helps children engage in reading and writing activities in more sophisticated ways.

Once children know the names of some letters and are somewhat phonemically aware (they can at least isolate the beginning sounds in words), they begin to learn about the relations between printed letters and the sounds they represent. Learning about letter sounds extends children's phonemic awareness and enhances their learning as they engage in reading and writing. Reading and writing, in turn, extend children's knowledge of letter–sound relationships. Thus the multiple experiences that children have with printed language become mutually supportive and reciprocal in nature.

Over time, skill in phonemic analysis and developing letter-sound knowledge help children to understand the *alphabetic principle*—the idea that the letters in printed words represent the sounds in spoken words. Insight into this principle allows children to learn about the workings of the alphabetic code. Early in development, children learn to attend to and use letters and sounds at the beginnings of words and then letters and sounds at the ends of words—rather than going

---

[1]The progression of skill development we describe for the alphabetic code is largely, although not entirely, consistent with Ehri's (2005) theory of word learning.

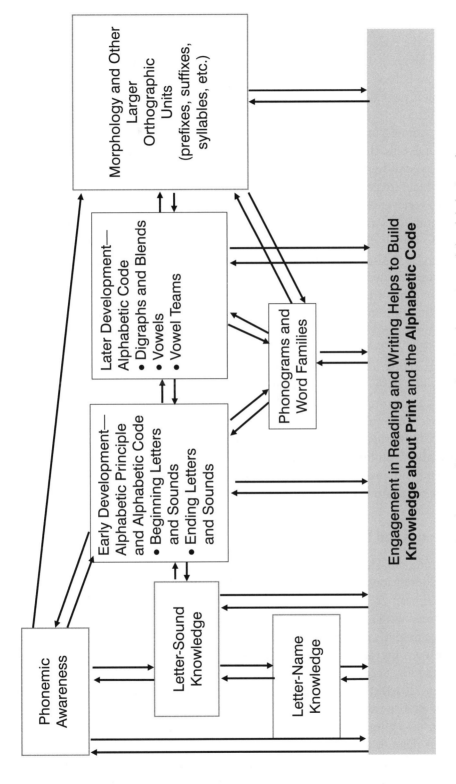

FIGURE II.1. Developmental progression in learning about print and the alphabetic code.

from the beginning, to the middle, to the end, as might seem logical. Letters and sounds at the ends of words are easier to attend to than those in the middle partly because the medial sounds are influenced by (coarticulated with) both the sound that comes before them and the sounds that come after. (An explanation of coarticulation is provided in the discussion of the development of phonemic awareness in Chapter 5.)

Engagement in appropriately challenging reading and writing activities helps to further extend the child's understanding of, and facility with, alphabetic coding. Ultimately, children come to recognize and make productive use of phonograms/ rimes, which are at the center of word families. Depending in part on the instruction they receive, children may learn about phonograms and word families before they acquire knowledge about some of the other, later developing aspects of the code (i.e., vowels and digraphs and blends), or, more likely, they will learn about those aspects of the code as they are also learning how word families work. Again, all of these relationships are reciprocal in nature; growth in one area stimulates growth in other areas.

As the children progress, they will benefit from learning about other aspects of written language, such as that words are often composed of more than one meaningful part (i.e., prefixes and suffixes modify the meaning of the root word). With enough guidance and engagement in reading and writing they will also come to recognize other, larger orthographic units such as frequently occurring syllables (e.g., *ple*, *tion*). Recognizing these larger chunks helps children identify unfamiliar words more effectively and efficiently. As a result, children are likely to read and write more and build their sight vocabularies more quickly. This larger sight vocabulary, in turn, allows children to read even more effectively and efficiently, which, again, leads to more improvements in overall reading ability and the ability to devote more attention to meaning construction as opposed to word identification.

Alphabetics and RTI

Most young children who are identified as being at risk in an RTI process demonstrate limitations in the skills that are the focus of this section of the book, and many will need greater guidance in developing these skills than will children who learn to read with relative ease. In fact, it is widely believed that the development of phonemic analysis and phonics skills is a major stumbling block for children who struggle with literacy acquisition. These findings were summarized by Adams in 1990 and more recently by Snow et al. (1998), the NRP (2000), and Pressley and Allington (2015). Further, there is substantial evidence, including evidence from our own studies cited in Chapter 1 (Scanlon et al., 2005; Scanlon et al., 2008; Vellutino et al., 1996), that children benefit from expert and responsive instruction that helps them to build these foundational skills.

As implementation of RTI procedures has become a common practice, particularly in the primary grades, we have become aware that schools sometimes adopt highly manualized and scripted published programs to address children's alphabetics needs (Scanlon, Anderson, & Goatley, 2015) and that teachers are often directed to deliver these programs with fidelity. We argue against such practices, as much instructional time can be lost to teaching children things that they already know and to teaching children things that they are not ready to learn (McKay & Teale, 2015).

In addition to these concerns, as noted in Chapter 2, one important principle of the ISA is that the instruction offered to struggling readers should be as coherent as possible. Therefore, if schools are considering the adoption of supplementary programs for their struggling literacy learners, we encourage them to examine the alignment between their core instruction and any supplementary phonemic awareness or phonics programs to ensure that the programs are congruent with the core language arts instruction that is offered in their classrooms. We have known for a long time that coherent instruction improves literacy learning outcomes (e.g., Allington & Johnston, 1989; Mosenthal et al., 2004; Wonder-McDowell et al., 2011). Moreover, it is important to ensure that the supplemental instruction is responsive to what the children know and are able to do and that the children understand the utility and application of what they are learning to authentic reading and writing. It is also important to convey the reality that, in English, the alphabetic code is not entirely reliable and that children need to learn to be somewhat flexible in their decoding attempts.

Part II of this book focuses on helping teachers become highly knowledgeable about the developmental course of phonemic awareness and phonics skills in order to enable them to effectively identify what their students are ready to learn and how the various component skills might be most effectively taught in isolation and applied in context. To assist in the decision-making process with regard to where to focus instruction about the alphabetic code, Figure II.2 provides a decision tree with page references for various portions of the current text in hopes that, as teachers plan instruction for children at various points along the developmental continuum, they can quickly reference segments of this text that are applicable.

In the following chapters we discuss the progression through each step in some detail. However, as we become immersed in the details of each process, it is important to keep in mind how all the processes fit together. They are intricately related and are mutually supportive; they are important only to the extent that they support the development of meaningful reading and writing. It is very easy for teachers, whether they teach beginning readers and writers or older children who struggle, to focus primarily on these foundational processes, possibly losing sight of their goal—to help children understand the texts they read and to be able to write meaningful texts. In fact, because this book necessarily devotes so much attention to these foundational processes, we fear we might contribute to this tendency to lose sight of the desired outcome: children who read and write for understanding and enjoyment.

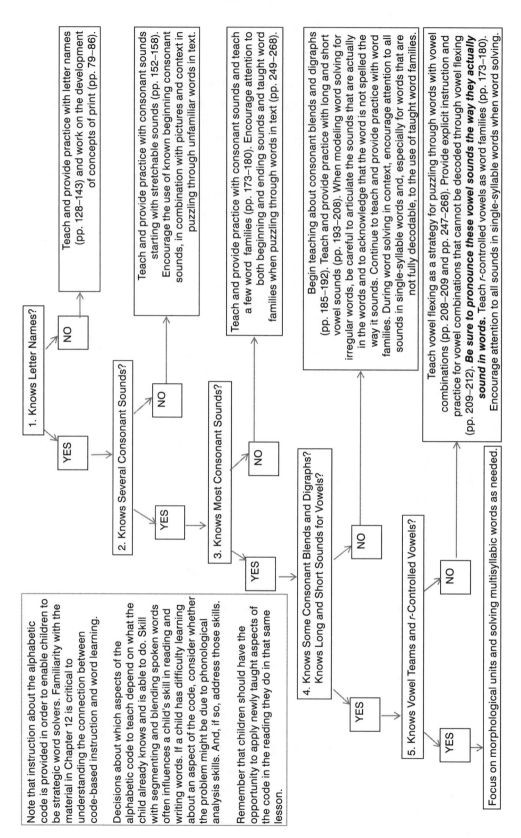

FIGURE II.2. Decision tree to guide instruction about the alphabetic code. Page numbers refer to the present volume.

The decision tree contains the following text elements:

Note that instruction about the alphabetic code is provided in order to enable children to be strategic word solvers. Familiarity with the material in Chapter 12 is critical to understanding the connection between code-based instruction and word learning.

Decisions about which aspects of the alphabetic code to teach depend on what the child already knows and is able to do. Skill with segmenting and blending spoken words often influences a child's skill in reading and writing words. If a child has difficulty learning about an aspect of the code, consider whether the problem might be due to phonological analysis skills. And, if so, address those skills.

Remember that children should have the opportunity to apply newly taught aspects of the code in the reading they do in that same lesson.

1. Knows Letter Names?

YES / NO

NO → Teach and provide practice with letter names (pp. 128–143) and work on the development of concepts of print (pp. 79–86).

2. Knows Several Consonant Sounds?

YES / NO

NO → Teach and provide practice with consonant sounds starting with stretchable sounds (pp. 152–158). Encourage the use of known beginning consonant sounds, in combination with pictures and context in puzzling through unfamiliar words in text.

3. Knows Most Consonant Sounds?

YES / NO

NO → Teach and provide practice with consonant sounds and teach a few word families (pp. 173–180). Encourage attention to both beginning and ending sounds and taught word families when puzzling through words in text (pp. 249–268).

4. Knows Some Consonant Blends and Digraphs? Knows Long and Short Sounds for Vowels?

YES / NO

NO → Begin teaching about consonant blends and digraphs (pp. 185–192). Teach and provide practice with long and short vowel sounds (pp. 193–208). When modeling word solving for irregular words, be careful to articulate the sounds that are actually in the words and to acknowledge that the word is not spelled the way it sounds. Continue to teach and provide practice with word families. During word solving in context, encourage attention to all sounds in single-syllable words and, especially for words that are not fully decodable, to the use of taught word families.

5. Knows Vowel Teams and r-Controlled Vowels?

YES / NO

NO → Teach vowel flexing as a strategy for puzzling through words with vowel combinations (pp. 208–209 and pp. 247–268). Provide explicit instruction and practice for vowel combinations that cannot be decoded through vowel flexing (pp. 209–212). *Be sure to pronounce these vowel sounds the way they actually sound in words.* Teach r-controlled vowels as word families (pp. 173–180). Encourage attention to all sounds in single-syllable words when word solving.

YES → Focus on morphological units and solving multisyllabic words as needed.

78

Purposes and Conventions of Print

Deciding where to place this particular goal was a bit difficult because, as becomes evident below, there are aspects of the print conventions and print awareness notions that are not exclusively related to the development of alphabetic knowledge. However, because it would be extremely difficult, if not impossible, for children to develop skill with alphabetics if they did not understand the basic purposes and conventions of print, we ultimately concluded that this goal needed to be discussed before presenting the other goals related to the development of alphabetic skills.

The Purposes of Print

Some children are identified as at risk of experiencing reading difficulties at the beginning of kindergarten largely because they have had very limited prior experience with print. For these children, it is important to frequently discuss and model how print is used for communication. Following are some examples of things that a teacher might do to facilitate an understanding of the communication value of print[1]:

Teacher Writing

While texting or writing a note to a parent or to another teacher, the teacher might explain that she or he is writing to tell that person . . . (a particular thing).

Writing Names on Papers and Belongings

When asking children to write their names on papers or other belongings, the teacher should explain the purpose of doing so (so that everyone knows to whom it belongs).

Reading to Children

- When reading aloud to children, the teacher might periodically explain that, since the author couldn't be there to tell the story, he or she wrote it down instead.
- The teacher might start by looking at the pictures in the book with the children and explaining that the words on the page(s) tell the story that goes with the pictures.
- With each reading of a book, the teacher might stop at different points and ask the children to say what the author has told them so far or what they think will come next in the story.
- The teacher could also introduce a wordless book (e.g., *Good Dog, Carl* [Day, 1997]) and suggest that they all (the teacher and the children) write a story that goes with the pictures.

When questions come up in conversation, the teacher might model how she or he can use reading to find the answer—using either print or digital resources.

Shared Writing

Children should have multiple opportunities to express their thoughts in print.

- Early on, the teacher might do the writing and record the children's thoughts while the children look on. After reading aloud what a particular child has dictated, the teacher might ask, "Is that what you want it to say?" (If necessary, the teacher and the child might need to collaborate to make the child's intended message clear.)

---

[1]Note that in this section the discussion is limited to the purposes and conventions of print goal. There are many other goals that can be addressed in (shared) reading and writing activities.

- The teacher should demonstrate how the writer goes back and reads portions of the text that have already been written so that the writer remembers what he or she wants to say next.
- Some teachers engage their students in writing a class letter to parents at the end of each week to tell them about the class's experiences. Once the letter is completed, the teacher leads the class in shared reading of the letter a few times, and a copy of the letter is then sent home with the children or is posted on the class's webpage. The children are encouraged to share the writing piece at home so that parents will know what is happening in school.

Using Print for Record-Keeping Purposes

Even at the early stages of the development of print knowledge, children can either write or use a name card to sign up for activities or express preferences. For example, children can:

- Sign their names on an attendance list or place their name cards in the "present" box. (Early in the year, it may be necessary to make name cards distinguishable, for example, by having different colored name cards for children whose names start with the same letter.[2])
- Sign up for a turn at a specific center.
- Write their lunch preferences on a lunch count list. (*Note*: Early on, it is helpful to have models to which the children can refer. For example, if pizza is on the lunch menu, a labeled picture of a slice of pizza would be provided.)

Conventions of Print

Different writing systems have different conventions regarding how print is organized and displayed. Children who are just beginning to learn about the writing system for their particular language sometimes need explicit guidance regarding the conventions of that language. Conventions in the English writing system include such things as the following.

- There are special kinds of marks on paper (and other media) that are called letters. By themselves the letters are fairly meaningless, but, when placed next to each other in the correct sequence, they form words.
- The word *word* refers to a unit of meaning.
- Printed words are separated by spaces.

---

[2]Some teachers put children's pictures on the name cards early on, but this defeats the purpose of helping children learn that print is a form of communication.

- Print is organized from left to right on a line and from top to bottom on a page.
- Words are organized into larger units of meaning called *sentences*.
- There are other markings in written language (punctuation marks and the use of print size, italics, etc.) that signal intonation and phrasing.
- Sentences are strung together to convey larger messages.

Print Conventions and the CCSS

The CCSS for print concepts for kindergarten and first grade (NGA & CCSSO, 2010, p. 15) are listed in Table 4.1. Most of these concepts are addressed in this chapter. However, we treat the learning of letter names (Standard RF.K.1.d) in a separate chapter (Chapter 6). It is also of note that the CCSS include print concepts among the Reading Standards: Foundational Skills (K–5) but make no mention of print concepts and conventions in the writing standards. This oversight is a bit surprising, as engaging young children in writing provides particularly effective opportunities to draw their attention to foundational print conventions that, obviously, have application to both reading and writing.

Proficient readers are often so familiar with these conventions that they don't even think about them and so may neglect to explain them to early literacy learners. Whereas children who have been read to frequently and who have had the opportunity to experiment with writing often begin to understand some of these conventions before they start kindergarten, children who have had very limited print experience are sometimes baffled by these arbitrary conventions. For these children, it is important to teach these conventions explicitly. Such explicit teaching about print conventions is also important for children whose primary language has different conventions (e.g., Chinese, Arabic, Korean, Hebrew).

TABLE 4.1. CCSS Print Concepts Standards for Kindergarten and First Grade

Standard

RF.K.1 and 1.1. Demonstrate understanding of the organization and basic features of print.

K.1.a. Follow words from left to right, top to bottom, and page by page.

K.1.b. Recognize that spoken words are represented in written language by specific sequences of letters.

K.1.c. Understand that words are separated by spaces in print.

K.1.d. Recognize and name all upper- and lower-case letters of the alphabet.

1.1.a. Recognize the distinguishing features of a sentence (e.g., first word, capitalization, ending punctuation).

Print Conventions and ELs

Many alphabetic languages share several of the English print conventions, including that there are letters that represent sounds, that together letters form words that are separated by spaces, and that words are strung together to form sentences. European languages also share the directionality conventions of English. Thus children who are learning to read and write English after having learned or begun to learn to read and write in a European alphabetic language will have knowledge that will facilitate their learning of English. However, some non-European alphabetic languages, such as Arabic and Hebrew, are written and read from right to left rather than from left to right. Thus children coming from those language backgrounds may find the competing conventions challenging to negotiate. Conventions pertaining to punctuation also vary across languages. For example, in Spanish, a question is signaled by an inverted question mark at the beginning of a sentence and by a "regular" question mark at the end of the sentence. For non-alphabetic languages, such as Mandarin and Cantonese, there are many points of difference from English with regard to the print conventions that children need to understand. An extensive discussion of these differences in print conventions across the world's languages is beyond the scope of this book. They are mentioned here mainly to alert teachers to be mindful of the fact that languages do differ, sometimes substantially, with regard to print conventions and to encourage them to try to learn about the conventions of ELs' first languages so that they understand, plan for, and respond more effectively to students' potential sources of confusion. A text entitled *Learner English: A Teacher's Guide to Interference and Other Problems* edited by Swan and Smith (2001) is an excellent resource in this regard.

Developing an Understanding of English Print Concepts and Conventions

Shared Reading[3]

When reading to children, the primary focus should always be on the meaning of the text. In the early primary grades, it is helpful to read large-print texts (e.g., big books, language experience charts, morning messages) with the children every day. During shared reading, it is important for the teacher to do the following:

- Point to the words while reading. The reading should be done with natural intonation and phrasing but at a somewhat slower pace than might be used when reading for other purposes. Slowed reading, coupled with pointing, will give the children the opportunity to observe the left-to-right and

---

[3]As we use the term, *shared reading* refers to the teacher and the children reading a single text together—both the children's and the teacher's voices are heard.

top-to-bottom sequencing of print. On occasion, it is helpful to mention the "return sweep" one does while reading. That is, when readers get to the right-hand end of a line of print, they return to the left-hand side of the page—but one line down.

- Talk explicitly about important print concepts. For example, the teacher might discuss the number of words in the title of a book, the number of letters in a character's name, and so forth.
- Occasionally discuss the directionality of print explicitly (e.g., "When we read, we always start on this side") and the purpose of punctuation marks (e.g., "This little dot is called a period. Authors put periods in to tell us when they are done with one idea. When we are reading and we see a period, it tells us to stop for a second and think about what we just read").
- Share the reading with the children by encouraging them to chime in while the adult reads. Repeated readings of the same text will help the children realize that the same page of print sounds essentially the same each time it is read.
- Encourage children to point to the words during shared reading. Once the text is somewhat familiar to the children, giving them the opportunity to point to the words while the group reads the text chorally will help them attend to the sequencing of print. This will also contribute to the development of the all-important *concept of word* (see the box entitled "Development of the Concept of Word").

Activities such as these should not supplant the focus on the meaning of the text.

Shared Writing

In order to promote the understanding of print concepts while writing, the teacher could do the following:

- Explicitly talk about where on the page one starts to write and about the direction one follows when continuing to write.
- Talk about the spacing between letters and words and how the spacing helps the reader/writer to know where one word ends and the next one begins.
- Talk about when upper-case and lower-case letters are used.
- Talk about the use and purpose of punctuation marks.

KEEP IN MIND   Sometimes teachers use terms to refer to some of these print concepts and conventions that are intended to make the concepts more memorable but may actually contribute to confusing the children—especially if they are shaky on the concepts and if they are receiving instruction in multiple settings (as children in an RTI process often do) in which the teachers use different terms for the same concepts. For example, we've encountered teachers who refer to the spaces between letters in a word as "spaghetti spaces" and the spaces between words as "meatball spaces." Other teachers use pom-poms and pipe cleaners to reference the different-sized spaces. These are cute ideas, but if a child were to receive instruction from both teachers and had yet to really grasp the purpose of spaces, he or she is likely to become more rather than less confused by the experience! Teachers who share responsibility for teaching the same children should also share critical terminology.

Development of the Concept of Word

Perhaps the most central of the concepts that emergent readers need to grasp in order to begin to build their reading and writing skills is an understanding of what a word is. Clay (1991) indicated that the concept of word is a pivotal insight needed to move forward in literacy learning. And, as Adams (1990) pointed out, it is in considering words that alphabetic and phonological skills become useful. Words are the basic units of meaning from which larger messages are constructed. During shared reading activities, it is the words to which the teacher points.

Research suggests that children develop an understanding of what a word is through engagement with memorized printed texts (typically predictable patterned texts) and an awareness of beginning consonant letters and sounds (Flannigan, 2007; Morris, Bloodgood, Lomax, & Perney, 2003). As opposed to being an all-or-nothing accomplishment, the concept of word is thought to develop in stages (Mesmer & Williams, 2015). At the earliest stage, children demonstrate an emerging awareness that print, rather than pictures, carries the meaning, but they do not yet understand how print it is organized into words and do not yet point to individual words as they recite a memorized text. Children in the second stage understand that letters are grouped together in meaningful ways and that these groupings are separated by spaces. When operating on a memorized text with only monosyllabic words, children at stage 2 can finger-point read with accuracy and can use beginning sound information in conjunction with rehearsal to locate specific words within a line of text. They cannot maintain accuracy, however, if the text contains multisyllabic words as well. For example, after shared reading of a highly patterned text, *One Bee Got on the Bus* (Dowd, 1996), we observed a child accurately finger-point read (saying each word as he pointed to it) four of the six pages.

Six bears got on the bus.
Five bunnies got on the bus.
Four butterflies got on the bus.
Three bats got on the bus.
Two bugs got on the bus.
One bee got on the bus.

Which pages were read accurately? Those that had only one-syllable words. Children in Stage 2 do not yet distinguish between spoken syllables and words, and they assume that each is represented by a bound set of letters on the page. It is not until Stage 3 that the concept of word is fully consolidated. At this stage, children are able to accurately finger-point read memorized text that contains multisyllabic words, such as the text above, and can reliably use letter-sound knowledge to locate words within the text. These children have come to understand that each grouping of letters represents an individual word, regardless of the number of syllables contained in the word (Mesmer & Williams, 2015).

Evaluating and Documenting Children's Progress

Figure 4.1 presents the group snapshot that might be used to track children's understanding of the purposes and conventions of print. Understanding of the various concepts can be demonstrated during shared reading and writing activities; it is not necessary that the children be able to read and write independently in order to be credited with understanding the purposes and conventions of print. This snapshot is used to document whether the child reliably demonstrates that he or she understands such conventions as the following:

- *Print as communication.* The child's understanding of the fact that print is a form of communication can be demonstrated in a variety of ways, such as when a child chooses to write to someone for the purpose of conveying information, or when a child asks to have printed language read to him or her ("What does that say?").

- *Left-to-right and top-to-bottom directionality.* In English, print is followed from left to right and from the top to the bottom on a page. Close observation of what the child does while engaged in emergent reading of memorized texts will allow the teacher to note the child's understanding of these conventions. So too will children's responses to questions during shared writing. For example, the teacher might ask, "I've run out of room on this line, where should I write the next word?"

- *The concepts of letter and word.* Partly because some of the earliest words they learn are also letters (*I* and *a*), it can take children a while to fully understand the differences between words and letters. This understanding is usually evaluated through direct questioning. For example, the child might be asked to count the number of letters or words on the page of an emergent-level book. The ability to engage in finger-point reading of a memorized emergent-level text, pointing and saying the correct word, also provides evidence that the child has developed a concept of what a word is. (See the next bullet point.)

- *One-to-one match.* Children who are just beginning to learn to read often start by learning to read patterned, predictable, emergent-level books. These books usually have one to four words on a page. Once the child has learned the pattern of the book (e.g., "I see a . . .") he or she is able to read the book by repeating the patterned phrase and labeling the accompanying picture. A child who is able to accurately point to each word as he or she reads it and does so accurately with words that are composed of more than one syllable has developed the ability to do one-to-one print-to-speech matching.

- *Purpose/use of punctuation.* Punctuation is used to convey meaning within and across sentences. In evaluating young children's understanding of the purposes and uses of punctuation, focus on the most basic, earliest forms of punctuation encountered (many highly literate adults continue to struggle with aspects of punctuation). To be considered proficient in this context, the young child should demonstrate that he or she understands that, in reading, the reader's voice reflects the ending punctuation (rising with a question mark, adding emphasis with an exclamation point, etc.) and that, in writing, sentences end with a punctuation mark and that different punctuation marks are used for different kinds of sentences.

- *Capitalization* has reference only to writing on the snapshot. A child would be rated as proficient if, with regard to capitalization, he or she reliably capitalizes the first letter (and only the first letter) in the first words in sentences and in proper names.

Group Snapshot—Purposes and Conventions of Print						
Student names						
Print as communication	Reading					
	Writing					
Left to right	Reading					
	Writing					
Top to bottom	Reading					
	Writing					
Concept of word	Reading					
	Writing					
Concept of letter	Reading					
	Writing					
One-to-one match	Reading					
Purpose/use of punctuation	Reading					
	Writing					
Capitalization	Writing					

Key:

◻ *B—Beginning* indicates that instruction has addressed the objective but that the child has only a preliminary understanding or capability with regard to that particular objective.

⊠ *D—Developing* indicates that the child has some understanding of the objective but does not reliably demonstrate that understanding or capability or is not yet automatic (fluent) with the skill.

⊠ *P—Proficient* indicates that the child reliably and automatically demonstrates the understanding or capability.

FIGURE 4.1. Group snapshot for purposes and conventions of print

CHAPTER 5

Phonological Awareness

ALPHABETICS GOAL 2

The child will have a conceptual grasp of the fact that words are made up of somewhat separable sound segments. Further, the child will be able to say the individual sounds in words spoken by the teacher and blend separate sounds to form whole words.

The development of skill with the alphabetic code requires that children develop important understandings about the nature of *oral* (spoken) language. That is, they need to understand that spoken words are composed of individual sounds and they need to learn to attend to and manipulate those sounds. The ability to do so will enable them to learn about the connections between the sounds in spoken words and the letters in printed words. Some children develop insight into the phonological nature of spoken language with relatively little guidance and will not need the type of thoughtful and explicit instruction described in this chapter. However, many children who have difficulty with literacy acquisition will benefit from explicit and responsive phonemic awareness instruction. To enable teachers to be responsive to the skills of their students, we discuss some of the intricacies of phonology as the chapter unfolds and why it can present a challenge for some children.

Phonological Awareness and the CCSS

The CCSS identify standards for phonological awareness in grades K and 1 only. However, older children who struggle with literacy acquisition may benefit from

---

Terminology

Phoneme—the smallest unit of sound that distinguishes between the meanings of words. For example, *can* and *cane* differ by one phoneme (short *a* vs. long *a*). *Can* and *cane* each have three phonemes.

Phonology—the study of the unconscious rules governing the production of speech sounds.

Phonetics—the study of the ways in which speech sounds are articulated (i.e., what parts of the mouth are used in what way to produce particular sounds).

Phonics—the system by which the sounds in spoken language are represented by the letters (or other symbols) in printed language.

Phonological awareness—the ability to reflect on and manipulate the component sounds of spoken words (e.g., syllables, onsets and rimes, phonemes).

Phonemic awareness—a particular type of phonological awareness: the ability to reflect on and manipulate the phonemes in spoken words. Phonemic awareness is the most important type of phonological awareness relative to reading and writing development.

---

the types of instruction, described later in this chapter, that support the development of these skills, as well. All of the phonological awareness standards except one are addressed in this and/or subsequent chapters. Table 5.1 lists the CCSS for phonological awareness for kindergarten and first grade (NGA & CCSSO, 2010, p. 15), along with the page numbers in this book on which particular standards are addressed.

Phonological Awareness and ELs

The existing evidence suggests that children who are learning English as an additional language benefit from explicit phonological awareness instruction much as do children who are native speakers of English, and at least one study (Lesaux & Siegel, 2003) suggests that the effects of bilingualism on early literacy skills may actually be positive. In fact, recent research suggests that phonological awareness generalizes across languages (Branum-Martin, Sha, & Gamaat, 2015). That is, being or becoming phonologically aware in one language facilitates phonological awareness in a second language.

However, it is important for teachers to be aware that some English phonemes do not occur or are not distinguished in other languages (Swan & Smith, 2001). As a result, English phonemes that are not part of a student's native language may be particularly difficult for the student to notice and attend to, and they are likely to confuse those phonemes with a close phoneme that does occur in their language. Interventions for ELs are more effective when they pay particular attention to the English phonemes that are not a part of the students' native language (August

TABLE 5.1. CCSS Phonological Awareness Standards for Kindergarten and First Grade

Standard	Pages
RF.K.2 and 1.2. Demonstrate understanding of spoken words, syllables, and sounds (phonemes).	100–122
K.2.a. Recognize and produce rhyming words.	101–111
K.2.b. Count, pronounce, blend, and segment syllables in spoken words.	100
K.2.c. Blend and segment onsets and rimes of single-syllable spoken words.	111–115
K.2.d. Isolate and pronounce the initial, medial vowel, and final sounds (phonemes) in three-phoneme (consonant–vowel–consonant, or CVC) words.	116–122
K.2.e. Add or substitute individual sounds (phonemes) in simple, one-syllable words to make new words.[a]	
1.2.a. Distinguish long from short vowel sounds in spoken single-syllable words.	Addressed in Chapter 10
1.2.b. Orally produce single-syllable words by blending sounds (phonemes), including consonant blends.	113–115
1.2.c. Isolate and pronounce initial, medial vowel, and final sounds (phonemes) in spoken single-syllable words.	116–122
1.2.d. Segment spoken single-syllable words into their complete sequence of individual sounds (phonemes).	116–122

[a]This standard is not addressed, as it is not clear to us how this standard could be usefully addressed without reference to letters. The ability to add and substitute phonemes in the context of word building and word reading are more advanced skills that draw on the phonological processes addressed in this standard and are discussed in Chapter 10.

et al., 2014). Swan and Smith (2001) provide listings of English phonemes that do and do not occur across a variety of common languages.

Phonemic Awareness Versus Phonics

Many people confuse the concepts of phonemic awareness and phonics. Therefore, even though definitions of these terms are provided in the "Terminology" text box, a more thorough discussion of the distinction and relationship between them is warranted.

In its purest form, phonemic awareness involves the ability to analyze and manipulate the sounds in *spoken* words and has nothing to do with the written representation of words. Phonics, on the other hand, involves the connections between the sounds in spoken words and the letters that represent those sounds in written form. It is possible for a child to be quite phonemically aware but know little or nothing about phonics.

Proficient readers (e.g., teachers) sometimes have difficulty accurately analyzing words at the level of the phoneme when the words have more letters than sounds (e.g., *though*—which has two sounds) and when the words have more sounds than letters (e.g., *box*—which has four sounds). To assist teachers in becoming attuned to the sounds in spoken words and to help them keep the distinction between phonemic awareness and phonics in mind, we encourage them to consider the examples in Figure 5.1 and, for each pictured word, to count and articulate the individual phonemes and to consider the features of the words and the sounds in the words that make them more or less difficult to segment into individual sounds.

Teachers need to be sensitive to the sounds that actually occur in spoken words in order to be effective in guiding children to attend to those sounds. Otherwise, they may provide children with guidance and feedback that only serves to confuse

Words and the phonemes that compose them

Explanation and elaboration

/s/ /u/ /n/

It is relatively easy to articulate the individual sounds in the word *sun* because each of the consonant sounds can be articulated without the addition of a vowel sound (i.e., /ssss/ and /nnnn/). However, some teachers have a habit of adding an unnecessary *schwa* (short-*u*) sound when articulating these sounds (they say "*suh*" rather than /sss/ or "*nuh*" rather than /nnn/). We encourage teachers who are "*schwa*-sayers" to own up to their bad habits and to try to eliminate the *schwa* sound whenever possible.

/f/ /i/ /sh/

The word *fish* has three sounds but four letters. In discussing this word in professional development sessions, there is usually at least one teacher in the group who will argue that a word like *fish* should not be used in phonemic awareness activities because it has a digraph (*sh*). Our response, however, is that /sh/ is a common sound in spoken language and that, since we are not focusing on the written word, there is nothing wrong with using *fish* in phonemic analysis activities.

/n/ /o/ /z/

The last sound in the word *nose* is /z/, but it is represented by the letter *s*. Because it is often difficult for literate people to ignore the spellings of words, teachers illustrating how to say the individual sounds in words will sometimes incorrectly articulate the sounds in accord with the way the word is spelled (/n/-/o/-/s/) rather than the way it sounds (/n/-/o/-/z/). Since maintaining a focus on the sounds is critical when working on phonemic analysis skills, we frequently remind teachers to try to avoid letting the spellings of words interfere with their perception of the sounds that compose the word. We find ourselves frequently saying "Let the letters go!"

/f/ /o/ /k/ /s/

Fox is another example that illustrates a discrepancy between the number of letters and the number of sounds. There are four sounds in *fox* but only three letters. Sometimes in a group of teachers there will be individuals who argue that the last sound in fox is /ks/—but this is, obviously, two sounds. To convince teachers of this, we typically ask them to decide whether the words *fox* and *socks* rhyme. When they realize that they do rhyme, they concede that *fox* has four phonemes.

FIGURE 5.1. Phonemic analysis "consciousness raising" for teachers.

them. This will, of course, be especially problematic for children who are struggling to develop early literacy skills.

Why Is Phonemic Awareness Important?

Children who understand that spoken words are composed of small units of sound and who can manipulate those units (e.g., listen to the sounds /m/ /a/ /t/ and blend them to make the word *mat*, or separate *mat* into its component sounds) are generally more successful in the early stages of learning to read than are children who do not understand this concept and cannot, therefore, manipulate those sounds (e.g., Brady, Shankweiler, & Mann, 1983; Bryant, MacLean, Bradley, & Crossland, 1990; Fletcher et al., 1994; Vellutino et al., 1996; Wagner, Torgesen, & Rashotte, 1994). A child who understands that words or syllables are composed of somewhat separable sounds will more readily come to understand that the sounds in spoken words are represented by the letters in printed words. Understanding this relationship between sounds and letters is thought to be one of the fundamental tasks facing the beginning reader and writer (Adams, 1990).

For some children, the realization that speech can be segmented into words, words into syllables, and words or syllables into phonemes (individual sounds) takes a good deal of time to develop. Other children appear to develop this insight into spoken language quite easily and without explicit instruction (Scarborough & Dobrich, 1994; Torgesen, Wagner, & Rashotte, 1994). Generally, children who demonstrate phonemic awareness without having had explicit instruction come from literacy-rich and language-rich backgrounds. However, coming from such a background does not guarantee that a child will develop phonemic awareness easily.

Phonemic Awareness and Reading Problems

Children who experience significant difficulty in learning to read tend to have difficulty in developing sensitivity to the phonemes in spoken language. Many researchers believe that this slow development of phonemic sensitivity is an important *cause* of reading difficulties. Numerous studies have found that measures of phonemic awareness, administered in kindergarten, are strong predictors of reading success in first grade and beyond (Scanlon & Vellutino, 1996; Torgesen & Burgess, 1998; Yopp, 1988). However, it should also be noted that learning to read helps children become more sensitive to the sound structure of words. Thus phonemic awareness helps children learn to read and spell, and learning to read and spell helps children to become more phonemically aware (Quinn, Spencer, & Wagner, 2015). In short, as noted in the Introduction to Part II, the two processes are reciprocal.

Instructional Influences
on the Development of Phonemic Awareness

Many studies (e.g., Ball & Blachman, 1991; Blachman, Ball, Black, & Tangel, 1994; Bradley & Bryant, 1991; Schneider, Roth, & Ennemoser, 2000) have demonstrated that explicit instruction designed to promote phonemic awareness has a positive effect on the reading and writing performance of the children who receive such training, both in the short term (immediately after training) and in the long term (1–5 years after training was provided). Further, positive effects have been noted in a variety of instructional groupings (one to one, small group, and whole class). While there is clear evidence for the importance of helping children to become phonemically aware, the National Reading Panel (2000) concluded that training in phonemic awareness alone is not as effective in promoting reading and writing abilities as is training in phonemic awareness that is coupled with explicit instruction in letter–sound correspondences and in the application of the alphabetic code.

Why Is It Difficult for Some Children
to Notice/Attend to Phonemes?

People who are proficient readers and writers in an alphabetic language often find it difficult to imagine how anyone would have difficulty noticing the phonemes in spoken language. It just seems obvious to them. However, people who are proficient readers and writers in languages that do not use an alphabetic writing system are generally not as phonemically aware. Their languages are no less phonemic than English, but they simply don't notice the phonemes because there is really no need to; the phonemes are not represented in their language's writing system (Read, Zhang, Nie, & Ding, 1986). Thus it is not surprising that many children with very limited literacy experience will not be phonemically aware. Many such children will begin to develop this insight when their attention is drawn to the sounds in words through their engagement in reading and writing activities and through involvement in learning songs and poems that emphasize sound similarities (e.g., alliteration and rhyme). However, for a variety of reasons some children need much more explicit and focused instruction in order to become aware of the component sounds in spoken words.

In what follows, we describe some factors that may contribute to children's difficulty with attending to the phonemic nature of spoken language:

A Natural Inclination to Focus on the Meaning of a Word
Rather Than Its Sounds

Children, like proficient readers in nonalphabetic languages, are naturally inclined to attend to the meanings of words. After all, the concept of a *dog* is much more interesting than the sounds that comprise the word. If you ask a young child how many sounds are in *dog,* he or she is apt to say "woof, woof" rather than "three."

The Fleeting Nature of Speech Sounds

The sounds in words are rather fleeting. It takes substantially less than a second to articulate the first sound in *ball* or the first sound in *sun.* As a result, it can be hard to draw children's attention to the individual sounds. When attempts are made to do so, they are differentially effective depending on the characteristics of the sound. Thus, for example, some consonant sounds can be stretched or articulated over a protracted period of time without distortion. Examples of stretchable sounds include /ssss/, /rrrrr/, /ffff/. However, many consonant sounds cannot be "stretched" without distortion. These sounds, including those associated with the letters *b, d, g,* and *t,* are referred to as *stop-consonant sounds* because their production requires that the air flow be briefly stopped during articulation. As a result of this stoppage of the airflow, it is impossible to elongate the pronunciation without distorting the sound. For instance, when teachers attempt to draw children's attention to the initial sound in the word *boy,* they are likely to say /buh/ with an emphasis on the /uh/ portion. Children who are not yet attuned to the phonemic qualities of spoken language might well attend to the /uh/, which takes longer to articulate than the /b/, which is fleeting. Table 5.2 presents a listing of the letters representing stretchable and stop-consonant sounds. Note that the letters *w, x,* and *y* do not appear on the list. The letter *x* is not on the list because it actually represents two sounds, /k/ and /s/, and as such is a consonant blend. For the letters *w* and *y,* most teachers are accustomed to pronouncing these sounds in isolation as (*wuh*) and (*yuh*), respectively. The addition of the schwa sound (uh) makes these sounds seem more like stop consonants, as their sounds cannot be elongated without distortion. In fact, however, both sounds can be stretched without distortion.

TABLE 5.2. Letters Representing Stretchable and Stop Consonant Sounds

Stretchable	Stop
Soft *c* (as in *city*)	*b*
f	Hard *c* (as in *cat*)
l	*ch*
m	*d*
n	Hard *g* (as in *game*)
r	Soft *g* (as in *gym*)
s	*j*
sh	*k*
th	*p*
v	*q*
z	*t*

The sound for *w* would sound like the /oo/ sound in *too* and the sound for *y* would sound most like the long-*e* sound.

The Problem of Coarticulation

Another reason that phonemes are not particularly obvious is that the phonemes in words are hard to separate from one another. For the sake of efficiency, the articulators (the parts of the mouth that move in order to produce the intended sounds) are preparing to say the next sound in a word while they are still articulating the previous sound. As a result, there is no clear point of demarcation between one sound and the next. The sounds are literally blended together. This blending is referred to as *coarticulation*.

Examples of Coarticulation

To get a better sense of coarticulation, try these exercises:

- **Say the words** *see* and *so* out loud a few times. Are the sounds you hear at the beginnings of those two words the same? Your answer is, of course, yes. Now, say the same words again (*see, so*) but notice the position of your lips as you make the /s/ sound in each word. Is your mouth position the same? Probably not. Typically, when pronouncing the /s/ in *see,* your lips are stretched back a bit in preparation for pronouncing the /E/ (long-*e*) sound. When pronouncing the /s/ in *so,* your lips are more rounded in preparation for pronouncing the /O/ (long-*o*) sound. In this case the change in mouth position doesn't result in a noticeable change in the /s/ sound. However, for some changes in mouth position, and for some phonemes and phoneme combinations, the change in the movement of the articulators does affect sound—as illustrated next.

- **Say the words** *at* and *ant* out loud. Listen to the vowel sound in each word. Pretend you don't know how the words are spelled. Do the vowels sound the same? Probably not. For most people the two sounds are actually quite different. The /a/ in *ant* is sort of "twangy" as a result of the articulators preparing to produce the /n/ sound. In producing the /n/ sound, air is pushed through the nose. Therefore, while producing the /a/ in *ant*, some of the air is pushed through the nose as well. On the other hand, in pronouncing the /a/ in *at,* all of the air is pushed through the mouth. The path of the air, which is changed by the position of the articulators, changes the sound.

Similarity of Many Phonemes

Because children tend to rely on what their mouths are doing as they articulate sounds, it is sometimes difficult for them to distinguish between two sounds that are articulated in almost the same way. In many cases, the only difference in the articulation of two sounds is in whether or not the vocal cords vibrate. Such sounds

Sound pairs that differ only in voicing	
Voiced	Unvoiced
/b/	/p/
/d/	/t/
/v/	/f/
/g/	/k/
/j/	/ch/
/z/	/s/

Other confusable pairs	
/l/	/r/
/m/	/n/

(Note: Both sounds in each pair are voiced. They are confusable because there is only a slight change in mouth position when articulating one or the other member of the pair.)

FIGURE 5.2. Pairs of phonemes that are easily confused.

are said to differ in *voicing*. For example, the sounds /f/ and /v/ are articulated in the same way *except* that the /v/ sound is voiced (the vocal cords vibrate), whereas the /f/ sound is not voiced.

As illustrated in Figure 5.2, several pairs of phonemes in English differ only in voicing. Children often confuse these sounds—particularly in their writing. Children who make these types of substitutions are more phonemically aware than teachers sometimes realize.

There are some clear instructional implications related to these potentially confusable sound pairs, such as:

- In planning instruction to promote phonemic awareness, it is important to initially avoid asking the children to discriminate between sounds that are potentially confusable, because this makes the task more difficult. For example, if children were asked to sort groups of pictures by similarities in their beginning sounds, it would be much more challenging to sort a set consisting of *van, fork, fox,* and *vase* than to sort a set consisting of *mat, fork, fox,* and *mop.*
- In children's writing, particularly in early writing, substitutions within these minimally contrasted pairs (e.g., substituting *t* for *d,* or *b* for *p*) are common. Teachers who understand the origin of these substitutions and who recognize that they are close approximations will provide children with more effective feedback.

Assessing Phonological Awareness

As with most skills, in order to plan instruction, it is important to know what the student(s) already know and are able to do. Documenting current skills and abilities can be accomplished either through explicit assessment of skills and abilities or through careful documentation of skills observed during instruction. In this chapter, we provide a snapshot for phonological skills (see Figure 5.11, p. 123) to assist in the documentation process. This checklist can be used to guide informal assessment of phonological skills and instructional planning.

Before turning to the assessment and instructional activities, however, a brief discussion of the use of written spelling as an index of phonological and phonemic awareness is provided because, at least for children who have some understanding of the writing system, an assessment of written spelling is an efficient way to gather preliminary information regarding children's degrees of phonological awareness.

Using Written Spelling to Assess Phonemic Awareness

Although *phonemic awareness* refers to the ability to analyze and manipulate the sounds in *spoken* words, written spelling can be used as an indicator of a child's phonemic analysis skill. For beginning readers and writers to spell words that they have not committed to memory, they need to analyze the sounds (phonemes) that make up the word and then represent those phonemes with letters. Because measures of written spelling can be administered fairly quickly and to several children at once, they are an appropriate first step in analysis of phonemic awareness for children who know something about the writing system.

A child who accurately spells the word *jet* when asked to do so is likely to be fairly phonemically aware. So, too, is the child who spells *jet* with a g *(get)* or *jet* with an a *(jat),* or *jet* with both a g and an a *(gat).* Obviously, the latter spellings are at odds with the conventional spelling for *jet.* However, they all show that the child has noticed all of the phonemes in the word—choosing g rather than j because they notice the /j/ sound at the beginning of the name of the letter g and choosing a rather than e because the sound of short e can be heard in the name of the letter A.[1] A child who produces this type of spelling is sufficiently phonemically aware and does not need explicit instruction in phonemic awareness. (Of course, the child still needs to learn about conventional spelling.)

A child who cannot sound-spell simple words may or may not be phonemically aware. Problems with sound spelling may be due to lack of familiarity with the alphabetic code *or* to lack of phonemic awareness *or* both. Thus poor performance on a measure of sound spelling signals a need for further assessment of the child's phonological skills. Good performance on such a measure signals that the child may not need explicit instruction in phonemic awareness.

Many teachers find developmental spelling assessments useful for gaining initial insights into children's phonemic analysis and phonics skills. The Primary Spelling Inventory from *Words Their Way* (Bear, Invernizzi, Templeton, & Johnston,

---

[1]A child's inclination to use the relationships between letter names and letter sounds is discussed more fully in subsequent chapters.

A Note about Sound Spelling

Once children have learned something about the alphabetic writing system and before they have learned the conventional (correct) spellings of many words, they often write words by thinking about the sounds they hear in them and then representing those sounds with letters. Several different terms have been used to describe this approach to spelling, including *invented spelling, inventive spelling, kindergarten spelling,* and *temporary spelling.* We prefer the term *sound spelling* because it more clearly conveys to children what they are expected to do when attempting to write words that they don't yet know how to spell.

2015) is widely used for this purpose. This assessment is administered much like a traditional spelling test. However, children are asked to spell words that have not been "studied," and the teacher analyzes the elements that are represented in the children's spelling attempts, not just whether or not the words are spelled conventionally. Teachers can use their analyses to make initial judgments about what an individual child already understands about phonemic analysis. For example, if a child represents most or all of the beginning sounds for the dictated words but little else, the teacher can probably conclude that the child does not need phonemic awareness instruction focused on helping her or him to attend to beginning sounds and that she or he is probably ready for instruction that focuses attention on the ending sounds in words. Such an assessment would, of course, also provide evidence of the child's understanding of letter–sound correspondences.

Brief Assessment of Phonological Awareness for Children Whose Spellings Do Not Provide Much Information about Their Degree of Phonological Awareness

Children who show no evidence of phonemic analysis skill in their sound spellings may, nevertheless, be at least somewhat phonemically aware. Further assessment of their skills would need to be conducted in a context in which they are not required to write. Teachers can learn a great deal about children's phonemic analysis skills by using the group snapshot presented at the end of this chapter as a systematic guide in evaluating which types of skills the children demonstrate. For example, the teacher might start with an intermediate skill such as onset–rime blending (described later), demonstrate what is expected, and then administer a few items providing feedback on each. If the child is unsuccessful, the next step would be to move to an easier skill, such as sorting by ending sound (also described later). Again, the teacher would explain and model the task and then have the child try a few items while providing feedback. Based on how readily the child performs the task, the teacher would next move to a more or less challenging skill.

Grouping and Pacing

Some children need little or no explicit instructional guidance in order to become sensitive to the individual phonemes in spoken words. Others need some guidance but then make rapid progress and have no further need for that sort of instruction. Still others need more prolonged engagement in carefully sequenced instructional activities. Initial assessment followed by ongoing monitoring (via anecdotal records or checklists/snapshots) can help to ensure that instruction is appropriately responsive.

Activities for Promoting (and Assessing) Phonological Awareness

Described next are some methods for helping young children become attuned to the sound structure of spoken language. Although the activities are presented in somewhat of a list form, this presentation format is used primarily for the sake of clarity. We anticipate that teachers will draw on different instructional techniques as the need arises and will think of the exercises presented throughout the remainder of the chapter as mutually reinforcing activities.

Blending and Segmenting Syllables

Typically, the earliest emerging phonological analysis skill is the ability to blend and segment the syllables in multisyllabic words. This skill emerges early (for most children by the age of 4 or 5) largely because, unlike phonemes, which are coarticulated, syllables are more distinctive and are more physically apparent via the movement of the mouth. This is so because every syllable contains a vowel sound, and vowel sounds are open-mouth sounds. As a result, there is slight movement of the jaw for each syllable. Because the ability to blend and segment syllables are early and easily acquired skills, we do not address them in this chapter. Instead, we focus on the phonological skills that have proven to be challenging for children who experience difficulty with literacy acquisition.

Some of the instructional activities are sequenced, reflecting research that suggests that there is a clear developmental progression. The progressions described can be used to differentiate instruction for individual children or groups of children. The phonological awareness snapshot (see Figure 5.11, p. 123) is designed to help teachers keep this progression in mind.

Sensitivity to Sound Components in Texts

Using the Group Snapshot

In using the phonological awareness group snapshot, the goal is to make note of whether children demonstrate particular skills and knowledge with sufficient ease that they would be expected to be able to do it reliably in the future. As children are engaged in the activities described in this section, the teacher makes note of those children who reliably:

- *Complete the rhyme in known text.* When reading aloud a familiar text to the children, the teacher reads the first portion of a rhyming couplet and then pauses to let the children supply the rhyming word.
- *Identify rhyming words in text.* When the teacher reads a rhyming couplet, the child indicates which two words rhyme.
- *Identify alliterative words in text.* When the teacher reads a portion of text that contains several words that begin with the same sound, the child can identify words that have the same beginning sound.

Reading/Singing/Reciting Stories, Songs, Nursery Rhymes, and Poems

Although the activities described in this section are most often used in a whole-class context, they are appropriate to use in small-group and one-to-one instructional settings as well. Too often, in a whole-class setting, the children who are at greatest risk for reading difficulties do not participate fully in language activities. An observer will often notice that when such children do engage, they do so by shadowing (i.e., copying) the responses of the children who are not at risk.

Children who become phonemically aware without explicit guidance tend to spontaneously engage in the kinds of language play encouraged in the activities described in this section. The goal of the modeling and guided practice described is to encourage children who do not do these kinds of things spontaneously to engage in productive language play.

READ BOOKS THAT PLAY ON THE SOUNDS IN LANGUAGE

Perhaps the easiest and most pleasant way to begin to attune children to the sounds in spoken language is through the use of books, poems, and songs that include rhyme and/or alliteration (many words that have the same beginning sound). There are many such children's books available. Yopp (1995) has developed an annotated bibliography of books that are well suited to this purpose. Additional lists of such books are provided by Adams, Foorman, Lundberg, and Beeler (1998) and Yopp and Yopp (2009). Examples of these books are:

All About Arthur (Carle, 1974)
Alphabears (Hague, 1984)

"I Can't," Said the Ant (Cameron, 1961)
Sheep in a Jeep (Shaw, 1986)
Six Sleepy Sheep (Gordon, 1991)
There's a Wocket in My Pocket (Seuss, 1974)
Rhyming Dust Bunnies (Thomas, 2009)

While the children listen to books, poems, and songs that highlight the sound structure of language, teachers can encourage them to listen for rhyming words and/or words that have the same sound at the beginning. Repeated readings of such texts will give the children more opportunity to become attuned to the sound similarities in the text. If children are having difficulty noticing those similarities, the teacher can emphasize the similar-sounding words while reading.

Yopp and Yopp (2009) and Adams et al. (1998) suggest several ways in which the word play in books can be extended to engage children in actively considering the sounds in words. For example, the teacher might do the following:

- After the children have heard the text a few times, read it to them again, but stop before reading the second word in a rhyme pattern to allow the children to provide the rhyming word.
- Periodically stop after reading a rhyming couplet and ask the children to identify the rhyming words.
- Comment on certain groups of words that occur in the text, for example, "The author called the little girl 'Rrrrosy Rrrrobin Rrrrrross' [Seuss, 1963, p. 42]. What sound do you hear at the beginning of all of those words?"
- Involve the children in creating additional verses that follow similar sound patterns.

KEEP IN MIND   Although not directly related to the specific goal of helping children develop phonemic awareness, it is useful to present nursery rhymes, poems, and lyrics in print that is large enough for the children to see.

SING SONGS THAT PLAY ON THE SOUNDS IN WORDS

Because rhyme is a prominent characteristic of many songs, singing and listening to songs will help attune children to the phonemes in spoken language. Songs that engage children in active manipulation of the sounds in words will be most effective in moving the children forward. Manipulating the sounds in words in the ways suggested by the following songs[2] can be fairly challenging for children who are just beginning to become phonemically aware.

---

[2]These songs can be found on CDs by Raffi, Nancy Cassidy, and many other children's recording artists. Dr. Jean Feldman also has a collection of CDs, including many songs that are useful for promoting phonemic analysis (see *www.drjean.org*).

"Willoughby, Walloughby. . . . "
"Down by the Bay"
"The Name Game"
"Apples and Bananas"

The children will need several opportunities to learn the song before they are expected to engage in manipulating the sounds. For example, some classroom teachers play these songs during transitional activities (such as during cleanup time or snack time or while the children are involved in cutting, pasting, or coloring activities). This helps to promote familiarity with the songs and encourages sound play.

Once the children are fairly familiar with a given song (and can at least sing along with the recording comfortably), invite them to add their own verses. It may be necessary to provide support in constructing these additional verses, as exemplified for the song "Down by the Bay." Here is the first verse:

Down by the bay
Where the watermelons grow
Back to my home,
I will not go
For if I did,
My mother would say:
"Did you ever see a <u>bear</u>,
<u>Combing his hair</u>
Down by the bay?"

In this song, only the underlined words change in subsequent verses. The first and last underlined words always rhyme.

Once the children have sung the song several times, perhaps over a period of a few days, the teacher might model how to make up new verses (e.g., "Did you ever see a <u>car</u> parked on a <u>star</u>?"). The teacher might then encourage the children to suggest verses. Initially, to make this easy for children, the teacher might ask for just the first word of the rhyming pair and generate the second word of the pair him- or herself. A sample dialogue appears below.

Sample Instructional Dialogue

TEACHER: Today we are going to make up some new parts for this song. We can pick an object and make a rhyme with it. I'll do one first to show you what I mean. My object is a ball. So I have *ball,* then I need to think of a word that rhymes with *ball* . . . a word that sounds the same at the end. I know! *Ball—hall.* Those words rhyme. I am going to use those words to make a new part for our song. How about "Did you ever see a *ball* rolling down the *hall*?" Let's sing the song with that verse.

Now, let's do a verse with a fruit. What fruit would you like to use?

CHILD: Pear!

TEACHER: OK! First I'll have to think of a word that rhymes with *pear*. I know—*chair*! *Pear* and *chair* rhyme—they sound the same at the end. *Pear* and *chair*. Now let's think of what the *pear* could be doing with the *chair*? How about sitting on it? Did you ever see a *pear* sitting on a *chair*! Let's sing a verse with the rhyming words *pear* and *chair*.

Once the teacher has modeled this approach several times, she or he should encourage the children to generate the rhyming words and to think of how the two words will be related in the song. Children can also be encouraged to think of new verses at other times and try to remember them for the next time the class sings that particular song. Silliness is an important element in the appeal of this activity.

LEARN, RECITE, AND MODIFY RHYMES, CHANTS, AND POEMS

Well before the concept of phonemic awareness became an important focus in thinking about developmental reading, jump rope, hand clapping, and nursery rhymes and poems were commonly used to entertain children and to engage them in language play. Rhymes and poems help children shift their focus from attending to the message to noticing the sounds in the words that are used to convey those messages.

Once children have learned and can recite a given rhyme or poem, they are often delighted by "playing" with it and changing the verse. For example, for the nursery rhyme "Jack Be Nimble," once they have learned it, children might be invited to modify it by making a new rhyme, perhaps by assuming that Jack was slow instead of quick.

Jack be nimble,
Jack be slow,
Jack jump over
The _____ [Purple bow, or farmer's hoe, or elephant's toe].

Note

In the examples given in this section, some words are likely to be unfamiliar to many kindergarten children. This activity could be used to support vocabulary development as well as phonemic awareness—although we are not suggesting that teachers should get into extensive discussions about every word that may be unfamiliar.

This activity could be made easier for children by presenting pictures (which should include objects that rhyme as well as some that do not). The children would then choose between and among the pictures. Children who find this activity difficult might be given only two choices (e.g., a purple bow or a red car). As they gain proficiency, children might be asked to choose from a larger set of pictures.

For children who do not make progress with the rhyme and alliteration activities described thus far, more explicit instruction, using words that are not presented in meaningful contexts, is useful. By eliminating the meaningful context, we give the children more opportunity to focus on the sounds in the words. The sound sorting activities described in the next section are among the easiest phonological awareness activities and provide a useful starting point for instruction.

Sound Sorting: Sorting Pictures or Objects by Sound Similarity

Using the Group Snapshot

Four different sorting principles are used for sound sorting: beginning sounds, rhyme, ending sounds, and medial sounds. As the children are given the opportunity to attempt sorts based on each of these principles, the teacher should note on the snapshot (p. 123) the child's level of proficiency (Beginning, Developing, Proficient). To be considered Proficient with a skill, the child should be able to do the sorting reliably and fairly quickly.

The activities described in this section are included in many programs designed to promote phonemic awareness. The teaching that goes on with these activities is more explicit and more focused than the sensitivity to sound activities described in the previous section. However, the general objective is the same: to help children notice sound similarities and differences in words.

The general technique entails providing children with a group of objects or pictures of objects that can be sorted by sound similarity in a specified part of the words. For example, children might be given pictures of a *mat*, the *moon*, a bar of *soap*, and a *mouth* and be asked to put together the three that have the same sound at the beginning and/or to move the one with a different beginning sound away from the others.

Materials

Developing materials for sound-sorting exercises takes some thought. Therefore, we have developed sets of pictures for use in sound sorting and made them available on the website associated with this book (see the box at the end of the table of contents). These picture sets follow the guidance we provide below related to the various sorting principles. For example, there are picture sets that are useful for sound sorting focused on stretchable beginning sounds. These picture sets can be printed on card stock, cut apart, and used over and over again. Alternatively, the picture sets for a given day can be copied onto plain paper and each child can be given a sheet containing the pictures. The children would then cut up the sheet into individual pictures in preparation for the day's sorting activities.

There are other potentially useful materials available as well. For example, pictures for use in sorting activities can be found in *Words Their Way* by Bear et al. (2015). There are also numerous sets of materials for promoting phonemic awareness that can be purchased, some that use miniature objects rather than pictures.[3] When using purchased materials, it is important to carefully analyze the materials before using them as, all too frequently, pictures or objects are included in a set to which they do not belong (e.g., an object starting with the /sh/ sound included among objects beginning with the /s/ sound). The guidelines provided below can assist in that analysis.

Things to remember when developing (or selecting) materials to use for sound sorting activities include the following:

- Choose pictures of objects that are relatively unambiguous in terms of the names that might be applied to them.
- Choose pictures of objects that have one-syllable names.
- Always apply the same name to a picture. If you initially labeled a picture *rug*, it will confuse children if you later use the same picture but decide to call it *mat*.

Especially for introductory purposes:

- Choose objects with names that contain a relatively simple phonemic structure in the part of the word that will be the focus of the activity. For example, for a beginning sound sort, the words *fork, fox, rope,* and *fish* would be a good group to use because the beginning sounds are single consonants. Words with consonant blends, such as *flag, frog,* and *stick,* would be more challenging to analyze.
- Choose words in which the targeted phonemes can be easily stretched or emphasized without distortion (e.g., the initial sounds in these words can be stretched—*rrrrope, ffffox, mmmmoon*) so that the children's attention can be drawn more effectively to the sounds in that part of the word.
- Use contrasts that are very distinct so that the differences in the sounds are easier to notice. For example, the sounds /f/ and /r/ are quite different from one another, whereas the sounds /f/ and /v/ are quite similar (they differ only in voicing). Thus it would be easier for a child to notice that *rope* has a different beginning sound in the set *fork, fox, rope, fish* than to notice that *van* has a different beginning sound in the set *fork, fox, van, fish*.

---

[3]We advise against using miniature objects for phonological awareness activities as they have too much play value and therefore may keep the children from focusing on the task at hand: thinking about the sounds.

As children begin to demonstrate the ability to detect similarities and differences in the sounds in words, the restrictions on word selection can be relaxed, and word sorts can include stop consonants (i.e., *ball, top, box,* and *bike*).

Think Sounds, Not Letters

In working to attune children to the sounds in spoken words, it is important for the teacher to think about the sounds in the words that are being analyzed, not the letters. For example, the word *shoe* has two sounds but four letters and there is nothing particularly challenging about attending to the sound represented by the *sh* digraph. Therefore, words beginning with /sh/, since it is a stretchable sound, could be included in early phonemic awareness activities such as sorting by beginning sounds (e.g., *shoe, shirt, shell, man*).

Sequence of Instruction for Sorting Activities

Research has demonstrated that there is a progression in the order in which children become sensitive to (aware of) the sound components in words. The easiest sound components for children to attend to and learn to manipulate in single-syllable words are *onsets* and *rimes*. The next easiest component is the ending sound. In one-syllable words, the most challenging part for a child to attend to is the middle sound—usually the vowel sound and individual sounds that are parts of consonant blends (Fox & Routh, 1975; Treiman & Zukowski, 1996).

Terminology

Onset—the portion of a spoken word or syllable that precedes the first vowel. The onsets in the following words are underlined: <u>some</u> <u>tr</u>ick <u>shr</u>ink.

Rime—the vowel and what comes after it in a spoken word or syllable. The rimes are the portions of the words that are not underlined in the examples above.

Based on the accumulated research (see Burgess, 2006, and Quinn et al., 2015, for reviews), a sequence of instruction is presented in this section. Early on, children should be asked to sort words based on the sound components that are easiest for them to attend to (onsets and rimes). In our experience many children find it easier to attend to rimes initially than to onsets (beginning sounds). For other children it appears that onsets are easier. Therefore, no confident recommendations can be made about whether to start with onsets or rimes. The best advice is probably to try both and determine which sorting principle a particular group of children appears to find easier and to focus on the targeted sound component until the children can easily sort based on that principle. Then switch to working with the other sorting principle that was initially more challenging (whether onset

TABLE 5.3. Recommended Order for Sorting Principles

Order	Sorting principle	Sample picture set
1	Rime (rhyme) Onset (beginning sounds)	*cat, hat, mat; pin, fin, tin* *moon, mat, mouse; soap, sun, sock*
2	Ending sounds	*pail, ball, seal; moon, fin, van*
3	Middle sounds	*coat, soap, home; map, rat, pack*

or rime). Continue to work with that new principle until the children can sort easily based on that principle as well. When children can easily sort based on both onset and rime, begin to work on sorting by ending sounds. Finally, when children are able to easily sort pictures based on similarity in ending sounds, they should begin to work on sorting pictures based on similarity in medial sounds. Table 5.3 provides a summary of the order in which the sorting principles should be pursued.

Odd-One-Out Sorting Activity

For an initial introduction to sorting by sound commonalities, the *odd-one-out* activity is useful because it allows children to focus on just a few words at a time. In this activity, children are presented with groups of pictures, one group at a time. In each group, all of the pictures except one have the same sound(s) in a specified part of the word. The children are asked to figure out which word doesn't have the same sound (does not belong).

A fairly detailed description of the odd-one-out activity, using beginning sounds as the sorting principle, follows. The same format can be used to introduce and practice the other sorting principles. In general, children should work on a given sorting principle until they are both fast and accurate before moving on to a new sorting principle.

KEEP IN MIND   Children are most likely to attach the intended label to a picture if the teacher labels it immediately when it is presented. Sometimes teachers hold back and wait to see if the children can label the pictures. Often the children will suggest a different label than the one intended. Once they've decided that the picture shows a shark, for example, it may be hard for them to remember that the teacher called it a fish.

BEGINNING-SOUND ODD-ONE-OUT SORT

For this activity, collect several groups of pictures. Each group should contain two or three pictures that begin with the same sound and one picture that begins with a different sound (see Figure 5.3). For initial demonstration and practice purposes, it is best to choose items for which the beginning sound can be easily elongated

FIGURE 5.3. Pictures for phoneme sorting. Note: Pictures are *seal*, *sun*, and *mop*.

(stretched) when it is pronounced (i.e., words starting with the sounds for *f, l, m, n, r, s, sh, th, v, z*). Using stretchable sounds makes it easier to demonstrate the sorting principle of interest. Also, keep in mind that it is important that the children assign the correct labels to the pictures (the labels you intend). This can be ensured by saying the names of the pictures frequently. Finally, it is important to note that no printed letters are used in these activities and no mention of letter names is made. In the sample instructional dialogue below, when letters appear between slash marks (e.g., /fffff/), it signals that the teacher is to articulate and elongate the sound of the letter.

Sample Instructional Dialogue

TEACHER: I have three pictures here. One of them doesn't belong in the group because it has a different sound at the beginning. This is a *sssssseal*, this is a *sssssun*, and this is a *mmmmmop*. (*Points to each picture while labeling it.*) When I say *sssssun* and *sssssseal*, do you hear that they both have /sssss/ at the beginning? *Sssssun, sssssseal*?

CHILDREN: Yes.

TEACHER: Now when I say *mmmmmop*, do I make that /sssss/ sound? *mmmmmop*.

CHILDREN: Yes? No?????

TEACHER: That's right, *mmmmmop* doesn't have the /sssss/ sound, so I'm going to move the *mmmmmop* away from *sssssun* and *sssssseal* because the beginning sound in *mmmmmop* is different from the beginning sounds in *sssssun* and *sssssseal*. *Mmmmmop* doesn't have /sssss/ at the beginning. We hear /sssss/ in *sssssun* and in *sssssseal*. (*Points to each picture while naming it.*) So I'm going to put them together because they have the same sound at the beginning. Now you try one. (*Lays out three new pictures and points to each while naming it.*) Here are *fffffan, rrrrrake*, and *fffffox*. Two of these sound the same at the beginning, and one of them has a different sound at the beginning. Let's see if we can figure out which one has a different sound at the beginning. *Fffffan, rrrrrake, fffffox*.

CHILDREN: Fan?

TEACHER: No, let's think about this one together. First we'll say each word. *Ffff-fan, rrrrrake, fffffox*. (*Encourages the children to join in labeling the pictures and stretching the beginning sounds.*) When we say *fffffan,* what is the first sound we make? Let's all make the first sound in *fffffan.* /fffff/. So *fffffan* has /fffff/ at the beginning. Now let's try *rrrrake* and think about what sound we make first when we say *rrrrrake.* /rrrrr/. Do *fffffan* and *rrrrake* both have /rrrr/ at the beginning?

CHILDREN: No!

TEACHER: So, *ffffan* and *rrrrake* have different sounds at the beginning—and I am going to move them apart.

Now, let's try *ffffox.* Do you hear the same beginning sound as in *fffan?* Or do you hear the same sound you hear at the beginning of *rrrrake?*

> **KEEP IN MIND**   When stretching words for children, particular emphasis should be placed on stretching the part of the word to which the children are to attend. So, for the example in Figure 5.4, it is helpful to say ffffan, not fffffaaaannnn. The latter rendition of fan would be appropriate at a later time when children are attempting to analyze all of the sounds in a word—as, for example, when they are writing.

The teacher should provide the children with several examples of sorting by the beginning sound. Gradually, as the children demonstrate that they understand the task, the teacher should begin, on subsequent items, to reduce the elongation of the beginning sounds when saying the names of the pictures. When the children can readily and accurately sort without the teacher elongating the sounds, the items used can be expanded to include words that begin with stop consonants (e.g., *b, d, g, h, k*). Although adding a *schwa* sound (the /uh/ in /buh/) is unavoidable when producing stop sounds in isolation, the teacher should be careful to minimize it as much as possible because otherwise it may dominate the sound of the consonant—thereby making it harder to focus on the consonant sound.

Sorting Boards

Once children understand the general principle of separating pictures by whether or not they have the same sound in a particular part of the word, sorting boards can be used to provide additional sorting practice. The same sorting principles

FIGURE 5.4. Beginning sound sort. Note: Pictures are *fan, rake,* and *fox.*

would be used. The sorting boards contain two or three columns, each headed by a picture that begins (ends, etc.) with a different sound. The children are then given a packet of pictures that have the same beginning (ending, etc.) sound as one of the pictures heading a column. One by one, children then place the pictures with the same sounds in the appropriate column. In using the sorting boards, children should be encouraged to say the name of each picture as they consider its placement. If they have difficulty deciding in which column to place a picture, they should be encouraged to name the pictures already in the column under consideration. Once the children have learned how to do this type of sorting, they can use these sorting boards fairly independently, perhaps as a center activity.

An example of a sorting board for a beginning-sound sort is presented in Figure 5.5. The two pictures at the top are posted on the board when the child begins to work with it. The pictures at the bottom are given to the child in a packet. The child is to sort the pictures into two groups by beginning sounds. Clearly, it is important to make sure that the children have the correct label for each picture before asking them to do the sort.

Phoneme Blending and Segmentation

Phoneme Blending and Reading

Learning to blend phonemes is generally easier than learning to segment the phonemes in a word. Practice with phoneme blending is helpful because, when beginning readers attempt to decode a word that they do not recognize immediately, one strategy they may use is to (1) identify the individual letters, (2) think of the sound each letter represents (or could represent), (3) hold the individual sounds in memory while other sounds are retrieved, and finally (4) blend all of the individual sounds together. Difficulty with the blending process (or any of the other processes involved) may interfere with retrieval of the name of the printed word and, ultimately, with comprehension of the text. Providing children with practice in blending individual (spoken) sounds into words may make it easier for them to handle the blending process while reading. In addition, having children blend individual sounds into words will help to attune them to the fact that words are composed of separable sounds. In turn, this idea should help children develop the ability to segment words at the level of the phoneme (which then assists with sound spelling).

Phoneme Segmentation and Writing

In order to write effectively at the early stages, children who do not know the conventional spellings of words must be able to segment words into their component sounds. For example, when children first begin to truly use the alphabet to communicate in writing, they often print the letter representing the first, or the most salient, sound in each word they want to write. To do so, the child must be able to focus on the individual sound in the word and to think of it as

FIGURE 5.5. Beginning-sound sorting board. Note: Column headers are *rain* and *sock*; pictures to sort are *saw, soup, rug, ring, roof, sun,* and *rope.*

being somewhat distinct from the remainder of the word. Then the child might articulate the sound, try to think of which letter makes that particular sound, and, finally, write the letter. The activities described in this section help the child to both attend to and isolate the individual sounds in words. When children have learned a bit about letters and their sounds, they are ready to coordinate these understandings and to begin to apply their phoneme segmentation and letter-sound knowledge in writing.

Sound Blending

> ### Using the Group Snapshot
>
> Four different types of blending activities are described below. On the snapshot (p. 123), these activities are listed in order of their difficulty. As with earlier portions of the snapshot, the child's level of proficiency (Beginning, Developing, Proficient) should be periodically documented. To be considered Proficient with a skill, the child should be able to do the blending reliably and fairly quickly. Children who are identified as being proficient on a given skill should move on to the skill that is next in the sequence of development.

A puppet or a picture of a character (like a robot or a space alien) are typically used in blending exercises. The children are told that a character has a strange way of talking: He spreads out the sounds in his words too much. It becomes the children's job to figure out what the character is trying to say—sort of like a guessing game. Three or four pictures are then put in front of the children. The character (through the teacher) then names one of the pictures using his funny (segmented) speech. The children attempt to figure out which of the pictures he named. In our research, we have typically used finger puppets that "need some help learning to talk." Children typically love these blending activities. The puppets are very popular and usually have names and personalities. These activities can have a playful tone but clearly need to stay focused on the instructional purpose: developing awareness of the phonemic nature of spoken language.

Sample Instructional Dialogue

TEACHER: We are going to play a game with this puppet and some pictures and words. This puppet has a strange way of talking. He says the sounds in his words very slowly. Because he says the sounds so slowly, we really have to think about what he is trying to say.

Here's how we start the game. I will put out [three or four] pictures [see Figure 5.6]. The puppet will tell which picture he is thinking of, and you get to figure out which picture it is. That means you'll need to put the sounds he says together to make a real word.

Let's try one. First, I'll tell you what the pictures are: *mouse, man, fox, fan*. (*Points to each picture while naming it.*) Now the puppet is going to name one of these pictures in his very slow way. We'll put together the sounds he says to figure out the word. Now we'll listen to the puppet. He says /ffff/ /an/. If we put /fff/ /an/ together, it says *fan*. So that's how this game works.

KEEP IN MIND If only one of the pictures displayed for this activity started with an /f/ sound or an /m/ sound, the children would not have to blend the component sounds in order to produce the correct response. All they would need to do is decide which of the pictured items started with /f/ or /m/.

FIGURE 5.6. Sample pictures for onset–rime blending. Note: Pictures are *mouse, man, fox,* and *fan.*

Now he's going to name another picture. Listen and see if you can tell which picture he is naming. /mmm/ /an/. (*Pauses for about 1 second between segments.*)

CHILDREN: *Mouse!*

TEACHER: You remembered the first sound he said, /mmm/. But listen to both parts of the word. /mmm/ /an/. /mmm/ /an/. (*Makes the pause between the segments a bit shorter so that they will be easier to blend.*)

CHILDREN: *Man!*

TEACHER: *Man!* Yes! When you put /mmm/ /an/ together, it makes the word *man.*

Table 5.4 illustrates the progression of difficulty for sound-blending activities. It is important to note that when blending tasks are first introduced, the children are given several pictures to choose from when deciding on a response. The pictures serve as a scaffold for the children, making it easier for them to understand the phonological skill that is the focus of the activity. However, in order for children to develop the level of blending skill necessary to support their ability to puzzle through unfamiliar printed words, they need to become proficient with blending without relying on picture choices. In moving from instruction using

---

Individualizing Blending Challenges in a Group or Classroom Context

It is easy to make blending tasks more or less challenging to fit a child's current capabilities. For example, in a group activity, the teacher might ask one child to blend an onset–rime combination and another child, who is a bit more advanced, to blend individual phonemes. Some children might be asked to blend words with stretchable sounds, whereas others will be asked to blend words with stop consonants. A child who is struggling might be given sound segments that are only minimally separated, whereas a child who is progressing more quickly might be asked to blend segments that are presented with longer separations between them. However, teachers need to keep in mind that children who routinely demonstrate different instructional needs should probably be in different instructional groups.

TABLE 5.4. Progression of Difficulty for Blending Activities

Onsets and rimes with picture choices	As for the sorting activities described previously, blending activities should initially focus on onsets and rimes. When the puppet speaks, he provides the onset and the rime segments of the intended word. Thus, if he wanted to say the word *fan*, he would say /f/ /an/.
Onsets and rimes without picture choices	Once the children are able to blend onsets and rimes, as demonstrated by choosing the correct picture in the set displayed, the next level of difficulty engages them in onset–rime blending when no picture choices are available. The game-like aspect of the activity can be maintained when there are no picture choices if the teacher shows the picture of the object named *after* the children have correctly identified it.
Single phonemes with picture choices	If the children can blend onsets and rimes without picture choices, the puppet should begin to speak in individual phonemes: /m/ /ou/ /s/. Once again, picture choices are made available in order to make the task a bit easier. For example, the teacher might display pictures of a *mat*, a *leaf*, a *mouse*, and a *light*. The puppet would name one of the pictures using his unusual speech pattern: /m/ /a/ /t/. The children must figure out which picture the puppet is naming. (Note: To make the process efficient, the teacher might replace only the picture just named on each successive turn.)
Single phonemes without picture choices	If the children can identify the correct picture with the picture choices displayed, the task should be made a bit more challenging. The teacher holds all of the pictures so that the children can't see them, then the puppet peeks at one of the pictures, uses his segmented speech to name it, and the children try to guess at which picture he has looked. This activity can be made more game-like if the child who successfully blends the sounds is given the card to hold.

picture choices to no picture choices, it is important to continue to use words that are in the children's spoken vocabularies.

Phoneme Segmentation

Phoneme segmentation is, for most children, the hardest of the phonemic analysis tasks. For that reason, it comes last in the sequence of instructional procedures for promoting phonemic awareness. There are more difficult phoneme manipulation tasks, such as reversing the sequence of phonemes in a word (e.g., given the word *top*, the child would need to say *pot*), but it is not clear that developing proficiency on such tasks has any real utility for the child—aside from being a lot of fun for some children, of course.

Language Play

In a classroom setting, keep the puppet or pictured character used for phoneme blending activities and some picture cards available as a free choice or center activity. The children may not be accurate in the way they segment and blend the words, but at least they will be thinking about the sounds in words. Over time, this language play may benefit them.

Moving from Blending to Segmenting

Some children find it quite easy to learn to segment words into phonemes, whereas others find it much more challenging. Participating in phoneme-blending activities is likely to make learning to segment easier because the blending tasks provide a lot of modeling of how words can be segmented. Practice with blending activities also makes phoneme segmentation seem like fun for many children. As the children begin to become facile at blending sounds to make words, they will usually be eager to take a turn at controlling the puppet and talking the way the puppet does. This sort of playful practice is useful and should be encouraged.

Phoneme (Sound) Counting/Segmentation

Phoneme counting involves segmenting a word into its individual phonemes and using counters to track the number of sounds.

TYPES OF WORDS

Initial instruction and practice for phoneme counting should use words with only two sounds, both of which are stretchable (e.g., *me, say*), and the child should not be required to separate the rime portion of the word into individual phonemes. For example, segmenting the word *me* into individual phonemes requires the child to separate the onset from the rime (/m/ /e/). This type of segmentation is comparatively easy. Segmenting a word like *in,* on the other hand, requires breaking up the rime portion (there is no onset in the word *in*). Once children are successful with segmenting two-phoneme words with stretchable consonants, they should begin work on words with stop consonants. The general instructional sequence for introductory lessons is presented in Table 5.5. Sample lists for each type of word used in sound-counting activities are provided in Figure 5.7.

**TABLE 5.5. Progression of Difficulty for Sound-Counting/
Segmenting Activities**

Degree of challenge	Types of Words to Use
Easiest	Two-phoneme words with onsets and rimes and stretchable consonants (e.g., *me*)
	Two-phoneme words with stop consonants (e.g., *go*)
	Three-phoneme words with stretchable consonants (e.g., *sun*)
	Three-phoneme words with stop consonants (e.g., *bat*)
Most challenging	Three- or four-phoneme words that include consonant blends (e.g., *fly, stop*)

Two Phonemes		Three Phonemes		Consonant Blends
Stretchable	Stop consonants	Stretchable	Stop consonants	
me	bow	safe	bat	fly
so	by	foam	bite	stop
new	boo	face	bike	smile
my	do	fame	cap	frog
shoe	day	man	cake	snow
say	guy	mane	dot	flag
lie	go	mice	good	plane
low	cow	moss	gate	sweep
lay	hay	fan	hike	grape
moo	high	noon	kite	prize
mow	tie	news	keep	fry
may	who	nice	pot	float
knee	he	mall	pack	glue
she	key	name	tape	block
ray	pay	knife	tight	ski
row	pie	some	tap	bread
sew	toe	zoom	top	crib
zoo	tie	feel	take	stick

Note. Within a column words need not be used in order.

FIGURE 5.7. Words for phoneme counting.

MATERIALS

Phoneme-counting activities were originally described by Elkonin (1973). He used "sound boxes" to provide children with a graphic representation of the process of segmenting words. As children articulate each phoneme in a word, they are taught to move a counter into the box that represents that sound. Because Elkonin was the first to introduce this procedure for sound counting, many now refer to this method as *Elkonin boxes*. Because the technique has been found to be so successful in helping children learn to segment words at the level of the phoneme, and because the sound boxes provide for an easy and straightforward transition between sound counting and sound spelling, Elkonin boxes have been incorporated into many early intervention and early literacy programs.

Typically, a sound-counting activity begins with providing each child with a piece of (laminated) paper on which connected squares have been drawn. Initially, the number of squares corresponds to the number of phonemes in the words that will be used for sound counting. Often, a small symbol is drawn in or under the leftmost box to indicate that it is the "beginning box." We usually use a star to signal "start." (Although no letters are used at this point, sequencing the sounds in words from left to right will help the child to understand the left-to-right directionality of print.) The teacher provides each child with a small number of counters (poker chips, counting cubes, etc.). To start with, the teacher has the same materials as the children, perhaps in a bigger version depending on the number of children in the group. Table 5.6 summarizes the instructional sequence for sound counting; Figure 5.8 provides an example of Elkonin boxes.

TABLE 5.6. General Instructional Sequence Focused on Sound Counting

Teacher	Children
Models saying the sounds and moving the counters.	Watch.
Says individual sounds.	Move counters.
Moves counters.	Say individual sounds.
Watches.	Say sounds and move counters.

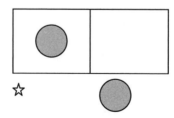

FIGURE 5.8. Illustration of Elkonin boxes.

Sample Instructional Dialogue

TEACHER: Before, we were practicing listening to the sounds in words. Now we are going to figure out how many sounds there are in some words that we use all the time. If we know how many sounds there are in a word, it will help us decide how many letters we might need to use when we write that word.

Let's think about the word *me*. When I say the word *mmmmeeee*, I start with the /mmmm/ sound and then I make the /eeee/ sound. So *mmmmeeee* has two sounds: /mmmm/ and /eeee/.

I can use these boxes to help me count the sounds. The first box has a star in it to help me remember it is the box for the first sound in the word. The star will help us remember that this is where we *start*.

Let's try using these boxes to help us count the sounds in *mmmmeeee*. When I say *mmmeee*, I start by saying /mmmm/, so I put a counter in the start box. Then, when I say /eeee/, I put a counter in the next box. (*Demonstrates.*) Now, let's all say the sounds in the word *mmmeeee*. (*Encourages the children to use their counters as teacher uses hers or his.*). Me /mmmm/—/eeee/. (*Puts a counter into the correct box while articulating each sound, briefly stopping between the two sounds.*)

CHILDREN: (*Move the counters into each box, with teacher guidance as necessary.*)

TEACHER: (*Provides encouragement.*) Now I'll just say the sounds, and you move the counters into your boxes just as I'm saying the sounds. /mmm/ /eeee/.

CHILDREN: (*Move the counters and receive feedback from the teacher.*)

TEACHER: Now, who would like to say the sounds in *me* for us while the rest of us move our counters?

VOLUNTEER CHILD: /mmmm/ /eeee/.

OTHER CHILDREN: (*Move the counters.*)

TEACHER: Now, let's all say the sounds in *mmmeee* and move the counters into the boxes as we say each sound.

"How Would Stretch Say It?"

One of the teachers with whom we've worked (A. Daley) used a puppet named Stretch when she worked with her kindergarten groups. During blending activities, Stretch articulated the individual sounds, and the children would identify the word that Stretch was attempting to say. Stretch's memorable way of talking was very helpful to the children when, at a later point, they were attempting to write. If they demonstrated difficulty with segmenting the sounds of the words they wanted to write, the teacher would simply ask "How would Stretch say it?" This simple prompt reminded the children of the process and engaged them in doing the sound analysis more independently (and lightheartedly) than they otherwise might have done.

As the children become more adept at this exercise, the teacher should gradually withdraw his or her support. The goal is for the children to be able to count the sounds in two-sound words (articulate the sounds and move the counters) independently. The teacher should continue to use words with stretchable sounds until the children can segment them easily and are therefore ready for more challenging words. Some children will be ready for the more challenging words sooner than others. In this case, individual children can be asked to segment and count the sounds in different words.

When the children are facile with counting the sounds in two-sound words that have stretchable consonants, they should be asked to count sounds in two-sound words with stop consonants. Later, they would work with words that have three sounds with stretchable consonants, then three-sound words with stop consonants, and so on. (Samples of appropriate words are provided in Figure 5.7.)

When it is clear that the children understand the process, it is time to remove the scaffold of having the same number of boxes as there are sounds in the words. In order to apply their segmentation skills to authentic writing, they need to be able to determine the number of sounds in the words they want to write. At this point the children can have a standard set of boxes (four or five boxes) and use as many boxes as they need to represent all of the sounds in the words—realizing that there will often be boxes left over.

Transition from Sound Counting to Sound Spelling

Once children are able to use the counters to represent the sounds in words, the sound boxes can be used to assist them in figuring out spellings for words they want to write.

SINGLE LETTER SOUNDS

Initially, the teacher might use the sound boxes to teach and reinforce the sound of an individual letter. For example, if the children are learning the sound of the letter *m*, the teacher might display three sound boxes and provide a marker (or a letter tile) with the letter *m* on it. The teacher would say a series of words, each of which has the sound of *m* in either the beginning or ending position, and then model the process of stretching the word, thinking about where the /mmm/ sound was heard, and then moving the *m* marker into the box that represents the position in the word where the /mmm/ sound is heard.

After modeling the process with a few words (making sure that sometimes the /mmm/ sound occurs at the beginning and sometimes at the end), the teacher would invite the children to participate in the sound analysis and decision making concerning the location of the /mmm/ sound. By initially representing only one sound in the word, the process will be more manageable for the children.

FIGURE 5.9. Sound boxes representing each sound in the word *she*.

FIGURE 5.10. Lines representing each sound in the word *plane*, with the silent-*e* appended but without a line (because it does not represent a sound on its own).

KEEP IN MIND Sound boxes are used to represent sounds, not letters. If a sound is represented in print by two letters (e.g., *sh, th, ch*), both letters would be written in the box for that sound (see Figure 5.9). Silent letters, such as the silent-*e*, should not be placed in sound boxes (because they do not represent a sound).

Ultimately, the children should be able to figure out how many boxes would be needed for a given word and then to figure out which letters should go into each of the boxes. When children begin to use this skill when they are writing, we would encourage them to start by thinking about how many sounds they hear in a word, then drawing a line for each sound (as drawing boxes would take too much time), and then writing in the letters for the sounds on the lines. For example, if a child who has had some experience with using sound boxes wanted to write the word *plane*, he or she would start by thinking about how many sounds there are. Then the child might draw a line for each sound and then place the letters that represent those sounds on the lines. Depending on where the child is in his or her knowledge of phonics (and orthography), he or she might add the silent-*e* at the end—but not on a line (see Figure 5.10).

Fiddling with Phonemes, Playing with Language at Odd Times

The activities described below can be squeezed into odd moments of the day. These activities typically should not be attempted unless the skills on which they build have already been introduced explicitly and practiced. For teachers who are working with children in an intervention setting, the "talking like the puppet" activity could be used to practice phonemic analysis skills while traveling through the hallways.

Line Up by Sound

Have children line up for PE, recess, and so forth in accordance with whether or not a certain sound (not letter) occurs in their names. For example, the teacher might ask children whose names begin with the /sss/ sound to line up first. *Sara* and *Sam* would line up, but not *Sean,* because his name starts with the /sh/ sound. For children with more advanced skills, the teacher might line children up by whether they have a particular phoneme anywhere in their name. The teacher might say "if you have an /mmm/ in your name, line up" in which case *Sam, Amy,* and *Max* would all line up.

Talking Like the Puppet

Occasionally the teacher or other children can pretend to be the robot or space person or whatever prop was used for the sound-blending activity. The teacher might use a segmented version of the child's name (e.g., "/T/ /o/ /m/, please bring me a pen") or object (e.g., "Tom, please bring me a /p/ /e/ /n/"). Such language play may encourage children to engage in similar play when the teacher is not present.

Evaluating and Documenting Children's Progress

Figure 5.11 presents the group snapshot for phonological skills. This checklist can be used to track children's development of phonological skills. Although the skills are presented in list form by necessity, it is important to remember that the various instructional techniques are mutually reinforcing. Teachers are encouraged to draw upon different techniques as needed. Within each set of instructional activities (e.g., sorting, blending) the tasks are sequenced to represent a developmental progression. In general, children should demonstrate success on the easier task within a sequence (e.g., blending onsets and rimes with pictures) before moving on to the next most challenging task (e.g., blending onsets and rimes without pictures). Children should be considered proficient when they can reliably and quickly demonstrate a particular skill.

Group Snapshot—Phonological Skills					
Student names					
Sensitivity in text					
Complete rhyme in known text					
Identify rhyme in text					
Identify alliteration in text					
Sound sorting					
Beginning sound					
Rhyme					
Ending sound					
Medial vowel					
Sound blending					
Onset–rime w/ pictures					
Onset–rime w/o pictures					
Single phonemes w/ pictures					
Single phonemes w/o pictures					
Sound counting/segmentation					
Two phonemes, stretchable consonants					
Two phonemes, stop consonants					
Three phonemes, stretchable consonants					
Three phonemes, stop consonants					
Words with consonant blends					

Key:

◻ *B—Beginning* indicates that instruction has addressed the objective but that the child has only a preliminary understanding or capability with regard to that particular objective.

◩ *D—Developing* indicates that the child has some understanding of the objective but does not reliably demonstrate that understanding or capability or is not yet automatic (fluent) with the skill.

⊠ *P—Proficient* indicates that the child reliably and automatically demonstrates the understanding or capability.

FIGURE 5.11. Group snapshot for phonological skills. Adapted from Scanlon and Anderson (2010). Copyright by the International Literacy Association. Adapted by permission.

CHAPTER 6

Letter Naming
and Letter Formation

ALPHABETICS GOAL 3

The child will be able to name and print all 26 letters of the alphabet, both upper- and lower-case versions, accurately and rapidly.

The CCSS (NGA & CCSSO, 2010) call for children to know the names of all of the letters of the alphabet by the end of kindergarten, to be able to print many of them by the end of kindergarten, and to print all of them by the end of first grade. In fact, current research suggests that it would be ideal for children to know most of the letter names (18 upper-case and 15 lower-case) by the end of preschool to ensure successful literacy acquisition (Piasta, Petscher, & Justice, 2012). However, this does not mean that if we could simply get preschool teachers to drill their students on letter names we could avert reading difficulties! Rather, young children learn letter names in a variety of ways and through a variety of activities. And knowledge of letter names is a simple-to-measure indicator of a lot of things that lead to the development of letter-name knowledge, including:

- Having spent time in an environment (at home or at school or both) that values literacy and provides opportunity to interact with literacy materials (books, paper and writing/drawing tools, puzzles, magnetic letters, etc.).
- Being interested in learning and motivated to learn about print.
- Having access to supportive adults who are responsive to and supportive of the child's emerging literacy skills.

Although there can be no doubt that explicit instruction focused on letter-name knowledge will help preschoolers learn the names of letters, if the approach makes learning about the letters seem like work rather than play, and if it is done in such a way that children feel overwhelmed and/or frustrated, efforts to improve this knowledge base are apt to backfire with at least some children, who will conclude that print-related activities are to be avoided at all costs.

Further, children who enter kindergarten lacking in letter-name knowledge are certainly not destined to experience reading difficulties. Rather, their future success in reading depends, at least in part, on the experiences they have with print and the effectiveness of those experiences in attuning them not only to the elements of print but also to the interrelationships between spoken and written language. In fact, research demonstrating that instructional experiences in kindergarten make a big difference for children who arrive with comparatively little early literacy experience provides a strong argument for initiating intervention efforts in kindergarten (O'Connor et al., 2005; Scanlon & Vellutino, 1996, 1997; Scanlon et al., 2005, 2008).

The speed with which children can name the letters in kindergarten is also a strong predictor of their growth as readers (as measured by oral reading fluency measures in first grade; Stage, Sheppard, Davidson, & Browning, 2001). This relationship may suggest that slow letter naming is an indication of some uncertainty about the names of the letters. This uncertainty requires children to expend more of their cognitive energy on this lower-level skill, and, as a result, children have fewer cognitive resources to devote to word solving and fewer successful experiences with word solving. Thus it is important to help children become fluent with letter names as soon as possible.

The goal identified for this chapter involves both the learning of letter names and letter formation, but there is substantially less research focused on the teaching and learning of letter formation early in the process of literacy acquisition. Nevertheless, engaging children in learning to form letters has the clear potential to help them to learn the critical features of the letters (e.g., what makes a *B* a *B*?) they are learning to name and what features distinguish one letter from another.

Learning Letter Names and ELs

Children who are learning English as an additional language may encounter different challenges in learning the names of letters in English, depending on their levels of literacy in other languages. For example, if a child had already learned letter names in Spanish, he would need to learn new names for many of the alphabetic symbols that are shared across languages. The name of letter *J*, for example, is pronounced *hota* in Spanish and represents the phoneme /h/. On the other hand, many letter names in Spanish bear similarity to their English counterparts, but several of these have an extra syllable added to the letter's name in English (e.g., the Spanish names for the letters *l, m, n,* and *s* would be pronounced *elay, emay, enay,* and *esay,* respectively).

Assessing Letter Knowledge

Small-group and individual intervention settings provide the teacher with more opportunity to individualize instruction, making it possible to develop a more optimal instructional plan for teaching individual children about letters. In fact, a summary of the research on teaching the alphabet revealed that alphabet instruction was more effective when done in small-group rather than whole-class settings (Piasta et al., 2012). It is likely that one of the reasons for this is that instruction can be more responsive to the knowledge and skills of the children in the group. To make instruction more responsive, it is important to first determine which letters the child can already recognize, name, and/or produce and for which letters, if any, the child knows the corresponding sound(s). For children who know little about the alphabet, it is also important to take into consideration which letters may hold significance for them (e.g., because the letters are in their names or in the names of friends, pets, siblings). As the school year progresses, it is important to document growth in the letter-level skills.

Although complete individualization is not possible for the classroom teacher, initial assessment of letter-level skills nevertheless provides important information that contributes to grouping decisions. Periodic assessment of letter-level skills during the course of the year provides important information concerning whether children are in appropriate groups, whether they are making progress or need more intensive instructional support, and whether the class, as a whole, is making sufficient progress.

Initial Evaluation of Letter-Level Knowledge

Table 6.1 provides an overview of the type of assessment that might be done to evaluate letter-level knowledge. To make the evaluation as efficient as possible, we recommend that teachers do the following:

- Assess letter naming first.
- Assess recognition for any letters the child cannot name.
- Assess production (printing) for any letters the child can name.
- Assess letter–sound association of any letters for which the child was able to name *both* the upper- and lower-case versions.
- Assess use in decoding of any letter for which the child knows the sound.

The assumption of this approach to assessment is that any letter(s) a child can name, he or she will also be able to recognize; therefore, it is not necessary to

TABLE 6.1. Assessment of Letter-Level Skills

Letter-level skill	How the skill is measured	Example
Letter recognition	The child is shown a small group of letters and is asked to point to the one named by the teacher.	The teacher displays *B S M T O* and says, "Point to the *T*." (*Note*: If a correct response seems like a lucky guess, include the letter in another set and ask the child about that letter again.)
Letter naming (identification)	The child is shown an individual letter and asked to name it. The teacher notes whether the response is correct and, if so, whether it is fast (no hesitation).	The teacher shows the letter *B* and asks, "What is this letter called?"
Letter production	The child is asked to print individual letters.	The teacher provides the child with pencil and paper and says, "Make the letter *B* for me." (*Note*: Be sure that models of the letters are not in sight.)
Letter–sound association	The child is asked to say the sound made by a letter presented in print. (*Note*: Do not name the letter when asking for its sound. The letter name often provides a good clue to the letter's sound.)	The teacher displays or points to a single letter and asks, "What sound does this letter make?"
Use in decoding	The child is asked to decode words comprising the letter being evaluated and other known elements or orthographic units that are identified for the child.	The child is shown a word family, such as *at*, and is told, "This is *at*." Then the teacher puts a *b* (or whatever letter is being evaluated) in front of the *at* and asks, "If I put this letter in front of *at*, what will the word be?"

evaluate the child for recognition of those letters. Similarly, it is assumed that the child will not be able to print letters that he or she cannot identify; therefore, only letters that the child can identify are evaluated for production (printing). Letter-sound knowledge is typically acquired only after the child can identify (name) the letter. Thus letter-sound knowledge should usually be assessed only for letters that the child can already identify.

Use in decoding would be assessed only for letters for which the child knows the sounds. The child's ability to use letter sounds in decoding words can be evaluated informally by noting the child's success as he or she reads. Our goal in conducting assessment in the way described is to make the assessment as efficient as possible and, at the same time, avoid asking children to try to do many things that they are not yet ready to do—thereby potentially undermining their confidence. The group snapshot for alphabet knowledge can be used to document children's progress with respect to letter naming, letter production, and letter sounds. This snapshot can be found at the end of this chapter (Figure 6.7, p. 144).

Note

Occasionally children are taught (and learn) letter sounds instead of letter names. If this is true for a given child, it will be evident during a letter identification assessment, as the child will provide the letter sound rather than the letter name when asked to identify individual letters.

Alphabet Knowledge and Decoding Assessment

In the online supplement to this book, we provide an assessment tool that follows the guidelines listed above and provides the materials, protocols, and instructions for administration (see the box at the end of the table of contents).

Choosing Letters for Instruction

Although intervention teachers have the luxury of being able to plan instruction that is more closely tied to the knowledge and skills of the children, it is useful for both classroom and intervention teachers to give careful consideration to the order in which letters are taught.

Recommendations for Working with Children Who Know Very Little about the Alphabet

• *Avoid similar letters.* It is important to choose letters to teach that are as different as possible from one another in terms of their appearance and their sounds. For example, it would make sense to avoid teaching the letters *b* and *d* at the same time or in close proximity to one another because they look alike and the names of the letters rhyme. Also, teachers might want to avoid teaching *j* and *k* together because their names rhyme. When teaching letter sounds, teachers should avoid teaching sounds for letters such as *d* and *t* at the same time because of the similarity in their sounds (they only differ in voicing).

• *Begin with upper-case letters.* Upper-case letters are preferable because their features are more salient and they are less visually confusable. It is potentially very confusing for a child to have to learn the upper- and lower-case versions of letters simultaneously when the two versions of the same letter are very dissimilar in appearance (more than half of the letters have different-looking upper- and lower-case versions). Research indicates that children are 16 times more likely to know the name of a lower-case letter if they know the name of the upper-case letter (Turnbull, Bowles, Skibbe, Justice, & Wiggins, 2010).

• *Teach letters that are important to children.* Children are typically very interested in learning the letters in their names, and they tend to learn those letters first, especially the first letter in their first name (McKay & Teale, 2015).

• *Teach more frequently occurring letters first.* Some letters, such as *a, s, t,* and *m,* occur more frequently than others, such as *j, x,* and *z.*

Optimal Order of Instruction for Teaching the Alphabet

We have frequently been asked to provide guidance on the optimal order in which to teach the alphabet and have declined to do so because there is no evidence that any particular order is necessarily better than another. Further, we feel that the order of letter instruction should be tied to the instructional materials in use, as children would ideally see the letters they are learning in books and other texts soon after the letter has been introduced. The logic we provide for how to select letters for instruction for children who know little about the alphabet is, we think, most important. Further, virtually all of the research with which we are familiar indicates that what we *should not* be doing in the process of teaching the alphabet is teaching a letter of the week in a whole-class context. In their book *No More Teaching a Letter a Week,* McKay and Teale (2015) make a very cogent argument, based on a substantial amount of research, for retiring that practice.

Sequence of Objectives for Learning about Letters

In general, children demonstrate letter-related skills in the following sequence:

1. Recognition
2. Naming
3. Letter–sound association
4. Use in decoding

If a child has no knowledge of a given letter, instruction should focus initially on recognition of the letter. Once a child can reliably and quickly recognize a letter, she or he is ready to begin working toward reliable and quick naming of that letter. Activities that engage children in printing the letter (production) can help them learn to recognize and identify the letter. However, their ability to print the letter on request without referring to a visual model ("Print the letter *T* for me") will typically occur after the children can both recognize and name the letter. Once children know the name of a letter, they are ready to learn the letter's sound and ultimately to use that letter in reading and writing.

Children Do Not See Letters Backwards

Children often confuse certain pairs or groups of letters (e.g., *b/d, u/n, p/q*). Such confusions were once thought to indicate that a child somehow saw things differently or that the image was rotated or reversed as it traveled from the eye to the brain, or vice versa. Nearly 40 years ago, however, Vellutino and his colleagues demonstrated that such confusions arise from difficulties in remembering what visually similar letters are called. In other words, children who make errors such as substituting *b* for *d* are not having difficulty with the visual aspects of the process; it is the *verbal memory* aspect of the task that is problematic for them (Vellutino, 1979).

Rationale for the Sequence

Many teachers are initially uncomfortable with the idea of teaching about letter names and letter sounds separately and/or with the idea of teaching upper-case letters before lower-case letters. These recommendations apply primarily to children who begin with very little letter knowledge. Teaching about both upper- and lower-case letters and letter names and letter sounds simultaneously has the advantage of providing new information for all or most of the children in the class. Thus the children who already know the names of many letters probably learn about letter sounds in this instructional context. Those who know some capital letters probably learn the lower-case version of those letters. However, those who know little, if anything, about the alphabet are faced with a huge amount of information and, potentially, little guidance concerning what they are to accomplish in these instructional episodes.

For example, if a teacher were using a "letter-of-the-week" instructional format (not an approach we recommend, as noted above), she or he might introduce the upper- and lower-case printed versions of the letter *B*, tell the children that both of those letters are called *be,* and that they both make the /b/ sound that we hear at the beginning of *ball* (see Figure 6.1). Note that the children need to be somewhat phonemically aware in order to attend to the onset in the word *ball*. Also note that it is likely that children who know little about the alphabet will be insensitive to the importance of orientation with regard to letters. Add to these potential points of confusion the various ways in which an individual letter might be presented (in

FIGURE 6.1. *B*/ball illustration.

different fonts and by different hands). Clearly, the child who comes to instruction knowing little about the alphabet has more to learn in a letter-of-the-week context than does a child who already knows quite a bit about the alphabet. To expect the same instruction to lead to the same learning outcomes for children with very different starting points is obviously foolish but, in our experience, all too common. Instruction will be much more effective and efficient when it is guided by knowledge of what children already know and what they are ready to learn next. Further, in alignment with the philosophy that drives the implementation of RTI, children who are lagging behind classroom expectations need more instructional support than do their classroom peers (instruction in smaller groups and/or for more time).

Note

It is not necessary to work on recognition of all letters before moving on to identification of letter sounds for some of them. In general, the intention is to work forward from the child's current knowledge base. However, it is reasonable to work toward the ability to name both the upper- and lower-case versions of a given letter before beginning to work on the sound of that letter.

Letter Recognition

Whole-Alphabet Activities

There are a variety of useful ways to familiarize children with the entire alphabet and to attune them to the fact that specific forms are associated with particular names.

• *Singing the alphabet song.* While singing, the teacher and/or the children should point to the printed letters. In a small group, each child might have his or her own alphabet strip to use while singing the song. Such an activity requires careful teacher monitoring to ensure that the child is, in fact, pointing to the letter that is being named in the song. It is also important to slow the song down enough so that the children who most need the practice actually hear the names of the individual letters. We have all met children who believe that one of the letters in the middle of the alphabet is called *"elemeno"* (L-M-N-O). For children who know very little about the alphabet, most of the song initially sounds like a string of meaningless syllables (*ay-bee-cee-dee-eee-ef-gee*)—which it is for them. Early on, particularly for children in intervention settings and for those with limited alphabetic knowledge, it is helpful to use letter strips that include just the upper-case letters.

- *Singing to a specific letter.* Once children have learned the alphabet song, a focus on specific letters can be accomplished by singing the song up to a specific letter and then stopping at that letter. For example, the teacher might decide to sing to the letter *K*. The group would then sing the song and point to the letters, as usual, but stop at the *K*. The teacher might also discuss the letters that come before and after *K*. The purpose of this activity is to draw attention to individual letters. The song can, of course, be sung a number of times, and children can be invited to choose which letter to sing to.

- *Singing to the missing letter(s) and filling it (them) in.* In this activity, the children are provided with alphabet strips with a few letters missing (see Figure 6.2). The group sings to the first missing letter and then fills it in by selecting from a small group of letters provided, as illustrated in the figure. Then the song is begun again and continues to the next missing letter, and so forth. (The teacher may need to show a model of the letter for which the children are looking.)

- *Reading and discussing alphabet books.* Children who have had little print exposure prior to school will enjoy listening and reacting to alphabet books almost as much as younger children do. Because such books typically devote an entire page (or more) to each letter, they are a great resource for focusing the child's attention on individual letters. They are also helpful for teaching about letter–sound correspondences. Further, it has been demonstrated that reading alphabet books to children leads to more print-specific discussion than does reading other types of books (Justice & Piasta, 2011; Smolkin, Yaden, Brown, & Hofius, 1992). In addition, alphabet books have the potential to contribute to vocabulary development both for native speakers of English and for children who are ELs, as many alphabet books include pictures of a number of concrete objects on the page for each letter. Pointing to and naming those objects and the printed word associated with each of them, and perhaps discussing some of the objects a bit (their use, where they might be found, etc.) can help to expand the children's vocabularies.

FIGURE 6.2. Missing letter illustration.

A Note about Font

To reliably recognize a letter, a child needs to learn which features of the letter are characteristic of the letter per se and which features are irrelevant. For example, the *T*'s presented in Figure 6.3 appear in different fonts, and some contain features that are not critical to the *T*'s identity.

T T 𝕋 I 𝒯 T

FIGURE 6.3. Font illustration.

Hand-printed letters and highly embellished fonts in books add even more variations through which a child must sort to determine which features define the letter and which features are merely stylistic variations. Children who learn to identify the letters of the alphabet without explicit and focused instruction generally extract the essential elements or critical features of letters either through their supported attempts to write or through exposure to multiple examples (Gibson & Levin, 1975). In other words, they learn what gives *T* its "*T*-ness." However, it is important to accelerate the pace of letter learning for children who begin kindergarten with limited letter-name knowledge. Thus the letters used in the earliest phases of instruction should, ideally, consist only of the features that define the letter. For example, all but the last example among the letters in Figure 6.3 would be poor choices for introducing the letter *T* because they include unnecessary features or features that are necessary but are not sufficiently salient. The last example, comprising only the critical features of the T, is clear.

In considering instructional materials for beginning readers, teachers should look critically at the font used in the books that children are asked to read. Ideally, it would be crisp and unembellished. Teachers should also note whether the "sticks" on the letters (the ascenders and descenders) sufficiently distinguish between similar-looking letters and should avoid fonts that feature the "typewriter" a and g (as printed here). Below is an example of the type of primary font that is often found in books intended for beginning readers:

a   b   d   p   n   h

Compare the font above to the example below, which is a very good primary font that was found for free on the Internet using the search term *primary font*.

a   b   d   p   n   h

Clearly, it will be easier for children to learn the letters that are presented in the second example because the height of the ascenders makes it easy to distinguish *a* from *d, n* from *h,* and so on.

Teaching about Specific Letters

Materials Needed

A short text with large print (a book or a poem) that contains several instances of the letter to be taught should be selected. In a Tier 2 or Tier 3 intervention setting, it would be ideal to use materials that are routinely available in the child's classroom.

Use a letter card containing the individual letter. The letter should be large enough for all of the children in the group to see, and the font should be unembellished, containing only the critical features.

Introducing the Letter

• Present the letter to be taught on a card (the letter *M* is used in the following examples). Provide all of the children in the group with a card that has the selected letter on it. Tell the children what the letter is and have them repeat the letter name.

• While leaving the letter in view, introduce the text.

• Tell the children that the words in the book contain many *M*'s and that, after the book is read, they are going to look for all of the *M*'s.

• Explain that knowing the letters helps us to read and write.

• Engage the children in a discussion of the book before beginning to read. Encourage anticipation (prediction) and personal reactions to the text.

• Read the text to the children, pointing to the words while reading. Read with natural phrasing and intonation (not word by word).

• While reading, engage the children in discussing and reacting to the text.

• After reading, briefly discuss various (meaningful) aspects of the text.

• Focus in on the letter by saying something like: "Let's look for all of the *M*'s. There were a lot of *M*'s in this book!"

• Do a letter search, encouraging the children to find the focal letter on each page. Frequently use the name of the letter during the letter search (i.e., "There's an *M*" and "You found another *M*!"). Also encourage the children to use the name of the letter. Unless the name of the letter is used frequently, some children will treat this activity as a visual matching task rather than as a letter-naming activity. (Once several instances of the focal letter have been located, ask children to find a few instances of letters that were taught previously.)

Figure 6.4 provides an illustration of a book that would be useful for teaching about an individual letter and explaining its utility.

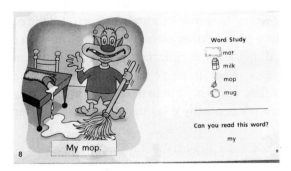

To the left is an example of a book that might be used to teach the letter M. Notice the following:

- The font is clean and unembellished.

- There are enough capital M's for the children to engage in recognition activities (letter hunts for the M).

- The story is interesting despite the fact that there are only a few words per page.

- There are opportunities to develop comprehension skills, including:
  - Using pictures to support meaning construction.
  - Engaging in making predictions ("What do you think will happen [after the spill]?").
  - Relating text to real life ("Who does the clean-up when there's a spill at your house?").

FIGURE 6.4. Example of a book that might be used while teaching the name of the letter *M*. From *Ready Readers, Monster Mop*, by Aimee Mark, illustrated by Cameron Eagle. Copyright 1997 by Pearson Education, Inc., or its affiliates. Used by permission. All rights reserved.

KEEP IN MIND   The purpose of the letter hunt activity is to give children many opportunities to connect the printed letter to the letter's name. Do not have children count the letters, because counting would keep them from thinking about the letter's name.

Practicing Letter Recognition

When the children can reliably find instances of the letter with the letter card in view, practice letter recognition without the letter card in view. If a child has difficulty recognizing a letter without the letter card present, the letter card should be provided again.

Look for opportunities to have the children find the letter(s) they are learning in other contexts (e.g., on a bulletin board or calendar, on displays while walking through the hallway). Direct children's attention to these displays and encourage them to try to find the target letter. Our purpose in having children look around the environment for letters they can recognize is to encourage them to become attuned to the fact that they are often surrounded by print and that they are beginning to acquire the skills to make some sense of it. Further, the children will, hopefully, think about the letters more frequently if they are attuned to their presence in a variety of contexts.

Games for Promoting Letter Recognition

Once some letters have been introduced for recognition, simple games can be constructed to reinforce recognition.

- *Letter bingo.* Customized bingo games can be created using only the letters that the children are learning or have learned. For each bingo card, make three or four columns, each with three or four boxes. Print one letter in each box (letters can be used more than once, if necessary, to provide enough letters to fill the card). The teacher can call the letters while the children place markers on the letters as they are called. The teacher should monitor the children's performance to ensure accuracy. Also, to promote children's ability to name the letters, they should be encouraged to name each letter as they cover it. (There needn't be any winners or losers with this game—the children are generally delighted to simply cover up all of their letters.)

- *Parking lot game.* In this game, a parking lot is drawn on a piece of paper that includes two rows of parking spaces with four or five spaces in each row. One of the letters that the children are learning is printed in each of the parking spaces in such a way that, when the paper is placed in front of the child, all of the letters will be properly oriented (right side up). Several different parking lots are made, all with the same letters but with the letters in different locations on each. To play the game, each child is provided with a different parking lot sheet and a toy car that fits in the parking spaces. Then the children are directed to park their cars in different spaces according to the letter named by the teacher (e.g., "Everyone park your car on the letter *M*"). To encourage letter-name retrieval, a child who has "parked" his car might be asked, "What parking space is your car in?" Figure 6.5 provides an example of a parking lot game board. Blank versions of the game board are available in the online supplement to this book (see the box at the end of the table of contents).

Letter Identification

When the teacher notices that a child quickly and accurately recognizes given letters, the focus should shift to letter naming. For many children, once they can reliably recognize a letter, they are also able to identify it. However, for some children, it takes a good deal of additional practice to be able to retrieve the names of given letters. An additional goal for letter identification is for the child to become able to name letters quite quickly so that, as the reading they engage in becomes more demanding, slow letter identification skills will not limit the other processes. Thus

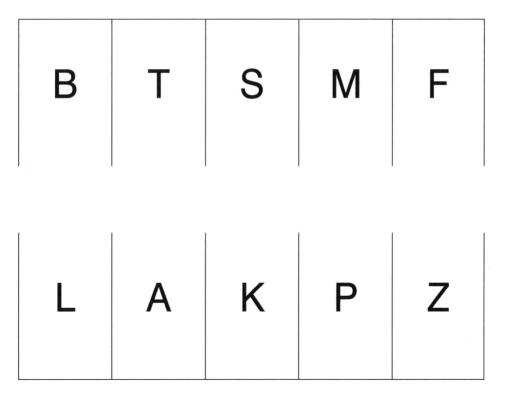

FIGURE 6.5. Parking lot game board.

the goal of the letter-naming activities is not only accurate identification but fluent (fast) identification.

Introducing Letters for Identification

In preparing to teach in a small-group or intervention setting, the teacher should choose four or five letters that the children can recognize but not name reliably or quickly. During instruction, the teacher would show each letter, name it, and ask the children to repeat the name. If a child makes a mistake, the teacher would provide the correct letter name and point out the salient features of the letter. If appropriate, the teacher would point out how the misidentified letter differs visually from the letter the child named. Before moving on, the children should be asked to repeat the name of the letter. The same letters are presented a number of times, in a different order each time, to provide children with the opportunity to practice the letters' names.

Practicing Letter Identification

Children who are just beginning to learn about the letters often forget letters that were learned previously. As new letters are presented, it is important to frequently review previously learned letters. Below are some suggested activities for providing additional practice with letter identification:

- Provide each child with a collection of the letters he or she knows (perhaps in an envelope). Once every couple of days the children should be invited to go through their letter cards and name all of the letters they *already* know. This activity can be used as an opportunity to evaluate letter identification skill, but the most important purpose is to promote fluency with letter identification.

- Occasionally choose a word in the text that is being read and ask the children to name all of the letters in the word. For example, while pointing to the word *cat,* the teacher might say, "Here is the word *cat.* Tell me the names of the letters you see in the word *cat.*" Or the teacher might say: "What is the first [middle, last] letter you see in *cat*?" or "Spell the word *cat* for me by telling me all of the letters in *cat* starting with the first one." (Until the children have print directionality firmly established, the teacher should always point to the letters when using words such as *first* and *last* in reference to print.)

KEEP IN MIND Classroom teachers often work with several children at once, even in a small-group setting. In such situations it is sometimes hard to ensure that all of the visual materials (in this case, letters) are oriented properly (right side up) for every child in the instructional group. Proper orientation of letters is especially important in letter study because some letters are easily confused (e.g., *b/d, u/n, p/q, b/p*).

Matching Games for Promoting Letter Identification

Use letters that the children are currently learning for identification and fluency (and additional letters they can already identify reliably and fluently, if necessary, to make the game fun). As children begin to be able to identify a fairly large number of letters, it will sometimes be useful to include both upper- and lower-case versions of the same letter in these games. In this case *T* and *t* would be a match, as would *T* and *T*.

A Common Parental Concern

Perhaps one of the most common parental concerns that primary-grade teachers encounter relative to literacy development has to do with young children's inclination to confuse visually similar letters (e.g., *b* and *d*, *p* and *b*, *u* and *n*). Many parents believe that such confusions are a sign of a serious reading difficulty that is sometimes referred to as dyslexia.

The difficulty that some children experience with remembering what name to apply to two things that look a lot alike (e.g., *b* and *d*) is partly due to the fact that, until children encounter print, most of the objects they learn to label are called by the same name regardless of how the object is oriented in space. Thus, a pen is a pen regardless of whether its writing end is pointed to the top, bottom, left, or right of the perceiver's visual field. With letters, it is necessary to remember the symbol's orientation, as well as its other critical features, in order to recall the proper label. One of the questions in the parent booklet mentioned in Chapter 3 (p. 70) addresses this common concern.

To help children overcome difficulties with commonly confused letters, teachers can provide a model of the upper- and lower-case versions of the two confusable letters and encourage the children to refer to the model whenever they are uncertain about a letter's identity ("Check your b–d chart"). An example of such a model is provided in Figure 6.6. Many early primary-grade teachers have found it useful to have such a model posted on all four walls of their classroom so that children can refer to it easily from wherever they are seated. A copy can also be sent home.

FIGURE 6.6. *B*/*D* example. Adapted from Scanlon and Anderson (2010). Copyright by the International Literacy Association. Adapted by permission.

Use letter cards to play games of Go Fish or Concentration (Memory). In playing such games, make sure that the letter cards are always properly oriented relative to the children. For example, if two children will be involved in a game of Concentration, make sure they are both on the same side of the table. Further, make sure that the cards are always being viewed right side up. A small dot at the top of both the front and the back of each card will help—particularly if the children are frequently reminded that they need to keep the cards turned so that the dot is on the top. Also, in all games, make sure that the children name each letter as it is used. The purpose of playing the games is, after all, to help the children connect printed letters to their names and to become fluent in doing so.

Evaluating and Documenting Children's Progress in Letter Identification

Children's accuracy in identifying letters can be evaluated through the use of a formal assessment or through observation of individual children's responses in routine instructional interactions. If informal observations are used, the teacher can note when the child can quickly and accurately name given letters over a couple of sessions. The group snapshot for alphabet knowledge, included at the end of this chapter (Figure 6.7, p. 144), can be used for capturing this information in small-group instructional situations. The first column (REC/ID [Recognition/ Identification]) would be used to capture letter-naming skill. Children who can recognize but not name a letter would be considered to be at a beginning point in development. Children who can name the letter but are not automatic or reliable across several days would be rated as developing. Children who are reliably fast and accurate in naming a letter would be considered proficient.

Letter Production

Any writing activities attempted with children will be much more time-consuming and difficult for them if they need to expend a lot of cognitive energy forming the letters. Therefore, it is useful to help children learn to form the letters efficiently and legibly.

Introducing the Letter

Learning to print letters can help children attend to the critical features of the letters they are learning and, therefore, assist the children in learning the letters' names. Thus instruction designed to help children learn to print letters, although it comes *after* our discussion of helping children to learn letter names, is something that would occur *while* children are learning letter names.

KEEP IN MIND To support efforts to provide congruent instruction, if a child in an intervention setting does not have an established method for printing a letter, it is reasonable for the teacher to teach the method employed in the child's classroom.

To help children learn to print a given letter, the teacher might:

- Provide children with a large-print version of the letter.

- Explain that they will be learning to write the letter.

- Trace the letter with her or his finger as the children watch, explicitly describing the process while tracing. For example, in describing how to print the letter *T*, the teacher might say, "This is how we make an upper-case *T*. We make a straight line down. Then a *T* needs a straight line across the top. So we make two lines when we make a *T*, a straight line down and then a line across the top of the *T*."

- Invite the children to trace the letter several times while again providing a verbal description of the process for printing the letter. As illustrated in the example above, the teacher should be sure to use the name of the letter many times while guiding the children through letter formation.

- The teacher can model the printing of the letter on a chalkboard or dry-erase board while the children watch. Once again, it is essential to provide a verbal description and to say the name of the letter several times.

- Have the children print the letter on paper, a chalkboard, or a dry-erase board, guiding their initial printing attempts with the same verbal descriptions. The children should name the letter each time they write it.

- If a child has difficulty producing a recognizable letter, the teacher can assist him or her by guiding the child's hand (while the child holds the pencil) to form the letter. Allowing children to write large versions of letters early on may make it easier for them to attend to and produce the critical features.

Note

Dry-erase boards are especially appealing to children for these kinds of activities. They enjoy both the opportunity to write and the opportunity to erase. Teachers can capitalize on this appeal by having erasure time serve instructional purposes. For example, if several letters were printed on the dry-erase board, the children could be directed to erase one letter at a time (e.g., "Erase the *T*, erase the *M*," and so on).

In letter production, in our opinion, the focus should be on general form, not on details. The goal is clearly recognizable letters, not necessarily beautiful ones.

It is also important that the child, ultimately, be able to print letters fairly quickly. If children have already learned to form some letters fluently (as is often true of the letters in their names), it may be difficult for them to alter the letter formation while remaining fluent. A decision about whether to attempt to change their approach to forming particular letters should rest on a determination of whether this approach will reduce their writing fluency in the future. The purpose of handwriting instruction (especially in an age where most things are done on the computer) is to ensure that letter formation does not interfere with the process of communication (Graham, Harris, & Fink, 2000). In an intervention setting, perfect handwriting should not be a focus. (This does not, however, mean that neat and legible handwriting shouldn't be encouraged.)

KEEP IN MIND   Until children can form letters effortlessly and automatically, they should have ready access to an alphabet strip to use as a model. And they should be taught how to use the alphabet sequence, if need be, as an assist in finding the letter they want to use in their writing.

Games and Other Activities for Practicing Letter Formation and Letter Names

Children should be encouraged to print given letters many times until it is apparent that they do not need to refer to a model of the letter when they print and that they can form the letter fairly quickly. Children should print letters that are being focused upon several times during a given lesson, and they should name the letter each time it is printed. Below we describe several engaging ways to provide practice with letter formation.

Tic-tac-toe is a particularly motivating way to engage the children in practicing letter formation (and several other foundational literacy skills, as will be discussed in subsequent chapters). For purposes of learning the names of letters and how to print them, the game can be played in a couple of different ways.

- *One letter.* To work on just one letter, each player in the game would use a different colored marker. On his or her turn, he or she would each print and name the targeted letter. The winner of the game would be determined by having three letters of the same color in a row.
- *Two letters.* Each player would have a different letter, which each would print and name on his or her turn. The winner of the game is determined by having three of the same letters in a row (as in tic-tac-toe with *X*'s and *O*'s).
- *Multiple letters.* In this version, each player uses a different colored marker. On their turn, players each choose from a set of letter cards and name and write the letter they pick. The winner is determined by having three (different) letters of the same color in a row.

In order for tic-tac-toe to support letter-name learning, children need to name the letter as or after they write it. Teachers have found it useful to have dry-erase boards dedicated to tic tac toe. They make the game grid on the board using masking tape so that all that the children need to do when they play is write in the letters. Having dedicated boards allows the teacher to ensure that the boxes are large enough to easily contain the children's writing and that instructional time is not lost to erasing and redrawing the grid.

Sticky note bingo. A bingo game of the sort described on p. 136 can be played using sticky notes (Post-its) to cover the letter. After covering the letter, children print the letter on the sticky note—peeking under it if need be to recall the correct formation.

Print in a Variety of Media

A variety of media for printing can be used to maintain the children's interest. For example, the children might be asked to print:

- Using different colors or kinds of markers on paper
- In whipped cream or shaving cream on the table or desk
- Using a wet sponge brush on a chalkboard (although these are rapidly disappearing from our schools!)
- Using markers on dry-erase boards
- In sand or salt on a cookie sheet
- Using drawing toys such as Magnadoodles or Ghostwriters or a paint program on a computer or tablet.

Remember to have children say the letter names as often as possible during these activities.

Evaluating and Documenting Children's Progress

Teachers can observe and record children's proficiency in producing a particular letter, either informally by observing them as they write or by explicitly asking them to print particular letters. To qualify as proficient, the child needs to be able to print the letter quickly and accurately and without needing to refer to a model of the letter.

Figure 6.7 presents the group snapshot for alphabet knowledge. This snapshot can be used to document the progress of children within a group in letter recognition and identification, letter production, and letter sounds as discussed in the next chapter.

Group Snapshot—Alphabet Knowledge															
Student Names															
	REC/ID	Print	Sound	REC/ID	Print	Sound	REC/ID	Print	Sound	REC/ID	Print	Sound	REC/ID	Print	Sound
A															
a															
B															
b															
C															
D															
d															
E															
e															
F															
f															
G															
g															
H															
h															
I															
i															
J															
j															
K															
k															
L															
l															
M															
m															
N															
n															
O															
P															
Q															
q															
R															
r															
S															
T															
t															
U															
V															
W															
X															
Y															
Z															

Note that when the upper- and lower-case versions of a letter are essentially identical in appearance, it is not necessary to evaluate the two versions separately. Therefore, the snapshot does not provide space to do so.

Key:

◻ B—*Beginning* indicates that work with this letter has begun.

◪ D—*Developing* indicates that the child can perform the task but is slow and/or sometimes inaccurate but does not reliably demonstrate that understanding or capability or is not yet automatic (fluent) with the skill.

◩ P—*Proficient* indicates that the child reliably and automatically demonstrates the skill.

FIGURE 6.7. Group snapshot for alphabet knowledge.

From *Early Intervention for Reading Difficulties: The Interactive Strategies Approach, Second Edition,* by Donna M. Scanlon, Kimberly L. Anderson, and Joan M. Sweeney. Copyright © 2017 The Guilford Press. Permission to photocopy this figure is granted to purchasers of this book for personal use or use with their students (see copyright page for details). Purchasers can download enlarged versions of this figure (see the box at the end of the table of contents).

CHAPTER 7

Letter–Sound Association

To puzzle through unfamiliar words, children need to know about the relationships between printed letters and their sounds. This chapter focuses on helping teachers to (1) understand letter–sound relationships from the perspective of a novice reader, and (2) teach children the conventional letter–sound relationships for consonants. Thus, with regard to the CCSS, this chapter focuses mainly on RF.K.3a. Teaching about letter–sound relationships for vowels will be addressed in Chapter 10.

The Link Between Letter Names and Letter Sounds

For many consonants, the name of the letter provides information about the letter's sound. For example, in the following letters, the initial phoneme in the letter's name is the sound represented by that letter—*b, d, j, k, p, t, v, z,* and also the soft sound of *g* (as in *gym*) and the soft sound of *c* (as in *city*). For other consonants, the final phoneme in the letter's name is the sound represented by the letter (*f, l, m, n, r, s, x*). For all of these letters, knowing the letter name provides useful information about the letter's sound. This is one of the reasons why we stress the utility of helping children learn the names of the letters before expecting them to learn the sounds. Table 7.1 illustrates the link between letter names and letter sounds by writing out the name for each letter.

TABLE 7.1. The Link between Letter Names and Letter Sounds

Letter sound at the beginning of letter name	Letter sound at the end of letter name	Letter sound not in letter name
B (*bee*)	F (*ef*)	C (as in *cat*)
C (*see* as in *city*)	L (*el*)	G (as in *give*)
D (*dee*)	M (*em*)	H (*aich*)
G (*jee* as in *gym*)	N (*en*)	W (*double you*)
J (*jay*)	R (*ar*)	Y (*why*)
K (*kay*)	S (*es*)	
P (*pea*)	X (*ex*)	
T (*tea*)		
V (*vee*)		
Z (*zee*)		
Q (*kyou*)		

When young children write, they often use letter names as a source of information about letter sounds (Bear et al., 2015; Read, 1971). Thus, if a child wants to write the word *cat* and does not already know how to spell it, she or he is likely to start the word with a *k* because the first sound heard in the word *cat* is also the first sound heard in the name of the letter *k*. Obviously, in order for children to be able to do this type of complicated analysis, they need to know the name of the letter and be somewhat phonemically aware (i.e., able to notice the similarity in the onsets in the word *cat* and in the name of the letter *k*).

It is also interesting to note (and very predictable, given what is known about the development of phonemic awareness) that children tend to learn the sounds of letters in which the letter sound is in the onset of the letter name (e.g., *b, k, t*) more readily than the sounds of letters in which the letter sound is embedded in the rime (e.g., *s, m, f*; Treiman, Sotak, & Bowman, 2001). This is at least partially because children tend to be able to separate syllables into onsets and rimes (/b/ /e/) before they are able to segment the rime portion of a word into its separate phonemes (/e/ /s/).

For some consonants, of course, the letter sound is not contained in the letter name (*h, w,* and *y*). The letter–sound associations for these letters are notoriously difficult for young children to learn. However, it is often in the children's attempts to use these letters in spelling that we see the strongest evidence of their inclination to use letter names as a resource. Thus a child might spell the word *was* as illustrated in Figure 7.1. In this example, the *y* is used to represent the /w/ sound, consistent with the first sound in its name (*why*). The *z* is used to represent the /z/ sound heard at the end of the word *was*.

Vowels are more complicated than consonants. Long vowel sounds are, of course, very transparent. The sound is the same as the name of the letter. Short

FIGURE 7.1. Sound spelling of *was*.

vowels, however, present children with greater challenges because, for most vowels, there is little relationship between the name of the letter and the short vowel sound associated with it. For example, for the letter *e*, the short sound is not heard in the name of the letter. Rather, the short-*e* sounds like the beginning of the name of the letter *a*.

In fact, for the vowels *e, i, o,* and *u,* the short vowel sound associated with the letter is actually heard in the name of the vowel letter that immediately precedes it in the alphabet.

Note

The discussion of vowels in this section is some of the most challenging text in this book. Try as we might, we were not able to make it simpler. Therefore, a few suggestions are in order:

- Do the exercise described below *out loud*. You really need to hear the letter sounds and the letter names in order to understand the points being made.
- If you do not engage in these exercises in a workshop or class setting, do them with a friend or colleague. Sometimes what confuses one person will be clear to someone else.
- Realize that expending the effort to understand these relationships will help you to better understand aspects of your students' literacy development. When teachers understand what children are doing and why, they have the potential to provide much more effective feedback and guidance to the children.

These letter–name, letter–sound relationships are typically very difficult for literate people (such as teachers) to notice because they have been so well trained in the conventional letter–sound relationships that they seem natural. Some insight into these relationships can be gained using Table 7.2 and following the directions provided below.

Say the sound of the vowel in the middle column of the table (don't say the word—just the vowel sound it contains). As you are saying the short vowel sound, begin to say the name of the letter in the right-hand column. Do not stop—glide

TABLE 7.2. Links between Vowel Letter Names and Short Vowel Sounds

Letter used in conventional spelling	Short vowel sound as heard in . . .	Vowel letter name containing that sound
E	Short e, as in pet	A
I	Short i, as in pit	E
O	Short o, as in pot	I
U	Short u, as in putt	O

right from the short vowel sound into saying the name of the letter. *Do this out loud and pay attention to how your mouth moves.* Most people notice that the sound of the vowel in the center column occurs at the beginning of the name of the letter in the right-hand column.

The left-hand column in Table 7.2 has the letter that is usually used to spell the short vowel sound (that is, the short-*e* sound is spelled with an *E*). If you try to glide from the sound of the vowel in the middle column into the name of the letter in the left-hand column, you'll find that you can't really glide easily into the name of the letter. Again, pay attention to how your mouth moves. You'll probably notice much more movement. That's because the *short sound of the vowel is not contained in the name of the vowel.*

What does all this mean for children? It means that children who are beginning to include vowels in their writing and do not yet know the conventional spelling for the short-*e* sound are likely to spell it with an *A*. They would write *pat* when writing about their *pet*. A teacher who did not understand the reason for the use of the letter *a* in this context might well provide feedback focused on helping children to isolate the middle sound in the word *pet*. In other words, the teacher is apt to operate on the assumption that the difficulty in spelling this word is due to inaccurate phonemic analysis rather than to not knowing the conventional spelling of the short-*e* sound. Children are likely to be confused by this feedback because they actually did isolate the /ĕĕĕĕ/ (short-*e* sound), which the teacher so helpfully articulates by way of feedback. The problem is they just don't know how to spell the short-*e* sound.

The tendency for beginning readers to produce unconventional spellings by using letter names (or parts of letter names) to represent sounds has been widely documented in the research arena and across multiple languages (Ellefson, Treiman, & Kessler, 2009) but, in our experience, surprisingly few primary grade teachers are aware of what the children are doing when they produce spellings such as *yz* for *was* or *wk* for *duck* (the beginning sound in the name of the letter *w* is /d/). Understanding the origins of these spellings, and doing so quickly, will allow teachers to provide more productive feedback for children. For example, for the *wk* spelling, the teacher might say "You noticed that /d/ sound at the beginning of *duck*. The letter that we use for that sound is the letter *d*." Or, if the sound and the key word for *d* have already been taught, the teacher might say "You noticed that

/d/ sound at the beginning of *duck*. Let's look at our key words and find the one that has the same sound that we hear at the beginning as *duck*."[1]

Selecting and Using Key Words (Mnemonics)

Key words are often used to help children learn and remember letter–sound relationships—and they can be especially useful for the hard-to-remember relationships discussed above. However, for key words to be helpful, they need to be "good" key words. That is, they need to provide clear and representative examples of the sounds on which we want the children to focus. An example of the key word alphabet chart used in ISA research studies appears in Figure 7.2. Our purpose in presenting this chart is not to suggest that ours is necessarily better than others that are available. It is just an example of what a well-planned and constructed (key word) alphabet chart might look like.[2]

In developing these key words, several considerations played a role. These considerations may be useful to teachers as they consider the utility and appropriateness of the key words they utilize or are considering. Thus we share our thinking as follows:

For the short-*a* sound

- Avoid words in which the *a* is followed by an *n* (*ant, antlers, ankle*), an *r* (*arm*), or an *l* (*alligator*) because, as a result of coarticulation, these letters tend to change the sound of the *a* such that it is not a good example of the short-*a* sound.

For the short-*e* sound

- Avoid words like *elephant* and *envelope* because, for the child who is just learning, the first syllables in those words are the same as the names of the letters *l* and *n*, respectively. Thus a beginning reader might think that *l* is the first letter in *elephant*. To avoid this problem, we named the elephant on our key word chart *Ed the Elephant*.[3]
- Avoid the word *egg*. Many people pronounce the word *egg* such that it sounds very much like a (non)word spelled with a long-*a* spelling pattern

---

[1] In providing this example, we do not mean to suggest that every unconventional spelling that a child produces should be corrected. Whether or not an unconventional spelling should be addressed in this way depends on a variety of factors.

[2] Teachers refer to such charts by various names (letter chart, alphabet chart, key words, etc.). Consistent terminology should be used across instructional settings.

[3] We elected to use an elephant as our key word for *E* because, although young children may think that it begins with an *L*, it does begin with a true short-*e* sound and there are no other picturable objects that begin with a true short-*e* sound.

A a	B b	C c	D d	E e	F f	G g	H h	I i
J j	K k	L l	M m	N n	O o	P p	Q q	R r
S s	T t	U u	V v	W w	X x	Y y	Z z	

FIGURE 7.2. ISA key words.

(*aig*). (For doubters, note that *Craig* and *Greg* rhyme for many speakers of American English—although there are certainly regional variations.) Teachers using a set of key words with *egg* for *e* have drawn a smiley face on the egg and named it *Ed* to address this problem.

For the short-*i* sound

- Avoid words in which the *i* sounds more like a long *e*. For example, some people pronounce the word *igloo* such that it sounds like *ee-gloo* and *iguana* such that is sounds like *ee-guana*. Our key word for short-*i* is *itchy*.

For the short-*o* sound

- Avoid words in which the *o* sounds more like an *au*. For example, some people pronounce the word *ostrich* in such a way that it sounds like *austrich*.
- Do not use the word *orange* because the *r* changes the pronunciation of the vowel.

For all consonants

- Avoid words in which the focal letter is included in a consonant blend because it is harder for young children to attend to and isolate the initial sound in a word if it is part of a blend. *R* blends are especially problematic for the letters *t* and *d* because when either of these letters is combined with *r* at the beginning of a word, the sound of the focal letter (*t* or *d*) cannot be isolated. (For example, the word *train* and the nonword *chrain* sound the same when pronounced. Neither of them includes a recognizable /t/ sound.)

Another characteristic of key words that may make them more useful to children is the integration of the letter and the picture representing the key word. Ehri, Deffner, and Wilce (1984) found that when letters and key words were integrated (as ours are), children seem to learn the letter–sound correspondences more readily.

An additional consideration that guided the development of our key words was familiarity. If children are familiar with the concepts that the key words represent, they will be better able to attend to the key word as it is intended to be used: to help them remember the letter–sound correspondence rather than having to learn about the concept as well. For example, *house* and *cat* are familiar but *iguana* and *leopard* are less so for most children. A related concern is that it is easier to analyze the phonemes in a known word than in an unfamiliar word (Metsala, 2011).

Letter Sounds and Key Words and ELs

The issue of using familiar words as key words may require extra attention for ELs as their English vocabulary, in general, may be more limited. For these children, as well as for children whose language may be limited for other reasons, it will be helpful to imbue the keywords with meaning beyond the context of the key word chart. For example, if *octopus* is used as the key word for *o,* it would be helpful, perhaps, to show a video clip of an octopus or to read a book such as *An Octopus Is Amazing* (Lauber, 1990). If *yarn* is used for *y,* using yarn in a measuring project in math or demonstrating knitting or crocheting would imbue it with meaning and thus help to make it more memorable. For a word to become part of a child's spoken vocabulary, it generally helps if the child encounters the word several times and across contexts (as is discussed in Chapter 15).

KEEP IN MIND If a child is receiving reading instruction in more than one setting, the key words used in the different settings should be the same. The purpose of key words is to assist memory. If children are taught several key words (because they are receiving instruction in more than one setting), then they are, essentially, being asked to learn more than children who are receiving instruction in only one setting. This is also a concern as children move from one grade to the next. Children who have learned the letter–sound correspondences so well that they no longer need key words will not have to recall the key words at all. Those who still need the key words often have to learn a whole new set when they move from one grade to the next. This is neither useful nor fair to the children!

Teaching and Practicing Letter Sounds

Children are ready to learn a letter's sound as soon as they can reliably identify the upper- and lower-case versions of the letter. To begin instruction on letter sounds, teachers should demonstrate that the letter tends to make the same sound in different contexts in which it occurs. If a set of key words is to be used, the key word should be included when initially introducing the sound of the letter. A sample dialogue for teaching the sound of the letter *s,* using *sun* as the key word (see Figure 7.3), is provided below. Note that, for the first few letter sounds taught, it makes sense to begin with stretchable sounds as this makes it easier to draw the children's attention to the sound.

FIGURE 7.3. Sun key word picture.

Sample Instructional Dialogue for Introducing Letter Sounds		
Materials needed: Letter *S* on a card, word cards with words beginning with the letter *S* and the /s/ sound (e.g., *sun, soup, sock, seat, some, said*) card with key word for *S*.		
Teacher	**What the teacher says**	**Comments on the activity**
Says:	"We are going to learn about the sound that the letter *s* usually tells us to make in words. When we see an *s*, it tells us to make the /ssss/ sound."	Notice the explicit language.
Shows letter *s* and says:	"/sssss/."	Note the advantage of stretchables.
Shows the word *sun* and says:	"Here is the word *sun*. It has an *s* at the beginning. The *s* tells us to make the /ssss/ we hear at the beginning of *ssssun*."	
Shows a picture of a sun with the letter *s* next to it (or in it, depending on the key words in use) and says:	"Here's a picture of a *sun*. We are going to use this picture to help us remember the sound that the *s* makes. So when we see the letter *s*, thinking of a sun can help us remember the sound of *s*. The word *ssssun* has an *s* at the beginning, and the *s* tells us to make the /ssss/ sound that we hear at the beginning of *sssssun*."	Repetition of key points is useful when new information is being introduced.
Shows several other printed words that start with *s* and for which the children know the meaning, and says:	"Here are some more words that have *s* at the beginning: *ssssoup, sssssock, sssseat, ssssome, ssssaid*."	Elongating the beginning sound makes it easier for the children to attend to.
Points to the *s* in each word and says:	"These words all have an *s* at the beginning."	
Points to each word while saying it.	"The *s* makes the same sound in all of these words: *sssoup, sssock, ssseat, sssome,* and *sssaid*. "Do you hear the /sss/ at the beginning of each of these words? *Sssoup, sssssock, ssssseat, sssssome,* and *ssssaid*."	

After this introduction, the children should be invited to think of words that have the /sss/ sound. The teacher might write each word the children suggest on a chart large enough for the children to see and draw their attention to the *s* in the word. The words should be grouped by the relative position of the *s* in the words (beginning, middle, or end of the word). If a child suggests a word that has the /s/ sound but no *s* (e.g., *city, celery*), the teacher should acknowledge that the words do begin with the /ssss/ sound but explain that the word does not happen to have an *s* and that the letter at the beginning of that word will be learned/discussed at a different time. To honor the children's contributions, words that start with the target sound but not with the target letter could be put on a separate list for later consideration.

Practicing Letter–Sound Associations for Consonants

Activities designed to reinforce letter–sound associations should typically focus on the sounds of letters that occur at the beginning of words until the children are very facile with those associations. Later, the focus can be shifted to the sounds in other parts of the word. In small-group instructional settings, different skill levels among individual children may be accommodated by asking different children to focus on different parts of the word.

Following are several activities that can be used to provide practice in applying developing letter-sound knowledge.

Sorting by Beginning Letter Sound

This activity is very similar to the sound-sorting activity described in Chapter 5. In order to sort pictures of objects by the beginning letter sound, children must be able to isolate the beginning sounds in spoken words. For this activity, the teacher would do the following:

- Select several pictures of objects that either do or do not start with the sound of the letter that is the focus of instruction. Avoid objects that start with the target sound but not with the letter. Also avoid objects that start with the letter but not the sound that is being targeted (e.g., *sugar* starts with *s* but not with the /sss/ sound) and avoid words with consonant blends at the beginning.

- Name each object and have the children decide whether it starts with the sound of the target letter.

- Have the children place all pictures that start with the target letter under a printed version of the letter.

- Later, when the children have learned about several letter sounds, have them sort groups of pictures according to the initial letter in the word. They might use a sorting board such as the one illustrated in Figure 5.5 (p. 112), with letters heading the columns rather than pictures.

"What's My Beginning Letter?"

This activity helps prepare the children to effectively apply their letter-sound knowledge in writing. Rather than thinking about multiple aspects of the writing process, they can concentrate on thinking about what letter to use to spell the first sound in a word. In this activity the teacher would do the following:

- Give children three or four letters for which they are learning the letter sounds.

- Hold up a picture, name it, and ask the children to find the beginning letter of the word. Each child should be allowed enough time to pick out his or her letter before the other children give their responses. (The teacher would ask the children to keep their choices private until everyone has decided which letter to select.)

- Remind children who need the key words to use them by saying something like: "Think of the sound that you hear at the beginning of the word I say and look at the pictures of our key words [*pointing to an available display*] and think about which one starts with the same sound as the word I said. Then look at the letter that goes with the picture, and you'll know which letter to choose."

As the children become more proficient with this exercise, the teacher might ask them to write the beginning letter for the word on a piece of paper or on a dry-erase board instead of picking the letter from a set of alternatives (e.g., "If I wanted to write the word *tub*, what letter would I write first?"). Having the children write the letters is a more challenging task and translates more directly into writing.

KEEP IN MIND   If we want children to make good use of key words, we need to show them how to use them (by modeling and thinking aloud) on several occasions. It is also important to:

- Provide them with guided practice in using the key words.
- Encourage them to use the key words during both reading and writing.
- Notice when they use the key words spontaneously and help them reflect on the utility of doing so (e.g., "I saw Sara look up at our key words when she wasn't sure what sound that *W* made. That helped, didn't it, Sara?").

In order to provide all children in an instructional group with the opportunity to do their own thinking, teachers have found it useful to provide the children with "offices" in which to work. The office is constructed from two manila folders stapled together in such a way that, when opened and set on the table, they form a three-sided enclosure in which each child can work.

Strategic Emergent Reading

To help children understand how letters can help them identify unfamiliar words, they need instruction and guided practice in applying their letter-sound knowledge in puzzling through words encountered in text. To address this need, the teacher might do the following:

• Explain to the children that they are learning about the sounds of letters because the letters will help them figure out words when they are reading.

• Engage the children in reading emergent-level texts that highlight the letter under study.

• In reading these texts, explicitly model how to use the letters in combination with other available clues for word identification. For example, if the text says *I saw a mouse* and is accompanied by a picture of a mouse-like critter, the teacher might say something like: "Hmm, that's a puzzling word. I know it's going to start with an /mmm/ sound because I see that letter *m* at the beginning of the word. In the picture I see a rat or a squirrel or something. But I know it must be something that starts with /mmm/. So that helps me decide that the word must be *mouse*."

As the children engage in either shared or supported reading, encourage them to use the letter sounds they know to try to anticipate the beginning sound in upcoming words.

Emergent-Level Texts

Emergent texts are those designed to enable children to get a sense of the reading process but that do not require them to read in a conventional way. Such texts usually include repetitive language and pictures that closely parallel the print. Some emergent-level texts provide opportunities to focus on particular letters (see for example, *Monster Mop* in Figure 6.4, p. 135).

Sound Boxes

Elkonin boxes, described in Chapter 5, can be used to reinforce letter–sound associations. The children are given a counter with the focal letter on it or a letter tile. Then the teacher dictates words, one at a time, and the children decide whether they hear the sound of the focal letter at the beginning, middle, or end of the word, and they place the marker in the appropriate box.

Writing Helper

During shared writing activities, as the teacher writes, she or he should invite the children to help by saying which letter should be written for the beginning, middle, or end (depending on children's skills) of particular words. For example, if the teacher is writing a caption for a picture a child has drawn, the teacher might ask the child to say what the first letter would be for words that start with letter sounds that the child has learned. Again, it is important to remind children to use the key words they have learned for a particular letter sound if they cannot immediately recall the letter that represents the sound.

Personal Dictionaries

In our kindergarten intervention groups, each child developed his or her own personal dictionary that contained a page for each letter of the alphabet and the associated key words that were used in the classroom.

As the children learned the sound for each of the letters, they put pictures of things that start with that letter on the appropriate page in the dictionary. To save time, the children were given several pictures that had been cut from newspapers, magazines, old phonics books, and so forth, and told to select a few to paste into their picture dictionaries. (Note that in intervention settings, time for drawing and coloring should be strictly limited so as to fully capitalize on the intensity of the small instructional grouping.)

As children progressed, they were encouraged to label some of the pictures that they put in the dictionaries. Because the dictionary is a long-term project and because it is in book form (and, therefore, may be considered "published"), the spelling that appears in the book should be conventional. To accomplish this in a small-group setting, individual children, supported by the teacher, might work out the spelling of the word on a piece of scrap paper, and then each child can copy the conventionally spelled picture label into his or her dictionary. Some children also enjoy copying words that start with a given letter onto the appropriate page of their dictionary by referring to a published children's dictionary. As the children's literacy skills progress, the captions for the pictures can become longer and include some of the high-frequency words that the children are learning.

The personal dictionaries should represent an ongoing project for the children. The goal should *not* be to fill up the entire page on the day that page is begun. Rather, the children should be encouraged to add entries over time. These dictionaries can be sent home with the children at the end of the year with the invitation to continue to add pictures over the course of the summer. This may encourage the children to continue to think about the relationships between the sounds in spoken words and the letters in printed words. Blank personal dictionaries with the ISA keywords are available in the online supplement to this book (see the box at the end of the table of contents).

Games for Reinforcing Letter Sounds

A variety of simple games can be redesigned to help reinforce letter–sound associations:

- *Letter bingo.* Each playing card has letters on it, and the caller says sounds.
- *Picture bingo.* Each playing card has pictures beginning with particular sounds, and the caller says letter names. Or each playing card has letters on it, and the caller says words. The child covers the letter for the first sound in the word.

- *Picture post office.* A "post office" is set up with three or four "mail slots," each identified with a letter. The children have cards to mail. Each card contains a picture whose name begins with one of the letters on the post office slots. The children can check their own accuracy if the correct pictures are pasted into the box under each slot.
- *Parking lot.* The parking lot director (teacher) names objects, and the children park their cars on the letter that comes at the beginning of the word named.
- "*I spy* (with my little eye something that begins with the letter __)." The children are given the first letter in a word and perhaps some meaning-based clue. They are encouraged to guess the word. When they offer guesses that are wide of the mark, there should be discussion about why their guesses don't fit the clues.

Useful Resource

Words Their Way by Bear et al. (2015) contains an abundance of appealing games and activities that provide practice with letter sounds.

Evaluating and Documenting Children's Progress in Letter-Sound Knowledge

Periodically, teachers might opt to use a formal early literacy assessment to document children's skills with respect to letter sounds. For ongoing documentation, teachers can observe and record children's proficiency with letter sounds, as well as other aspects of alphabet knowledge, informally through instructional interactions. To qualify as proficient, a child needs not only to be able to quickly and reliably provide the sound for a particular letter and/or to identify the letter that represents a particular sound (which is what is assessed on most formal assessments) but also to be able to apply this knowledge when engaged in reading and writing.

Note

The Alphabet Knowledge Assessment available in the book's online supplement provides a means of assessing letter-sound knowledge (see the box at the end of the table of contents).

The group snapshot for alphabet knowledge (Figure 6.7, p. 144) can be used to document the progress of children within a group in letter recognition and identification, letter formation, and letter sounds.

CHAPTER 8

The Alphabetic Principle and the Alphabetic Code

Early Development

ALPHABETICS GOAL 5

The child will understand that the letters in printed words represent the sounds in spoken words and will understand how to use beginning and ending consonants in reading and spelling words.

In order to progress as readers and writers, children need to understand how to use the alphabetic code to decipher printed words. In the previous chapter we discussed teaching letter–sound relationships. In this chapter we focus on ways to help children learn how to apply that knowledge. Children develop proficiency with alphabetic coding at different rates and, depending on the materials they read and the instruction they receive, they learn about different aspects of the alphabetic code in different sequences. The ISA is not tied to a particular curriculum. Therefore, although in what follows we suggest a sequence for teaching about aspects of the code and provide a rationale for that sequence, we recognize that the curricula in place will play a large role in determining how instruction proceeds. In this and the next chapter, we offer approaches to helping children to develop various decoding and spelling skills but stress that the order in which particular skills are taught and practiced will, to a great extent, be determined by what the children already know and by the materials that they will be reading. In other words, *the sequence in which we present the skills is not necessarily the sequence in which the skills should be taught.*

159

In this chapter we describe instructional activities that help children to develop a conceptual understanding that the letters in printed words represent the sounds in spoken words and to understand how to apply this insight in emergent reading and writing. In Chapter 9 we discuss teaching children how to productively use phonograms (e.g., *at, in, ight*) that are the basis for word families (e.g., *mat, fat, cat*). In Chapter 10 we discuss ways to further the development of skill with decoding (reading) and encoding (writing) by teaching children about consonant digraphs, consonant blends, short and long vowels, and vowel digraphs. Chapter 11 concludes the alphabetics section with a discussion of instruction around larger orthographic units and multisyllabic words.

Early Development of Skill in Using the Alphabetic Code

Grouping and Pacing

The instruction described in this section is appropriate for children who know at least a few letter sounds and who are able to attend to the beginning sounds in spoken words. These skills generally develop in kindergarten or before. Older children who do not yet demonstrate these skills will benefit from instruction designed to promote phonemic awareness (Chapter 5) and knowledge of letters and their sounds (Chapters 6 and 7).

Sequence of Development

Generally, understanding of the alphabetic principle and skill with the alphabetic code develop gradually and in a predictable sequence. The sequence tends to parallel the sequence described for phonemic awareness:

1. Beginning letters and sounds
2. Ending letters and sounds
3. Middle letters and larger orthographic units (chunks)

Therefore, in teaching children about the alphabetic principle, we begin by engaging them in making (building), reading, and writing words that involve changes only in the beginning letter (e.g., *mat, fat, sat*). These activities are useful both for introducing the alphabetic principle and for giving children practice with the letter sounds they are learning. Once children appear to be proficient with beginning letters, we work on the ending sounds in written words, once again using word building, word reading, and written spelling activities. When children are proficient with reading and spelling words that require changes just at the beginning or end, they are prepared to attend to the middle letters/sounds in words. At this point, some approaches call for teaching about word families while others focus on vowel sounds. In our lineup of chapters we address word families first. However, it is important to clarify that the ordering of Chapters 9 and 10 is, to some degree, arbitrary.

Teaching the Concept
of the Alphabetic Principle: Beginning Letters

Sample Instructional Dialogue for Introducing the Alphabetic Principle	
Materials needed:	Three or four letters for which the children know the sounds and a phonogram that, when combined with the individual letters, will produce three or four words.
Teacher	**What the teacher says**
Says:	"When we read, the letters tell us what sounds to make. They help us figure out what each word is."
Displays the word *it* and says:	"This little word is *it*. I can put a letter in front of the word *it*, and I will have a new word."
Puts an *s* in front of *it* and says:	"When I put an *s* here, *it* becomes *ssssit*. The *s* tells us to make the /sssss/ sound, and when I put /sssss/ and /it/ together, it makes the word *sssit*."
Displays the letters *f, b,* and *l* and says:	"I can change *ssssit* to *ffffit* by changing just one letter. *Ssssit* and *fffffit* have different sounds at the beginning of the word, so I need to change the beginning letter. So, I'll take the *s* away. Now the word is *it* again. I need to put another letter in front of *it* to make the word *ffffit*. "What letter makes the sound that you hear at the beginning of *fffffit*?"
Reinforces or scaffolds or, if necessary, models by saying:	[Reinforces.] "Yes, the letter *efffff* makes the /fffff/ sound." Or: [Scaffolds.] If you are not sure what sound each of these letters makes, you can look at your key words. Which letter has a key word that starts like *ffffit*?" Or: [Models, if necessary.] If I am not sure what letter to use to make *ffffit*, I can look at my key words to find one that starts like *ffffit*. I've only got three letters here, so that makes it easy. I'll start with the letter *b*. I look up at the key word chart and I find the *b*. The key word for *b* is *ball*. /b/b/b/ is the sound at the beginning of ball. That is not the same as the beginning sound in *ffffit*. So *b* is not the letter that I need. Next, I'll try *f*. I go to my key words and find the *f* and I see that the key word for *f* is *fan*. *Fffffan* and *fffffit* have the same sound at the beginning. So *f* is the letter I need."

Guided Practice: Changing Beginning Letters to Build, Read, and Spell Words

Once the concept of the alphabetic principle has been introduced, children should be provided with guided practice in applying it. Three practice activities are used: word building, word reading, and written spelling. The teacher should explicitly demonstrate the task before asking the children to do it.

Word Building

This is the easiest of the practice activities and so should be used first. The children are given a single phonogram (such as *it*, *an*, or *op*) that can be used to form several different words. The teacher names the phonogram and then asks the children to make words by changing just the beginning letter. For example, the teacher might use letter tiles to show the word *make* (see Figure 8.1) and say "This is the word *make*. If I take the *m* away, all I have left is *ake*. If I add one of these other letters, I can make a new word. If I put a *b* in front of *ake*, I have the word *bake*."

Once the process has been demonstrated, the children can be asked to form the words that the teacher dictates using the same phonogram. As needed, they should be encouraged to refer to the key words that have been taught to help them recall the sounds for the letters. Word building is relatively easy for the children because the number of letters that might be used to form the new word is limited and the key words are readily available for reference.

Word Reading

In this activity the teacher changes the beginning letter in the word, while the children watch, and asks the children to read the new word. This task is somewhat more challenging than the word-building activity because the children need to recall both the sound of the beginning letter and the sound of the phonogram and then blend the sounds together. Until the children learn the routine for this activity, the teacher would guide their attention by saying something like, "This word is *sit*. If I take the *s* away, and put an *f* at the beginning instead, what will my new word be?"

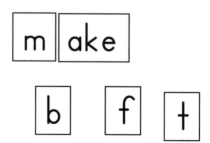

FIGURE 8.1. Word building with *ake*.

Written Spelling

In this activity children are asked to spell the words they have been building and reading. For children at this point in development, the phonogram would be left in view, and they would be expected to refer to it in order to properly spell the word dictated by the teacher. Their major task is to analyze the word spoken by the teacher and then to decide which letter to use to represent the beginning sound in the word.

The Role of Phonograms and Word Families in Early Decoding and Encoding Activities

In the activities described above, we use phonograms to form multiple words in a word family by changing just the beginning letter. In these early activities it is unlikely that the children will actually learn the phonogram that is the central component of the word family, because most of their attention is drawn to the beginning of the word, which is the only part that changes. The goal in the activities that focus on beginning letters is for the children to become facile with using the beginning letters as cues when they are attempting to read and spell words.[1]

Ultimately, however, it is important that children learn that words containing the same sound pattern often share the same phonogram. Once children learn a number of frequently occurring phonograms and understand how the phonograms can be generalized, they will be better able to efficiently analyze and identify unfamiliar words. A more thorough discussion of teaching to promote the effective use of phonograms for reading and writing words in a family is provided in the next chapter.

Independent Practice: Real Word or Not?

Once children have learned to build and read words by changing the beginning letter, additional independent practice can be provided by giving children a phonogram and several individual letters and asking them to make two lists of words using that phonogram: real words and words that are not real. Teachers sometimes use a letter slide for this activity to encourage the children to be a bit more systematic (see Figure 8.2). Teachers have also found the letter slide useful when working with children who fidget a lot with letter tiles or letter cards.

Note that we are not recommending that children be simply asked to read nonsense words, as to do so has the potential of undermining a child's developing understanding of how to construct meaning while reading. By asking the child to determine whether or not a word is a real word, we are, in fact, helping to establish the understanding that the words we read should make sense. Asking the question "Is the word I just said a real word?" is an important step in self-monitoring, cross-checking, and, ultimately, self-correction. We return to this topic in Chapter 12, when we discuss word-solving strategies.

---

[1]Note that when children are reading words in the context of a book or other text, they will have additional sources of information to support their word-solving efforts.

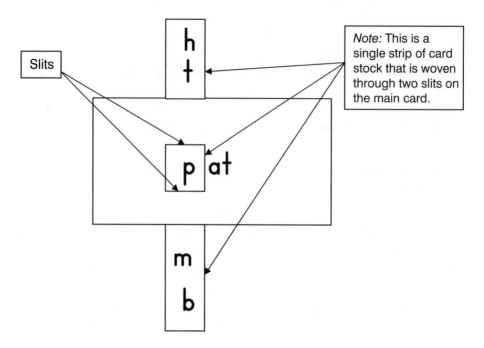

FIGURE 8.2. Example of a letter slide.

Strategic Emergent Reading and Writing

It is easy to assume that children understand the connections between phonics activities and literacy—because they are so obvious to us! However, such assumptions should not be made. It is important to explicitly help children understand the relationship between decoding and constructing the meaning of printed language. Some suggestions for helping children to make these connections while reading to and with them are provided next.

To promote word solving during shared reading, the teacher might:

• Periodically point to individual words in the text and draw the children's attention to the beginning letter. Ask them to use the first letter to decide what the first sound in the word will be.

• Identify a character or object in the picture and ask the children to try to find the printed word for it. ("Can you find the word *bear* on this page? What letter do you think it will start with?") In order to find the word, the children must first attend to the initial sound in the spoken word, think of what letter represents that sound, and, finally, examine the printed words to find one that starts with that letter. Of course, for children at this point in development, we would only ask them to find a specific word on a page when there was only one word with that beginning sound.

To promote effective sound spelling during shared writing, the teacher might:

• Encourage the children to participate in isolating the beginning sound in the word that is about to be written and then deciding what letter should be used to represent that sound.

• Write the first letter of the upcoming word and ask the children to figure out what the word will probably be, based on information provided by the context and by the first letter.

Throughout the activities discussed above, children would be frequently reminded to refer to the key word chart as needed until reference to the chart becomes habitual and/or the children no longer needed to rely on key words to remind them of the letter–sound correspondences.

Teaching the Concept of the Alphabetic Principle: Ending Letters

Grouping and Pacing

In the ISA, teachers continue working on single-consonant sounds using initial consonant substitution with phonograms until children are quite facile with the sounds for most of the consonant letters. When children know these sounds well, and when they are able to attend to the ending sounds in spoken words (i.e., sort by ending sound), they are ready to learn to build, read, and spell words by making changes to both the beginnings and ends of words.

Sample Instructional Dialogue for Teaching Children to Attend to Ending Sounds in Word Reading		
Materials needed:	Six or seven consonants for which the children know the sounds and a single vowel (see Figure 8.3, p. 166).	
Teacher	**What the teacher says**	**Comments on the activity**
Says:	"When we read, the letters tell us what sounds to make. We have already practiced reading words with different beginning sounds. Now we are going to learn to pay attention to the letters at the ends of words, too. Paying attention to *both* the beginning and ending sounds will help us figure out even more words when we read."	Reminding students of what they have *already* learned supports motivation and promotes the expectation that they will learn more.
Displays the letters *s, a,* and *d* next to each	"This is the word *sad.* I can change one letter and make the word *mad.* "Watch, I take the *s* away and put an *m* at the beginning, and that makes the word *mad.*	Changing just one letter at a time makes the task easier. The teacher

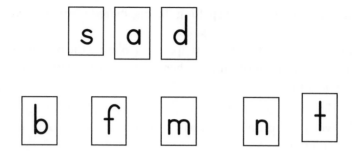

FIGURE 8.3. Word building beginning and ending sounds.

other to form the word *sad* and the remaining letters below, as in Figure 8.3. Says and models:

"Now I will change *mad* to *man*. I need to think about the sounds in *mmmmaaaannnn* and decide which letter I need to change. *Mmmmaaannnnn* has an /mmmm/ sound at the beginning, so the *m* needs to stay. So, I'm going to think about the end of the word *mmmmaaannnn*. I hear the /nnnn/ sound at the end of the word *mannnnnn*—so I'll need to change that ending letter to the letter that makes the /nnnn/ sound—that's the letter *n*." [The teacher might elongate the pronunciation of the name of the letter *n* to emphasize the /nnnn/.]

articulates the kind of thinking that the students will need to do in order to successfully build the words the teacher names.

Guided Practice: Changing Beginning and Ending Letters to Build and Read Words

Following this initial introduction, the teacher would engage the children in collaboratively making (building) several additional words by changing just one letter at a time. Thus the teacher might ask the children to change *bad* to *mad*, *mad* to *man*, *man* to *mat*, *mat* to *fat*, *fat* to *fan*, and so on.

Phonemes That Are Easily Confused

In Chapter 5 we discussed the fact that there are multiple pairs of phonemes that differ only in voicing (e.g., /b/-/p/, /d/-/t/, see Figure 5.2, p. 97). For children who are just beginning to learn how the alphabetic code works, it would be best to avoid asking them to make changes that require them to distinguish between easily confused phonemes. Thus in word building, for example, changing *mad* to *mat* (or vice versa) requires much more precise analysis of the ending sounds than would changing *mad* to *map*, as the final sounds in these two words are more readily distinguished.

In subsequent lessons the children would be engaged in word building, word reading, and written spelling of words in which changes are made at either the beginning or end of each word to form a new word. In word building and written spelling activities in early lessons, the teacher should emphasize the part of the word that needs to change by stretching the sound if possible and/or by saying it somewhat louder. As the children's skills increase, this type of teacher scaffolding should be reduced and ultimately eliminated.

Independent Practice: Making Words

Once children have learned to build and read words by changing the beginning and ending letters, additional independent practice can be provided by giving children a single vowel for which the sound has been taught and several individual letters. The children would be asked to make a list of as many real words as they can make, keeping the vowel in the middle.

Strategic Emergent Reading and Writing

Children who are able to build words by making requested changes to both the beginning and ending sounds/letters are ready to apply that knowledge while reading and writing. Thus, in addition to drawing the children's attention to the beginning letters as they puzzle over unfamiliar words, they should be encouraged to attend to the ending letters as well to confirm their attempt at identifying the word. Note that many emergent-level texts provide so much support for word identification through a combination of the context, the pictures, and the beginning letters that children are often able to effectively word solve without needing to attend to the ending letters. However, once a word is accurately identified, they can be encouraged to check the ending letter to confirm that the word has indeed been accurately identified ("Did you check the ending letter/sound to make sure it matches your word?").

Strategic Reading: An Example

We once observed a kindergartner reading an emergent-level text with a picture of a log laying on the ground. The text read "Look at the log." The child read it as "Look at the land." Because the teacher had just begun to draw the children's attention to the ending sounds in words, she was able to reinforce what the child had done right ("I see you are thinking like a reader. We do see land in that picture and the word does begin with *l*") and to extend the child's thinking about how to use print ("Remember, we've been talking about how we need to look all the way through to the end of the word to make sure that our word has the right sound at the end.").

In writing, children who are beginning to attend to ending sounds in isolated word-study activities should be encouraged to engage in analyzing and spelling the final sounds in words both during shared writing and in their own independent writing. Teacher modeling of this more complete analysis of the printed word is, of course, important.

KEEP IN MIND   When children hesitate over reading or spelling a word, it is appropriate to scaffold their attempts by referring to the key words that are being used to support letter-sound learning. For example, the teacher might say:

- "If you can't remember what sound that letter makes, check your key words."
- "If you are not sure what letter will make the sound that you hear at the end of that word, check your key words."

The purpose of this type of scaffolding is to build independence in reading and spelling unfamiliar words.

Evaluating and Documenting Children's Progress

Figure 8.4 presents the snapshot for the skills discussed in this chapter. The application of the skills discussed are considered both in terms of the child's performance in isolated word work and in terms of the child's ability to apply the developing skills in the context of reading and writing meaningful text. Children would be considered proficient with given skills when they are reliable and automatic (fluent) in demonstrating the skill. For reading and writing isolated words, children would not be considered proficient until they are able to make changes to the words without needing the scaffold of teacher emphasis on the part of the word that needs to be changed.

Note that in the *Writing words in text* section of the snapshot we have included "Represents middle sound with a vowel." This is included here because, when a child is proficient with all of the other skills listed on this early development snapshot, it is likely that the child is also representing some medial vowel sounds. However, often the letters chosen to represent the vowel will be unconventional unless the vowels have been explicitly taught. Thus, to be considered proficient on this skill, the child would need to consistently, but not necessarily accurately, include a vowel in sound spellings.

Group Snapshot—Alphabetic Code, Early Development					
Student names					
Reading isolated words					
Initial consonant substitution					
Final consonant substitution					
Writing isolated words					
Initial consonant substitution					
Final consonant substitution					
Reading words in text					
Uses initial consonant sound					
Uses final consonant sound					
Writing words in text					
Represents beginning sound in word					
Represents ending sound in word					
Represents middle sound with a vowel					

Key:

◻ *B—Beginning* indicates that instruction has addressed the objective but that the child has only a preliminary understanding or capability with regard to that particular objective.

⊠ *D—Developing* indicates that the child has some understanding of the objective but does not reliably demonstrate that understanding or capability or is not yet automatic (fluent) with the skill.

⊠ *P—Proficient* indicates that the child reliably and automatically demonstrates the understanding or capability.

FIGURE 8.4. Group snapshot for early development of skill with the alphabetic code.

CHAPTER 9

Phonograms
and Word Families

ALPHABETICS GOAL 6

The child will develop the ability to use phonograms and word families to read and spell orthographically related words.

Orthography refers to letters and spellings and the representation of speech in writing (Venezky, 1998). Many languages, including English, have alphabetic orthographies in which letters or letter combinations represent the phonemes of the spoken language. In alphabetic orthographies, certain spelling–sound patterns, involving multiple letters and sounds, tend to occur with some regularity. For example, the letter string *ight* occurs in several different words, such as *light, slight, might,* and *night.* Proficient readers process these spelling patterns as units rather than processing all of the letters individually. In addition, English is more regular at the level of the phonogram (Kessler & Treiman, 2003). Processing these larger orthographic units allows the reader to read and spell more efficiently and fluently.

In Chapter 8, phonograms and word families were used to teach and provide practice with letter sounds at the beginnings of words. In this chapter, the focus is on teaching the phonograms and word families themselves. If children do not yet have fairly good skills with the initial consonant substitution discussed in the previous chapter, it will be more productive for them to continue working on those skills than to engage in the activities discussed in this chapter.

Phonograms and Word Families and the CCSS

Although the CCSS make no mention of phonograms and word families, helping children learn to use them will enable them to learn to read and spell many words. Therefore, the instruction discussed in this chapter has the potential to support both the phonics and word recognition standards and the fluency standards. The following foundational skills standards (NGA & CCSSO, 2010, p. 16) are addressed in this chapter:

- FS.K.3.d. Distinguish between similarly spelled words by identifying the sounds of the letters that differ.
- FS.1.3.g and 2.3.f. Recognize and read grade-appropriate irregularly spelled words.

Phonograms and Word Families and ELs

The written representation of words varies across alphabetic languages with regard to the regularity of the spelling–sound relationships. The English orthography is considered to be one of the most irregular, whereas Spanish, Italian, and German, for example, are quite reliable in terms of the spelling–sound relationships. In fact, studies suggest that most children learning to read in these more reliable orthographies can learn to decode just about any word by the end of first grade. Individuals who have learned to read and write in these more consistent orthographies will likely find learning to read and write English a bit confusing initially because they are so accustomed to the one-to-one grapheme–phoneme correspondence that characterizes their first language. It may well be helpful to explicitly point out to such individuals that they need to think differently about how to decode words. For example, in working with a student who has reasonable command of oral English, the teacher might explain: "I know when you read Spanish, the letters tell you what sounds are in the word. In English, sometimes the letters and sounds don't match." For children with less oral language skill, it would be useful for someone who speaks the child's language to translate this idea. The fact that the English writing system is filled with irregularities can also serve as a rationale for ELs, as well as all beginning readers, for learning and using larger orthographic units to read and spell words.

Phonograms as Decoding and Encoding Units

As children learn more and more words, they begin to become attuned to (and are often taught) recurring spelling patterns (e.g., *ing, ook*). Over time, they come to use these patterns in attempting to read and spell words. For example, children who can easily read the words *look* and *took* are likely to find it easier to identify the word *cook* than children who only know the sounds for each of the letters that make up the word *cook*. The children might have learned *-ook* as a *phonogram,* or they might have learned to use an analogy strategy that allows them to apply what they know about the pronunciation of *look* and *took* in their attempts to read the word *cook*. Either way, they are learning to use these larger orthographic units in attempting to figure out words, and this makes their attempts more efficient. As students engage in more and more reading and writing, these units become consolidated in their memories (Ehri, 2005), and they become able to use these units when attempting to identify words with more than one syllable. Thus, for example, children who can readily read the words *thing, ring,* and *sing,* and who can read *look* and *took,* might be able to effectively puzzle out the word *cooking.*

In this chapter we discuss teaching children to use phonograms to decode (read) and encode (spell) words. As we use the term, *phonogram* refers to frequently occurring spelling patterns that represent the rime portion of a syllable (the vowel and what comes after it). Teachers often use the term *word family* to refer to both the spelling patterns and the group of words that can be formed using the phonogram. As it is unclear whether children will benefit from understanding the distinction between a phonogram and the family of words that can be generated from the phonogram, we think that the general term *word family* is appropriate to use for instructional purposes. Other terms, such as *chunk* or *decoding key,* are also used for these elements. For instructional purposes, it is important that, at least for beginning readers, one term be used rather than a variety of terms. Further, the same term should be used in all settings for children who receive reading instruction in more than one setting.

Research done by Ehri (1998) suggested that children need to be fairly familiar with individual letter–sound correspondences and how they are used in encoding and decoding before they can learn to effectively use larger orthographic units such as phonograms. However, more recent research suggests that in languages such as English, which is characterized by a good deal of irregularity in spelling–sound correspondences, it may be beneficial for children to learn larger orthographic units, such as phonograms, from early on (Ziegler & Goswami, 2005). Ultimately, it is important for children to learn that words containing the same sound pattern often share the same spelling pattern, and vice versa. When children learn a number of common spelling patterns and have learned how spelling patterns can be generalized, they will be better prepared to efficiently analyze and identify words that they do not immediately recognize, and they will also be more strategic in their attempts to spell words.

Phonograms are more efficient decoding and spelling units both because they allow the reader to avoid potentially tedious letter-by-letter processing and because the pronunciation of the vowels in words that contain phonograms is often more reliable than the pronunciation of individual vowels, as determined by letter-by-letter decoding and spelling "rules."

Figure 9.1 provides a list of phonograms from which more than 500 primary-grade words can be derived. The list includes 37 phonograms identified by Durrell (1963), plus a few others that teachers felt should be added.

Note that some of the phonograms listed here (e.g., the *r*-controlled vowels and *aw*) will also be discussed as vowel digraphs in the next chapter. If a vowel digraph can be used to generate multiple words, it can be treated as a word family. Thus, *aw* is treated as a phonogram because it comes at the end of several common words—for example, *saw, raw, claw, paw,* and *jaw*. However, *au* is not treated as a phonogram because additional letters would need to be added to the end to form words.

Selecting Phonograms for Instruction

The phonograms selected for instruction should be composed of letters for which the child already knows the names. Further, they should be drawn from books the children will read in the near future, ideally shortly after instruction and practice with the phonogram. To help children see the utility of learning phonograms and to provide sufficient practice, it is useful to use books in which the instructed phonogram occurs several times. In our intervention studies, we recommended that the earliest phonograms taught should be as distinct from one another as possible so that the children would be more apt to treat the phonogram as a unit rather than to analyze it letter by letter. For example, if the first few phonograms taught were *an, ap,* and *at,* the child would need to attend very carefully to the final letter in order to distinguish them from one another. On the other hand, if the first few phonograms taught were *an, op,* and *it,* the child could more readily process them as units because they look so different from one another. Thus the recommendation to use distinctly different phonograms early on is to help the children develop an understanding that not all words need to be read letter by letter.

ack	eat	ice	ock	uck
ail	ell	ick	oke	ug
ain	er	ide	op	ump
ale	est	ight	ore	unk
ame		ill	or	ur
an		in		
ank		ine		
ap		ing		
ar		ink		
ash		ip		
at		ir		
ate		it		
aw				
ay				

FIGURE 9.1. Phonograms that can be used to form over 500 primary-grade words.

However, we know of core reading programs that take a different approach to the early teaching of phonograms. For example, they introduce several phonograms with the same short vowel (e.g., *at, ap, an*) consecutively, then move on to a second vowel (e.g., *op, ot*). A program that takes such an approach would presumably be providing books in which the most recently taught phonograms appear with some frequency. We see opportunity to apply the phonic elements that are being taught in isolation as the most crucial issue in supporting the development of skill with using these larger orthographic units in word solving.

Teaching Children to Read and Write Words Using Phonograms

The teaching of phonograms is fairly common in the primary grades, and the approach to instruction that we have frequently seen is one in which the teacher introduces a new phonogram and then engages the children in generating a list of words that can be built with the phonogram. The list is commonly created on chart paper, and these charts are displayed around the room for future reference. Although there is certainly value in this approach, there is a risk that, for children who are slower to acquire these skills, this activity won't really help them learn the phonogram because most of the attention during the construction of the list is on the onsets of the words, as that is what changes. To help children learn phonograms to the point at which they can use them productively in their reading and writing, we advise that, once a new phonogram has been introduced and used to build some words, further work with it should include one or two phonograms that were previously taught. The phonograms would initially be taught and practiced in a word building activity. Thereafter the teacher would engage the children in reading words that she or he builds with the phonograms and, later still, the children would write the words.

Sample Instructional Dialogue for Word Building with Phonograms		
Materials needed (for each child in the group):	• The new phonogram to be taught (*ot* in this example) plus one or two previously taught phonograms (if available). We'll use *ap* in this example. The phonograms should be on cards (or, if letter tiles are being used, the letters making up the phonogram should be taped together). • Several individual letters that will allow several different words to be built with each phonogram (the letters *l, n, m, t, c,* and *h* in this example).	
Teacher	What the teacher says	Comment on the activity
Shows new phonogram and says:	"We are going to learn about a new word family today. Remember, a word family is a	The teacher names the word family several times to help the children store it in memory. She

	group of words that all have the same spelling pattern. The family we are learning about today is the /ot/ family. Words in this family all have the letters *o* and *t* at the end. Those letters together sound like /ot/.	or he also gives the children a purpose for learning word families.
	"We'll see lots of words in the /ot/ family in our reading, and you'll use /ot/ words in your writing, too. So, learning this and other word families will help us with our reading and writing."	
Shows several consonants for which the children have been taught the sounds and says:	"We are going to use these letters to make some words in the /ot/ family. You may remember the sounds for these letters, but if you don't, you can check our key words to help you remember the sounds."	The activity at this point is similar to the initial consonant substitution activity described in Chapter 8 and so shouldn't require much teaching or practice.
Says:	"Let's make the word *pot*. Sometimes people cook in a *pot*. How would I make the word *pot*?"	In working with children with limited vocabulary, if the teacher thinks the children might not know the meanings of the words used, she or he could show pictures for the words that are picturable.
Provides feedback.	"Right. I put a *p* in front of *ot* to make *pot*."	
Says:	"How would I make the word *not*? I am *not* standing up."	
Says:	"How would I change *not* to *tot*? Sometimes a baby is called a *tot*."	The teacher would provide feedback with each change.
Shows *ap* phonogram and says:	"Now let's make a word from our /ap/ word family that we learned before. How would I change *tot* to *tap*? I *tap* the table with my finger. *Tap*."	The *ap* word family doesn't share any letters with the *ot* word family. Using distinctly different word families early on is intended to encourage the children to process the phonograms as units.

After a few more examples—for example, changing *tap* to *nap, nap* to *not, not* to *lot, lot* to *lap*—the teacher would give each child the word families and individual letters and would engage them in building words that the teacher dictates. It is important, when working with only two word families, not to ask the children to make changes in a highly predictable sequence, such as changing the beginning letter, then the phonogram, then the beginning letter, and so forth, as this may diminish the children's attention to the word families. A reasonable sequence for this pair of word families would be *tot* to *tap, tap* to *nap, nap* to *not, not* to *lot, lot* to *lap, lap* to *map, map* to *cap, cap* to *cot, cot* to *hot.*

After the children have engaged in word building and seem fairly confident with it, the teacher would use one set of the instructional materials to make words one at a time, as the children watch, and for each word the teacher would ask different children to read the word. At a later point, the children write words dictated by the teacher. For this written spelling activity, it is often helpful to start by creating a column for each of the phonograms that will be used. Then the teacher dictates words, and the children decide in which column each word belongs and write the dictated word in the correct column. Teachers sometimes use a graphic of a house and talk about these charts as two- or three-family houses; the children need to decide in which family each dictated word belongs (see Figure 9.2).

KEEP IN MIND   Before calling on a child to read a word in this, as well as all of the other activities that call for children to read words in isolation, the teacher should provide enough time for all of the children to think of the word. If the teacher too quickly calls on the first child to raise a hand, which is a fairly common practice, those children who need more time to process will lose the opportunity to do the necessary thinking. Similarly, if the teacher directs a child to read the word before she displays it (e.g., "The next one is for Michael"), the other children in the group may attend less to the word.

FIGURE 9.2. A two-family house used for word family practice.

Further Phonogram Practice

Once a phonogram has been introduced and practiced, the children can be asked to generate as many real words as they can using the phonogram and make a list of them. Alternatively, they could be asked to systematically use a set of consonants, blends, and/or digraphs to try to form words with the phonogram and to read each resulting combination and make a list of all of the real words and nonwords that are formed. When using the word family houses described above, one of us (JMS) has used the idea of a "garage" for the nonwords. In this case, as children generate words, the real words go into the house, and the nonwords go into the garage.

Note

Making decisions about which combinations yield real words and which result in nonwords is, potentially, a helpful activity in promoting self-monitoring when the children read continuous text. If a decoding attempt results in a nonword, they are more likely to notice it.

Maintaining a Focus on Phonograms

After each phonogram has been introduced and practiced, the goal is for children to use it in decoding words they do not immediately recognize and in spelling words for which they have not memorized the conventional spellings. The activities described next are designed to promote the use of phonograms for these purposes.

The Phonogram Display

The phonograms that have been introduced and practiced should be prominently displayed for the children to refer to during reading and writing. For this display, we recommend that the phonograms be organized by the vowel they contain. Long and short vowel phonograms should be grouped separately. Phonograms that have neither a long nor a short vowel sound (e.g., the *a* in *all*) would also be grouped separately. An example of a phonogram display is provided in Figure 9.3. Note that the key words for the short vowel sounds are included in the display as an extra scaffold. (We discuss the teaching of vowels in Chapter 10.)

Note that by grouping the phonograms by vowel sound, the phonogram chart provides the children with an additional clue about how the phonogram will be pronounced, so it is important for the teacher to explain the organization of the display. In addition, for phonograms with which children have particular difficulty, it is helpful to provide a familiar high-frequency word to facilitate their recall of the sound of the phonogram (see Figure 9.3). This is especially helpful for phonograms that are contained in high-frequency words that the children can readily identify.

Reading Connected Text

While reading, when children encounter a word they do not immediately recognize and the context is not sufficiently helpful to allow word identification, they should be encouraged to see whether there are any familiar phonograms contained in the word. The vowel or vowels in the word should serve as a point of reference for looking for known phonograms. Ideally the children would remember the phonograms that they have learned. However, if they don't, the phonogram display will facilitate their attempts to make use of the phonograms. The children would be guided to find the first vowel in the word they are attempting to identify and then check the phonograms in the column for that vowel. If the word in question contains more than one syllable, more than one phonogram that has been taught may help the children to identify the word. For example, if the phonograms displayed in Figure 9.3 had been taught and the children encountered the word *entering*, they could make progress toward identifying the word by recognizing the three phonograms contained in the word (*en*, *er*, and *ing*). Children should always, of course, be encouraged to determine whether their decoding attempts make sense in the context of the text they are reading.

Spelling

Children should be encouraged to use phonograms in attempting to spell words when they do not know the conventional spelling. In order to do so, the children would first determine the number of syllables that are contained in the word they

Word Families We Know

A	E	I	O	U
at	en	it	ot	up
an	ess		op	ug
ain	eet	ite	oat	ute
ame	ean	ight (night)	ope	
ay (play)			old	
all	er	ir	or	ur
ar		ing	oy	
			ook (look)	

FIGURE 9.3. Phonogram/word family display for children.

wish to spell (by counting the number of "beats" in the word). Often, it is helpful to have the children draw a line for each syllable in the word. Over time, and with teacher guidance and support, for each syllable the children would learn to:

- Determine what the initial sound(s) is (are) and how it (they) should be represented in print.
- Think about whether they know any phonograms that sound like the remainder of the syllable. If so, that phonogram should be used to complete the spelling for that syllable.

Subsequent syllables in the word would be analyzed in a similar fashion.

Children will become more efficient in using phonograms in their spelling if they periodically have "spelling tests" in which they use a phonogram-based spelling strategy. For example, by referring to the "Word Families We Know" display illustrated in Figure 9.3, the children might be asked to spell *mess, feet, shop, coat, raining,* and *daylight.* While the use of phonograms as one spelling strategy will certainly, on occasion, lead to unconventional spellings (e.g., some children will provide *daylite* as the spelling for *daylight*), the use of phonograms will considerably improve the initial spelling attempts of many children.

Games for Promoting Fluent Use of Phonograms

The games described next can be used in centers and/or for practice at home.

- *Phonogram guessing game.* The clue giver thinks of a word containing one or more of the phonograms on the chart and provides a clue concerning the meaning of that word (e.g., "I'm thinking of something kids usually don't like to have to clean up"). The children try to think of a word that fits the clue and contains one of the phonograms. If they cannot think of the word with only the meaning clue, the clue giver would provide another clue that focuses attention on a smaller group of phonograms (e.g., "The word I'm thinking of has one of the word families that start with *e* in it"). If the children are still unable to think of the word, the clue giver might point to the phonogram contained in the word, tell the children that the word belongs to that word family, and then remind the children of the meaning clue initially provided.

- *Go Fish.* Go Fish games can be created using words derived from phonograms that have been taught. In this game the children ask for words containing a specific phonogram. Thus, a child might ask for a word in the *ake* family (pronouncing the phonogram rather than naming the letters). A match is created by having two words with the same phonogram.

- *Tic-tac-toe.* For this game the children are provided with two or more phonograms that have been taught. On each turn, the player has to think of a word using one of the phonograms and write it in the square of choice. Repetitions of words are not allowed. All words need to be real when pronounced (although if the children are playing without an adult, there may be unconventional spellings of real words). Children use different colored markers to write the words, and the winner is determined by the colored entries on the game board.

● *Phonogram hunt.* Children are given a text in which they are to go on a "word family hunt." That is, they are invited to see how many phonograms they can find in the text. The text may be covered with a transparency or plastic sheet protector, and children can underline or circle all of the words belonging to the families they have learned. Alternatively, they might use a dry-erase board to keep a running list of all the words with known phonograms that they find. This game helps to increase children's awareness of phonograms and their ability to use them productively for reading and spelling.

● *Great big words.* The children are encouraged to find words that contain a large number of phonograms. A cumulative list of words containing several phonograms might be maintained with an eye toward finding a really big word by the end of the school year. The children can be on the lookout for such words in their classroom as well as at home.

Evaluating and Documenting Children's Progress

Figure 9.4 presents the group snapshot for phonograms and word families. The snapshot allows teachers to document proficiency relative to both isolated practice activities, which is the context in which the word families are explicitly taught, and the application/use of word families in the context of reading and writing meaningful text. For children to be considered proficient with respect to the isolated practice activities, they need to be able to quickly and accurately build, read, and spell words composed of taught word families and easily learn new phonograms as they are introduced. With regard to application, to be considered proficient in reading, the children need to readily decode words in taught word families when they are encountered in context. For writing, children would be considered proficient if they reliably spell words using appropriate word families that have been taught. Of course, children would not be considered proficient in any of these skills if only a few word families have been taught and learned. Rather, children should know quite a few word families and should be readily expanding their repertoires.

Group Snapshot—Phonograms and Word Families						
Student names						
Practice in isolation	Word building					
	Word reading					
	Written spelling					
Application	Reading					
	Writing					

Key:

◻ *B—Beginning* indicates that instruction has addressed the objective but that the child has only a preliminary understanding or capability with regard to that particular objective.

⊠ *D—Developing* indicates that the child has some understanding of the objective but does not reliably demonstrate that understanding or capability or is not yet automatic (fluent) with the skill.

⊠ *P—Proficient* indicates that the child reliably and automatically demonstrates the understanding or capability.

FIGURE 9.4. Group snapshot for larger orthographic units and multisyllabic words.

CHAPTER 10

The Alphabetic Principle and the Alphabetic Code

Later Development

ALPHABETICS GOAL 7

The child will understand how to use all of the letters in printed words as an assist in determining the pronunciation of the word. Similarly, the children will learn to represent all of the sounds in a spoken word with an acceptable letter when writing.

The content discussed in this chapter builds from the content discussed in the first five alphabetics goals (print concepts and conventions, phonological awareness, letter names, letter sounds, and early development of skill with the alphabetic code). As noted in the previous chapter on phonograms and word families, the instructional elements that are the focus of this chapter are likely to be addressed either simultaneously with or somewhat before instruction focused on phonograms and word families—depending on the instructional materials in use. However, it is important to note that the evidence that exists, limited as it is, suggests that, at least for students who experience difficulties in the early stages of literacy acquisition, greater gains in the development of decoding skills occur when children are first taught to decode words on a letter-by-letter basis (Ehri, Satlow, & Gaskins, 2009). As also noted, however, there is remarkably little research on this topic, and there are theorists who advocate for introducing phonograms and other larger orthographic units sooner rather than later owing to the many irregularities in spelling–sound correspondences that characterize the English language (Ziegler & Goswami, 2005). Despite these differing points of view, there is agreement that, in order to become proficient readers, students need to be skilled in using letter–sound correspondences to puzzle through words, *and* they ultimately need to learn multiletter patterns and use those larger orthographic units in puzzling through unfamiliar words encountered while reading. Many of the patterns readers come to recognize automatically are learned through repeated, successful engagement in word solving and extensive amounts of reading. The additional phonics skills addressed in this chapter, once learned, will enable successful word solving.

Recent Research on the Role of Written Spelling in Orthographic Word Learning

In the last few years, several studies have been published that indicate that children learn to identify written words more quickly when a portion of the instruction engages them in spelling the words in writing; spelling them orally did not have the same impact (e.g., Shahar-Yames & Share, 2008; Ouellette, 2010). In teaching students new phonic elements, we have always stressed that it is valuable to have students build, read, and spell (in writing) words containing the phonic elements that are under study. This recent research reinforces our sense that the act of spelling words assists children in the process of word learning.

In this chapter we discuss ways to further the development of skill with decoding (reading) and encoding (writing) by teaching children about consonant digraphs, consonant blends, short and long vowels, and vowel digraphs. For children who experience difficulty with learning the alphabetic code, vowels typically present the biggest challenge.

Phonics Skills and the CCSS

The CCSS place high expectations on the phonics achievement of young children. For example, by the end of kindergarten, children are expected to "associate the long and short sounds with common spellings (graphemes) for the five major vowels" (RF.K.3.b; NGA & CCSSO, 2010, p. 16). Although some are strongly opposed to the phonics skills expectations articulated in the CCSS (e.g., Carlson-Paige, McLaughlin, & Almon, 2015), our experience with kindergarten intervention suggests the expectations may not be unreasonable, assuming that the instruction that the children receive is well organized, coherent, and provided by teachers with sufficient expertise. We say this because we found, in the study we published several years ago (Scanlon et al., 2008), that many of the kindergartners who qualified for and received kindergarten intervention knew the long and short sounds of the vowels and their common orthographic representation (e.g., the VCe pattern for long vowel sounds) by the end of kindergarten.

These were children in high-needs schools who qualified for intervention owing to limited early literacy skills (letter-name knowledge and phonological awareness) at kindergarten entry. Further, the intervention they received was not very intensive. They were taught in groups of three for half an hour two or three times per week for approximately 25 weeks. This rather limited amount of intervention (25 to 30 hours in total), combined with solid classroom instruction, enabled many of the children to attain a fairly high level of phonics skill by the end of kindergarten.

In addition to Standard RF.K.3.b, this chapter also addresses instruction to support multiple phonics and word recognition standards in the first- and second-grade standards. Table 10.1 lists the CCSS for phonics and word recognition for first and second grade (NGA & CCSSO, 2010, p. 16), along with the page numbers in this book on which discussion related to each standard begins.

Later Development of Skill in Using the Alphabetic Code

Grouping and Pacing

The activities described in this section are intended for children who

- Know the names of most of the letters and the sounds of most of the consonants.
- Can build and read words using initial and final consonant substitution.

TABLE 10.1. CCSS Phonics and Word Recognition Standards for First and Second Grade

Standard	Pages
RF.1.3 and 2.3. Know and apply grade-level phonics and word analysis skills in decoding words.	124–214
RF.1.3.a. Know the spelling–sound correspondences for common consonant digraphs.	185–192
RF.1.3.b. Decode regularly spelled one-syllable words.	170–180
RF.1.3.c. Know final -e and common vowel team conventions for representing long vowel sounds.	193–212
RF.1.3.g. Recognize and read grade-appropriate irregularly spelled words.	Chapters 12 and 13
RF.2.3.a. Distinguish long and short vowels when reading regularly spelled one-syllable words.	193–212
RF.2.3.b. Know spelling–sound correspondences for additional common vowel teams.	208–212
RF.2.3.e. Identify words with inconsistent but common spelling–sound correspondences.	208–212
RF.2.3.f. Recognize and read grade-appropriate irregularly spelled words.	272–295

- Are at least beginning to be able to segment single-syllable words into their individual phonemes.
- When writing, can represent the prominent consonants with an acceptable letter and are beginning to include vowel markers (i.e., they frequently represent long vowels with the vowel letter; e.g., CAK for *cake*) and occasionally represent short vowel sounds with a letter that is unconventional (e.g., PAT or PNT for *pet*) or don't represent short vowel sounds at all.

If children are on track to achieve the end of kindergarten phonics expectations, they will need to meet the grouping and pacing criteria listed above long before the end of kindergarten, as many children need a good deal of instruction and practice with decoding and spelling to become proficient with vowels. While some children will move very quickly through the content discussed in this chapter, others will move more slowly and will need many more repetitions and reinforcements. *It is important to remember that education is about teaching children, not about teaching the curriculum regardless of what the children are learning.*

Assessment for Grouping

One of the most efficient ways of evaluating children's skills with the alphabetic code is through an evaluation of their written spelling. Bear et al. (2015 or any earlier version) provide developmental spelling inventories that can help teachers identify groups of children who have similar understandings about the workings of the alphabetic code. Once such groups are identified, instruction can be more explicitly targeted to what the children in the groups are ready to learn.

Consonant Combinations

Consonant Digraphs

When two letters together represent a single sound, the letter combination is called a *digraph*. The English writing system includes multiple consonant digraphs (e.g., *ss* as in *class, ff* as in *sniff, ch* as in *inch, th* as in *the*). The pronunciation of some digraphs is quite transparent, for example, the *ff* in *sniff* in which the two letters, together, represent a single phoneme /f/. There are also some frequently occurring digraphs that represent the sound of only one of the letters in the digraph (e.g., *ck*). In addition, there are some frequently occurring digraphs that are not at all transparent in that neither of the letters in the digraph, by itself, represents the sound of the digraph. The most frequent of these are *th, sh,* and *ch*. Double letter digraphs (such as *ff*) generally do not need to be explicitly taught. However, the most frequently occurring digraphs that are not doubled letters *(th, sh, ch, wh, ck)* may need to be explicitly taught and practiced as decoding elements. Only one digraph would be introduced on a given day/lesson.

Two Sounds for *th*

The *th* digraph represents two sounds. For one, the vocal chords vibrate a bit as the sound is pronounced (e.g., the /th/ sound in the word *the*), whereas for the other pronunciation the vocal chords do not vibrate (e.g., the /th/ sound in the word *thing*).

In teaching a digraph, the teacher would start by showing the children several words that include the digraph, read the words to them, and draw their attention to the fact that the two letters together represent a single sound. For digraphs to which it applies, it is important to point out that the sound represented by the digraph is different from the sound that either of the letters makes alone. The children should be encouraged to listen to each of the words and to isolate and say the sound of the digraph.

For use in word-building and word-reading activities, the digraph should be treated as a single decoding element (see Figure 10.1). Some teachers do this by printing the digraph on a card, others tape two letter tiles together. Using the letter cards in Figure 10.1, the children might be asked to change *tap* to *chap, chap* to *chat, chat* to *mat, mat* to *pat, pat* to *pack,* and so on.

Consonant Blends

In a consonant blend the sounds of two or three consonants are blended together, but the individual sounds of each of the consonants are still fairly discernable (*cl, cr, bl, br, fr, scr, sm,* etc.). In the ISA, we teach blending as a process rather than teaching every possible consonant blend as a unit because there are far too many blends.

WHEN ARE CHILDREN READY TO LEARN ABOUT CONSONANT BLENDS?

The concept of blending consonants can be introduced when children know the sounds of most, if not all, of the single consonants and can use those consonant

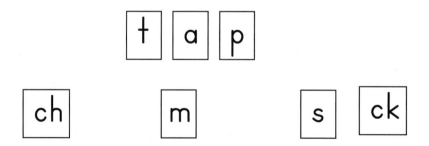

FIGURE 10.1. Word building with digraphs.

sounds in decoding and spelling single-syllable words. At the very least, children need to know the sounds of the individual consonants in the blends which they are learning.

ORDER OF DIFFICULTY FOR CONSONANT BLENDS

Some blends are easier for children to analyze and read than others. As with all instruction, it is helpful to begin with the clearest, easiest examples and to move to more challenging items once the children are facile with the easier ones.

- *Easiest blends.* Because it is easier to draw children's attention to consonant sounds that can be elongated (stretched) without distortion (e.g., *s, m, n, f, r, l*) than to stop consonants (e.g., *p, b, d,* hard *c* [as in *cat*], and hard *g* [as in *goat*]), it makes sense to start teaching the blending process with a blend in which both consonants are stretchable (*sm, fr, sl, fl, sn,* etc.). The specific blends selected for instruction should be determined by the reading the children will do in the near future (the same day or the next day). Work with a variety of blends composed of stretchable consonants should continue until the children are fairly proficient with them.

- *More difficult blends.* Consonant blends that have a combination of stretchable and stop consonants (*pr, br, bl, cl, sc, st,* etc.) are somewhat more challenging because it is difficult to draw children's attention to the stop consonant portion of the blend.

- *Most difficult blends.* Some of the most challenging consonant blends in the initial position are *dr* and *tr*. These are challenging because the stop consonants *d* and *t* are not easily detected in these blends due to coarticulation. That is, because of the way that the mouth positions itself to make the /r/ sound as it is articulating the /d/ or /t/ sound, the sounds of the *d* and *t* are distorted. (This is the reason why a child might spell the word *drip* with the letters *jrip* or *jip* or spell *truck* with the letters *chrk*.)

Confusing Writing System

We once observed a kindergarten child reading an emergent-level book about a toy bear. The story unfolded something like this. "My bear can sit. My bear can swing. My bear can swim. My bear can dry." The child read the book quite comfortably until the very last page, which showed the bear hanging on a clothesline. The child puzzled over the last word for a bit and then said, "It's not *dry* because it doesn't start with a *j*."

Some of the most challenging consonant blends in the final position are those in which a nasal consonant (i.e., *m* or *n*) precedes a stop consonant (e.g., *t, p*).

These are difficult because children use changes in mouth position as clues to the sounds in words. The subtle changes in mouth position when the nasal consonant is present or absent are hard to detect. This can be experienced by saying the words *wet* and *went* or *rap* and *ramp* and carefully attending to the various parts of the mouth that are involved in the pronunciation. Most would agree that the mouth movements for each pair of words are very similar. Difficulties with nasal + stop consonant blends will be most apparent in the children's writing, where they will typically fail to include the nasal consonant. Thus, *jump* may be spelled *jup,* and *hand* may be spelled *had.*

Note

In pronouncing a "nasal consonant," air flows through the nose (nasal passage) instead of through the mouth. The sounds for *m, n,* and *ng* (which is a single phoneme) are the only nasal consonants.

CONSONANT BLENDS AND ELs

Consonant blends are relatively uncommon in the first language of many ELs (e.g., Arabic, Farsi, Spanish, Turkish, and many South Asian languages; see Swan and Smith, 2001). The relative lack of these structures in the ELs' first language can make it difficult for them to perceive and produce English blends. These difficulties result in mispronunciations in spoken words. Thus students might pronounce *breakfast* as *breffess* or *hand* as *han.* Or they may add short vowel sounds to the consonant sounds in the cluster. For example, *stop* might be pronounced *estop,* and *spring* might be pronounced *espering.*

TEACHING CHILDREN TO READ AND WRITE WORDS WITH CONSONANT BLENDS

Word building, word reading, and written spelling can be used to teach and practice the use of consonant blends. The first step in helping children to learn to read consonant blends is to make sure that the children can blend spoken consonant sounds to form words (see Chapter 5). The next step would be to teach and provide practice with printed representations of consonant blends at the beginnings of words, starting with word building. For this initial instruction, it is helpful to use groups of words that can be formed with one or the other of the single consonants in the blend, as well as a combination of the two (or three) consonants (see examples in Figure 10.2 on p. 190). Often during initial instruction, we use a family of words in which the phonogram remains constant and the focus is on changing and modifying the elements of the blend.

When the children can build, read, and spell words with blends in which both consonants are stretchable, the focus of instruction can shift to blends in which only one of the consonants is stretchable and, over time, to the more challenging blends. Here it is important to note that the goal is NOT to teach all possible blends, but rather to teach a process for reading and spelling blends. Once the process is understood, with practice the children will gradually learn to handle the more challenging blends. Also, aside from early lessons where the focus is on the process of blending, other aspects of the alphabetic code can be addressed in the alphabetics segment of a lesson. Thus, for example, children may be asked to build, read, and/or spell words that involve all of the elements of the code that have already been taught and that, in the teacher's opinion, need more practice.

Step 1: Phoneme Blending		
Teacher	What the teacher says	Comments on the activity
Says:	"Many of the words that we read have two consonant letters together, and each letter makes its own sound. When we see these words, we need to think of the sound made by each letter and then blend them together. We'll start by practicing blending with Stretch [or whatever character is used in phoneme analysis activities]. Stretch is going to say some words one sound at a time, and you need to figure out what Stretch is saying. We are going to work with words that have two consonant letters together."	After this introduction, the teacher articulates the sounds in several words that contain (stretchable) consonant blends. After the sounds for each word are articulated, the children attempt to blend them to form a whole word. Ideally, the children should be able to do this type of blending before they are asked to do the more challenging task of looking at the letters, thinking about the sounds they make, and then blending them to form words. By the time children are learning about consonant blends, they shouldn't need the picture choices to successfully complete the phoneme blending. However, if they struggle, continued work on phoneme blending with words containing consonant blends is warranted, perhaps with picture choices if necessary to support the development of this skill.
Examples of words with two stretchable consonants for phoneme blending: *flake, snow, smile, frog, fly, slide, smoke, sleep, flat, free*		

Step 2: Decoding of Consonant Blends (Using the *ip* Phonogram)		
Teacher	What the teacher says	Comments on the activity
Displays and says:	"Some of the words we are going to make today have consonant blends in them. That's when there are two consonants, like *s* and *l,* next to each other. When you read words like that, you make the sound of each letter and then blend them together."	The letters to be used in word-building activities are displayed. All of the consonants to be used in the initial consonant blends are stretchable.

	Initial word	**Change to**	**Change to**	**Change to**	**Change to**	**Change to**
Easiest blends (both initial consonants are stretchable)	sip	lip	slip	sip	lip	slip
	lake	fake	flake	fake	lake	flake
	mock	sock	smock	mock	sock	smock
	sag	nag	snag	nag	sag	snag
More difficult blends (one stretchable and one stop consonant)	boom	loom	bloom	loom	boom	bloom
	camp	ramp	cramp	ramp	camp	cramp
	gain	rain	grain	rain	gain	grain
	pay	lay	play	lay	pay	play
	pill	sill	spill	sill	pill	spill
	sack	tack	stack	tack	sack	stack
	tick	sick	stick	sick	tick	stick
DR and TR blends	dip	rip	drip	rip	dip	drip
	dug	rug	drug	rug	dug	drug
	tack	rack	track	rack	tack	track
	tail	rail	trail	rail	tail	trail
	tap	rap	trap	rap	tap	trap
	tip	rip	trip	rip	tip	trip
Three-letter blends	sip	tip	rip	trip	strip	trip
	lit	sit	pit	spit	split	lit
	sand	stand	strand	stand	sand	stand
	seam	team	steam	stream	steam	seam

FIGURE 10.2. Word sets for practicing consonant blends.

Displays phonogram and says:	"All of the words we are going to make now have these two letters: *i* and *p*. When they are together in a word, they sound like this— /ip/. There are a lot of words in the /ip/ word family. Let's make some words with /ip/."	The *ip* phonogram can be printed on a single card rather than on two separate letter cards.
Says:	"If I put an *l* in front of /ip/, what word would it make?"	The teacher places an *l* in front of *ip* for all children in the group to see.
Provides feedback.	"Right, the word would be *lip*."	If the children cannot respond accurately at this step, they are not ready to work on consonant blends. They need continued work with single consonants.
Demonstrates blending consonants.	"Watch, now I am going to put an *s* in front of *lip*. So I have the /sss/ sound and then *lip*. /ssss/ /lllliiip/—when I put them together, it will sound like . . . *slip*."	The teacher should move through these steps slowly so that the children can see what she or he is doing.
Removes the *s* from the blend and says:	"Now, if I take the *s* away, I would have . . . *lip* again."	The teacher should pause to give the children the opportunity to think about what the word will be when the *s* is removed.
Adds the *s* again and says:	"If I put the *s* back on, it would be . . . *slip*."	Again, the teacher should pause briefly before saying the word *slip* so that the children have the opportunity to think of it on their own.
Removes the *l* and says:	"Now, what will happen to the word *slip* if I take the *l* away?"	The teacher should, again, give the children enough "think time" before answering the question.
Adds the *l* back and asks:	"Now, what word do I have if I put the *l* back again?"	
Explains.	"So, when we see a word with two consonants together, often we will need to make the sound of each consonant and then blend them together to try to figure out what the word is."	
Reminds children of exceptions.	"There are some times when this doesn't work. You already know, for example, that when *c* and *h* are together, you usually don't hear the sound of either the	The teacher might remind the children of any other consonant digraphs that have already been taught.

| | *c* or the *h*; instead, you hear the special sound that *c* and *h* make together." | |

Step 3: Word Building

Teacher	What the teacher says	Comments on the activity
Presents letter and phonogram cards and says:	"We are going to make some words in the /ip/ word family. You need to listen carefully to the words I say and put letters at the beginning of the word so that you make the word I say. Sometimes you'll need one letter at the beginning and sometimes you'll need two letters."	The teacher should provide the children with the phonogram and the letters needed to make all of the words in the family.
Dictates words in the set.	"Make the word *sip*." "Change *sip* to *lip*." (Refer to the sample word set in Figure 10.2, p. 190)	The teacher watches as children attempt to build the words and provides needed scaffolding, which may include elongating sounds, reminding the children to use the key words, and so forth.
Provides feedback and reinforcement.	Sample comments: • "You stretched that word when you were trying to figure out what letter[s] you needed and it worked!" • "I noticed you looking at the key words when you weren't sure what letter to use. That helped, didn't it?"	The teacher would continue to work with the children on sets of words that include consonant blends composed of stretchable consonants until the children appear to be fairly proficient. With slight modifications, the sample comments provided to the left could be used as scaffolds (e.g., "Stretch that word to figure out what letter you need").

Step 4: Word Reading

The teacher forms words with one or both elements of the consonant blends and asks the children to read them. Assistance is provided as needed.

Step 5: Written Spelling

The teacher presents the phonogram to be used for word formation, tells the children that all words will be in that word family, and then dictates words with one or both elements of the consonant blend that is the focus of the activity. The children write the words on paper or on a dry-erase board.

Vowels

Learning to decode and encode vowel sounds is significantly more complicated than learning to decode and encode consonant sounds. This is true for several reasons, including the following:

• Within a word or syllable, the sound of the vowel tends to be influenced by (coarticulated with) the surrounding consonants.

• There are no clear-cut acoustic boundaries between vowels (e.g., there is very little difference between the sounds for short *e* and short *i*).

• Vowels are pronounced differently by people from different locales. For example, when people are perceived to have accents, it is usually because of the way they pronounce their vowels.

• Most of the "rules" for representing vowel sounds in print are quite unreliable. For example, the "silent-*e* rule" only works about 50 or 60% of the time (Clymer, 1963).

• The printed representations of many vowel sounds, other than the short vowels, are complex.

  ○ It generally takes more than one letter to represent the vowel sound.

  ○ Sometimes the two letters are separated by one or more consonants, as in *cake* and *time*.

  ○ Sometimes the two letters represent more than one vowel sound. For example, the *ea* combination is used to represent the long *e* in *bead*, the short *e* in *bread*, and the long *a* in *great*.

  ○ Moreover, sometimes the same vowel sound is spelled in many different ways. For example, all of these words have the long-*a* sound: *cake, great, weigh, play, rain, prey, ballet*.

Because of this complexity and unreliability, in the ISA we teach the children to be *flexible* in decoding vowels. We teach that when they encounter a vowel, they should be prepared to try different pronunciations if their first attempt does not result in a real word that makes sense in the context of what they are reading.

Vowels and ELs

English has a greater variety of vowel sounds than many other languages. So, here again, ELs may find it challenging to perceive and produce the sounds of the English language. Further, for ELs who have learned to read in a language that uses the same letters used in English, the pronunciations associated with the vowel letters may well be different from what they learned in their first language. Therefore, to become proficient in reading and writing English, they will need to learn new associations to those letters. Yet another challenge for ELs is the lack of regularity in the sound–spelling system of English that is especially prominent with vowel sounds.

Instruction for Short Vowels and Long Vowels with the Vowel–Consonant–*e* Spelling Pattern

To help children develop flexibility with vowels, we teach the most common spellings for the two most common sounds of each vowel letter when we begin to teach about a given vowel. That is, we teach the long and the short sounds for the vowel on the first day that we begin to work on sounds for that letter. This is not as challenging for the children as it may initially seem because, by the time we teach the sounds for a particular vowel, they already know the name of the letter and may have already been using the vowel letter in their writing. It would not be unusual, for example, for a kindergartner to use the letters *A* and *T* to spell the word *ate*, or the letters *B* and *I* to spell the word *buy*. Thus children generally have a sense that the letter *A* can be used to represent the long-*a* sound before we begin to teach the vowel sounds. From our perspective, it makes sense to build from this knowledge and teach one additional association for each vowel (i.e., the short vowel sound). Moreover, over the many years that we have recommended this approach to teaching vowel sounds, teachers have consistently reported success.

A suggested order for introduction of the vowel sounds is provided below. This order is based on the similarities between and among the vowel sounds (the vowels whose short vowel sounds are most different from one another are taught first, as it is easier to discriminate one from the other) and on the usage frequency of the vowels. Teachers who are using a core program or phonics series obviously should follow the progression recommended by that series for teaching short vowel sounds. However, since many published programs teach all of the short vowels before the long vowels, it will be necessary to deviate somewhat from the program guidelines in order to teach for flexibility.

The suggested order is as follows:

• Long and short sounds for *a*, using long-*a* words spelled with the silent-*e* pattern (as in *make* and *late*). This pattern is sometimes referred to as the vowel–consonant–*e* pattern and is abbreviated as VC*e*. (The spelling pattern that characterizes many one-syllable, short vowel words is the consonant–vowel–consonant [CVC] pattern.) Note that these spelling patterns are sometimes referred to as *syllable types*.

• Long and short sounds for *i*, using long-*i* words spelled with the VC*e* pattern.

- Review of long and short sounds for both *a* and *i*.

- Long and short sounds for *o*, using long-*o* words spelled with the VC*e* pattern.

- Review of long- and short-*a*, -*i*, and -*o* sounds.

- Long and short sounds for *e*, using long-*e* words spelled with the double-*e* pattern (because there are very few long-*e* words spelled with the VC*e* pattern).

- Review long and short vowel sounds and spellings for *a*, *i*, *o*, and *e*.

- Long- and short-*u* sounds, with the long-*u* spelled with the VC*e* pattern. Note that it is important to initially introduce long-*u* words that have a true long-*u* (*mute* and *cube*) rather than words with an /oo/ sound, as in *toot* (and *tube*, *rude*, *dude*, *blue*, etc.). Of course, the latter type of long-*u* words are quite common and should ultimately be included in practice activities.

- Review vowel sounds and spellings taught thus far.

Ideally, as each vowel is taught, the children would be provided with enough practice to allow them to really learn the sounds for the vowel and how the sounds are often represented in print. The children should not be rushed on to the next vowels in the sequence before they are fairly secure with those that have already been taught.

Lists of words that can be used for teaching and practicing each of the vowel sounds are provided in Figure 10.3. The first page of Figure 10.3 provides lists for teaching about individual vowels. The second page provides lists for reviewing vowels once more than one vowel has been taught and practiced. The words on each list are intended to be used in the order in which they are listed for word building, as doing so requires a change in just one phoneme as the children move from one word to the next. This serves to reduce the level of challenge a bit and, therefore, increases the likelihood that the children will be able to focus in on the new skill they are learning. However, as children's skills develop, it is not necessary, and probably better, not to strictly adhere to the ordering of these lists. Below we describe procedures for teaching about the vowels.

Note

We try to avoid referring to the silent-*e* *rule* because the silent-*e* is far from entirely reliable and therefore does not really constitute a "rule." Many one-syllable words that end in *e* do not have the long vowel sound (e.g., *have*, *come*, *give*, *one*, *some*, *live*). Some teachers refer to the *e* at the end as a clue that the other vowel in the word might make the sound that is the same as its name.

(text resumes on page 198)

Long and short *a*	Long and short *i*	Long and short *o*	Long and short *e*	Long and short *u*
mat	bit	mom	seed	cube
mate	bite	mop	feed	cub
fate	kite	mope	fed	cut
fat	kit	mode	wed	cute
fad	hit	mod	weed	jute
fade	him	rod	week	jut
made	dim	rode	seek	but
mad	dime	robe	seen	cut
sad	time	rob	teen	cute
Sam	tide	sob	ten	mute
same	hide	sop	men	muse
tame	hid	top	met	fuse
tape	rid	tone	meet	use
tap	ride	cone	beet	us
cap	wide	con	bet	bug
cape	wine	cop	bed	hug
came	win	cope	fed	hub
cane	pin	hope	feed	cub
can	pine	hop	feet	cube
man	dine	pop	meet	tube*
mane	line	pope	met	tub
make	fine	rope	net	
take	fin	rode	need	
tame	sin	rod	seed	
game	sit	cod	weed	
gate	site	code	wed	
hate	side	cob	red	
hat	ride	lob	reel	
rat	ripe	lobe	peel	
rate	rip	lone	pen	

Tube does not have a true long-*u* sound. Rather it is pronounced with the double-*o* sound as in *toot*. However, since the children ultimately need to learn to decode words with this spelling–sound relationship, it is fine to include it once the children are fairly secure with the more rule-based spelling–sound correspondence for long *u*.

FIGURE 10.3. Word lists for working on long and short vowel sounds. Note that, for any given lesson, only a portion of a list would be used. This keeps the amount of time devoted to this aspect of a lesson reasonable and reduces the number of letters that the children need to manage. *(page 1 of 2)*

Review of *a* and *i*	Review of *a, i,* and *o*	Review of *a, i, o,* and *e*	Review of *a, e, i, o,* and *u*
bit		feed	cute
bat	cot	fed	cut
fat	cat	fad	cat
fate	fat	fade	cop
fame	fit	made	cope
tame	fin	mad	cape
time	fine	bad	cap
dime	pine	bid	tap
dim	pane	bide	tip
Tim	pan	ride	dip
tin	pad	rode	did
tan	pod	rod	deed
fan	cod	nod	deep
fin	code	need	keep
fine	rode	weed	beep
mine	rod	wed	bop
mane	rid	wet	top
man	ride	get	tap
can	ripe	got	tab
cane	rope	lot	cab
cape	robe	let	cub
cap	rob	net	cube
tap	rib	not	tube
tip	rig	rot	tub
sip	rag	rob	sub
sap	tag	robe	sun
sat	bag	rope	sin
sit	big	hope	tin
site	bin	hop	tan
kite	win	top	teen
kit	wine	tap	ten
hit	line	tape	men
hat	like	take	met
hate	lake	tame	meet
	rake	time	mat
		Tim	mate
		Tom	fate
			fit

FIGURE 10.3. *(page 2 of 2)*

Teaching Children to Decode and Encode Long and Short Vowel Sounds

Below we illustrate the process we use for teaching about the long and the short sounds of a vowel simultaneously. We begin with a brief overview of the process and then provide a more detailed explanation in the form of a sample script for each step. The instructional routine is abbreviated once the first couple of vowels have been taught.

- *Locating vowel sounds.* This involves having the children listen for the vowel sounds to be taught and deciding whether the sound occurs at the beginning, in the middle, or at the end of given words. The purpose here is to ensure that the children are able to notice and isolate the vowel sounds.

- *Comparing and contrasting vowel sounds.* This is a sound-sorting activity in which the children listen to spoken words and sort them into long and short vowel groups. Some teachers use pictures as an initial step in the sorting process. The comparing and contrasting step is, again, intended to attune children to the sounds of the vowels before they begin to attend to the written representations of those sounds.

- *Explaining the silent-*e *generalization.* This involves providing an explicit explanation of how the silent-*e* works. Because the silent-*e* is one of the most common ways of representing the long vowel sound, it is important that children understand the generalization well.

- *Introducing the short vowel key word.* The short vowel sounds are among the hardest letter sounds for children to remember. Therefore, encouraging children to actively use the key words is important. Early on, children benefit from explicit guidance in how the key words can support their reading and writing efforts.

- *Word building.* This involves making words that the teacher dictates, using moveable letters.

Terminology

Note that it is not necessary for children to use the terms *long* and *short* in reference to the two sounds of a vowel. Indeed, some children are confused by these terms because they suggest that the pronunciations differ in duration, which they generally don't. What children most need to know is that each of the vowel letters commonly represents two sounds and how each of those sounds is commonly represented in print. However, if children receiving instruction in an intervention setting are hearing these terms in their classroom (or vice versa), making this connection explicit should help to support the application of skills across settings.

- *Word reading.* This involves reading words that the teacher either writes or makes using moveable letters. At least early on, we recommend using moveable letters, as this makes the changes from one word to the next more evident.

- *Written spelling.* This involves writing words dictated by the teacher.

Each of these instructional steps is elaborated more fully below.

Step 1: Sample Instructional Dialogue for Locating Vowel Sounds		
Rationale:	It is important that the children be able to notice the targeted vowel sounds in words. By asking them to decide whether the targeted sound comes at the beginning, middle, or end of the word, we are able to determine whether they are ready for the more challenging task of using letters to represent those sounds.	
Materials needed:	A large-print letter *a* and the picture for the key word to be used for the short sound of *A*.	
Teacher	**What the teacher says**	**Comments on the activity**
Says:	"We are going to start learning about vowel sounds. Vowels are special letters. One of the things that makes them special is that every word has to have a vowel in it. Another thing that makes vowels special is that every vowel can make more than one sound. The vowel letter that we are going to start with is the letter *a*."	
Displays letter *a* and says:	"Sometimes when there is an *a* in a word, the sound it makes is the same as its name, /ā ā ā/. Listen for the /ā ā ā/ sound at the beginning of these words: *aaaage, aaaache, aaaate, aaaape*."	The teacher elongates the long-*a* sound in each word as she or he says it. (*Note*: An *a* [or any vowel] with a straight line over it—/ā/— denotes the long sound. The line is called a macron.)
Says:	"Now listen for the /ā ā ā/ sound at the end of these words: *maaaay, plaaaay, saaaay*."	The teacher elongates the long-*a* sound as she or he says each word.
Says:	"Sometimes the /ā ā ā/ sound is in the middle of a word. Listen for the /ā ā ā/ sound in these words: *maaaake, gaaaame, taaaape*."	The teacher elongates the long-*a* sound as she or he says each word.
Asks:	"Listen to this next word and tell me where the /ā ā ā/ sound is—at the beginning, in the middle, or at the end: *aaaape*?"	The teacher might use Elkonin boxes as a support/scaffold to ensure that every child has an opportunity to respond. Each child

		would have three boxes and would place a marker in the first, middle, or last box.
Provides feedback.	"Yes, the /ā ā ā/sound is at the beginning." Or: "Listen again—*aaaape*—we hear the /ā ā ā/ sound at the beginning of *aaape.* The /ā ā ā/ sound is the first sound I make when I say *aaape.*"	
Continues with activity, adding new words.	*make, play, aid, tape, ace, say, shake, fame, ape, safe, tray,* etc.	The teacher says each word and provides feedback. Practice continues with various one-syllable long-*a* words until the children don't need the teacher to elongate the sound and are fairly quick at locating the sound in words with two or three sounds.
Says:	"So far we've learned that a lot of times when there is an *a* in a word, it means we are supposed to say its name. But sometimes we are supposed to make a different sound /ă ă ă/—like the sound we hear at the beginning of the word *aaaapple* [or whatever key word is to be used]."	The word used to introduce the short vowel sound should be the key word that will be used to remind the children of the vowel's sound. The teacher should show the picture of the key word when she or he mentions its first sound. (*Note*: An *a* with a curved line over it—ă) denotes the short-*a* sound. The curved line is called a *breve*.)
Directs:	"Everyone say the sound of *a* that comes at the beginning of the word *aaaapple.*"	
Asks:	"Now listen to the word *aaaat.* Do you hear the /ă ă ă/ sound at the beginning or at the end of the word *aaaat?*"	The teacher elongates the short-*a* sound when presenting the first couple of items.
Provides feedback.	"Yes, the /ă ă ă/ is at the beginning of the word *aaaat.*" Or: "Listen again to the word *aaaaaat.* The /ă ă ă/ sound is at the beginning."	If the response is incorrect, the teacher should say the word again, elongating the vowel sound even further.
Continues:	"How about the word *maaat?* Is the /ă ă ă/ sound at the beginning, in the middle, or at the end of the word *maaat?*"	The teacher should provide practice with locating the short-*a* sound in different words until the children are facile at locating the sound in words.

Reduces support and continues:	"Where is the /ă ă ă/ sound in the word *add*?"	Ideally, the children should be able to identify the location of the vowel sound without the teacher elongating it for them. The teacher should reduce the amount of elongation as quickly as possible while still ensuring the children's success. The teacher may need to do different amounts of elongating for different children.
Continues with activity, adding new words.	*cap, as, back, add, sat, mad, axe, tap, bat, sad, at, pack, act, had,* etc.	The teacher says each word and provides feedback. Practice continues with various one-syllable short-*a* words until the children no longer need the teacher to elongate the sound and are fairly quick at locating the sound in words with two or three sounds.

Note: Short-*a* with coarticulation problem: If the children can easily locate the short-*a* sound in the words listed above, have them try some short-*a* words in which the vowel sound is altered somewhat by the nasal consonant. Examples of these words include *am, ran, an, and.* Although these are not good examples for introductory purposes, ultimately the children need to categorize these words as containing the short-*a* vowel sound.

	Step 2: Sample Instructional Dialogue for Comparing and Contrasting Vowel Sounds
Rationale:	In order to ultimately use letters to represent vowel sounds, the children need to be able to distinguish between the two sounds associated with the vowel.
Preparation:	Steps 2 and 3 should occur in the same instructional episode, so be sure to allow enough time for both.
Materials needed:	A chart with two columns, one headed by a familiar word with the long-*a* sound in the middle and one headed by a word that has a short-*a* sound in the middle. We'll use *tap* and *tape* as column headings in this example. A highlighter is also used in this activity. (*Note*: Do not use words with an *n* or an *m* following the vowel for the headings of the columns because these letters distort the sound of the vowel a bit, and this may confuse the children. All of the words used for the long-*a* column should be spelled using the silent-*e* pattern. Lists of words for these activities are provided in Figure 10.3 (pp. 196–197).

Teacher	What the teacher says	Comments on the activity
Points to each word that will be the header for the short-*a* or long-*a* column as it is said.	"We are going to make a chart with words that have the /ā ā ā/ sound and words that have the /ă ă ă/ sound. In the first column on the chart, I have written the word *tap* and in the second column I've written the word *tape*."	If this activity occurs on a different day from Step 1, it may be helpful to have the children locate the sound of the short- and long-*a* in the words at the top of each column.
Says:	"Now I'm going to say another word, and I want you to decide if the middle sound in the word I say sounds like the middle sound in *taaap* or if it sounds like the middle sound in *taaape*."	This is an auditory activity at this point. Therefore the teacher would not have the printed word visible to the children.
Presents words.	"The first word is *maaaake*. Does the middle sound in *maaaake* sound like the middle sound in *taaaaap* or the middle sound in *taaape*?"	At least on the first couple of items, the teacher should emphasize the middle sounds in the words by elongating them. However, the goal should be to reduce or remove this scaffold as soon as the children are ready. (*Note*: If children struggle with determining in which column a word belongs, it may be necessary to revert to more focused phonemic analysis instruction before proceeding with the decoding instruction.)
Writes the word in the appropriate column as the children look on, engaging the children in the process of spelling the word as much as possible.	"What's the first sound we hear in *make*? And what letter do we need for that /mmm/ sound? And we know the middle sound is . . . ? And the last sound in *make*?"	The words on the list should be conventionally spelled. So, for long-vowel words, the teacher would add the *e* and say something like "In the dictionary [book] spelling for *make*, there's an *e* at the end—so we'll put that on."

Asks:	"Our next word is *cat*. Which column does *cat* go in? Does the middle sound in *cat* sound like the middle sound in *tap*? Or like the middle sound in *tape*?"	Again, if need be, the teacher should elongate the vowel sounds in the words to help children make their decisions.
Continues.	*face, cat, bake, gate, nap, dad*	The teacher says additional words, asking children to decide in which column to place each word and engaging the children in interactive writing of the words until four or five words have been added to each column. It is not necessary to have the same number of words in each column.
Says:	"Now let's read our lists and see what we notice about the letters in these words."	The teacher should read down the first column, pointing to each word as she or he reads.
Asks:	"What do you notice that's the same in all of these words?"	Generally children quickly notice that all of the words have an *a*. If they don't, the teacher should direct their attention ("What letter do you see in every word?").
Confirms:	"Yes, all of the words under *tap* have an *a*."	
Says:	"Now let's read the words in this next column. See if you can figure out what's the same in all of these words."	The teacher reads down the column, pointing to each word as she or he reads.
Asks:	"What did you notice that's the same in all the words in this column?"	Sometimes a child will notice just the *e*'s or just the *a*'s. If the teacher is working with an individual, it may help to have the child highlight all of the vowels in the word to make the pattern more apparent. In a group, with group effort, usually both the *e*'s and the *a*'s are noticed—but it may help, nevertheless, for the teacher to highlight all of the vowels to emphasize the pattern.

Step 3: Sample Instructional Dialogue for the Explanation of Silent-e		
Rationale:	English orthography (the writing system) is quite complicated. It is helpful to provide children with clear explanations about some of the conventions of the orthography.	
Preparation:	Step 2 should immediately precede this step the first time the explanation is given. It may well be necessary to repeat this explanation, perhaps in abbreviated form, on several occasions.	
Materials needed:	The chart that was created during Step 2.	
Teacher	**What the teacher says**	**Comments on the activity**
Explains.	"For all of the words on this list that have that /ā ā ā/ sound, there's an *a* in the middle and an *e* at the end. All of the words on this other list have an *a* in the middle but no *e* at the end. They all have the /ă ă ă/ sound because they don't have an *e* at the end."	The teacher points to the words in each list as she or he explains the similarities and differences.
Continues.	"The *e* doesn't make a sound in these words. It is silent. When something is silent that means it is not making any sound. Even though the *e* is silent, it still has an important job. It is a clue we can use when we are thinking about how a word might sound. When the *e* comes at the end of words like these, it tells us we should probably say the name of the vowel that's in the middle of the word."	The teacher points to the words in the column under *tape*.
Note that if children are receiving instruction in more than one setting, it is important to use the same terminology for the silent-*e* generalization across settings so as not to confuse them.		
Continues.	"When there's no *e* at the end, and there's only one vowel in the word, that usually means that we are supposed to say the vowel's other sound. For the letter *a*, that's the /ă ă ă/ sound."	The teacher points to the words in the column under *tap*.

Step 4: Sample Instructional Dialogue for the Discussion of the Key Word		
Rationale:	The short vowel sounds are among the hardest letter–sound correspondences to remember. Key words, when used effectively, allow children to independently remind themselves of the vowel sounds.	
Materials needed:	The picture for the key word for the letter *A*.	
Teacher	**What the teacher says**	**Comments on the activity**
Shows vowel key word and says:	"We are learning that, when we are looking at the letters in a word and trying to figure out what the word will sound like, we need to think carefully, especially about the vowel letters. The letter *a* may be telling us to make the /ā ā ā/ sound, or it may be telling us to make the /ă ă ă/ sound. If there's an *e* at the end of the word, we try the /ā ā ā/ sound first. If there's no *e* at the end, we try the /ă ă ă/ sound. It's easy to remember that /ā ā ā/ sound because it is just the same as the letter's name. But the /ă ă ă/ sound is harder to remember. To help us remember the /ă ă ă/ sound, we have this picture of an ăăăpple [or of whatever key word is used]. "The word *aaapple* starts with that /ă ă ă/ sound. So, if you are looking at the letter *a* and you can't remember its other sound, then you could find the letter *a* on the key word chart and look at the picture that goes with it. The /ă ă ă/ sound at the beginning of *aaaaaapple* will remind you of the other sound of *a*."	

Step 5: Sample Instructional Dialogue for Word Building	
Rationale:	In word building, the children are given a fairly small set of letters with which to work. This simplifies the task of building the words. We are, in essence, providing the children with a scaffold by limiting the letter set from which they are to choose.
Preparation:	Word building can be done with a single large set of letter cards that all of the children can see, or each child might be given a set of letters with which to work. Often teachers use both large cards and letters for individual children. That way each child can work on a given word independently, and then the children can check their attempts against what is displayed with the larger cards.
Materials needed:	Word list for long-*a* and short-*a* words and the moveable letters needed to make the words that will be used in the lesson. Figure 10.3 provides lists of words that can be used. For any given lesson, teachers would choose only a segment of a given list.

Teacher	What the teacher says	Comments on the activity
Says:	"Now we are going to use these letters to make some words. Today, all of the words we are going to make will have an *a* in them. Sometimes the words will need that silent-*e* to show that the sound of the *a* is just like the sound of its name. Sometimes, we won't need an *e* at the end because the sound of the *a* will be /ă ă ă/, like in *aaaapple*."	The children are provided with all of the letters they will need to make the words that will be dictated.
Makes the word with the letter tiles and says:	"Let's have everyone use three letters to make the word *mat*. *Mmmaaat*. Change *mat* to *mate*. Change *mate* to *fate*. Change *fate* to *fat*. Change *fat* to *fad*. Change *fad* to *fade*," etc.	Early on the teacher should provide as much support as the children need—stretching the sounds, isolating and articulating sounds individually, reminding them to use the key words, and so forth. The teacher should also monitor children's attempts at each word and provide corrective feedback as needed (commenting on what they did right and what needs further thought). However, the goal is for the children to be able to independently analyze and represent the sounds as soon as possible. Therefore, the teacher should always be thinking carefully about which aspects of the task the children need help with and which aspects they might be able to handle alone.

Step 6: Sample Instructional Dialogue for Word Reading	
Rationale:	After building the words during Step 5, the children are familiar with the words that they will be asked to read. They have been "primed," so to speak. As a result, it will be easier for them to identify these words than it would have been without the word-building step.
Preparation:	In this activity, the teacher uses moveable letters to form the same words that the children were making during the word-building activity.
Materials needed:	Letters large enough for all of the children in the instructional group to see; the word list for long-*a* and short-*a* words (in Figure 10.3).

Teacher	What the teacher says	Comments on the activity
Says:	"Now I am going to make some words, and I want you to figure out what each word is. Remember to check for that silent-*e*. Also remember, if you are not sure about the sound of one of the letters, you can use your key words to figure it out."	Drawing from the words on the long-*a* and short-*a* word list (and other words the children may see in texts they will be reading soon), the teacher uses the moveable letters to form words that the children attempt to read. The teacher again provides scaffolding on an as-needed basis by reminding the children to attend to the presence or absence of the silent-*e* and by guiding them to use the key words.

Step 7: Written Spelling		
Rationale:	Spelling out an entire word can be very challenging, as it requires being able to do both the phonemic analysis and the alphabetic coding component. Having children spell words that they have been working on in other ways helps to build their confidence and competence and to increase their proficiency with the types of analysis required for spelling.	
Materials needed:	Word list for long-*a* and short-*a* (in Figure 10.3) and writing materials (paper and pencil, dry-erase boards and markers, etc.).	

Teacher	What the teacher says	Comments on the activity
Says:	"Now we are going to write some words. All of the words we write will have the letter *a* in them. You need to listen to the words carefully and decide whether the word has an /ā ā ā/ sound. If it does, you need to be sure that the word you write ends with a silent-*e*. If the word has a short-*a* sound, /ă ă ă/, then you don't need to put an *e* at the end."	The teacher should monitor the children's spelling of each word and provide any needed scaffolding. The children should discuss their decisions (e.g., about whether or not to include a silent-*e*). Discussions of these decisions will help to make the reasoning more prominent to the children and therefore, hopefully, more generalizable.

Similar procedures might be followed as each new vowel is introduced and practiced. However, as children demonstrate that they understand the processes involved, it may not be necessary to spend as much time or do as much explaining as the example above indicates.

Learning the alphabetic code is challenging for some children, especially learning about vowel sounds, as the spelling–sound correspondences for vowels are particularly unreliable. Therefore, helping the children to become very familiar with the two most common sounds for the major vowels will enable them to develop the flexibility (to try alternate pronunciations for vowel letters) they ultimately need in puzzling through the unfamiliar words they encounter while reading, as there are many words in written English that do not "follow the rules" that are often taught.

Organizational Tip

Some teachers make a sheet with the letters needed for the words used for practice activities. Each child is given a sheet, which he or she cuts apart in preparation for the word-building activities. After the letters are used, they can be stored in an envelope or snack bag to be used by the child on subsequent days. When they are fairly proficient with spelling and reading the words on the list, the children can take the list and the associated letters home for additional practice.

Instruction for Vowel Digraphs

When two vowels occur next to each other in a word, they usually represent one sound. Teachers sometimes teach students, "When two vowels go walking, the first one does the talking." Unfortunately, this "rule" does not work for many words, including some of the highest frequency words (e.g., *been, great*). Perhaps a better "rule" would be "When two vowels are together in a word, usually only one vowel sound is heard." Or, "When two vowels go walking, somebody says something."

Vowel Flexing in Word Solving

We have encouraged teachers to teach children to be flexible with the vowel sounds for many years. Many teachers are initially skeptical about children's ability to use this strategy. However, every teacher who has reported back after teaching this strategy has indicated that the strategy is very useful. In fact, one experienced teacher who was working with fourth-grade children identified as learning disabled reported that she thought it was the most powerful decoding strategy she had ever taught her students.

Usually when two vowels are together in a word, the sound of one of them is heard. Most often it is the long sound of the first vowel (e.g., *bean, rain, boat*). Sometimes it is the short sound of the first vowel (e.g., *head, been*). Occasionally, it is the long sound of the second vowel (e.g., *great, break*).

Sometimes, of course, two vowels together signal a sound that is different from the sound made by either letter individually (e.g., *oy, au, ei*). Still other vowels are influenced by the letter that immediately follows—this is especially true of *r*-controlled vowels (*ar, er, ir, or,* and *ur*) in which neither the long nor the short sound of the vowels can be distinctly heard.

For purposes of instruction, the various kinds of vowels are handled differently in the ISA.

ai	ea	ie	oa	ue
ay	ee		oe	ui
	eu*			

*As in *pseudo.*

FIGURE 10.4. Vowel combinations that can be decoded with vowel flexing.

VOWEL DIGRAPHS THAT CAN BE DECODED WITH VOWEL FLEXING

Figure 10.4 presents a listing of the vowel digraphs that can usually be decoded by trying the long and short sounds for each of the vowels, including the /oo/ sound for *u* as in *blue.* These digraphs do not require explicit instruction beyond teaching the two sounds of the vowel and the vowel flexing strategy, which is discussed in Chapter 12. *Practice with vowel flexing must occur in context, as only context will allow the reader to determine if the decoding attempt is accurate.* Teaching children to be flexible with vowel sounds (e.g., trying the long sound of the first vowel in the pair first, then trying the short sound of the first vowel, and then trying the long sound of the second vowel would allow the reader to effectively puzzle through words like *bead, head,* and *great.*

VOWEL DIGRAPHS THAT MAY NEED TO BE EXPLICITLY TAUGHT

Several digraphs represent vowel sounds that cannot be identified via vowel flexing. Some of the digraphs include two vowels (e.g., *au* and *oi*) and some include a vowel and a consonant (e.g., *oy* and *ow*). The vowel digraphs that may need to be explicitly taught include:

- Digraphs with only one common pronunciation:

  au aw ew oi oy

- Digraphs with two common pronunciations:

oo	ou	ow
(as in *look* and *boot*)	(as in *out* and *soup*)	(as in *now* and *snow*)

- *r*-controlled vowels: When a single vowel is followed by the letter *r*, the sound of the vowel is altered (coarticulated) such that is it hard to distinguish the sound of the vowel from the sound of the *r*. Therefore, *r*-controlled vowels are generally taught as decoding units as, linguistically, they represent single phonemes.

ar   er   ir   or   ur

INSTRUCTION FOR VOWEL DIGRAPHS THAT CANNOT BE DECODED USING VOWEL FLEXING

Children's knowledge of these various vowel digraphs and the ease with which they acquire new knowledge about the alphabetic code should determine the amount of emphasis that is placed on teaching these decoding details. It may be, for example, that simply showing and discussing a word or two that includes the vowel combination will suffice to allow the child to successfully puzzle through words with that combination, especially when they are encountered in a meaningful context. However, some children may need the type of practice that is provided in the word-building, word-reading, and written spelling routines described previously.

Note that it would be difficult to use some of these vowel digraphs in word-building exercises because sometimes there are several different ways a given sound might be spelled (e.g., the sound at the end of the word *drew* could be spelled with an *ew*, a *ue* [as in *blue*], or an *oo* [as in *too*]). In this example, the *ue* spelling does not need to be explicitly taught, since it can be solved through vowel flexing. However, the *ew* and the *oo* may need to be explicitly taught. In doing so, we advise starting out by teaching and providing practice with the different spellings in separate lessons, incorporating other vowel sounds in a given lesson so that the students get some practice in working with the vowel combination. Thus, for example, if the *ar* and *oi* vowel digraphs have already been taught, the teacher could introduce the *ew* combination, talk about the sound it typically represents, and introduce the key word (*chew*) and the picture mnemonic (see Figure 10.5). Then she or he would engage the students in word building, word reading, and written spelling for words containing one of the three vowel digraphs. Words used for such exercises might include: *new, coin, car, flew, far, point, part, stew, join,* and *brew*. (Note that for students who are at a point in development at which they are ready to learn vowel digraphs, it is not necessary to change only one part of the word at a time, as is done in the lists provided in Figure 10.3. Note also that it is useful to point out to students that the *oy* spelling of /oi/ generally only occurs at the end of words.)

In a subsequent lesson, the teacher might introduce the double-*o* spelling that represents the same sound as *ew*, talk about the fact that it represents another way that the /oo/ (as in *boot*) sound is spelled, introduce the key word, and then engage in word building, word reading, and written spelling with the new spelling pattern while incorporating other previously taught spelling patterns. For example, the following words might be used: *food, corn, chart, tooth, moon, short, zoo, worn,* and *sharp*. Note that until children have committed to memory spellings of words with more than one potential spelling, it will not be possible for them to determine which spelling to use. Therefore, the alternative spellings should not be included in a single lesson.

For vowel digraphs that have two common pronunciations, students need to learn both pronunciations and need to be encouraged to be flexible in decoding the combination—alternating the sound until a word is identified that fits the context in which the word is encountered. For these vowel digraphs that need to be explicitly taught, it may be helpful to introduce and teach the key words for vowel digraphs that are depicted in Figure 10.5. Note that for some of the phonemes that have two common spellings, such as *oi* and *oy* for the /oi/ sound, the pictures are described by a phrase that incorporates words with both of the spellings. Thus, for the /oi/ phoneme, we have a picture of a *noisy boy*. For the /au/ phoneme that can be spelled as *au* as in *sauce* or as *aw* as in *straw*, we have a picture of a child *drinking sauce with a straw.*

FIGURE 10.5. Key words for vowel digraphs that may need to be explicitly taught.

THE SCHWA SOUND

In words with more than one syllable, one or more of the vowels may not represent any of the traditionally taught sounds, but instead may represent the *schwa* sound (e.g., the first vowel sound in the words *about* and *oven*). Every vowel letter is pronounced as a schwa sound in some words. If a child has tried both sounds for a particular vowel and is still puzzling over a word, it may help to suggest that he or she try the "*uh*" sound.

Vowel Flexing and Word Learning

In Chapter 12, we discuss the use of vowel flexing as an important tool for word solving. Children are taught that, when they encounter an unfamiliar word in text and their first attempt doesn't result in a word that fits the context, one of the things they can do to solve the word is to "Try different sounds for some of the letters, especially the vowels." For example, if they are puzzling over the word *great*, they would be encouraged to try the long sound of the *e*, the short sound of the *e*, and then to move on to the long and the short sounds of the *a* until they identify a real word that makes sense in the context of what they are reading. In order to be able to approach vowel digraphs in this way, children need to be very familiar with the two sounds of each of the vowels, and they need to view vowels as "decision points" that often require them to do some thoughtful problem solving.

Diphthongs

Some may wonder where diphthongs fit in our approach to teaching about vowel sounds. A diphthong (pronounced di*f*-thong) is a vowel sound that changes quality due to changes in mouth position during pronunciation. For example, in pronouncing the diphthong /oy/, the mouth position is initially similar to the one used in pronouncing a long-*o* sound, but then changes to the position similar to that used in pronouncing the long-*e* sound. The sound that is emitted changes accordingly. The English language has several diphthongs, including the /ou/ sound as in *shout* and the long *a (ay-ee)* and long *i (i-ee)* sounds. In teaching about vowel sounds, we do not make distinctions between diphthongs and monophthongs (vowels that don't change quality during pronunciation).

Evaluating and Documenting Children's Progress

Figure 10.6 presents the group snapshot for the aspects of the alphabetic code discussed in this chapter.

The order in which aspects of the code are listed on the snapshot is not intended to indicate an order for instruction. Rather, as we have indicated elsewhere, decisions about what to teach when should be driven by when the elements come up in the texts that the students will be reading. When children are taught about an aspect of the alphabetic code in isolation, they should have the opportunity to apply that knowledge in text shortly thereafter.

Using the snapshot:

- *Consonant digraphs.* Because there is a limited set of common digraphs, students would be considered proficient when they are fast and accurate in reading and writing words with the digraphs *ch, th, sh, wh.* The digraph *ph* is comparatively rare and may only need to be taught incidentally when it comes up in text.

- *Consonant blends.* There are a large number of blends, and we do not advocate teaching all of them explicitly. Rather, students should be taught a process for working with consonant blends and would be considered proficient when they can read and spell words containing blends that have not been explicitly addressed in instruction.

- *Short and long vowels.* Children would be considered proficient when they readily apply the generalization that in words with the CVC pattern the short vowel sounds will most often occur, while the long vowel sound will more often occur in words with the VC*e* spelling pattern. In writing, proficiency would be demonstrated by reliably including the silent-*e* when the word contains a long vowel sound (even if the long vowel is conventionally spelled with a different spelling pattern). The point here is that learners understand the conventions of the CVC and VC*e* patterns even though they are far from entirely reliable.

- *Other vowel patterns via vowel flexing.* This is a skill that we can only observe during reading and will be most useful to the child while reading connected text. Proficiency would be recorded when the learner is reliably able to identify words in which vowel flexing can be usefully applied.

- *Other vowel patterns.* These are patterns that cannot be decoded via vowel flexing and therefore need to be explicitly taught. Proficiency would be recorded when the learner knows and uses many taught patterns reliably.

Group Snapshot—Alphabetic Code, Later Development												
Student names												
		Isolated	In text	Isolated	In text	Isolated	In text	Isolated	In text	Isolated	In text
Consonant digraphs (*sh, ch, th . . .*)	Reading										
	Writing										
Consonant blends (*fl, st, br . . .*)	Reading										
	Writing										
Short vowel sounds in CVC words	Reading										
	Writing										
Long vowel–silent-e pattern (VCe)	Reading										
	Writing										
Other vowel patterns via vowel flexing	Reading										
Other vowel patterns (*aw, ow, or, ar . . .*)	Reading										
	Writing										

Key:

☐ *B—Beginning* indicates that instruction has addressed the objective but that the child has only a preliminary understanding or capability with regard to that particular objective.

☒ *D—Developing* indicates that the child has some understanding of the objective but does not reliably demonstrate that understanding or capability or is not yet automatic (fluent) with the skill.

☒ *P—Proficient* indicates that the child reliably and automatically demonstrates the understanding or capability.

FIGURE 10.6. Group snapshot for later development of skill with the alphabetic code.

Morphological Units and Multisyllabic Words

In Chapter 9 we discussed the utility of teaching children to notice and use phonograms to read and spell words within orthographic word families for the purpose of helping them to develop fluency with word identification and spelling. In this chapter we again focus on fluency with word reading and spelling but now with a focus on helping children learn to handle words that are composed of (1) more than one meaningful part (e.g., *unhappy, happiness, unhappiness*), and/or (2) multiple syllables. Because both types of words come up early in children's reading and writing experience, it is important to provide guidance on how to handle them.

Vowels and Syllables

A syllable is a unit of pronunciation. Every syllable contains one and only one *vowel phoneme*—although that vowel phoneme may be represented by more than one letter. As discussed in the previous chapter, usually when two vowels are together in a word, they represent just one vowel phoneme. In attempting an unfamiliar word, it may help the child to look for the vowels in the word—recognizing, of course, that silent-*e*'s will sometimes cause problems with syllables. The reader may find it useful to group sounds around the vowels, thereby forming syllables. For example, with the word *recognizing,* looking for vowels allows the reader to accurately note that there are four syllables in the word. However, such an approach will not always work. For example, looking for vowels in the word *therefore* might lead one to expect three or four syllables (i.e., *the, re,* and *fore* or *the, re, for,* and *e*).

Words with Multiple Meaningful Parts

Morphology

The English language is morphophonemic in nature. Words are made up of units of meaning (morphemes) and units of sound (phonemes). In the terminology typically used by teachers and students, morphemes are referred to as *root words, prefixes,* and *suffixes.* Nunes and Bryant (2006) suggest that "Some of the most important correspondences between spoken and written language are at the level of the morpheme. . . . The system of morphemes, therefore, is a powerful resource for those learning literacy" (p. 157). Indeed, some of the important correspondences that Nunes and Bryant refer to account for some of the apparent irregularities in the spelling–sound correspondences in the English writing system. These irregularities, however, actually have the advantage of conveying and/or preserving meaning. For example, the past tense (*-ed*) endings in *looked, wanted,* and *played* are all pronounced differently (/t/ in *looked,* /ĕd/ in *wanted,* and /d/ in *played*). But the *-ed* carries the same meaning in all three words. The plural marker *-s* or *-es* presents a similar situation; sometimes it is pronounced as /ĕz/ as in *watches,* sometimes as /z/ as in *beds,* and sometimes as /s/ as in *tops.* But, despite these variations in pronunciation and spelling, the meaning of the ending remains the same.

By the time they begin kindergarten, most English-speaking children already have at least an implicit understanding of the morphemic nature of spoken language (Berko, 1958). This is evident in their tendency to overregularize irregular nouns and verbs (e.g., referring to multiple *deer* as *deers,* or forming the past tense of *go* as *goed*) and in some of the novel words they create (e.g., "crackering" soup, as cited in Carlisle & Goodwin, 2014). Because young children know how these morphemes work in spoken language, they can use this knowledge to their advantage in written language—at least once they have enough command of the alphabetic code to be able to focus on what are, essentially, orthographic and morphemic units.

There are two basic types of morphemes: free morphemes (root words) and bound morphemes (prefixes and suffixes). Bound morphemes include inflectional morphemes and derivational morphemes. Inflectional morphemes occur as suffixes and serve to change the grammatical role of the root word so that it appropriately fits the context of the sentence. They do not change the word's part of speech or meaning. Past tense and plural markers are examples of inflectional morphemes. Derivational morphemes change the meaning and/or part of speech of the root word and occur as either prefixes or suffixes. Derivational morphemes include *un-, re-, -less, -ly, -able,* and so on.

Morphology and the CCSS

The language standards of the CCSS address the need for young children to be able to use the most frequently occurring affixes (prefixes and suffixes) "as a clue to the meaning of an unknown word" (NGA & CCSSO, 2010, p. 27) and indicate in the foundational skills standards that, in first grade, children should be able to read words with inflectional endings (p. 16) and, by second grade, should be able to decode words with common prefixes and suffixes (p. 16). Thus, appropriately, the Standards focus on both the word meaning and the orthographic aspects of morphology; therefore, from our perspective, a discussion of morphology could or should be located in both this chapter, which focuses on word identification, and in Chapter 15, which focuses on word meanings. To avoid redundancy, however, we address the role of common affixes here and only briefly touch on the topic in Chapter 15.

Reading and Writing Words with More Than One Meaningful Part

In their review of the literature on morphological development, Carlisle and Goodwin (2014) suggest that morphological knowledge plays a greater role in children's spelling, word reading, and vocabulary knowledge in the upper elementary grades than in the primary grades. However, Berninger and colleagues (Berninger, Abbott, Nagy, & Carlisle, 2010) studied first through sixth graders and found that the greatest growth in morphological awareness occurred in the first three grades. Further, in a review of intervention studies, Bowers, Kirby, and Deacon (2010) reported that morphological interventions had a greater impact when offered in small-group contexts and with children who were experiencing literacy learning difficulties. In alignment with these findings, in the ISA, we have found it useful to explicitly teach about some of the most frequently occurring bound morphemes during the alphabetics segment of a lesson. Then, when children encounter words with known prefixes or suffixes in their reading, we encourage them to notice the prefixes and/or suffixes, and temporarily ignore them while attempting to identify the root word and then to add the prefix and/or suffix back in. When children are first starting to attend to suffixes and prefixes in their reading, we have them cover the prefix or suffix with their fingers, puzzle through the root word (which they may automatically recognize without the prefix or suffix), and then add the prefix or suffix back on.

Inflectional Endings

The first suffixes that children are likely to encounter in their reading and writing are the inflectional endings *-ing*, *-s* (or *-es*), and *-ed*. The various endings present different levels of challenge. The *-ing* ending is pronounced the same way in all contexts and so is a fairly easy ending for the children to grasp.

The *-ed* used to mark past tense is pronounced in different ways depending on the final sound in the root word. But its spelling is consistent, making it somewhat easier to teach and learn about than the plural marker, which is spelled in two different ways. The text box below provides details regarding the contexts in which the past tense and plural endings take on different pronunciations. (We provide this information *not* because children need to learn it but because we have frequently observed children asking for an explanation of why there is such variability in pronunciation.)

In general, if children pronounce past-tense inflections appropriately in their spoken language and if they understand that *-ed* tells us that something already

---

Pronunciations of Inflectional Suffixes

The pronunciation of past tense and plural endings depends on phonological characteristics of the ending sound of the uninflected form of the word, as illustrated below.

Pronunciations of Past-Tense Endings

Words ending in . . .	Pronunciation	Examples
/d/ or /t/	/ed/	*needed, wanted*
Unvoiced consonants other than /t/: /f/, /k/, /s/, /ch/, /sh/, /p/, and /th/	/t/	*sniffed, looked, dressed, washed, dipped*
All other ending sounds	/d/	*Rubbed, hugged, spilled, snowed, arrived, played*

Pronunciations of Plural and Third-Person Present-Tense Endings

Words ending in . . .	Pronunciation	Examples
Some unvoiced consonants: /f/, /k/, /m/, /p/, and /th/	/s/	*cuffs, kicks, cups, mitts, paths*
Voiced consonants (/b/, /d/, /g/, /l/, /m/, /n/, /ng/, /r/, /v/, and /th/) and all vowels	/z/	*bibs, mugs, buns, rings, bees*
/ch/, /s/, /z/, /sh/, and /x/	/ez/	*bunches, dresses, foxes*

happened, then they are likely to assign it the correct pronunciation. Once children have some experience with noticing and using the -ed inflection in their reading, they may well begin to use it in their writing as well. If they don't do so spontaneously, they should be encouraged to do so.

The -s (or -es) used to mark plurals and third-person present tense is pronounced in different ways as well. The determination of which pronunciation is assigned is, once again, based on the sound of the final phoneme in the uninflected form of the word (see the text box on the previous page). These inflectional endings are a bit more complicated because the same orthographic representations have two different roles to play (marking the plural and the third-person present tense) and because they are spelled in two different and seemingly arbitrary ways and take on three different pronunciations! Here again, however, we have found that it is useful to teach children that s and es are units of meaning that can be temporarily ignored and then added back on once the root word is identified. This usually allows them to assign the proper pronunciation to the marker because they know, implicitly, what the plural or third-person present-tense form of the root word sounds like in spoken language.

Won't Taking Off the -ed or -es Cause Problems for Long Vowel Words?

Teachers sometimes worry that by encouraging children to temporarily ignore inflectional endings we might impede that child's ability to accurately identify words with long vowel sounds. For example, if you ignore the es in the word *games,* you'll pronounce it as *gam.* This is certainly true but, as we discuss in the next chapter, thinking about the sounds in a word is only part of the process of identifying an unfamiliar word. Readers also need to think about whether the hypothesized pronunciation of the word makes sense in context and, if not, the reader needs to do some additional thinking by, for example, trying a different pronunciation for some of the letters, especially the vowels.

Derivational Morphemes

COMMON PREFIXES

The prefixes *un-* (meaning *not*) and *re-* (meaning *do again*) are the two most common prefixes and so are useful to teach early on. There are several additional prefixes that mean *not,* including *in-, im-, il-, dis-, non-,* and *ir-,* that occur quite frequently in written and spoken language. Although these prefixes may not come up in the texts that young children read themselves, they will come up in the texts that are read aloud to them and so might be taught for the purpose of helping children to expand their vocabularies (a topic that will be a focus in Chapter 15).

COMMON DERIVATIONAL SUFFIXES

Derivational suffixes change a word's part of speech. For example, adding -ly changes an adjective to an adverb (nice–nicely), and adding -ness changes an adjective to a noun (happy–happiness). Although is it not critical that young children understand how these suffixes function in terms of changing the part of speech, for purposes of word recognition and vocabulary growth it does help them to recognize these "chunks" so that they can, again, temporarily ignore them while attempting to decode the root word. Among the most common derivational suffixes are -ly (in what way or manner), -ment (action, result), -ness (state or quality), -less (without), and -ful (full of). The suffix -er is also quite common and signals multiple meanings (more [bigger], action [chatter], and a person who does an action [builder]).

Teaching Children to Use Meaningful Word Parts

The teacher explains that a single word sometimes has more than one meaningful part, using, as an example, a word with a prefix or a suffix that the children will soon encounter in their reading. The teacher would present the root word on a card and the prefix and/or suffix on separate cards and demonstrate how adding or removing the prefix or suffix changes the sound and meaning. The same prefix and/or suffix can be used to modify additional root words to further illustrate the process and further familiarize the child with the sound and meaning of the affix. The teacher should explain that noticing the parts will help readers to puzzle out words by letting them focus on one part at a time. Children should be encouraged to notice the affix, think of how it will sound, and then temporarily cover it up while thinking about what the rest of the word will sound like and then put the two (or more) parts of the word together. (When puzzling over a word with multiple meaningful parts in context, the children would be encouraged to also consider whether the pronunciation and meaning of the word make sense in the context in which the word is encountered.)

In any given lesson, only one new word part would be taught. However, as new word parts are taught, previously taught word parts can be integrated into instruction to help children become automatic in noticing and interpreting them and in using them to assist in their decoding of words with multiple syllables. Word-building activities using root words and the prefixes and suffixes that have been taught can be periodically revisited until the children are quite facile in using them. So, for example, if the prefixes re- and un- and the suffixes -ly, -ful, -ness, -ed, -(e)s, -er, and -ing have been taught, children might use several different root words to build and read multisyllabic words. For example:

build: rebuild, building, rebuilding, builder, builders
watch: watches, watchful, unwatchful, watchfulness

event: events, eventful, uneventful
swim: swims, swimming, swimmer
bright: brighter, brightly, brightness
happy: happily, happiness, unhappy, unhappily

When children read, they should be periodically reminded of the utility of thinking about, and temporarily ignoring, prefixes and suffixes while they puzzle through root words (see the "break the word into smaller parts" strategy in Chapter 12). When they write, they should also be periodically reminded to use the meaningful word parts they have learned.

Morphological Awareness and ELs

There are, of course, multiple ways in which morphological differences can have an impact on the learning of ELs in terms of both spoken and written language. For teachers who do not have expertise related to EL instruction, it is important to note that orthographic markers of meaningful distinctions such as number (e.g., singular and plural nouns) and verb tense (e.g., present, past, future) vary tremendously across languages and differ from English. For example, in Spanish, aspects of verb tense are typically marked within the word, whereas, in English, certain aspects of tense are represented in unique words. Thus, for example, in English the present tense of *I speak* would be translated as *hablo* in Spanish, and the future tense (*I shall speak*) would be translated as *hablaré*—no extra words, just a within-word modification.

Teachers who are teaching large concentrations of a given language group are encouraged to learn as much as they can about the first language of their students and to consider those language differences in planning and implementing their instruction. For example, it would likely be useful to be explicit about the differences in the way nuances in meaning are expressed between the two languages. Thus, for the future tense example above, the teacher might say "In Spanish, *hablo* and *hablaré* tell about speaking now (*hablo*) and speaking later (*hablaré*). So just the word is changed. In English, an extra word would be added instead (*I speak, I will/shall speak*)." If teachers are not able to access information about how the morphological components of their students' first languages may differ from English, they should, nevertheless, attempt to note which constructions tend to be difficult for students and provide explicit instruction related to those constructions.

Breaking Words into Parts That Are Not Meaningful

Many multisyllabic words are made up of syllables that do not have individual meanings. Readers can often find these syllables and decode the word if they attempt one or more of the following:

- For words with double consonants, break the word between the two consonants and decode each part (syllable).
- For words with the *consonant + -le* syllable structure (e.g., *ap-ple, lit-tle, scram-ble*), go back one letter from the *-le* and decode that consonant plus the *-le* as a syllable. Decode the first syllable and then decode the *consonant + -le* syllable by making the sound of the consonant and adding /ul/.
- For words with two different consonants together in the middle of the word, try breaking the word between the consonants (e.g., *basket, chimney, servant*).
- Try different pronunciations for the vowels—trying the long and short sound of the vowels alternately until a word that fits the context emerges. It may be helpful to tell/remind children that all of the vowels sometimes represent the /uh/ (*schwa*) sound, as in *about, effect, other* (as these words are pronounced in everyday conversation).
- For words that include spelling units that are not very decodable (e.g., *tion, sion, ture*), provide the pronunciation (e.g., "That part says *shun*" or "That part says *chur*") and explain that it will be seen in lots of words and is therefore useful to try to remember.

Decoding Multisyllabic Words

To initially make these approaches explicit, challenging words that are encountered while reading text can be written out and then analyzed briefly in isolation. It is useful to illustrate that multiple approaches can be applied together in attempting to decode a multisyllable word. It is also important to stress the need to think of words that would make sense in the context and to always confirm that the decoded word fits the context. For example, if the word *reignited* was encountered while reading a text about forest fires, the teacher might write the word on a dry-erase board and demonstrate for the students how they might go about figuring it out. Thus the teacher might say:

> "There are a lot of things we can try when we come to a puzzling word like this. Let's start by looking for any prefixes or suffixes we know. I see *re,* which we know means *again*. I also see an *ed* ending, which means it happened in the past. I am going to cover those two word parts up with my fingers while I look at the rest of the word. So, I've got *i–g–n–i–t*. Hmmm. If I'm still not sure what that word is, I can try breaking it apart between the two consonants. And then I can think about what the two parts will sound like. The first part is probably *ig,* because there is just that one vowel there. The second part could be *nit* or *nite,* because sometimes when we take the *ed* ending off it is really just the *d* that needed to come off. First I'll try *ignit, ignit.* . . . That doesn't sound like a word I've heard before. So let's try *ignite.* Ah! That's a word I

Is There Value in Teaching the Six Syllable Types?

In discussions about assisting children with decoding multisyllabic words, we are sometimes asked about the value of teaching children the six syllable types that characterize written English. The six types are:

1. Open: a syllable that ends in a vowel sound, such as in the words *say* and *me* or the first syllable in *robot*. They are referred to as *open syllables* because there is no consonant sound to "close" the syllable.
2. Closed: a syllable that ends with a consonant sound, as in the word *house* and *run* or the first syllable in *lemon*.
3. Vowel–consonant–*e* (VC*e*): a syllable with a long vowel sound that is signaled by the presence of the silent-*e*, as in the words *time* and *race* and in the second syllable in *outside*.
4. *R*-controlled vowel: a syllable that includes an *r*-controlled vowel such as in the words *part* and *for* or in the first syllable of the word *person*.
5. Vowel team: a syllable in which two vowel letters are together and represent a single vowel sound.
6. Consonant + -*le*: a syllable type that involves the pronunciation of the consonant sound that precedes the *le* plus /ul/, as in the words *little* and *table*.

All of these syllable types focus on the pronunciation of the vowel sound. We have not advised teachers to explicitly teach young children about all of these syllable types because it is not clear that thinking about syllable types will be as useful nor as generalizable for them as the approaches to vowels we do teach. For example, in the words *lemon* and *robot,* knowing about open and closed syllables will not assist the child in determining the proper pronunciation of the first vowel letter. However, children who have learned to be flexible with vowel sounds will know to try the other common pronunciation of the vowel if their first attempt at a word doesn't result in a real word that fits the context in which it was encountered. Similarly, flexibility with vowel sounds will assist children in negotiating vowel-team-type syllables. In this instance, it is important for children to know that *when two vowels are together in a word, usually only one vowel sound is heard.* With regard to *r*-controlled vowels, we do think it is useful to teach them (as indicated by our providing key words for them in Chapter 10, Figure 10.5, p. 211). However, we see no additional utility in teaching children that there is a specific syllable type for them.

We do, of course, teach the VC*e* generalization, as lots of practice with the application of that generalization is one of the ways in which we help children to become fluent and flexible with the vowel sounds. Finally, we do explicitly teach the consonant + -*le* syllable type, as that is the only way to explain to children why words such as *little* and *table* don't end with the long-*e* sound, particularly if children knew what an open syllable was supposed to sound like.

know! The author already used that word in this book when he was talking about how the fire got started. *Ignite* means to start a fire. Now, I need to put the other parts of the word back on. I'll start with the ending [uncovers the *-ed*]. So, now I've got *ignited*. That means it already happened. If I put the *re* back on, I have the word *reignited*. *Re* means again. The fire reignited—Oh! It started again!"

Spelling Multisyllabic Words

As noted in Chapter 5, it is fairly easy for even emergent readers to detect the number of syllables in a word. This skill can be put to good use when children attempt to spell words with more than one syllable, especially when children learn that every syllable contains a vowel sound and so every syllable in a written word must have at least one vowel letter. Early in the process of teaching children to spell multisyllabic words, we would start by having the children count the number of syllables in the word they are trying to write and draw a line for each syllable. They would then be encouraged to spell each syllable, being mindful that each syllable needs to have at least one vowel letter. They can also be encouraged to refer to their key word charts and/or phonogram charts if they need help in deciding which vowel letter(s) to use. Spellings constructed in this way will certainly not always be conventional. However, they will look more literate and will be more interpretable to the writer's audience. Thus, for example, a child who hasn't had this guidance might write BUTFL for *beautiful* (using the letters *b* and *t* to represent the syllables *be* and *ti,* respectively). A child who had been taught to count the syllables and to include a vowel letter in each syllable, on the other hand, might produce BEUTE-FUL, which, although still far from the conventional spelling, is more likely to convey the child's meaning.

Decoding by Analogy to Known Words

When proficient readers encounter an unfamiliar word, they typically do not consciously engage in the types of analysis discussed above. Rather, they are likely to identify the word by analogy to known words (e.g., the word *prattle* would be read effortlessly by analogy to words such as *battle* and *cattle*). Teachers should be alert for opportunities to move children toward this type of word-solving approach. For example, when a child encounters a word that is unfamiliar but very similar to one or more words that the child knows well, the teacher might comment, "You can figure out that word easily if you notice how similar it looks to. . . . " Initially the teacher would name the similar word. Over time, the teacher would reduce the support by asking, rather than telling, "Can you think of another word you know that looks like that one?"

KEEP IN MIND   Multisyllabic words may present a word identification challenge, but they can also present a vocabulary challenge. It is difficult for readers to ascertain that a word has been accurately identified if there is no word in their lexicon that corresponds to it. For that reason, a critical element of instruction is anticipating unfamiliar vocabulary and using it in prereading discussions. Since children differ widely in their vocabulary knowledge, it is important that teachers be alert to terms that may be challenging for some children and be prepared to individualize the vocabulary terms addressed. As the texts that children read become more challenging, a significant part of planning should involve teacher's prereading of the text selection and choosing multisyllabic words that are appropriate to focus on both for the purpose of decoding and for the purpose of building children's knowledge of word meanings.

Evaluating and Documenting Children's Progress

Figure 11.1 presents the group snapshot for morphology and multisyllabic words. Although presented in a list format, it is important to point out, once again, that instruction does not proceed from the top to the bottom of the list. Instruction related to multisyllabic words is not likely to move in a linear fashion but will be highly dependent on the instructional materials in use. Thus children should *not* be expected to demonstrate proficiency with all of the inflected endings, and then the derivational prefixes and suffixes, and so on. Rather, children should demonstrate an understanding of how these various word parts can be used to read and spell words. For example, a child who is considered proficient with respect to inflected endings will be able to read and spell new words that include those endings (assuming, of course, that the child can identify the root word). In other words, a child who is "proficient" knows quite a few of the morphological units, appears to make effective use of them in reading and writing, and is expanding his or her repertoire of morphological units easily.

To be considered proficient in puzzling through words with more than one syllable, children should demonstrate skill in recognizing that given words might be composed of more than one syllable and making reasonable attempts to break such words into smaller parts at reasonable boundaries. With regard to spelling, proficiency would be demonstrated if the child spells each syllable, including acceptable letters for each of the phonemes and including a vowel letter in each syllable. Recall that one major purpose for the group snapshot is to help teachers identify areas in which additional instructional emphasis appears to be needed.

Group Snapshot—Morphology and Multisyllabic Words						
Student names						
Inflectional suffixes (*-ing*, *-ed, -es*)	Reading					
	Spelling					
Prefixes (*re-*, *un-* . . .)	Reading					
	Spelling					
Derivational suffixes (*-ly*, *-ness, -er*, . . .)	Reading					
	Spelling					
Syllables	Reading					
	Spelling					

Key:

☐ *B—Beginning* indicates that instruction has addressed the objective but that the child has only a preliminary understanding or capability with regard to that particular objective.

☒ *D—Developing* indicates that the child has some understanding of the objective but does not reliably demonstrate that understanding or capability or is not yet automatic (fluent) with the skill.

☒ *P—Proficient* indicates that the child reliably and automatically demonstrates the understanding or capability.

FIGURE 11.1. Group snapshot for morphology and multisyllabic words.

PART III

Word Learning

Introduction

In Part II, we discussed the development of skill with the alphabetic code. The ultimate value in developing that skill is to enable a learner to quickly and accurately figure out the identity of printed words he or she has never seen before. A written word that a reader can identify quickly and accurately and in all contexts is said to be in the reader's *sight vocabulary*. Fast and accurate word identification is critically important to comprehension for both beginning and more proficient readers, because readers who know most of the words in a text can devote most of their thinking to understanding the text rather than to figuring out the words. In this part we focus on ways to help beginning and struggling readers learn words so well that they become part of their sight vocabularies.

Nagy and Anderson (1984) estimated that the print that students encounter in school consists of approximately 88,500 distinct word families (their definition of a word family is a group of words with clear and predictable relationships between form and meaning; e.g., *assume, assumed, assuming, assumption* would all be in a single word family). Nagy and Herman (1987) estimated that the typical fifth-grade student encounters 10,000 new word families in a year.

There is no way a teacher could possibly teach the huge numbers of words students must ultimately learn. Rather, children learn the vast majority of the words that ultimately become part of their sight vocabularies by effectively puzzling through and figuring out unfamiliar words that they encounter while reading. Share (1995) suggests that the ability to figure out unfamiliar words serves as a *self-teaching mechanism* that allows children to gradually increase the size of their sight vocabulary through reading. This is not to suggest, of course, that correctly identifying a word just once will necessarily allow it to become part of a reader's sight vocabulary. Rather, for most words, it is through multiple encounters with and correct identifications of the words that students come to learn them to the point of automaticity. Thus, the first time readers encounter an unfamiliar word, they may need to devote quite a bit of effort to thinking about what the word might be. On the next encounter, a bit less thinking may be needed for correct identification. On each subsequent encounter, readers are likely to be able to identify the word more and more easily and fluently until ultimately it becomes part of their sight vocabulary.

Exactly how a child comes to "know" a previously unfamiliar word has been the source of much debate over the years (Adams, 1990; Chall, 1967; Goodman, 1967; Pressley, 2006). And, although some experts assert that a consensus has been reached (Pressley, 2006), we are far from having reached scientific certainty as to how children accomplish this remarkable word-learning feat. However, there are a few points on which near unanimity exists:

- Children need to do extensive amounts of reading to build their sight vocabularies.
- Children need guidance and feedback while they are reading to become effective word learners (word solvers). However, the amount of guidance needed varies substantially among children.
- The texts that children read need to be somewhat but not too challenging if they are going to be useful in helping to build children's sight vocabulary.

These points of agreement, however, still leave unanswered the question of what readers actually do when they encounter an unfamiliar word in context. One of the reasons this question is so difficult to answer is that what readers do depends on:

Difficulties with Word Learning

Children in the early primary grades who are identified as being at risk of experiencing literacy learning difficulties, and especially those who do not accelerate with Tier 1 instruction alone, are particularly likely to demonstrate difficulties with word learning. Many children experience difficulty due to limitations in their ability to make effective use of the alphabetic code. However, as is discussed in some detail below, learning to read words encountered in context requires much more than alphabetic decoding skills. Rather, alphabetic skills and strategies need to be coordinated and orchestrated with other word-learning strategies, as well as with language skills and other knowledge sources. And children need to do a great deal of reading in order to encounter the many words they need to learn.

- Readers' knowledge and skills
- The text that they are reading and the types of supports that the text provides
- The instruction that they have received about how to approach unfamiliar words in text.

Characteristics of the Reader

Word solving is dependent on what readers know about the alphabetic writing system and on what they know about the language and concepts presented in a particular text. Although beginning readers are often taught the most common correspondences between letters and their sounds (as discussed in Part II, "Learning the Alphabetic Code"), it is important to keep in mind that written English is characterized by many, many irregularities in spelling–sound correspondence. Therefore, it is simply not possible for readers to rely exclusively on alphabetic information for the purpose of identifying unfamiliar words. Such an approach would lead to far too many inaccuracies in word identification—even for some of the most commonly occurring words, such as *have, was,* and *to* (which, if pronounced the way they are spelled, would result in words that rhyme with *brave, pass,* and *go*). Nevertheless, virtually all words consist of letters that at least partially signal their pronunciation. Therefore, knowing the most common correspondences between letters and their sounds and knowing how to apply that knowledge are critically important for building sight vocabulary.

Knowledge of the workings of the alphabetic writing system develops gradually and, at least for some children, requires explicit instructional guidance and practice.

- Readers who are just beginning to learn about letters and their sounds will make limited use of the alphabetic information in attempting to identify an unfamiliar printed word encountered in context because their alphabetic knowledge is limited and tenuous. Even if children know most or all of the common letter–sound correspondences, it is quite taxing to think about all of the letters in the word, the sounds those letters may represent, hold those sounds in memory, and then blend them together and say the resulting word. Moreover, the kinds of texts that beginning readers typically encounter provide many other sources of information that assist them in identifying unfamiliar words. For example, students at this point in reading development are often given texts that are repetitive (or predictable) and that have pictures that provide so much contextual support that they are able to "read" the text successfully by relying primarily on the pictures and the repetitive language (see Figure III.1). Children reading such texts do not necessarily need to attend carefully to the letter- and word-level information provided in the text.

FIGURE III.1. An example of an emergent-level text.

• Readers who are more familiar with the workings of an alphabetic writing system and more fluent at recalling the most common sounds associated with printed letters will find it less taxing to look through the word for more alphabetic clues about the word's possible identity. Such readers do not need texts that make heavy use of repetitive language patterns and pictures.

• Readers who have done quite a bit of reading and who have learned to read many words automatically will begin to recognize larger units of print, such as *bl*, *ink, er,* and so forth. These larger orthographic units will allow readers to be more efficient in puzzling through unfamiliar words. Instead of having to think about each separate sound in the consonant blend *bl*, these readers will process it as a unit or "chunk." Thus identification of the word *blinker* might require readers at this point in development to think about only three orthographic units rather than the seven letters that make up the word.

With regard to readers' familiarity with the language and concepts presented in the text:

• Readers must know the meaning of unfamiliar words encountered in text in order to know whether the word has been accurately identified. For instance, in reading a book about a farm that relies on repetitive language and pictures to make reading the text easier, children might read sentences such as

Look at the cow. Look at the horse.

quite easily because the pictures and the repetitive pattern are so helpful. However, if the text included the sentence

Look at the hen.

the children might experience difficulty because the word *hen* is less likely to be in their spoken vocabulary than the word *chicken*. Even though the word *hen* is relatively easy to decode (if one knows the most common letter–sound correspondences), children will not be able to conclude that their decoding efforts are accurate if they do not know the meaning of the word.

• Readers' sensitivity to the syntactic or grammatical aspects of a text also influences their ability to successfully puzzle through unfamiliar words. For example, the sentence "I have a _____" leads grammatically sensitive readers to expect either an adjective (e.g., *big*) or a noun (e.g., *cow*). This sensitivity will limit the number of options readers might consider and/or may signal them that an initial attempt at a word was inaccurate because it didn't fit the syntactic/grammatical constraints of the sentence.

• Readers' general knowledge (or schemas) for the circumstances or events portrayed in the text can also influence their ability to accurately identify unfamiliar words. For example, children who know a fair amount about farms are likely to more readily identify the last word in the sentence

Look at the goat.

because they know that goats are apt to be found on farms.

Characteristics of the Text

There are multiple kinds of texts that might be used to promote the development of reading skill. The variety and types of texts that children encounter may play a substantial role in their approach to word solving. Below we describe some of the types of texts that are often used in early reading instruction.

Predictable Texts

In the earliest phases of reading development, highly predictable texts are often used. Predictable texts generally have one line of print per page, which may be only a phrase (e.g., "The cow") or a complete sentence (e.g., "Look at the cow"). Generally, only one word changes from one page to the next, and that word is frequently something that can be illustrated pictorially. The picture on each successive page highlights the thing that changed. With this type of book, once children know the pattern (e.g., "Look at the _____"), they can rely primarily on the pictures to "read" the entire text. One advantage of these texts for emergent readers is that they help to build motivation for reading, because children can generally experience the positive feeling of success when they correctly "read." Another advantage is that these texts can be used to teach about print concepts, such as the concepts of *letter* and *word*. A significant potential disadvantage is that exclusive reliance on these kinds of texts can serve to confuse children about what it means to read, because many of these texts can be "read" primarily by looking at the pictures. They do not require that children devote much attention to the print. Extended use of such texts may ultimately serve to slow the reader's progress (Tunmer & Chapman, 1998).

Decodable Texts

Texts in which most of the words can be identified by applying knowledge of common letter–sound correspondences are often referred to as *decodable texts*— because most of the words can be sounded out. A decodable text might include a sentence like:

> Ben and Jen pet the cat.

In this sentence, all of the words except *the* can be decoded (if one knows the commonly taught letter–sound correspondences). The text might continue:

> The cat sits. Ben sits. Jen sits. Jen pets the cat. Ben pets the cat.

The advantage of this kind of text is that it provides practice with using the alphabetic code to decipher words. Such texts will be most useful when there is a match between the phonic elements recently taught and the phonic elements that are the focus of the text. A potential disadvantage is that the structure of the sentences in these texts tends to be quite different from typical spoken and written language (e.g., "Ben sits. Jen sits.") and thus may lead the child away from using syntax as a source of information in identifying words.

Early Sight Word Readers

Many high-frequency words are not entirely decodable, and they often occupy roles in sentences that make them hard to identify using contextual cues. Therefore, these words are often given special instructional attention. Several publishers have developed "sight word readers" to help to build automaticity with these words. These materials are intended to help make these frequently occurring words part of children's sight vocabulary. However, sight word readers are not all of a kind. Indeed, several series consist of books that look quite like the predictable texts described earlier. Thus the book *The Farm*, described in that section, contains text that repeatedly uses the phrase "Look at the _____." *Look, at,* and *the* are all high-frequency words. As noted above, in reading this text, beginning readers may attend very little to the printed words once they know the pattern, and therefore reading this text may not help them learn these high-frequency words. Although many series devoted to the teaching of high-frequency words feature predictable patterns, we are aware of at least one series, published by The Short Books (1999; *www.myshortbooks.com*), that varies the language structure in a way that encourages more careful attention to the print. These texts use a few high-frequency words over and over in the context of a single book, but the words are used in slightly different syntactic structures. As a result, readers need to attend more carefully to the words in order to read the text; such books seem more likely to help children build high-frequency sight vocabulary. For example, the book *The Farm* could be rewritten as:

Look at the cow. Look at the horse. Look! The pig. The cat. Look, look, look!

Clearly, this version of the text would require readers to attend more carefully to the print. As a further illustration, Figure III.2 presents two versions of the book *See My Pets*, only one of which is likely to help children learn the high-frequency words that are utilized.

FIGURE III.2. Two renditions of a book called *See My Pets*. The version on the left is much more likely to help children learn the words *I*, *see*, and *my* than is the version on the right. From Scanlon and Anderson (2010). Copyright by the International Literacy Association. Reprinted by permission.

More Advanced Sight Word Readers

For children who are a bit more advanced in their reading skills but who are having difficulty learning high-frequency sight words, we have found that books that
include many repetitions of very-high-frequency words help to facilitate the development of skill with these words. Books by Margaret Hillert and by Babs Bell
Hajdusiewicz (both originally published by Modern Curriculum Press), for example, are particularly helpful in this regard. Several of the books by Hillert involve
retellings of fairy tales such as Cinderella and Hanzel and Gretel. Because these
books emphasize the use of high-frequency words, the language patterns are far
from natural. For example, the book entitled *The Three Little Pigs* (Hillert, 1963,
p. 12) reads

> See my house. It is a little house. It is yellow.

However, because these books tell a story that is apt to be familiar to many
children (or that may be made familiar through read-alouds of the originals), and
because they look like small chapter books, the books are more appealing and
engaging for children than might be expected. We have observed that many children who are initially slow to develop high-frequency sight vocabulary show rapid
gains in this regard when provided with the opportunity to read some of these
books.

Strategy-Promoting Texts

Strategy-promoting texts is a term we have coined to describe texts that present
readers with problem-solving opportunities that promote the interactive use of a
variety of information sources for purposes of identifying unfamiliar words. Thus
readers may need to consider information provided by the picture, the general
context of the text, and the print in order to puzzle through an unfamiliar word.
Following are two examples taken from a series called Ready Readers (currently
published by Pearson Education).

The first example in Figure III.3 is taken from a book titled *My Room* (Spevack, 1997), in which the labels for several of the pictures are somewhat ambiguous and readers are required to attend to the print in order to determine the exact
word. For example, to confidently read the words "my rabbit" (as opposed to "my
bunny"), the emergent reader needs to think about at least three different sources
of information: the repetitive pattern in the book, the picture, and the printed
word *rabbit*. The second example presents a similar task within a somewhat more
challenging text. In this example, taken from the book *Eggs!* (Robinson, 1997),
readers who are relying primarily on the repetitive pattern of the text and picture
cues are likely to read "Look at the *fire*." Careful attention to the print, in conjunction with the other sources of information, is needed to accurately read the word

FIGURE III.3. Examples from strategy-promoting books. Left: From *Ready Readers, My Room*, by Judy Spevack, illustrated by Joan Holub. Right: From *Eggs!*, by F. R. Robinson, illustrated by Randy Verougstraete. Both copyright 1997 by Pearson Education, Inc., or its affiliates. Used by permission. All rights reserved.

smoke. Note that, although the word *smoke* adheres to commonly taught decoding generalizations, children reading this level of text have probably not attained that level of decoding skill and will therefore require multiple sources of information to solve the word. We have found that books such as these are particularly conducive to promoting the interactive use of a variety of informational sources for word solving. Indeed, the use of strategy-promoting books, which can be found in a number of different series intended for beginning readers, is quite central to promoting the interactive use of a variety of word identification strategies.

In our work with beginning readers, we have found use for all of the kinds of texts described above. The highly predictable and patterned books are particularly useful for children who know little about how the alphabetic writing system works. Occasional use of decodable books can be helpful for children who find it difficult to stabilize their knowledge of the alphabetic code. However, we do not use these texts exclusively for any extended period of time for fear that children will adopt an attitude toward reading that is exclusively code-focused. Because there are so many words in English that are not entirely decodable, it is important for children to learn to use other sources of information to check and confirm their initial decoding attempts. We have found that some children are slow to develop automaticity with high-frequency words. For these children, some series of sight word readers seems to be especially useful. However, in our early intervention programs we turn to strategy-promoting texts most frequently, and many kindergarten and first-grade classroom teachers have also found them helpful for the broad spectrum of children whom they teach. From our perspective, these texts capitalize on the advantages provided by many of the other kinds of texts described above, but do not suffer from their potential disadvantages.

Characteristics of Instruction

In addition to the characteristics of the child and the characteristics of the texts, the other major factor that influences children's ability to build their sight vocabulary is the instruction that guides their thinking about word solving. Whereas some children seem to learn to word-solve easily, without much instructional guidance, others need explicit guidance and extended opportunities for guided practice in order to become proficient word solvers. As Gerald Duffy (2003) puts it in his book *Explaining Reading*:

> Some students struggle with reading because they lack information about what they are trying to do and how to do it. They look around at their fellow students who are learning to read easily and say to themselves, "How are they doing that?" In short, they are mystified about how to do what other students seem to do with ease. (p. 9)

Because many children who struggle with learning to read have particular difficulty with learning to use the alphabetic code, schools and teachers often respond to these difficulties by emphasizing decoding strategies to the near exclusion of the other sources of word-solving information that texts provide. As a result, when these children encounter a word that is not fully decodable—a word such as *have,* for example, which, when decoded, would rhyme with *gave*—they have no other problem-solving strategies at their disposal. They are stuck. They have made no progress toward adding the word *have* to their sight vocabulary, and their ability to negotiate the remaining text is impaired.

On the other hand, some instructional approaches encourage children to rely primarily on the meaningful context in which a word occurs when attempting to solve unfamiliar words. Children are directed to attend to the alphabetic information provided in the word primarily to confirm their prediction of what the word will be. In fact, many children have been taught to think of a word that would make sense in the context in which the unfamiliar word is encountered, and then check the letters to see if they are consistent with their guess. Often a match on the first letter is considered a satisfactory match. Thus, for example, in reading the book *The Farm,* suppose a child reads the page that says "Look at the cow" as "Look at the calf" because he or she knows a lot about cows, and the particular cow pictured looks young to him or her. By some instructional philosophies, this error would be considered acceptable and would provide evidence that the reader was accessing the important sources of information for word identification. Further, because such an error did not substantially change the meaning of the text, teachers aligned with this instructional approach might decide that there was no value in redirecting the child's thinking on this particular word. This may be the appropriate reaction depending on the child's understanding of the alphabetic writing system. However, it is important to realize that a child who makes such an error has made little progress toward adding the word *cow* to the set of words that he or she can identify easily. Thus, the next time the child encounters the word *cow,* it will be no more familiar than the first time he or she encountered it.

A child who is reliably able to use the beginning letter in a word to guide his or her identification attempts is ready to learn how to use more of the available alphabetic information to word-solve. Directing such a child to consider both the beginning and ending letters in the word *cow,* as well as the general context and picture cues, would help to disconfirm *calf* and encourage the child to think about other possible identities for the word. Most likely, this guidance would lead to the accurate identification of the word in this particular example.

In the ISA, we explicitly teach word-solving strategies that are intended to help children negotiate such trouble spots by encouraging the use of as much of the alphabetic information as they are ready to handle, in combination with the contextual and pictorial cues that are available. Although there is little research that explicitly evaluates the specific effects of our approach to teaching word-solving strategies, because it has always been only one component of the larger instructional approach, testimonials from both classroom and intervention teachers suggest that it is an extremely important and powerful component and may be *the* most important contribution that the ISA makes to teachers' effectiveness with children who struggle with literacy acquisition. In fact, in a small study completed by Anderson (2009), which compared the effects of teaching teachers about just the content of the material covered in Part II of this text or just the content covered in Chapter 12 (strategic word learning), it was found that first-grade struggling readers whose intervention teachers learned about the strategic word-learning component outperformed students whose teachers learned the alphabetics content on measures of word identification and oral reading accuracy.

Although most of the words that children ultimately learn to identify will be learned through the use of word solving while reading, we encourage teachers to explicitly teach some of the most frequently occurring words (e.g., *have, the, was*) because these words are often difficult to identify strategically and because they occur so frequently that being able to identify them allows children to be more strategic. We discuss ways to promote the development of strategic word solving in Chapter 12; we discuss approaches to teaching high-frequency words in Chapter 13. The ordering of these two chapters is not intended to suggest that teaching children word identification strategies precedes the teaching of high-frequency words. Rather, teachers would address the two types of word learning instruction more or less simultaneously.

CHAPTER 12

Strategic Word Learning

WORD LEARNING GOAL 1

The child will develop flexibility and independence in applying code-based and meaning-based strategies to identify and learn unfamiliar words encountered in text.

Proficient readers are able to effortlessly identify virtually every printed word they encounter. Most of those words were learned through effective word solving while reading text. This chapter focuses on the development of effective word-solving skills that will enable readers to accurately identify unfamiliar words encountered while reading. Accurate identification of words in context, over time, helps readers learn the words so well that they become part of their sight vocabulary. Thus effective word-solving skills allow readers to "teach" themselves to read the vast number of words they must ultimately be able to identify without effort. Share (1995) refers to effective word solving as a *self-teaching mechanism*. According to Share, "the ability to translate printed words *independently* into their spoken equivalents assumes a central role in reading acquisition" (p. 155). He credits the use of letter–sound relationships to identify unfamiliar words as the primary path toward the attainment of reading proficiency. However, he argues that beginning readers need to develop a variety of word identification strategies that can be used to build their sight vocabularies. Although he places primary importance on decoding, Share acknowledges the significance of context in the word identification process. Indeed, he asserts that it is the individual's sensitivity to the constraints of the text, used in combination with a "willingness to test multiple alternative pronuncia-tions for 'goodness of fit'" (1995, p. 166), that allows even the partial decoding of unfamiliar words to take on a self-teaching value. Moreover, experiences with successful decoding help children become familiar with new letter–sound corre-spondences and patterns, thus expanding the power of the self-teaching mecha-nism (Share, 1995). According to the self-teaching hypothesis, automatic word recognition depends on both the number of times the child has been exposed to a particular printed word and the nature and success of the child's previous attempts to read the word. When children independently apply skills and strategies to read unfamiliar words encountered in text, they learn more words, and more about words, each time they read.

> **KEEP IN MIND**   Instruction in word-solving strategies has two major purposes. One is to enable children to identify particular words in particular texts at a given moment in time. The larger purpose is to help children to learn given words so well that they become part of the children's sight vocabularies. Thus word solving leads to word identification in a particular context. Successful word identifi-cation of a given word, across multiple contexts, leads to word learning.

To facilitate the development of effective self-teaching in the ISA, word identi-fication strategies are explicitly taught to beginning readers and to older children who demonstrate difficulties with word identification. Two general types of strate-gies are taught: code-based strategies, which focus on the use of letters and larger orthographic units to arrive at an approximation of the pronunciation of a word, and meaning-based strategies, which encourage children to focus on whether the attempted pronunciation produces a word that fits the context. When children have difficulty settling on what a word is, they are encouraged to utilize additional strategies. For example, readers might try alternative sounds for some of the let-ters, or they might read beyond the as yet unidentified word for additional contex-tual information that might inform their word-solving efforts. The goal is for chil-dren to learn to use both types of strategies in interactive *and* confirmatory ways.

Word-Learning Strategies and the CCSS

The CCSS do not directly address the process of strategic word identification and do not acknowledge that most words that ultimately become part of a reader's sight vocabulary are "self-taught." However, it is important to note that the attainment of the phonics and word recognition standards of the foundational skills stan-dards of the CCSS are critical to the development of the self-teaching mechanism. Children need to have well-developed phonics skills in order to be able to puzzle through and effectively identify unfamiliar words encountered while reading.

Word-Learning Strategies and ELs

Major factors contributing to learning to identify printed words via a self-teaching mechanism include that the words are in the developing reader's spoken vocabulary and that the reader has the syntactic/grammatical and semantic knowledge needed to determine that attempts at word identification which rely on phonics skills connect to meaningful words. This, obviously, presents a unique challenge for ELs. Teachers need to be sensitive to this challenge and need to provide more support and guidance for ELs than would be appropriate for children who speak standard English fluently. For example, it would be helpful to explicitly introduce the spoken forms of words that may be new to the children's vocabulary by using the pictures and context in the books they are preparing the children to read.

Approaches to Word Identification

There are three general approaches that children might use in identifying a word: a selective cue approach, a strategic approach, and an automatic approach. The strategic approach is the focus of this chapter. However, because many beginning and struggling readers initially rely heavily on a selective cue approach, we discuss that approach first. The automatic approach is, of course, the approach that is taken when a word is part of the reader's sight vocabulary.

The Selective Cue Approach

As children begin to learn a basic sight vocabulary, they are often inclined to attend to prominent cues to help them remember individual words. Sometimes the cues they choose have little or nothing to do with the printed letters in the words. They may, for example, attend to the overall shape of the word, to a picture (or even a smudge) that appears on the same page as the word, to the color of the paper on which the word appears, and so forth. Using these prominent cues, in many instances, will allow children to rapidly and accurately identify the word, but only if it appears in the same context and/or if the children have encountered no other words with similar visual characteristics. For example, many years ago, we had a child in our clinic who was able to reliably identify the word *not* when it appeared in isolation on a word card that his tutor was using for sight word practice, but he was consistently unable to identify the word when it appeared in the context of a book. After much debate about what the problem might be, we finally thought to ask the child. He told us that the way he identified *not* on the word card was by the presence of a small pencil dot that appeared on that card and no other. In other words, he wasn't even looking at the word; the errant pencil mark was sufficient for him to do what he understood was expected of him—speak the word *not* when that particular card was displayed. Gough, Juel, and Griffith (1992) found that attention to such selective cues was common among 4- and 5-year-olds.

Most primary-grade teachers have encountered children who can identify a word in one context but not in another and have found it rather mysterious. Understanding children's inclinations to use selective cues helps to demystify the behavior and has implications for how words are displayed on word walls and in other instructional resources. For example, early primary teachers often post word-wall words on cards that highlight the shape of the word or on different colored cards or using different color markers for different words. Although these shape and color cues may help children find a particular word on the display, these cues may also lead them to attend less thoroughly to the alphabetic information and thus impede their learning of the word.

Selective cue use is quite natural because children who are just beginning to learn to read do not yet know what features of words are most relevant for reliable identification. And, in fact, the use of selective cues can be an effective way of identifying words early on if the words that are being learned are fairly distinct from one another. Further, in some cases, selective cues may completely suffice—particularly for words that are very distinctive (e.g., a McDonald's sign that includes the golden arches) and that occur in limited contexts (e.g., the names of characters in Russian novels). However, as the number of written words that children encounter grows, reliance on nonalphabetic cues such as the shape of the word or on very limited alphabetic cues such as the first letter and the general context will lead to confusion. Children who do not analyze the words they are learning fairly thoroughly are likely to confuse similar-looking words such as *was* and *saw*; *on* and *no*; *of, from,* and *for*; and so forth. Reliance on a selective cue approach is likely to result in stagnation in the growth of sight vocabulary and confusion about the reading process more generally.

The Strategic Approach

Word identification strategies are deliberate (conscious) actions that readers employ in an effort to identify an unfamiliar word. To move children beyond the selective cue approach to word identification, the ISA focuses on helping children learn to use code-based and meaning-based word identification strategies flexibly and interactively while reading texts. The ultimate goal is for unfamiliar words to be learned so well that they can be identified effortlessly in all contexts (i.e., they can be identified automatically). In order for this automaticity to occur, readers need to carefully analyze the word both in terms of its phonological and orthographic characteristics and in terms of the way it is used in context. The instruction that children receive can play a critical role in the development of such a strategic approach (Brown, 2003). We encourage teachers in the early primary grades to explicitly teach and model strategic word solving and to help children internalize the strategies that are taught such that the children, ultimately, become skilled word solvers. To fully account for the complexity of the English writing system, two major types of strategies are taught: code-based strategies and meaning-based strategies.

What Is a Strategy?

Word identification strategies are a particular type of cognitive strategy. According to Dole, Nokes, and Drits (2009), "a cognitive strategy is a mental routine or procedure for accomplishing a cognitive goal" (p. 348). The goal of using word identification strategies is to accurately identify an unfamiliar word encountered in context.

Code-Based Strategies

Code-based strategies are taught because one major aspect of reading, for novice literacy learners, involves translating printed language into spoken language and translating speech into print. Ehri (1998, 2005) theorizes that, for the printed version of a word to be thoroughly stored in memory so that it ultimately becomes part of the reader's sight vocabulary, the reader needs to have mapped the sounds in the spoken word onto the letters in the printed word. That is, the reader needs to attempt to connect each of the sounds in the spoken word to one or more letters in the written word.

In order to effectively use code-based strategies, a reader must:

- Understand that spoken words are composed of smaller units of sounds (called *phonemes*) and have the ability to attend to and manipulate those phonemes.
- Be familiar with how the English alphabetic writing system works; readers need to understand that the phonemes in spoken words are represented by the letters in printed words.
- Over time, recognize that the alphabetic code for English is not entirely reliable and that there are alternative ways of pronouncing the same letter or letter combination, just as there are alternative ways to represent the same sound in writing (e.g., the long-*e* sound can be represented in multiple ways, including: *ee, ea, ei, ey,* and *y*).

Meaning-Based Strategies

Meaning-based strategies serve to direct and check decoding attempts by allowing readers to anticipate what an unknown word might be and/or to test whether an initial decoding attempt fits the context. The use of meaning-based strategies also allows readers to evaluate, on an ongoing basis, whether the text is making sense; if not, such strategies lead readers to institute some sort of "fix-up" strategy to recover meaning. In order to effectively use meaning-based strategies, readers must:

- Construe reading as a communicative process.
- Have sufficient background knowledge, vocabulary, and general language skill to notice when communication has broken down.
- Read materials that present some but not too much challenge; when a text is too challenging, readers are unable to build the context needed to enhance their word-solving efforts.

Interactive Strategy Use

In order to effectively puzzle through unfamiliar words, students generally need to use both code-based and meaning-based strategies in an interactive and confirmatory way. Because the English language includes many words that are not spelled in entirely predictable ways, decoding attempts often result in only an approximate pronunciation of the printed word. To settle on the actual pronunciation, the reader needs to think of a word that sounds like the result of the decoding attempt *and* that makes sense in the given context.

Children Tend to Learn What We Teach Them

Sometimes children who struggle with literacy acquisition come to believe that reading is about saying the words quickly and accurately and that writing is about accurately spelling and neatly writing the words. These beliefs may result from an emphasis placed on accuracy by the children's teachers. While we fully support and encourage teachers' efforts to address the needs of their students with respect to foundational skills, we also caution that this focus should not supersede a focus on understanding and enjoyment. Teachers need to emphasize that reading and writing are about *meaning making* if we want children to focus on meaning.

In the ISA we build the foundation for establishing an active use of meaning-based strategies through the interactions we have with children during read-alouds and in other contexts in which we seek to develop general world knowledge, vocabulary and language skills, and active engagement with the meaning of the texts that are read or heard.

The Automatic Approach

The goal of teaching children to be strategic in their attempts to identify unfamiliar words is to help them learn words so well that they become part of their sight vocabulary. Thus, although a strategic approach to word solving may result in accurate word identification, a word would not be considered to have been learned until the child could identify it effortlessly and in all contexts. That level of learning frees up the cognitive resources needed for meaning construction.

Reading Skill and Approaches to Word Identification

As children progress as readers, the proportion of words they identify using each of the three approaches shifts. Early on, most children use a selective cue approach to identify a small number of words. As children begin to understand how the alphabetic writing system works and how printed words are used to convey complex ideas, they develop (with appropriate guidance) the ability to be strategic in their word identification. At this point, most of the words they can identify while reading may be the result of using a strategic approach, although those that have been identified successfully on several occasions may be so familiar that they are automatically identified. Proficient readers identify the vast majority of words they encounter quickly and accurately, both because many of them are part of the readers' sight vocabularies and because, in the process of becoming proficient (which involves engaging in a great deal of reading), they have learned the numerous commonly occurring spelling patterns that occur in written English and therefore can decode many new words without needing to become consciously strategic. For example, many proficient readers will never have seen the word *sprat*; however, none are likely to have difficulty determining how it is pronounced. Proficient readers will on occasion, however, encounter words that require a strategic approach and perhaps even a few words (e.g., the names of certain medications) that they will identify via a selective cue approach.

Strategic Word Learning

There has been remarkably little research on word identification strategy instruction in terms of systematically testing which strategies are most effectively taught and when and how to effectively teach strategy use (Brown, 2003). However, summaries of the scientific research on literacy acquisition have generally concluded that it is critical for children to learn to use all of the graphic (letter) information in printed words as soon as possible (see Pressley & Allington, 2015, for a review) because *children who do not use all of the graphic information when attempting to read an unfamiliar word do not effectively store that word in memory* (Ehri, 2005; Share, 1995). As a result, when they encounter the word in the future, it may be no more familiar than it was the first time. Children who attend to all of the graphic information in printed words store more complete word information in memory and are more likely to successfully identify the word on subsequent encounters.

Because accurate word solving is critical to word learning, and because written English is not entirely decodable, it is also important that children learn to use the context in which the word occurs to direct and verify their decoding attempts. Thus children who rely too heavily on decoding strategies will produce many, many word identification errors when attempting to read unfamiliar words and will therefore not only fail to learn the words they are attempting but will also fail to make sense of the materials they read.

One of the biggest differences between children who experience difficulty with learning to read and those who learn to read with relative ease is in their abilities to use the phonological code. Strong readers learn to use the code more quickly than do children who struggle and who depend more on meaning-based strategies, presumably because their phonological skills are weaker and therefore are not as useful to them (Tunmer & Nicholson, 2011). However, because children who struggle do not make adequate use of the alphabetic code, they do not effectively store words in memory, and, as a result, their sight vocabulary develops more slowly, thus impeding their ability to read grade-level texts.

Such a finding might lead some to conclude that code-based strategies should be the primary focus of early reading instruction, at least for children who struggle with literacy acquisition. However, acting on such a conclusion has the potential to move the children away from focusing on the meaning of the things they read and may move them away from the expectation that what they read should make sense.

Based on the logic articulated above and on research on strategy instruction in the comprehension domain (Pearson & Gallagher, 1983; Roehler & Duffy, 1984), we developed an approach to word identification strategy instruction that teachers report is very effective for beginning[1] and struggling readers.[2] The strategies are taught explicitly, and the children are provided with extensive guided practice in applying the strategies. The ultimate goal is for the children to internalize the strategies so that they can effectively word-solve without teacher guidance. In order to help children internalize the problem-solving approach, we teach a small set of strategies of each type: four code-based strategies and four meaning-based strategies. Thus we do not teach an exhaustive list of all of the things an active reader might do in attempting to solve an unfamiliar word. However, the strategies that we do teach are representative of the kinds of things that readers might do. Our goal in keeping the strategy list fairly short is to make it more likely that readers

---

[1] The vast majority of the research on the ISA has involved the implementation of the entire approach. Therefore, we cannot attribute the effects of the ISA to the approach to teaching word-learning strategies.

[2] An extension of the ISA appropriate for older struggling readers has also been found to be effective in helping to improve oral reading accuracy and comprehension among fourth graders (Gelzheiser, Scanlon, Vellutino, Hallgren-Flynn, & Schatschneider, 2011). The Interactive Strategies Approach—Extended (ISA-X) is described in a forthcoming book by Gelzheiser, Scanlon, Hallgren-Flynn, and Connors.

will be able to learn the list well enough that they will be able to prompt their own word-solving attempts by recalling the strategies on the list.

Code-Based Strategies

Code-based strategies include using individual letters and larger orthographic units (digraphs, blends, phonograms, affixes, etc.) to figure out unfamiliar words. The aspects of the code to which children are expected to attend in utilizing the code-based strategies change as children's skill with the alphabetic code develops. Teachers are cautioned to be sure that children demonstrate the needed code-based skills in isolation before they are expected to apply them in the context of reading connected text (see Part II). For example, if children do not know the sounds that vowels represent, they would not be expected to attend to the vowels in words when attempting to identify a word in context.

We teach the following code-based strategies:

- *Think about the sounds of the letters in the word.* At the earliest points in development, children are taught to attend to just the beginning letter and sound in the unfamiliar word and to use that information in conjunction with pictorial or other contextual supports to identify the word. As children progress, the teacher focuses on encouraging them to use both beginning and ending sounds. Ultimately, children are expected to look all the way through the word, thinking about the sounds and blending them to make a word that fits the context.

- *Look for parts you know.* In using this strategy, readers look for word parts that have been explicitly taught (e.g., phonograms) or for word parts that are familiar (e.g., consonant and vowel digraphs, spelling patterns such as *tion*).

- *Try out different sounds for some of the letters, especially the vowel(s). Be flexible.* In using this strategy, students retrieve from memory alternate sounds for letters to determine which sound produces a meaningful word that fits the context. This strategy is particularly useful for vowels that have been taught and practiced. For example, in puzzling through the word *break,* the child might try the long sound for the *e,* the short sound for the *e,* and finally the long sound for the *a* before deciding that a real word that fits the context has been identified. The strategy of trying different sounds is also useful for the hard and soft sounds of *c* and *g* and for vowel digraphs that have more than one common pronunciation (e.g., *oo* and *ow*). This strategy can also be used to deal with silent letters in some letter combinations (e.g., *kn, gh, wh*).

- *Break the word into smaller parts.* This strategy is useful in identifying words with inflectional endings (*ed, ing, s*), words with other types of affixes, and multisyllabic words. By breaking a word into smaller parts, the decoding of an unfamiliar word can be somewhat simplified. As with other word identification strategies, this strategy would generally be used in combination with other code- and meaning-based strategies in efforts to accurately identify an unfamiliar word encountered in context. In initially teaching this strategy, the teacher would encourage students to cover known parts of unfamiliar words, attempt to decode the part of the word that isn't covered, rely on the context of the sentence and larger text to get a better idea of what the word might be, and, having formed a hypothesis about what the word is, read it with the covered part(s) added back in and check to see if the resulting word fits both the meaning and the syntax of the sentence. Because using the "break-the-word-into-smaller-parts" strategy requires facility with several other strategies, this tends to be one of the last strategies taught.

Meaning-Based Strategies

Meaning-based strategies include the use of picture clues and the context of the sentence and the larger text. We teach the following meaning-based strategies:

- *Check the pictures.* In using this strategy, students check the picture to see if there is information that is useful in identifying a puzzling word. This strategy is particularly useful for students who are just beginning to learn about the reading process and who do not yet have much ability to use code-based strategies to puzzle through unfamiliar words.

- *Think of words that might make sense.* In applying this strategy, readers use the meaning and syntax[3] of what has been read to generate a hypothesis about what a puzzling word is or to confirm the identity of an unknown word that has been identified using other strategies. Although it is sometimes possible to accurately identify an unfamiliar word encountered in context by relying solely on this strategy, this practice should not be encouraged because such an approach would not draw students' attention to the printed form of the word and would therefore not help students to add the word to their sight vocabularies.

- *Read past the puzzling word and then come back to it.* In using this strategy, students read on, often to the end of the sentence, to gain more insight into what the puzzling word might be. The strategy can be especially helpful when used early in a sentence or paragraph, when readers have not yet acquired much sense of what the sentence or paragraph is about. However, this strategy is also useful if the puzzling word occurs later in the sentence; sometimes reading the next sentence will help to clarify the identity of an unfamiliar printed word.

- *Go back to the beginning of the sentence and start again.* Sometimes when readers encounter an unfamiliar word, taking the time to puzzle over it causes them to forget what has already been read. In using this strategy, readers go back

---

[3]In the ISA, we do not try to get children to make a clear distinction between semantic (meaning) and syntactic (grammatical) sources of information for word solving, as the two sources are often intricately connected.

to the beginning of the sentence and start again to regain the context that the earlier part of the sentence provides. This additional context sometimes provides the needed information to confirm a hypothesis about the word's identity.

Teaching to Promote the Use of Word Identification Strategies

Although the ultimate goal is for children to learn to use the code-based and meaning-based strategies in a confirmatory way, we generally teach the strategies one at a time, since learning to use a new strategy takes effort. We explain what the strategy is, how it works, when to use it, and so on. Children are provided with a good deal of guided and independent practice with a strategy in order to ensure that it becomes part of their repertoire. However, we do not wait until children are proficient in the use of one strategy before introducing another. Rather, we provide focused practice with each new strategy as it is introduced and offer guidance in the interactive use of all of the strategies that have been taught.

KEEP IN MIND The way we talk about the process of identifying unfamiliar words may influence children's willingness to engage in the process. Referring to words as *hard* or *tricky* may lead some children to feel defeated before they even begin. So too might talking about being *stuck* on a word. Referring to unfamiliar words as *puzzling* or as *detective words,* however, may be a bit more motivating.

Resources That Support Strategy Use

Reading is a complicated process for beginning readers. Often they are asked to access a great deal of information as they read. For example, they may need to remember the word identification strategies they have learned, the sounds associated with each of the letters and letter combinations (including digraphs and phonograms) that have been covered, and the high-frequency words that have been taught. Meanwhile, they need to make sense of the text they are reading by drawing upon their prior knowledge and integrating it with the information in the text.

Early in reading development several of these knowledge sources are not automatically available. Therefore, it makes sense to provide resources to support children's processing. For the strategy component, as children develop a repertoire of strategies they can use, we provide a listing of the strategies and encourage them to refer to this list, if necessary, when trying to figure out a word. The list of strategies used in the ISA is provided in Figure 12.1. (A larger version that you can print out to use with students is available online; see the box at the end of the table of contents.) In the left-hand column is a symbol that is intended to serve as a mnemonic for the strategy listed in the right-hand column. Obviously, the mnemonics require

To figure out a word:

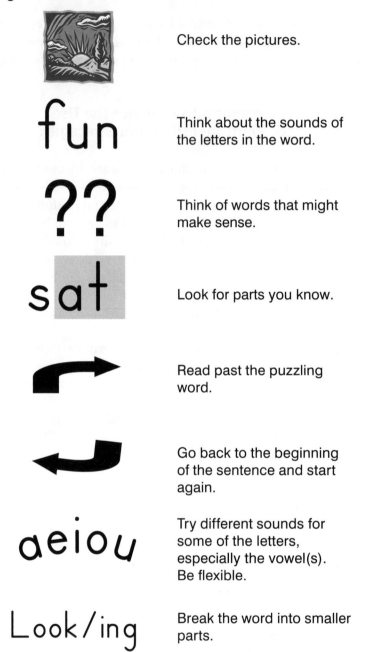

Check the pictures.

Think about the sounds of the letters in the word.

Think of words that might make sense.

Look for parts you know.

Read past the puzzling word.

Go back to the beginning of the sentence and start again.

Try different sounds for some of the letters, especially the vowel(s). Be flexible.

Break the word into smaller parts.

FIGURE 12.1. Word identification strategy list. Adapted from Scanlon and Anderson (2010). Copyright by the International Literacy Association. Adapted by permission.

a bit of explanation if they are to serve their intended function. For example, the children might be told that the little picture is a reminder that the pictures in a book might help them to figure out what a word is. The word *fun,* which serves as the mnemonic for the *think about the sounds in the word* strategy, is used, we might say, because you can figure out the word *fun* just by thinking of the sounds of the letters—and it is *fun* to figure out words by yourself.

KEEP IN MIND Strategies should generally be introduced one at a time. A strategy list containing only those strategies that have been introduced should be posted and made available to the children as they read. As new strategies are taught, they should be added to the list.

In addition to the strategy list, it makes sense to have other supports available, including the *key words* that are used to remind the children of the sounds that letters represent, the list of *word families* or *phonograms* that have been taught, and a *word wall* (perhaps personalized for individuals or groups) with the high-frequency words they have learned, and the Bb/Dd chart. We have observed that children who are provided with such resources and who are explicitly taught to use them when they encounter difficulty ultimately become more active and effective word solvers. Figure 12.2 provides an illustration of what the display of resources might look like for small-group instruction.

> ### Note
>
> Some teachers, when first told about providing a display of resources, have expressed the concern that the display will become a crutch for the children and will *prevent* them from learning. We have not seen this happen. And, once teachers gain experience with teaching with the resources with the purpose of helping children to internalize the strategies (as described later in this chapter), their concern about the resources being a crutch is alleviated.

The Components of Strategy Instruction

Research on strategy instruction in reading has, for the most part, focused on comprehension strategy instruction and has yielded a general consensus with regard to the critical components of strategy instruction (Duffy, 2003; Paris, Lipson, & Wixson, 1983; Pearson & Gallagher, 1983). In the ISA we have used the same general approach in the context of teaching about word identification strategies. In general, the components of strategy instruction involve (1) clear explanations of the strategies, (2) teacher think-alouds to model and illustrate the strategy, (3) guided practice in the use of the strategy, and (4) gradual release of responsibility for strategy use to the student for the purpose of promoting independent application. Each of these components of strategy instruction is described next.

FIGURE 12.2. Teaching space illustration.

Clear Explanations: Using Explicit Language to Communicate What the Strategy Is and When and How to Use It

Beginning readers and especially children who are struggling with the beginning stages of learning to read are often confused about how the process works. In explaining a strategy, it is important to try to take into account what each child understands about the process. Word identification strategies need to be explained from a child's perspective. This may be more difficult than it initially seems. It is often hard to explain how to do something that one does without conscious thought. Therefore, in preparing to teach a word identification strategy, teachers should think about how to explain the strategy *before* beginning instruction.

The *check-the-picture* strategy is typically taught first because, when highly predictable and patterned texts are used, it makes the least demands on children's literacy skills. In explaining this strategy, the teacher might say: "When you are reading and you come to a word you don't know, sometimes it helps to look at the picture. The picture might give you some ideas about what the word is." Explaining the strategy this way, rather than simply saying "Check the pictures," will help to make it clear that it is the *word* that needs to be identified and that the picture may provide an assist. Table 12.1 provides suggested introductory language for each of the eight strategies. Teachers are encouraged to introduce new strategies in preparation for reading a book in which the children will have the opportunity to use the new strategy.

As each new strategy is introduced, the teacher should demonstrate how the strategy would be applied and, when appropriate, how its use can be combined with previously taught strategies.

(text continues on p. 255)

TABLE 12.1. Sample Introductory Language for Each Strategy

Strategy	Suggested introductory language
Check the picture.	"When you are reading and you come to a word you don't know, sometimes it helps to look at the picture. The picture might give you some ideas about what the word is. "We have a picture here [point to the icon] to remind us that we could try checking the picture to help us figure out words."
Think about the sounds of the letters in the word.	"When we read, the letters in the word help us figure out what the word is. We have been learning the sounds of some of the letters, and now you are ready to use those letter sounds to figure out words in books. To start with, we are going to think about the first letter in our words, because that will give us some ideas about what the word might be. Thinking about the sounds that the letters make is a strategy that we will use a lot as we learn to read. "To remind us to use the *Think about the sounds of the letters in the word* strategy, we have the word fun here because it is *fun* to figure out words by thinking about the sounds of the letters in the word. "So, now we know about two things we can do to figure out words when we read: We can check the picture, and we can think about the first sound in the word. As we learn more about letters and their sounds we'll learn to use all of the letters to help us read words." (As children's skills with alphabetics increase, the teacher will want to encourage attention to other parts of printed words. In addition, as new strategies are introduced previously taught strategies should periodically be reviewed and connected with the new strategy.)
Think about words that might make sense.	"We read because we want to understand what the author is telling us. When we come to a word that we don't already know, it can help to think about what the author has been telling us because that will help us to think of words that might make sense. "Of course, when we come up with a word that might make sense, we'll need to figure out whether the letters in the word we are looking at would or could be in the word that we think would make sense. "To remind us to *Think about words that might make sense*, we have these two question marks [point to the icon] because when you are thinking about words that might make sense, you are asking yourself the question 'What word would make sense here?' Or, if you already have an idea of what a word might be, you ask yourself the question 'Would that word make sense here?'"
Look for parts you know.	(This strategy can be introduced after the children have been taught and had some practice with their first word family [and, if terminology other than word family is used (e.g., chunk, decoding key) that terminology should replace the word family terminology below.]) "Now that we've learned about the _____ word family, it will help us read some of the words in our book today. So, when we come to words that we don't already know, we can check to see if the word has any parts that we *do* know. Using word families can help us to do that. To find a word family, we need to look at the vowel and what comes after it. Looking for parts we know, like word families, is a strategy we can try when we come to words we don't already know. "To help us remember to *Look for parts we know*, we have the word *sat* with *part* of it highlighted (point to the icon and draw attention to the highlighted part)." (As appropriate, the teacher will want to encourage the use of this strategy in reference to other word parts that are familiar [e.g., consonant and vowel digraphs, spelling patterns such as *tion*].)
Read past the puzzling word.	"Sometimes when you are trying to figure out what a word is, it helps to read past the puzzling word. That means to keep on reading to see if the words that come after the puzzling word will give you more ideas about what the puzzling word could be. Then you can go back to the puzzling word and use your other strategies like thinking about the sounds and other parts you know to try to come up with a word that makes sense.

(continued)

253

TABLE 12.1. (continued)

Strategy	Suggested introductory language
	"We have this arrow [point to the icon] to remind us that when we are puzzling over a word and can't decide what it is, we can *Read past the puzzling word* to get some more ideas about what the word might be. The arrow is pointing in the direction we need to look to see the words that come after the puzzling word."
Go back to the beginning of the sentence and start again.	"Sometimes when you stop to puzzle over a word you might forget what you have already read in the sentence. Going back to the beginning of the sentence and starting again might help you figure out what the puzzling word is. After you've thought about the sounds and maybe some of the other parts you know, going back to the beginning and starting again may help you figure out a word that makes sense. "The arrow [point to the icon] is here to remind us that sometimes it helps to go back to what we've already read to see if it helps us figure out the puzzling word. When we *Go back to the beginning of the sentence and start again*, it can help us figure out the puzzling word."
Try different sounds for some of the letters, especially the vowel(s). Be flexible.	(It would be appropriate to introduce this strategy when the children have been taught about the long and short sounds of a vowel—even if they need to rely on the key word to remind them of the short vowel sound. We use the vowel *a* in the illustration below.) "We have been talking about how the vowel letter *a* sometimes sounds like /ă ă ă ă/ in words, like in aaaapple, and sometimes sounds like /ā ā ā ā/ just like its name. Knowing the two sounds can help us figure out some words because sometimes we need to try different sounds for some of the letters, especially the vowels. Trying different sounds means try one sound of the letter and, if it doesn't make a word that makes sense in the sentence, then we would try the other sound for the letter." When we do this, we are being *flexible* with the vowels. "People use the word *flexible* in different ways. We say that things that bend easily are *flexible*. When someone tries more than one way to solve a puzzle or a problem we say they are being *flexible*. When you try different sounds for a letter, you are being *flexible* with the vowel sounds. To help you remember to be flexible with the sounds of some of the letters, our picture here [point to the icon for the strategy] shows a line of letters that is flexible (or sort of bendy)."
Break the word into smaller parts.	(It would be appropriate to introduce this strategy in preparation for a book in which the children will encounter at least a couple of words that they do not yet know and that have more than one syllable. Start by showing the children how to break words into syllables in isolation [see Chapter 11]. Use words that have syllable patterns that are similar to, but not the same as, the words they will encounter in the book. For example, if the word in the book has a doubled consonant [e.g., *butter*], illustrate with a word that has a doubled consonant [e.g., *hammer*]. Or, if the children will encounter words with affixes that may be challenging to decode, teach about the affix [see Chapter 11] in preparation for reading the book.) "Sometimes when we see a word that is sort of long and we don't know what the word is, we can try breaking it into smaller parts, figure out what each part sounds like, and then blend the parts back together. If the word has two consonants in the middle, like this word [show *hammer*], we can try breaking it between the two consonants. To show you what I mean, I am going to draw a line between the two *m*'s. Then we can think about what the first part will sound like. [Give the children time to come up with *ham*.] OK, so we think the first part is *ham*. The next part is *m-e-r* [name the letters]. What do we think that part will sound like? [Give the children time to come up with *mer*. Or provide it if need be.] So now we've got *ham* and *mer*. Let's blend them together: /ham/-/mer/. What will that sound like? Is it a word? "When we use this new strategy of breaking the word into smaller parts while we're reading, we will also need to think about whether the word we come up with makes sense in the sentence. "To remind us of this strategy, we have the word *looking* (point to the icon). *Looking* has two parts, *look* and *ing*, and we have a line between the two parts to remind us that sometimes it helps to *Break the word into smaller parts*."

Eventually, the strategy prompts should evolve into a shorthand way of reminding children of how they might figure out an unfamiliar word. The children should be taught to use the mnemonics to trigger their memory for the strategies. However, when a strategy is first introduced, it is important to try to ensure that the children really understand what the strategy entails.

Think-Alouds: Modeling the Use of the Strategy

Teachers can use think-aloud techniques to help students understand the kind of thinking that a strategy involves. Research on the use of think-alouds in the context of comprehension strategy instruction indicates that they are most effective when they are explicit, leaving students little to infer about how the strategy should be applied, and when they are flexibly adjusted to reflect the demands of the text (Duke & Pearson, 2002). In a think-aloud, teachers talk about their thinking as they demonstrate their approach to solving a cognitive problem. During a shared reading activity, for example, teachers might occasionally puzzle through a word that they pretend not to recognize, or they might, in advance, cover up all or part of a word in the text. For example, in a think-aloud for the picture cue strategy, teachers might use a simple patterned/predictable book and put stickies over some of the words that change from one page to the next.

The teacher might say: "I have covered up some of the words in this book so I can show you how checking the pictures can help you figure out a word that you don't already know." Then the teacher reads through the book, pointing as she or he proceeds, until coming to the first covered word. At that point the teacher might say: "Hmmm. I don't know what that word is, so I am going to look at the picture to see if it gives me any ideas about what the covered word is. I see a _____ in the picture, so I think that the word may be. . . ." The teacher would then uncover the word to confirm, saying, "I was right. For this word, checking the picture helped me figure out what the word is!" Once the *think about the sounds* strategy has been introduced, the teacher might engage in the same type of think-aloud, except that she or he, with input from the children, would generate a short list of possibilities for the covered word and then uncover just the first letter to confirm what the word actually is.

When children have learned multiple strategies and are proficient in the use of several of them, the teacher might use multiple strategies during a think-aloud:

> "Hmmm, I don't know this word. I'm going to use my strategies to figure it out. I know lots of things I can try. I can look at the letters in the word and think about their sounds. Maybe I'll notice a word family or some other part I know. I can think about words that would make sense. Maybe the picture will give me some ideas."

Guided Practice and Gradual Release of Responsibility

Upon first attempting to use a given strategy, children need to work collaboratively to develop the thinking processes involved. The first few opportunities for children to use the strategy may be contrived to ensure that the utility of the strategy is very clear. For example, for the strategy of *trying different sounds for some of the letters, especially the vowels,* the first time the teacher asks the children to use this strategy, she or he might show a sentence containing the word *child.*

Jason is a child.

For children who know a fair amount about the alphabetic code, the most reasonable first attempt at the word *child* would be to pronounce it with a short vowel sound. After discussing that this decoding attempt did not result in a word that made sense in the sentence, the teacher would prompt the students to use the new strategy that had been taught (and perhaps reiterate the strategy). Once the word is successfully identified, the students and teacher would briefly reflect on the utility of the strategy.

Across many different reading episodes, teachers should provide the children with practice in using newly taught strategies in contexts in which the particular strategy will work effectively (e.g., when children encounter a word they do not immediately recognize, and the new strategy is likely to facilitate word identification, the teacher would suggest that they try the new strategy—by naming the strategy). Once children have experienced some success in applying the strategy, they need experience with attempting to use the strategy when it doesn't work. This will help them to understand the need to be flexible in applying the various strategies and to use multiple sources of information.

Thus, during guided practice, the teacher should act as a coach, initially advising children to try the strategy only when she or he is fairly sure that it will work and later encouraging them to try the strategy both when it will work and when it is not clear that it will work. Early on, when a strategy does not work, the teacher and children should reflect on the fact that the strategy did not work in that particular situation. For example, the teacher might say: "Hmm, sometimes checking the pictures does not help us to figure out the word. Later on, we will learn some other strategies that might have worked for this word." Or, "What other strategies do we know that we could try?"

Our goal is for the children to internalize the problem-solving strategies and to become independent in their use. One way to encourage internalization is to have them periodically rehearse the strategies they have learned initially by referring to the strategy list (and attending to the icons to remind them of the strategies), but later by relying on memory. For example, before reading a book, children might be asked: "What are some of the things we can do when we come to a word we don't know in this book?" In addition, when a child pauses on a word while reading, the teacher might say: "That word is puzzling you—what could you do to try to figure it out?" Engaging children in thinking aloud about the problem-solving strategies serves to enhance their awareness of the process (Prawat, 1989). When a teacher responds to difficulties in this way on a consistent basis, the children are likely to ask themselves the same questions when they encounter an unfamiliar word. They might say to themselves: "I don't know what that word is. What can I do to figure it out?"

KEEP IN MIND "Guided practice is something we too often skip. We teach, assume the teaching has paid off in learning, and then go straight to independent practice, the next step in the learning process" (Saunders-Smith, 2003, p. 50).

Independent Practice

The ultimate goal of strategy teaching is for children to be able to independently apply the strategies that are taught. To ensure that the children do, in fact, use the strategies when not engaged with the teacher, it is helpful to reflect on and discuss their strategy use when they are reading independently. Some teachers encourage children who are learning word identification strategies to use sticky notes to mark places in text where they have relied on strategies for word solving during independent reading. At a later point, the teacher conferences with the students about the places they have marked.

Encouraging Interactive Strategy Use

Although teaching the individual strategies is certainly important, it is critical that children learn to use strategies in combination and in mutually supportive and confirming ways. Thus, for example, a child who has learned to effectively use the strategy of *trying different sounds for some of the letters, especially the vowels,* might reasonably decode the word *read* such that it rhymes with *seed*. However, before settling on this pronunciation, the reader would evaluate whether that word fit the context in which it occurred and, if not, would try a different pronunciation (such as pronouncing it with the short-*e* vowel sound) and then check to see whether that word fits with the context. Thus interactive strategy use often involves an iterative process in which different pronunciations of individual words are checked against the reader's evolving understanding of the text. To illustrate this interactive and confirmatory use of strategies, teachers often find it useful to use a *cloze* task.

A description of how this procedure might be used with children who often make oral reading errors that do not fit the context of the passage is illustrated in Figure 12.3, using a page from the book *Six Fine Fish* (Dobeck, 1996). For this example, it would be useful to stress how just thinking about the meaning of the

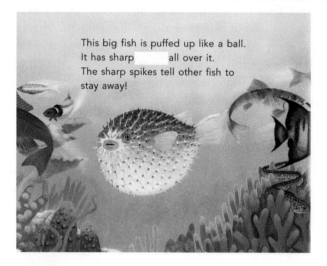

This big fish is puffed up like a ball.
It has sharp   all over it.
The sharp spikes tell other fish to
stay away!

Prior to meeting with students, the teacher selects a page in a book and identifies a word on the page that is fairly, but not entirely, predictable based on context. Covering the word with a sticky note (in this example, the word *spikes* is covered), the teacher reminds the students that often they can make some pretty good guesses about what a word will be if they read up to the word, think about what they know about the book so far, and look at what the pictures show. The teacher would then:

- Have the children read the text to the end of the sentence that contains the covered word.
- Ask the children to generate guesses about what the missing word might be. (In the current example, they might guess *points, things, spots, spikes, needles*, etc.).
- Make a list of the possibilities the children provide (trying to ensure that the list contains the covered word).
- Engage the children in a conversation about the other information they would need in order to figure out the covered word (perhaps by encouraging them to think of the strategies list).
- Reveal some of the print information to the children (in this example, uncovering the beginning consonant blend would be most appropriate; however, in other examples, it might be appropriate to uncover just the initial letter or possibly a word family). Encourage children to use the print information to narrow down the list of possibilities they generated.
- Ask them to think about what else they would need to ultimately confirm whether the hidden word is *spots* or *spikes*.
- Uncover the word and talk about the need to use lots of different kinds of information to figure out a word.

FIGURE 12.3. Illustration of a cloze activity to promote interactive strategy use. From *Ready Readers, Six Fine Fish,* by Maryann Dobeck, illustrated by Tom Leonard. Copyright 1996 by Pearson Education, Inc., or its affiliates. Used by permission. All rights reserved.

sentence gave the children some pretty good ideas about what the covered word might be. If the *read past the puzzling word* strategy had been taught, it would be appropriate to discuss this, as well as other strategies that were utilized.

Assessing, Reinforcing, and Planning from Strategy Use

As children progress, it is important to carefully evaluate the strategies they do and do not use effectively while reading. Some teachers find it useful to take running records for this purpose. However, because the use of running records can limit the teacher's ability to respond to the student's word-solving attempts, we do not encourage frequent use of them especially when teachers have the opportunity to work very closely with small groups or individual children and can thus observe and coach their word-solving processes. In these contexts, we encourage teachers to make note of the strategies they observe the children using, or neglecting to use, and to offer assistance and guidance as opportunities arise. For children who are first learning to be strategic word solvers, teachers should note which strategies are used spontaneously and which are used only with prompting. Such notations allow teachers to plan instruction more effectively. Thus, for example, if children are routinely and reliably using a particular strategy, that strategy probably does not need to be discussed at length or modeled in future lessons. If, on the other hand, children are using a particular strategy effectively but only when prompted to do so, the teacher needs to plan ways to promote independence in the use of that strategy. For strategies that children do not utilize effectively, even when prompted, additional explanation and modeling would be needed.

Word Identification Strategy-Focused Instruction

In this section, we describe how word identification strategy instruction, and the teacher thinking that goes along with that instruction, might unfold before, during, and after children engage in reading a book.

Strategy Instruction before Reading

Preparing to Read a New Book

Until children are routinely and effectively strategic, it is important to provide them with guidance and instruction in the use of word identification strategies prior to reading each new book. The characteristics of the books used for the purpose of promoting strategic reading are important to consider both because the level of challenge that the children encounter in each book will influence their ability to be strategic and because some books facilitate strategy instruction and practice more than others (see "Characteristics of the Texts" section in the introduction to Part III, pp. 231–235).

Selection of Texts That Will Be Somewhat Challenging

Generally, texts that children can read with 90–95% accuracy are considered to be appropriate for instructional purposes. A determination of which texts will fall in this range for particular children can be accomplished by taking running records (Clay, 1985; Johnston, 1997) on leveled texts and determining the highest text level (Fountas & Pinnell, 1996) at which the child is able to maintain this level of accuracy. Alternatively, following the sequence in a structured series of texts, such as a basal series or the Ready Readers (Pearson Publishing Company), may help to keep students in the appropriate range of challenge; some such series, such as the Ready Readers, attempt to systematically develop the decoding skills and high-frequency sight vocabulary that students need to negotiate upcoming texts.

Attention needs to be given to the level of challenge a text presents because, when there are many unknown words and/or when the content is too unfamiliar, it is extremely difficult, if not impossible, for children to be effectively strategic in working through it. A wide range of factors contributes to the level of challenge that a text provides for a particular child (see Mesmer, 2008). Teachers who work closely and thoughtfully with small groups of children will, ideally, come to know their students well enough that they are able to select books that provide sufficient challenge and thereby opportunity to observe and guide strategic processing but not so much challenge as to frustrate or overwhelm the child.

KEEP IN MIND   Children learn to read by reading. Some reading series engage children in reading and rereading the same passage or text for an entire week. If this is the only reading that children do, their rate of progress *and* their motivation are likely to be more limited than if a greater variety of texts are read and they therefore have more opportunities to be strategic in their word-solving efforts.

Preparing Children to Read a Specific Book

The supportiveness of the introduction of a new book should be based on the characteristics of the text and the skills and strategies of the children. If we provide more support than the children need to read a book, their opportunities to grow as readers will be limited because they will not have the opportunity to use their developing word identification strategies. If we provide too little support, they may become frustrated. Further, they will not be able to effectively apply their developing word identification strategies because, when a text is too difficult, children are unable to attend to whether or not what they are reading makes sense. Thus it may be difficult for children to determine whether word identification errors have occurred.

Several different approaches to the provision of support prior to reading a new book are presented below. The procedures are listed in order of their supportiveness, with the most supportive approaches listed first.

More
Support
↑

• *Read the text to the child(ren).* Children at the earliest stages of reading development often benefit from having a book read to them before they attempt to read it. This approach allows them to focus more of their attention on the printed words when they ultimately read, since they had the opportunity to enjoy and comprehend the text when it was read to them. However, it is important to keep in mind that, for children to become independent readers, they need to have the opportunity to engage in the strategic thinking and problem solving that reading a new book entails. If every text is read to them before they attempt it, which is the practice in some core programs, it will limit their opportunities to become strategic thinkers.

• *Introduce the book.* Previewing a book by looking at and discussing the pictures (sometimes called a *picture walk*) can help children develop schemas for the book and provide the teacher with the opportunity to introduce some of the language structures and concepts that will allow children to read the text more easily. Book introductions typically include several of the following components:

  ○ Introducing the title and author of the book.
  ○ Relating the book to something the children know about, care about, have read or heard previously, etc.
  ○ Collaborative wondering about what the book might be about; this often includes making predictions about what will happen in the text.
  ○ Flipping through the pages of the book and discussing what is happening and possibly refining predictions.
  ○ For books that include challenging language or language patterns, incorporating the language from the text into the discussion.

• *Teach important unfamiliar words and/or decoding elements before children read the text.* For a given text, it is generally possible to anticipate which words and/or decoding elements (e.g., word families) will be challenging for children. The important words or elements to teach ahead of time are those that both occur frequently in the text and would be difficult for children to figure out, given the contextual supports in the book and the children's current level of decoding skill. Teaching these words and/or decoding elements prior to having the children read the text will allow them to read more fluently on their first attempt.

• *Provide a brief book introduction and allow the children to independently preview the text before reading.* Children who have had extensive experience with book introductions can often gather a good deal of information about a text by flipping through the book independently before reading. The teacher might provide an overall schema for the text by briefly telling the children the topic of the text. For example: "Today we are going to read this book about snakes; before you read, look through the book a bit to see what you'll be learning about

Less   snakes." The children are then given time to preview the text on their
Support   own before reading.

KEEP IN MIND   It is possible to do too much in preparing children to read a new book. For example, we have observed teachers who teach far too many words from the book before asking the children to read. Only words that are important for understanding the text and that the children are unlikely to be able to figure out, given the contextual/pictorial support and their current word-solving strategies, should be taught prior to reading. We have also observed teachers routinely having children locate the most challenging language in the text prior to having them read the book. As a result, when the children come to this portion of the text while reading, their opportunities for problem solving will be reduced because they have already looked at and read the language. As an alternative, the teacher might use the challenging language during the book introduction but not directly draw the children's attention to the print. That way, the children will be primed for the unusual language but will have the opportunity to puzzle through it when they encounter it in print.

Strategy Talk

The nature of strategy discussions that are provided before a new text is read will depend on the children's point in development with word identification strategies. If new strategies have been taught recently, these might be reviewed fairly thoroughly, whereas strategies that the children understand and use well might only be briefly mentioned or not mentioned at all. Alternatively, if all of the strategies have been taught but the children need more support in effectively using some more than others, a brief lesson concerning the use of one or two strategies might be offered. Sometimes strategy talk before reading might involve having the children list the strategies they know in an effort to help them internalize the strategies so that they can call upon them when neither the teacher nor the list is available.

Strategy Instruction during Reading

Teachers should attempt to listen to individual children read as often as possible—particularly children who are identified as at risk for reading difficulties—because observing children's approaches to word solving provides opportunities for the teacher to coach and guide students' strategic behaviors and will inform the teacher's planning of future strategy instruction. In small-group contexts, teachers should listen to one child read during each reading opportunity. As a child reads, it is important for the teacher to attend to each of the components described below.

Allowing the Child Enough (Relaxed) Time to Puzzle through Difficult Sections of Text

It takes a good deal of time for young children to orchestrate the various strategies. If children are given assistance with puzzling through an unfamiliar word before they have had time to think things through, they may not develop the independence that is critical to becoming an effective word learner. Teachers need to think carefully about how to respond to children's difficulties when they read. As we've noted previously, children's development can be limited by providing either too little or too much assistance. The assistance given needs to take different forms for different students at different points in time (and in different contexts). Thus the recommendation to "allow the child enough time" does not come with an explicit recommendation concerning how long one should wait.

In some contexts it may be appropriate to provide assistance almost immediately—as when a child encounters a word that the teacher knows he or she cannot decode and the context is not helpful. In other situations, it may be appropriate to wait as much as 10 seconds or more if the child appears to be word solving productively.

When they are involved in partner reading or other group formats, children who need more time to puzzle through words may feel anxious about taking the time they need, and/or their partners may provide the word before they have had time to think it through. When children routinely have the words that they are puzzling over solved for them, their sense of efficacy with regard to reading may be undermined, and they may come to view themselves as unable to word-solve.

Rather than allowing a partner to provide the word that another child is puzzling over, it is helpful to encourage children to view taking the time to figure out a word as something positive ("It's fun to be able to figure out the word yourself—it's like being a detective"). If a child is not able to make progress with solving a particular word, the partner might be encouraged to make suggestions concerning different word-solving strategies to try, but it should be done only when the child who is reading indicates that he needs some ideas. For example, the teacher might say, "Take the time you need to figure out the word and let your partner know if you would like him or her to suggest a strategy that might work." This approach not only provides the reader with a bit more time to think but engages the partner in thinking about the strategies and can lead to productive conversations about how multiple strategies can be used to figure out the same word.

Noticing and Acknowledging Children's Strategic Word Solving

One of the values of listening to children read and noting their strategic word solving is that it focuses teachers' attention on what the children are doing to solve words—both when they are successful and when they are not. We have long known that guiding children's thinking and problem solving (and behavior) is more effective when we attend more to what they have done right than to what they have not done right. This principle applies to word solving as well. Teachers should look for occasions when children use one or more of the strategies spontaneously and attend to their efforts even if they are not entirely successful in identifying unfamiliar words. Indicators that a child is being strategic include the following:

- The child spontaneously corrects a word identification error.
- The child hesitates briefly over an unfamiliar word before identifying it accurately.
- The child refers to resources such as a strategy list, key word chart, or word wall for assistance in identifying a puzzling word.

When a child begins to demonstrate the inclination to be strategic, it is important to notice and name it. Examples of noticing and naming include the following:

- "I noticed that you looked at the key word chart when you puzzled through that word—that helped you remember the sounds of some of those letters and figure out what word would fit there."
- "I noticed you looking at your strategy list when you came to that puzzling word—that is a very good way to help you remember some of the things you could try when you need to puzzle through a word."
- "Wow! Good thinking! When you got to the end of that sentence you realized that something didn't make sense and you went back and reread the sentence and tried some different sounds for the vowels in that word, and it worked."

Gradual Release of Responsibility

In order for strategy instruction to have the desired effect, children ultimately need to become independent in strategy use. For some children, teachers will need to hand over responsibility for strategic word solving in a very planned and gradual way. Teachers should provide enough support for word solving to allow children to be successful but not so much support that they don't need to do much thinking. Thus, for example, in some cases it might be appropriate to suggest a specific strategy for a child to use; in other cases, patient waiting will be the most helpful thing to do. Following is an ordering of prompts that a teacher might provide or actions that a teacher might take that range from more to less supportive. In general, we want to provide the child with the least support possible while still ensuring success.

More
Support

↑

Less
Support

- Tell the child the puzzling word if there is little likelihood that, given his or her current skills, he or she could figure it out.

- Suggest a specific strategy or combination of strategies that is likely to work well for the child in the given context and help him or her apply the strategy if need be (e.g., "Think about the sound of the first letter in that word and then look at the picture to see if it gives you some ideas").

- Remind the child to look at the strategy list for ideas on how he or she might solve the word (e.g., "That word is puzzling you; look at your strategy list for some ideas on how to figure it out"). The purpose here is to teach the child to use available resources.

- Ask the child to think of the strategies that he or she could use without explicitly referring him or her to the list (e.g., "That word is puzzling you; what are some of the things you could try?"). Here, the purpose is to encourage the child to begin to internalize the strategies. The child may refer to the list if he or she wishes, but if the teacher believes that the child is beginning to internalize the strategies, the teacher may not want to direct him or her to the list.

- Wait patiently while the child puzzles through the word and try to notice what the child does to figure it out and explicitly name it (e.g., "You had to do some thinking on that word; I noticed that you covered up the ending while you were trying to figure it out—that worked, didn't it?").

- Wait patiently while the child puzzles through the word and then ask how he or she figured it out (e.g., "I noticed that you had to think about that word a bit; what did you do to figure it out?"). This reflection helps the child internalize the strategies by engaging him or her in talking about how he or she used them.

- Wait patiently while the child puzzles through the word and then briefly compliment him or her and move on (e.g., "I see you are really thinking like a reader!"). This is partly just a pat on the back, but it also helps to reinforce the notion that reading involves (is) thinking.

- Just let the child keep reading. Do not interrupt for strategy talk once a child seems to be secure in the use of a strategy.

Promoting Self-Regulation, Not Dependence

In the context of reading, *self-regulation* refers to the ability to independently notice and solve problems that arise with either word identification or comprehension. Teachers have a fair amount of control over whether children become self-regulated learners. In our experience, particularly in intervention settings, teachers are often inclined to do too much of the thinking for the students; as a result, the students come to depend on the teacher in ways that are counterproductive for their reading growth. When a child routinely looks at the teacher upon encountering difficulty with a word, it is usually a pretty good sign that the teacher has been too helpful to the child. It is important for teachers to reflect on what they do (or do not do) to promote self-regulation with regard to word learning. Many times fairly small changes in how the teacher reacts to a student's difficulties will lead to big advances in the student's ability to problem-solve independently. Table 12.2 provides a listing of some common student reading behaviors, along with the teacher behaviors and responses that either promote dependence on the teacher or promote independence of the teacher.

Encouraging Self-Correction among Children Who Are Capable but Disinclined

Some children who clearly demonstrate the ability to use word identification strategies when prompted by the teacher do not readily develop independence in using those strategies. They make many word identification errors and do not correct their errors unless prompted. These children can often be coaxed into independence by the institution of a brief period of competition between the student and the teacher. The competition involves tallying who notices an error first—the teacher or the student. The teacher, of course, waits until the child has read far enough into the text for the error to become evident—at least to the end of the sentence. Whoever notices the error first gets a tally mark. (The tally marks are drawn quickly in one of two columns on a piece of scrap paper; the record keeping should be a minor focus.) After a word identification error has been noted, the child is expected to make use of word identification strategies to repair it.

Generally, the teacher gets most of the tally marks the first time this competition is instituted. Within a few days, however, the child is usually getting most or all of them. At that point, the teacher should begin to fade the reinforcement system, dropping it altogether as quickly as possible. If the child asks to have it reinstated, the teacher can simply explain that it is just a little game played to help students remember to check themselves when they read. Since the child is already checking him- or herself, there is no need to play the game anymore.

The use of this "gimmick" for promoting self-monitoring should be reserved for those few children who truly understand the strategies and would be capable of noticing their errors if they had the mind-set to do so. This approach would not be appropriate for students whose word identification errors are caused by difficulties with comprehension of the text or for students for whom misidentified words are not part of their spoken vocabulary.

TABLE 12.2. Teacher Behaviors That Promote Dependence or Independence in Word Learning

Student reading behavior	Teacher response that promotes dependence	Teacher response that promotes self-regulation and independence
Child looks at the teacher upon encountering an unfamiliar word.	Teacher tells child word. Or Teacher gives a partial response (e.g., articulates the first sound in the unfamiliar word).	Teacher continues to look at word rather than making eye contact with the child. Or Teacher asks, "What could you try there?" Or Teacher prompts with a word identification strategy that has recently been taught.
Child reads many unfamiliar words with a rising (questioning) intonation.	Teacher confirms or disconfirms for the child ("Uh-huh" or "Nooo . . . ").	Teacher waits for the child to do the confirmation, saying nothing and keeping his or her eyes on the text. Or, if need be, Teacher prompts the child to confirm/disconfirm (e.g., "Keep reading [or reread] to see if that makes sense").
Child produces words that don't fit the context.	Teacher asks "Does that make sense?" before the child has read far enough along to realize that meaning has been lost. Or Teacher asks "Does that make sense?" *only* when it doesn't make sense.	Teacher does not comment on word identification errors until the child has read far enough along to notice that something doesn't make sense. Or Teacher asks, "Does that make sense?" both when it does make sense and when it doesn't; thereby making the question a genuine one rather than a signal that a word identification error has occurred.
Child seldom if ever self-corrects.	Teacher does all the monitoring for the child and prompts the specific strategies the child needs to use in order to solve word identification problems.	Teacher notices and acknowledges when the child self-corrects without being prompted to do so. And/or, teacher encourages the child to be independent in strategy use by briefly making error monitoring a bit of a competition between the teacher and the child (see *Encouraging Self-Correction* box).

Strategy Instruction after Reading

When children have finished reading a text, it is helpful to focus on the strategies they used effectively. For example, teachers might prompt them in one or more of the following ways:

- "What strategies do you think you used well today?"
- "What strategies do you think you need more practice with?"

- "Are there any strategies that you forget to use? If so, what can you do to remember to use that strategy?"
- "You puzzled through this word a bit and figured it out. Tell me how you did it."

It is also a good idea to name the things that the children did well.

- "I saw that you used the word family chart to help you figure out some words."
- "I heard a lot of people thinking like readers today. I notice that you are helping each other remember to use your strategies."
- "You guys are really getting good at being flexible with those vowel sounds!"

Evaluating and Documenting Children's Progress

Figure 12.4 presents a group snapshot for strategic word learning that can be used to track the development of word identification strategies among children in a small-group instructional situation. To document strategy use in any given lesson, the teacher might listen to an individual child read and make notes, using two-letter codes to represent each strategy, to record which strategies the child uses spontaneously or with prompting. Although it is certainly not always possible to determine which strategies children are using, especially for children who do a lot of their word solving in their heads, careful attention to the types of errors they make and to where their eyes go as they puzzle over a word can provide insights. By reviewing observational notations made over a week or so, the teacher would be able to update the snapshot for the children in each of her groups. Looking across the children's application of strategies, the teacher might notice patterns of use and nonuse that would inform planning for upcoming lessons.

In addition to documenting strategy use, it is also useful to document the ease with which children build their sight vocabulary through strategic word solving. The snapshot in Figure 12.5 is intended for this purpose. As with several of the snapshots, the primary purpose of this form is to prompt teachers' thinking as to which of the children in their groups might benefit from extra, more focused instructional attention. To use this form, the teacher would record observations of the ease with which sight words are acquired (*readily, slowly,* or *very slowly*). Such observations should be made at several points in time. This snapshot allows for this. Thus in the first column the teacher would record the date on which her or his ratings are entered for the group of children. She or he would then record a rating for each child in the column under that child's name. Ratings can be recorded up to 10 different times. Children who appear to be building their sight vocabulary slowly or very slowly relative to peers may be in need of more explicit instruction and/or more guided practice in the use of word identification strategies. Further, they clearly need more opportunities to read texts that are not too challenging.

KEEP IN MIND All of the discussion in this chapter has been focused on word identification strategy instruction. This is one major goal that is pursued in the context of engaging the children in reading text. The other major goal is for the children to become active, engaged comprehenders. For children who are at the early stages of learning to read and for those who are struggling with reading, it is easy for teachers to become so focused on facilitating the development of skill in word identification that the focus on meaning is lost—at least to the child. So, while in this chapter we discussed instruction that is intended to promote the development of skill in word identification that should occur before, during, and after children read a text, this instruction should not replace instruction intended to develop meaning-focused reading.

Group Snapshot—Strategic Word Learning, Use of Word Identification Strategies							
Student names							
CP—**C**heck the **P**ictures							
TS—**T**hink about the **S**ounds of the letters in the word	First						
	Last						
	Medial						
MS—Think of words that might **M**ake **S**ense							
LP—**L**ook for **P**arts you know							
RP—**R**ead **P**ast the puzzling word							
SA—Go back to the beginning of the sentence and **S**tart **A**gain							
DS—Try **D**ifferent **S**ounds for some of the letters, especially the vowel(s)							
BW—**B**reak the **W**ord into smaller parts							
IC – Use multiple strategies in an **I**nteractive and **C**onfirmatory way							

Key:

◻ *B*—*Beginning* indicates that instruction has addressed the strategy but that the child has only a preliminary understanding or capability with regard to its use.

⊠ *D*—*Developing* indicates that the child has some understanding of the strategy but does not reliably and/or spontaneously use the strategy.

⊠ *P*—*Proficient* indicates that the child reliably and spontaneously demonstrates use of the strategy.

FIGURE 12.4. Group snapshot for strategic word learning: Use of word identification strategies. Adapted from Scanlon and Anderson (2010). Copyright by the International Literacy Association. Adapted by permission.

Group Snapshot—Observations of Strategic Sight Word Learning						
Student names						
Builds sight vocabulary through strategic word identification while reading Code as: **R**eadily **S**lowly **V**ery slowly	Date					
	Date					
	Date					
	Date					
	Date					
	Date					
	Date					
	Date					
	Date					
	Date					

FIGURE 12.5. Group snapshot for sight word learning.

CHAPTER 13

High-Frequency
Word Learning

WORD LEARNING GOAL 2

The child will be able to read the most frequently occurring words accurately and quickly.

High-frequency words are those that occur very often in print (and in spoken language). Most high-frequency words refer to abstractions (i.e., they do not refer to things that can be seen or envisioned). As a result, they are relatively difficult to learn and often difficult to identify through the use of contextual cues. Further, many high-frequency words are not entirely decodable. For all of these reasons, it is useful to explicitly teach the most frequently occurring words and to provide sufficient practice so that children can identify them automatically.

Early Instruction of High-Frequency Words

The first words that children learn to read need special instructional consideration because the children have little or no conceptual framework for understanding the reading process and the role of printed words. Therefore, in this section we focus on ways to help children learn to read and write a small set of very-high-frequency words.

When we talk to kindergarten and first-grade teachers about teaching high-frequency words, we almost always get questions about how many words should be in this "small set." Since, to our knowledge, there is no research to guide a response to this question, we generally turn the question back to the teachers and ask about the expectations in their schools. In the first edition of this book, we reported that teachers' answers ranged from a low of 6 high-frequency words known by the end of kindergarten to a high of 100 words. In our kindergarten intervention work, in which we provided small-group instruction for half an hour twice a week to children identified as being at risk for literacy learning problems, it was not unusual for these children to know 50 or more high-frequency words at the end of kindergarten. So, clearly, even children who begin kindergarten with limited early literacy skills can learn quite a few high-frequency words by the end of the year. Because knowledge of high-frequency words provides children with so much access to reading materials and allows them to be strategic in learning new words, setting higher expectations for high-frequency word knowledge is probably in the children's best interest. That said, it is important to note that, in our approach, teaching high-frequency words entails much more than the drill-type activities that are often associated with teaching high-frequency sight words.

Note

Although the term *sight words* is often used when discussing high-frequency words, the two terms are not synonymous. As defined in Chapter 12, sight words are any words that can be identified automatically—without cognitive effort. While a proficient reader's sight vocabulary will contain many high-frequency words, it will also contain many, many words that occur with less frequency. Since the goal of instruction in high-frequency words is for these words to become part of the individual's sight vocabulary, both terms are used in this chapter.

High-Frequency Words and the CCSS

The ability to read "common high-frequency words" is only explicitly identified at the kindergarten level in the CCSS (RF.K.3.c; NGA & CCSSO, 2010, p. 16). In grades 1 and 2, the Standards call for children to be able to "recognize and read grade-appropriate irregularly spelled words" (RF.1.3.g and RF.2.3.f; NGA & CCSSO, 2010, p. 16). As we have noted previously, most words that eventually become part of a reader's sight vocabulary are learned through effective word solving while reading. The addition of irregularly spelled words to a reader's sight vocabulary can often be accomplished through effective word solving while reading, especially if the reader is fluent and flexible in the application of phonics skills. Thus, for example, an irregularly spelled word, such as *give*, can be effectively solved in context if the reader tries the different sounds that the letter *i* can represent. Thus irregularly spelled words are not likely to be as challenging to readers as they would be if the reader had only been taught conventional phonics skills, which would dictate that the word *give* be pronounced with a long-*i* sound. Of course, as discussed below, for children who are at an early point in their reading development, regardless of their age or grade level, it makes sense to explicitly teach and provide practice with some of the most frequently occurring words, as knowing these words enables the reader to engage in more effective word solving.

High-Frequency Words and ELs

Although there can be no doubt that ELs need to be able to automatically identify the most commonly occurring words in printed English, their ability to do so in a way that supports their ability to read and make sense of connected text requires that they know how these typically abstract words function in context. Therefore, in addition to providing opportunities for students to learn to recognize the printed versions of these words with automaticity, it is important to help children who are learning English as an additional language to understand how these words function in spoken and written language. Thus, for example, before attempting to teach children to identify the written word *the,* it may be useful to illustrate for them how the word functions in spoken language. For example, the teacher might introduce the printed version of the word *the* and begin by being very explicit in the use of the word—by providing several examples of the use of the word— emphasizing it with her or his voice each time. Thus the teacher might say: "This is the word *the.* We use it a lot. We say *the* car, *the* store, *the* hand, *the* paper. . . . We use *the* a lot when talking about things, and we will see *the* a lot in our reading."

The general point here is that it is easier to learn the identity of a printed word if the reader knows something about the meaning and use of the word.

Selecting Words for Instruction

A child who can identify few written words will generally be most interested in learning words that are important to him or her (e.g., his or her name, the names of family members or friends, words for feelings [e.g., *love, like, happy*], words for favorite toys, animals). Therefore, some of these words should be included in early sight word instruction. The most frequently occurring words, on the other hand, are neither important nor interesting to children. They are, nevertheless, important for children to be able to identify.

Multiple lists of high-frequency words exist, and for the most part the lists are pretty similar. The most recent compilation of high-frequency words is Fry's *1000 Instant Words* (Fry, 1999–2000), which, in our experience, many schools have adopted to guide their selection of the high-frequency words to teach. According to Fry, the 25 most frequent words constitute approximately one-third of any text, and the 100 most frequent words constitute approximately half of any printed text.

The full listing of the 1,000 most frequently occurring words can be readily found via an Internet search for "Fry Words." Several of the sites provide both listings of the words and pdfs for printing word cards suitable for display on word walls and for practice activities. Figure 13.1 presents the top 25 Fry words for purposes of illustration.

Some of the earliest words taught should be drawn from this list of very-high-frequency words. Other considerations in selecting words for early instruction include:

- The instructional materials in use in the classroom.
- The words the children are expected to know at the next grade level.
- The texts that are available for the children to read in the near future.

An additional consideration in selecting words for instruction is that a high-frequency word should *not* be introduced until the children can identify all of the letters in that word. Otherwise, the children are more apt to attempt to learn the word through the use of selective cues. Further, the first several high-frequency words that are introduced should be as different as possible from one another in terms of the way they look. Thus, for example, one would not want to introduce both *they* and *the* among the first several high-frequency words.

Teaching High-Frequency Words

For children who know few, if any, sight words, we would introduce only one new word at a time. In preparing to teach a new high-frequency word, it is important to have a text available that contains opportunities for children to read the word in context. It is often possible for the teacher to construct a text (such as the morning message) that uses the target high-frequency word several times and also carries a lot of meaning for the children. Many book publishers also have developed series of little books that, in a single book, use specific high-frequency words frequently enough that the children have the opportunity to become very familiar with them. As noted in the introduction to Part III, in our studies we have used the Ready

Words 1–5	the	of	and	a	to
Words 6–10	in	is	you	that	it
Words 11–15	he	was	for	on	are
Words 16–20	as	with	his	they	I
Words 21–25	at	be	this	have	from

FIGURE 13.1. Fry's (1999) 25 most frequent words.

Readers series (available through Pearson Learning) and felt that it was particularly useful. The Short Books, Inc., also publishes a very useful set of books for helping students to develop high-frequency sight vocabulary.

Introducing Words

The first several high-frequency words should be introduced very explicitly, presented in context and in isolation, and the children should be given a rationale for learning the word, as well as practice to support that learning. Thus the teacher might do the following:

- Choose a text in which the word appears several times. Read the text to the children, discussing the meaning, allowing the children to respond to it as usual.
- Point to the targeted word in the text that was read and say something like this: "Here's a word that the author used a lot in this book. The word is _____. This word is used in a lot of things we will be reading, so we are going to learn this word. That way, when we see it in other places such as in books or on some of our charts, we'll already know it."
- Write the word in large print on a card or chart paper, naming each letter as it is written. Invite individual children to name the word and to spell it while everyone in the instructional group is looking at the word.
- While leaving the word in view, invite individual children to find the word in several different locations in the book (or other text) that was originally read. As the children find the word, either they or the teacher should label the word (e.g., "There's the word *he*" or simply "*he, he, he*" each time the word is encountered).
- If a child chooses an incorrect match for the word, the teacher should discuss how the selected word is similar to, and differs from, the target word and talk about the letters in the word. For example, "The word you picked starts with *h,* just like the word *he.* I'm glad you noticed the *h*'s in those two words. Now let's look at the end of those two words. *He* ends with an *e.* Do you see an *e* at the end of this word [*her*] (*pointing to the end of the word*)? This is the word *her*; it has an *r* at the end. So the word you picked looks a lot like the word *he* that we are searching for. To make sure we have the right match, though, we need to look at the beginning and the end of the word and sometimes in the middle, too."

As illustrated in this example, when providing feedback following an incorrect response, we should always make note of what the child did correctly, as well as what aspect of the response needs more attention. If feedback conveys only inaccuracy, some children will lose their motivation to engage in the challenging activities that are being pursued.

When a child finds a correct match, the teacher might read aloud the sentence in which the matching word occurs, emphasizing the target word when it is read with both voice and pointing. Once children can find the word reliably with the model available, the word might be removed from view while the children continue to look for the target word in the text, as before. This approach encourages the children to try to internalize the orthographic representation of the word and to connect it to the word's pronunciation.

Group or Classroom Alternative

With a larger group of children, it is often useful to give each child a card with the target word on it. The cards for individual children do not need to be particularly big. However, the teacher should still use a large-print version as a model.

If children each have their own copy of the word, they can be given the choice of whether they want to refer to the model in the context of word search and word spelling activities. Children can also be encouraged to use the word card to find other instances of the word in print displayed around the classroom or school.

Making a Collection of the High-Frequency Words That Children Can Identify

When children are first learning some high-frequency words, they often enjoy having a collection of the words they have learned. Giving each child a special way to store her or his words is very motivating. Envelopes or small plastic pouches or boxes are often used for storage. Allowing children to decorate their collection device may encourage them to keep the words together and to practice them periodically. A variety of games can be played with word cards, so these collections can come in very handy.

Parents and caregivers should also be kept informed of the words the children are learning and be given suggestions for how they can help their children learn those words. For example, if a weekly newsletter is sent home with students, one section might be devoted to providing the parents with a list of the newest high-frequency words that have been taught and practiced.

Communication between classroom and intervention teachers concerning the words that children are expected to learn in the classroom is important, especially for children in a Tier 2 or Tier 3 intervention. Intervention teachers should consider initially teaching and practicing the most frequent words that their children do not yet know. Over the course of intervention, the ultimate goal is, of course, to ensure that each child knows the words they are expected to know at a given point in the school year. Therefore, intervention teachers should be helping children to add to their collections of known words, and the classroom word learning expectations should be given high priority.

Practicing Early High-Frequency Words

Reading and Writing

READING LITTLE BOOKS

Provide the children with the opportunity to read emergent- and beginning-level books that include the high-frequency words they are learning. (Sometimes it may be possible to create an appropriate book by building on a classroom theme and/ or modifying a book that has been read to the children.) Read these books several times with the children. Consider utilizing the types of sight word readers that were described in the introduction to Part III (see the example on the left side of Figure III.2, p. 233). Books of the sort described can be easily made using clip art.

REPEATED READING

The more children read, the faster they grow as readers. Children should frequently have the opportunity to read and reread books that are at an appropriate level of challenge for them. Books that have been read with the teacher should be made available for the children to read independently or with a partner. Ideally, children would be able to take these books home to read to family members as well. In addition, many publishers provide reproducible *Take Home* books that incorporate the same phonics skills and high-frequency words that the instructional series addresses. Children and families can be encouraged to accumulate such *Take Home* books in a folder at home so that children always have a ready source of appropriately challenging reading material. It is important to help parents understand the value of children reading the emergent-level books that they (appear to) have memorized. Otherwise, with the best interest of their child at heart, parents sometimes engage the child in interactions with books that are potentially counterproductive (e.g., some parents have reported that they cover the pictures or have children begin reading on the last page of the book and read the pages in reverse order!). Therefore, we suggest that teachers provide parents with insights into the purposes of having children read and reread these books and provide specific guidance on what parents can do while interacting with their children in this context (see Figure 13.2 for suggestions to parents of beginning readers). Additional information for parents or guardians can be found in our *Helping Your Child Become a Reader* resource (Scanlon, Anderson, Morse, and Yurkewecz, 2012), which can be accessed at the websites listed on p. 70.

WRITING

Be alert for opportunities to include the high-frequency words that have been taught in writing activities. The words that are in the children's sight vocabulary should be made available to them in list form, and they should be "given

Dear Parent,

Your child is beginning to learn to read. At this early point in development, children "read" books that provide them with the opportunity to develop familiarity with important skills but that do not require them to be able to read the words on the page in a conventional way. In fact, to a great extent, children "memorize" the repetitive refrains in these books and "read" them by using the pictures to remind them of what changes from one page to the next.

Parents are encouraged to spend some time listening to their children read these beginning-level books on a daily basis. When your child reads, encourage him/her to point to the words because this will help your child to:

- Become familiar with the directionality of print (that it goes from left to right).
- Begin to learn some of the words that occur frequently in the book by focusing his/her eyes on each word as it is said.
- Begin to use the letters at the beginnings of words to trigger his/her memory of what the text says.
- Understand that the pictures help to tell the story and may help him/her to remember what a particular word says.

It is also important to discuss the information presented in the book with your child so that he/she develops the understanding that we read for the purpose of understanding what we read. By discussing books with your child, even these beginning-level books, you can help to build your child's comprehension skills. Below are some examples of the kinds of conversation starters that you might use both when your child reads to you and when you read to your child.

Before reading,

If your child has read or heard the book before, you might ask questions such as these:

- "What was this story about?"
- "Is it like any other stories we've read?"

If your child has not read or heard the book before, then you might ask:

- "What do you think this book will be about?"

During reading, you might ask questions directly related to events in the story. Ideally, the questions would be rather open-ended:

- "Why do you think . . . ?"
- "What do you think would have happened if . . . ?"

During and after reading, you might share your reactions to the book and encourage your child to do so as well:

- "I liked the part where. . . . "
- "I thought it was funny when. . . . "

An important goal for parents is to support their children's interest in reading by making these early reading experiences enjoyable.

Sincerely,

FIGURE 13.2. Helping parents to support early reading development: An example.

permission" to spell these words conventionally in their writing by referring to the list. (Think for a moment about the message that is conveyed by a statement such as "If the word is on our list, you must spell it the right way whenever you use it in your writing" versus "Since the word is on our list, you will be able to spell using book spelling whenever you use it in your writing." The subtle difference in wording in these two statements could make a substantial difference in how a child approaches a writing activity.)

When using word lists to facilitate conventional spelling, try to ensure that the list is readily accessible to all of the children. We are all more likely to use resources if they are handy. Some teachers post the list prominently at the front of the room (in letters big enough for all of the children to see, regardless of where they are sitting). Other teachers post copies of the list at each table, often on all sides of the supply box that is kept there.

SENTENCE BUILDING

Once children can readily identify several words, use the words to create simple sentences. Some additional, more meaningful words would need to be added to the set in order to allow for the creation of these sentences. These additional words should be of interest to children and be very distinct from the other words in use for a particular sentence-building episode. These words might include the children's names or those of friends or family members, favorite animals, toys, and so forth.

Our first example of sentence building is appropriate for children who know very few words. The sentence used is *My doll is nice*. The major goal for this particular example is that children will have the opportunity to learn the words *my* and *is*, as these words occur more frequently than do *doll* and *nice*. While *doll* and *nice* receive as much attention in this activity as do *my* and *is*, *my* and *is* will be used more in other practice activities and so are more likely to be learned to the point where the children can identify them automatically.

For this activity, a sentence is written on a sentence strip (which could be just a strip of paper):

> My doll is nice.

The teacher would:

- Display one strip and read it with the children several times, while pointing to the words.
- Have individual children read the sentence a few times, while pointing.
- As the children watch, cut the sentence strip into words and display the words in a mixed-up order.

| nice. | | doll | | is | | My |

The teacher might then *think aloud* about how to reconstruct the sentence, as illustrated below:

Teacher	Think-aloud
Says:	"Hmm. I know the sentence said, 'My doll is nice.' So the first word I need is the word *my*. *My*. *MMMyyy*. It sounds like the first letter is *m*, so I'll need to look for a word that starts with *m*."
Finds the word *my* and observes:	"This word starts with an upper-case *m*. *My* is the first word in my sentence, so it needs to have an upper-case letter—so this must be the word *my*. So I am going to put it first. OK. The sentence said, 'My doll is nice.' My doll."
Says:	"The next word I need is *doll*. /d/d/d/*doll*. What letter makes that /d/d/d/ sound? Maybe my key words will help. I need to check to see if I know a key word that starts like /d/d/d/*doll*."
Directs children's attention to the key word chart and says:	"I see the key word *dog*—*dog* starts with a *d*—/d/d/d/*dog*, /d/d/d/*doll*—those words sound the same at the beginning, so they probably start with the same letter."
Points to the word cards and says:	"Let's see which of the words that I have left here starts with the letter *d*?"
Finds the word *doll* and says:	"I think this word probably says *doll* because it starts with a *d*. So now I've got *My doll*. (*Points to each word as it is said.*) 'My doll is nice. My doll is. . . .' I need to find the word *is*."
Points back and forth between the two remaining words and says:	"Hmm. I am not sure which one of these words says *is*. My doll is . . . nice. . . . Nice is the last word in my sentence so it should have a period."
Points to the word *nice* and says:	"This word has a period at the end and it starts with an *n*. *NNNNNice* probably starts with an *n*, so this word must be *nice*. So that word goes at the end of the sentence."
Points to *is* and says:	"This word that is left over must be *is*. Wait a minute! Is *is* one of our sight words. I wonder if this word is on our sight word list."
Finds the word on the list and says:	"There it is, this is the word *is*!"
Reads the entire sentence pointing to each word as it is read:	"Let's see if this all works. The sentence says: *My doll is nice.*"

Afterward, the teacher would mix up the words in the sentence again and invite the children to collaborate in reconstructing the sentence by arranging the words in the proper order. The teacher would provide prompts as needed with some of the strategies that were modeled earlier. Here are some examples of what the teacher might say:

- "What kind of letter will we need at the beginning of the sentence?"
- "What is the first sound you hear in *nice*?"
- "How could you figure out what letter will be at the beginning of the word *nice*?"

Note

The first several times that the children are engaged in these kinds of sentence-building activities, it may be helpful to leave an intact model of the sentence in view as the children do the reconstruction.

The teacher would gradually withdraw these supportive prompts as he or she notices the children being able to handle things on their own. As children collaborate with each other, the teacher should be sure to openly notice and encourage the problem-solving skills they demonstrate (e.g., "Jared stretched the sounds in that word when he was trying to figure out what it was").

Variations for Children with Larger Sight Vocabularies. As children progress, the sentences can be longer; eventually the initial sentence strip can be eliminated, and children can be challenged to form a meaningful sentence from a set of words. One teacher with whom we worked used sentence building as a center activity toward the end of the kindergarten year. She provided the words to build four or five different sentences. The words for each sentence were on different colored cards, so that it was easy to keep all of the words for a given sentence together. During their time at the sentence-building center, children were to take all of the cards of the same color and assemble a meaningful sentence. Different children could work on different sentences, or two children could collaborate. Once a meaningful sentence was assembled, the children wrote the sentence on their paper. When they finished with one sentence, they moved on to the next group of cards.

Below are the word cards for one of the sentences that the children might be asked to build. Clearly children would need to read all of the words multiple times before managing to build the meaningful sentence: *The cat likes to play with the hat.*

| with | cat | to | likes | play | hat. | The | the |

As should be evident from the preceding description, sentence-building activities provide practice with high-frequency words but also help to reinforce several print concepts (e.g., the first word in a sentence starts with a capital letter, the last word has a period or some other punctuation mark after it). They also provide children with opportunities to practice sound segmentation and letter–sound correspondences in a somewhat more meaningful way. Moreover, the process of reconstructing the sentence requires that children attend to the meaning of the sentence to ensure that it is properly ordered. Thus sentence building gives children the opportunity to exercise many important literacy skills. The teacher should be alert for opportunities to reinforce these concepts and the problem-solving strategies associated with them.

Lists and Games

The words that the children are learning can be used in a variety of games and activities that will help to build their fluency in identifying them. We describe several such activities, for which there are many possible variations, next.

PRACTICE READING THE LIST

Keep a list of high-frequency words that have been taught and ask the children to practice reading the list. For children who are just beginning to learn some high-frequency words, the words' positions on the list will likely serve to support children's ability to read the words and to find words they may want to use in their writing. However, the children need to be able to identify given words both in isolation and in context in order for the words to be considered to be known by them. Words that the children readily identify in isolation over several occasions need not be practiced as often, but they should be reviewed periodically—especially if the children are not able to automatically identify them in context. Children who continue to be uncertain about some of the words should be provided with additional practice with the most frequent of these words. Having children form the words using letter tiles or by writing them several times will help them to focus on the letters and the order of the letters that form a given word. Children should name the letters in the word and then name the word each time they build it or write it.

TIC-TAC-TOE

For this version of tic-tac-toe, each player uses a different colored marker to write high-frequency words in the squares of the board. For children who know very few words, each child might write the same word on his or her turn. As they write each word, children name the letters and then say the word. For children who know more words, the game would involve selecting a word card from a deck of cards containing words that have been taught. They would then read the word, write it in their selected square (naming the letters as they do so), and then name the word again. In both versions of the game, the winner is determined by having three words of the same color in a row.

PARKING LOT

The parking lot game described on pp. 136–137 can be used to reinforce sight word knowledge if the sight words are written into the parking spaces. The parking director then tells the players in which parking space to park. It is important that words be arranged differently on each player's parking lot so that children actually need to find the correct word rather than simply parking in the same relative position as their neighbor (see Figure 13.3).

CONCENTRATION (MEMORY)

Using a deck of cards that includes two copies of each of the high-frequency words under study, a traditional game of Concentration can be played. It is important that all players be on the same side of the playing surface so that all of the words are viewed in the proper orientation. The top or bottom of the word card should also be clearly marked so that when the cards are turned over the children are viewing them in the proper orientation. It is also important that each player, on

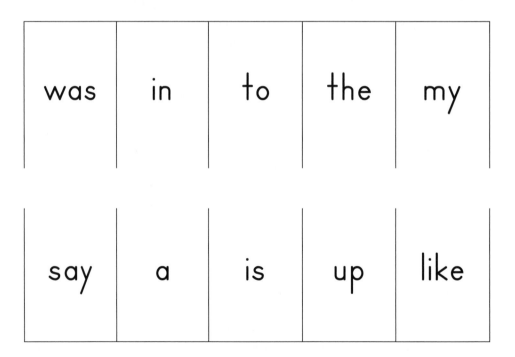

FIGURE 13.3. A parking lot game for high-frequency sight words.

his or her turn, says each word as it is turned over; otherwise some of the children will treat the game as a visual matching activity and come no closer to being able to identify the words automatically.

STICKY NOTE BINGO

Bingo boards with 12–16 squares are set up. Each square contains a high-frequency word. The caller says the word, and players cover the word with a sticky note and try to write the covered word from memory (on the sticky note). In preparation for the game, each child can prepare his or her own playing board by writing in the words that the teacher dictates in the square of his or her choice. When preparing the game boards, the words that are dictated should be displayed to ensure proper spelling. While playing the game, children should be encouraged to peek under the sticky note, if need be, to check the spelling. Children who misspell a word should be given a new sticky note and asked to write the word on it using a model and then use that sticky note to cover that word on their game board.

READING THE ROOM

Using a pointer or a flashlight, children are encouraged to search the print posted around the room for the high-frequency words they can read. (This assumes, of course, that the classroom has lots of poems, posters, language experience charts, and/or morning messages displayed.)

Later Instruction of High-Frequency Words and Building Automaticity

The development of accuracy and automaticity in identifying and spelling high-frequency words should be a particular emphasis for all children until they have mastered the most frequently occurring words. Remember that more than 50% of the words that one encounters in any given text consist of a fairly small number of high-frequency words (about 100 of them). Therefore, the 100 or so most frequently occurring words are of particular priority, because when children are able to identify and spell these high-frequency words effortlessly, they are able to devote more attention to the message of the text and, if necessary, to figuring out the less frequent (and often more meaning-bearing) words. Once children have begun to understand how the reading process works, they begin to learn new words through reading (as discussed in Chapter 12) instead of needing to have the words taught to them directly. Therefore, as children grow as readers, the high-frequency words that need the most explicit instructional attention are those that children are unlikely to be able to figure out, given their current word-learning strategies.

Grouping and Pacing

The instructional procedures described in this section are appropriate for children who already know a small set of high-frequency words (10–20). In general, the more words a child knows, the more quickly she or he will learn additional words. This is true for a variety of reasons but primarily because, as for virtually all learning situations, the more you know about something, the easier it is to learn more about that same thing. That said, it should be clear that, although we might start teaching high-frequency words by introducing only one new word at a time, as children progress, they can generally handle three to five new words in a given lesson.

Assessment for Instructional Grouping

In the early primary grades, children who are at similar points in their knowledge of high-frequency words often have similar instructional needs related to reading. Thus, assessing children's ability to read the words on a high-frequency list can provide useful information to guide grouping decisions. The Fry lists mentioned earlier can be used to make a rough determination of a child's high-frequency word knowledge. For administration, each list should be typed in primary font on a separate card or sheet of paper. We recommend that teachers break the first-100 word list into five lists of 20 words each (List 1 would include the first 20, List 2 the second 20, etc.). A record sheet for recording the child's performance would also be kept. Figure 13.4 provides an illustration of a record sheet on which a child's performance can be tracked across multiple administrations.

On the first administration, the assessment would begin with the first 20 words and continue until the child is unable to read more than half of the words on a given list (continuing past this point would be too frustrating for the child). Words identified both accurately and automatically should be marked with a checkmark (✔). Those identified accurately but more slowly should be identified with an X. When a child misidentifies a word, it is helpful to record what she or he says, as this will provide insights into the child's approach to word identification. On subsequent administrations, it is not necessary to readminister lists on which the child read all or nearly all (95%) of the words accurately and automatically. The words that the child reads accurately but slowly are words that should be selected for some of the practice activities described next.

Teaching High-Frequency Words

Selecting Words for Instruction

As discussed above, the earliest words taught should be highly distinct from one another because children's primary approach to word learning at the early stages is apt to be through selective cue use (i.e., using salient visual features, but often not the word's letters and sounds). By working with these words in a variety of ways,

Child's Name _____   Grade _____

First 20	Date	Date	Date
the			
of			
and			
a			
to			
in			
is			
you			
that			
it			
he			
was			
for			
on			
are			
as			
with			
his			
they			
I			
First 20 Total			

Second 20	Date	Date	Date
at			
be			
this			
have			
from			
or			
one			
had			
by			
words			
but			
not			
what			
all			
were			
we			
when			
your			
can			
said			
Second 20 Total			

FIGURE 13.4. Record sheet for tracking performance on a high-frequency word list across multiple administrations. Words are taken from Fry (1999).

children begin to attend to their letters and sounds in addition to their overall visual configuration. The potential confusability of words will remain an issue for a while as children's sight vocabularies grow. This, as well as other factors to consider in selecting high-frequency words for instruction, are discussed in Table 13.1.

Teaching High-Frequency Words in Preparation for Reading a New Text

In the ISA, the first time a high-frequency word is taught and practiced is in the context of preparing children to read a new book (see Chapter 12, p. 261). Teachers periodically remind children that learning these words is helpful because they are used a lot in reading and writing. When introducing a new word, it is presented on a card or sticky note. The teacher names the word, names and points to the letters in the word, and names the word again. Then the children do the same (name the word, name the letters, name the word), with teacher support as needed.

Logistical Tip

Our intervention teachers found it helpful to write the new words that would be taught for a given book on sticky notes and to place the notes inside the front cover of the book prior to the lesson. In preparing the children to read the book, the sticky notes are taken out and placed on the table. The words remain on the table during the reading. Children often find it useful to refer to these words while reading. After the book has been read, the words are reviewed and then placed back in the book, ready for the next time the book is used.

TABLE 13.1. Considerations on Selecting High-Frequency Words

Things to consider	Advice
Is the word likely to be easily confused with another word(s) that has recently been taught?	Avoid teaching visually confusable words in close succession. Children at the earlier stages tend to use the overall configuration of the word as a prominent cue for word identification.
How frequently is the word used?	Words that appear very frequently in print should be among the earliest words taught.
Do children have the decoding skills to identify the word on their own?	Words that follow regular spelling–sound correspondences that the children have already learned probably do not need to be taught explicitly. We want children to have opportunities to apply their decoding skills and to be strategic in their reading.
Will children encounter the word in continuous text in the near future?	Explicitly teaching high-frequency words prior to having children read a text containing those words helps them to be more fluent on the first reading. The high-frequency words will serve as anchors that allow children to be more strategic in analyzing other unfamiliar words in the text and in constructing an understanding of the text.

Practicing High-Frequency Words

Once a high-frequency word has been taught, it is incorporated into a set of words that will be practiced until children are fairly automatic in identifying them. Many of the practice activities described for children at the early stages of learning high-frequency sight words are appropriate for students who are a bit further along (see the section on "Practicing Early High-Frequency Words," pp. 278–285). However, as children progress, the number of words with which they work in practice activities will be larger. Practice activities include reading and rereading books, using a resource to spell high-frequency words conventionally while writing, and using various game-like word-reading drills.

For children who receive intensive intervention in very small groups or in one-to-one settings, we have found a word game we call Your Pile/My Pile to be helpful for practicing high-frequency words to the point of automaticity. This game is described next.

YOUR PILE/MY PILE: A GAME FOR PRACTICING HIGH-FREQUENCY WORDS

This game is designed to promote accuracy and automaticity in identifying high-frequency words that have already been taught. The game can be used as part of a small-group or one-to-one lesson but should only constitute a small part of the lesson. The game can also be suggested as a playful way to practice high-frequency words at home.

Selecting Words for the Game. High priority should be placed on the highest-frequency words in helping children build their sight vocabulary. Thus the most frequent words on high-frequency word lists should be among those learned first. It is also reasonable to provide practice on words that are of high priority for a particular child, either because of his or her interests or because of the text(s) that the child will be reading in the near future. Depending on children's current competence, the number of words in a drill may vary from a small number (i.e., from 3 to 5 words with several copies of each word included) to 20 to 30 words. Words for any given game should generally consist of the following:

- Some that the child routinely identifies accurately and relatively quickly.
- Some that the child can usually identify accurately but slowly.
- A few that have only recently been introduced to the child.

This combination of words serves to make the game manageable yet challenging enough to hold children's interest.

Preparing the Words for the Game. The words to be used should be written on cards. The cards should all be the same color, and the words should all be printed in the same color so that children do not try to rely on color cues as a means of trying to remember the word on a given card.

Preparing Children for the Game. It is important to explain to children why learning to recognize the words quickly will help them when reading. Explain that the more words they can recognize right away, the easier it will be to read stories and other kinds of books. It is also helpful to explain that the words that are being practiced are in a lot of different books and that learning those words will help them read and write many different things.

Explain How to Play the Game. Tell the child that you will present the words one at a time and that he or she is to tell what the word is as quickly as possible without making mistakes. Explain that, if he or she does make a mistake, you will tell him or her what the word is called, he or she will repeat the word (while looking at it), and then the word will go back in the teacher's pile for more practice. Further, explain that if the child can't identify a word, you might give him or her a hint to help him or her think about the sounds in the word, but that if you give a hint, the word needs to go back in the teacher's pile for more practice. Finally, if the child recognizes the word accurately, but it takes a long time, the word will also go into the pile for more practice. Words that the child recognizes quickly and accurately go into the child's pile for any given game. The goal is for the child to get all of the words into his or her pile. Often, in playing the game, teachers refer to the two different piles of words as *your pile* (the child's pile of finished words) and *my pile* (the teacher's pile of words that need more practice).

Playing the Game. Show the words one at a time, placing words in the child's pile if the child is accurate and relatively fast (for that child) in identifying the word. Words that the child identifies either inaccurately or slowly (taking longer than about 2 seconds) go into the teacher's pile for more practice. Once the teacher has gone through all of the words in the original deck, she or he picks up the cards in her or his (the teacher's) pile and continues on with the game—providing more practice on the words that the child was unable to name quickly and accurately on the first attempt. The game continues until all of the words are in the child's pile.

KEEP IN MIND   The major purpose of these drills is to help children get to the point at which they are both *fast* and *accurate* in identifying high-frequency words. Being automatic in their identification of the most frequently occurring words will allow children to devote more of their cognitive resources to constructing the meaning of the text and to puzzling through unfamiliar, less frequent words.

Eliminating Words from the Deck. For subsequent games of Your Pile/My Pile, words that the child routinely identifies accurately and quickly (within 1 or 2 seconds) can be removed from the deck and replaced with others. One way of easily tracking a child's knowledge of particular words is to mark word cards with a small checkmark if the child identifies the word quickly and accurately *the first time it is shown* on a given day. Generally, when words have three or four checkmarks, they can be removed from the deck. When words are removed from the deck, they can be added to the child's "Words I Know" chart (see p. 293).

Note

Putting checkmarks on the cards is done by the teacher after the lesson. This is not something that should be brought to the child's attention. We want the child to be thinking about the words, not the checkmarks!

Using "Words I Know" Charts and Word Walls to Encourage Automaticity with High-Frequency Words

Charts listing the high-frequency words that children have learned serve as important resources for them as they continue to practice accurate and rapid identification of these words and as they work toward internalizing the conventional spellings. At a classroom level, teachers often maintain word walls on which are listed all of the high-frequency words that the majority of the class is expected to know. In small-group and one-to-one intervention settings, teachers can develop similar "Words We Know" or "Words I Know" charts that include only the words that the children in the group or the individual child knows. These charts are useful in supporting the needs of children who might find the classroom word wall to be overwhelming.

Children should be given permission to spell words on the word wall and/or from their Words I/We Know charts conventionally (using "book spelling") by referring to the wall or the charts. Children are expected to spell the "Words I Know" words correctly in their writing, because allowing sound spelling of these high-frequency words is likely to slow down the process of getting these words to the point where they can be identified automatically. For example, the child who often spells the word *was* as *yz* is likely to have difficulty recognizing the word *was* accurately and quickly when he or she encounters it in text. Although sound spelling is an important contributor to the development of phonemic awareness and phonics knowledge, allowing children to use sound spellings for known high-frequency words is not recommended.

The use of the "Words I Know" chart to promote conventional spelling of these high-frequency words will highlight for children the fact that sound (invented) spelling is only a temporary means of facilitating communication.

> ## Invented/Inventive/Temporary/Kindergarten/Sound Spelling versus Conventional/Correct/Book Spelling
>
> Teachers in the primary grades use a variety of terms for the unconventional spellings produced by young writers, and we have been asked by many teachers to weigh in on what terminology is preferable. We feel that *sound spelling* is the most useful term because it most effectively communicates what the children are expected to do: think about the sounds in the words they want to write and then use letters to represent those sounds. Using terms such as *invented* or *temporary* convey nothing about the expected process, nor does *kindergarten spelling*—and that term has the potential to come across as somewhat demeaning, especially for older children who have yet to develop conventional spelling skills. We also feel that parents will be more accepting of the term and the practice of *sound spelling,* especially if teachers are careful to explain the role of sound spelling in literacy development: it helps children learn to attend to the individual sounds in spoken words (thus promoting phonological awareness), and it draws children's attention to letter–sound relationships (thus promoting the development of phonics skills).
>
> With regard to the terminology used to contrast with *sound spelling,* we encourage the use of *book spelling,* as it conveys the fact that words in books are spelled in standard ways and has the potential, with teacher guidance, to encourage children to use books as a reference when they are writing and using a word in a recently read text.

CHARACTERISTICS OF USEFUL CLASSROOM WORD WALLS

In order for classroom word walls to be effective for the children in the classroom, the words should be listed alphabetically by first letter, so that it is reasonably easy for children to find the word for which they are looking. Further, the words should be printed in a font that is large enough that the children can read them no matter where they are in the classroom—that is, so that children do not need to leave their seats to find a word on the word wall. Finally, it is important that most of the words on the word wall be printed on a standard background color with a standard color of ink so that children are not tempted to rely on something other than alphabetic features when they attempt to find a word.

CHARACTERISTICS OF USEFUL "WORDS I/WE KNOW" CHARTS

A "Words I Know" chart is an important resource for children who are slow to develop skill with high-frequency words. The words that are placed on these charts are high-frequency words that have been taught explicitly and that the teacher believes the children can identify accurately. In our intervention work, decisions about which words to add to a chart were often based on a student's performance in the Your Pile/My Pile game (see pp. 289–291). Early on, the "Words I Know" charts could be ordered in accord with the order in which children learn the words. Thus words that a child learned to read first would appear at the beginning of the list, whereas words learned more recently would be at the end. This ordering of the words gives the child who has yet to learn anything about alphabetization a positional cue for finding the words he or she wants to write.

Known high-frequency words should be moved to an alphabetized "Words I Know" chart as soon as the children know enough about the alphabet to effectively use if for locating words. This chart would look much like a classroom word wall except that the chart is much smaller, because the words need be visible only to the children in a small group or to the individual. Moreover, they would typically include fewer words than the classroom word wall. An example of a "Words I Know" chart appears in Figure 13.5, and a two-page version you can print out to

Words I Know

Aa and	Bb big	Cc can come	Dd down did does	Ee	Ff for	Gg good	Hh has him her	Ii is	Jj
Kk keep	Ll love	Mm make	Nn nice	Oo of on	Pp put	Qq	Rr run	Ss said says	Tt the to
Uu us	Vv very	Ww was want	Xx	Yy you yes your	Zz				

FIGURE 13.5. "Words I Know" chart. A chart of this type might be stapled on the facing pages of a manila folder. That is, the columns headed by A–E would be on the left-hand side, and the columns headed by F–J would be on the right-hand side. Such an arrangement would allow substantial space for adding words under each letter.

use with students is available online (see the box at the end of the table of contents). The online version can be stapled on opposing faces of a manila folder and used for tracking individual children's high-frequency word knowledge, for providing practice opportunities, and as a resource for conventional spelling.

The use of this chart should be clearly explained to children. They should be told that all of the letters of the alphabet are on the chart and that when they learn a word that starts with a particular letter, it will be put on the chart under that letter. High-frequency words that have already been learned can then be placed on the chart with an explicit discussion of where each word should be placed and why it belongs there. Teachers should also explain that when children want to find a word to use in their writing, they need to think of the sound at the beginning of the word and then think about what letter(s) might make that sound. Next, they need to find the word's first letter on the chart and read the words under the letter to see if the word they are looking for is there. This, of course, implicitly requires that children review some of the sight words they have learned as they read through the list and either accept or reject each word listed under a given letter.

For children who seem to have difficulty with reading and spelling the words on their "Words I/We Know" charts, it is helpful to make their personal charts of high-frequency words readily available. Some teachers tape a page protector to children's desks for their "Words I Know" charts. That way, the chart can be easily removed for updating. For children who have a larger sight vocabulary and for whom spelling is a major concern, teachers have found it useful to provide the words in a personal dictionary format, which is either kept in their desks (often in their writing folder) or attached to their desks with a string that allows it to hang off the desk out of the way but remain readily available when a child needs it.

"Spelling Tests" to Encourage Use of "Words I Know" Charts or Word Walls. Periodic administration of spelling tests, for which children are encouraged to refer to their charts, can help them learn to use a chart effectively. During the spelling "test," the teacher can walk the children through the process of finding the needed word on their charts as often as necessary. On these tests, every child has the opportunity to score 100% if she or he understands how to use the chart.

Guessing Games. There are a variety of ways to encourage children to make efficient use of word walls and "Words I Know" charts. For example, it is helpful to periodically play guessing games using the displays. Guessing games might take the form of the teacher providing verbal clues and the children using displayed words to assist them in guessing the correct response. For example, if the word *in* were on the word wall, the teacher might say something like "I'm thinking of a word that begins with *i* and is the opposite of *out*." Such activities can also contribute to vocabulary development.

KEEP IN MIND Procedures to ensure that every student has the opportunity to respond are easily incorporated into word wall activities. For example, in the guessing game described above, rather than having individual students make guesses, every child could be asked to write his or her guess on a dry-erase board before anyone is asked to share a guess.

Evaluating and Documenting Children's Progress

Figure 13.6 provides a vehicle for teachers to record their observations of children's acquisition of high-frequency sight words. The form allows space for teachers to record their observations of individual children multiple times over the course of a school year. For children in intervention settings, teachers will probably want to closely document their progress in learning high-frequency sight words. This can be done most easily by counting the number of words that appear on a child's individual "Words I Know" chart. Alternatively, for students who are not receiving intensive intervention, the high-frequency word assessment using the Fry lists (p. 287) can be periodically readministered and the highest numbered Fry list that the child reads with 90% or better accuracy can be recorded. Note, however, that children should not be considered to "know" a word unless they can identify that word both in isolation and when encountered in text. Children should not simply practice lists of high-frequency words that will be used for assessment, but should be learning words in preparation for use in meaningful contexts.

Group Snapshot—Observations of High-Frequency Word Learning						
Student names						
Number of known high-frequency words (can be identified automatically at sight). (Record the number of words on the child's "Words I Know" chart *or* the number of the highest 20-word list that the child reads with 90% accuracy. For example, if using the Fry list as suggested on p. 286, the teacher would record the first 20, the second 20, etc.)	Date					
	Date					
	Date					
	Date					
	Date					
	Date					
	Date					
	Date					
	Date					
	Date					
	Date					
	Date					

FIGURE 13.6. Group snapshot for high-frequency word learning.

PART IV

Meaning Construction

Introduction

Meaning construction is the goal of reading and reading instruction. As was highlighted in Chapter 1, reading is a complicated process that requires readers to draw on a wide array of knowledge sources and strategic processes. In order to understand a printed text, readers must be able to do much more than simply read the printed words quickly and accurately. They must also know what the words mean and understand the concepts to which they refer. Readers must be able to assemble the individual words into idea units, which become the building blocks for a more comprehensive understanding of the text. Ultimately, in order to fully understand a text, readers need to draw on and use their existing knowledge to interpret and construct the meaning of the text being read. Readers who need to devote a lot of attention to word identification and/or who have limited language skills, background knowledge, and/or ability to draw logical inferences will have limited ability to understand the things they read. Further, readers who do not actively think about the meaning of a text as they are reading are likely to have little recollection of what they have read.

In the previous chapters we have focused largely on the word-reading component of the reading process. Because this component is often a major stumbling block for children at the early stages of learning to read and for older struggling readers, it clearly needs to be addressed. However, the other processes need to be addressed as well, because, once skill with the alphabetic code is established, language, knowledge, and comprehension skills and strategies are the major determinants of reading comprehension. Further, unlike decoding skills, which represent a rather finite set of abilities, knowledge and language skills are limitless. Therefore, whereas children who begin school with limited early literacy skills may be readily helped to catch up to their peers with regard to their knowledge of the alphabetic code (because their abler peers stop growing), it is much more difficult to close the knowledge gaps that tend to be especially evident between more and less economically advantaged groups (Hirsch, 2006; Neuman, 2006). In fact, Neuman argues that "although the 'have-nots' gain knowledge, the 'haves' gain it faster. And by gaining it faster, they are able to gain more" (2006, p. 33).

There is also substantial concern that language and knowledge gaps develop as a result of reading difficulty because limited engagement in reading results in limited opportunities to acquire new vocabulary and language structures and to encounter and develop new knowledge. Stanovich (1986) described this phenomenon as the *Matthew effect*, which is a biblical reference to the notion that the "rich get richer and the poor get poorer." Although the research to date has yielded mixed results with regard to whether Matthew effects actually do arise for struggling readers (see Scarborough & Parker, 2003, for a review), it is hard to argue with the logic that such an effect could accrue.

In the chapters in this section, we focus on the knowledge, strategies, and dispositions that need to be developed and integrated in order for children to be able to make sense of the things they read (or listen to), and we discuss approaches to instruction that will help them do so. Three major goals are addressed in this section: (1) the development of fluent reading, (2) the development of vocabulary and more general language skills, and (3) the development of comprehension skills and strategies, as well as the general background knowledge that will enable children to construct the meaning of the texts they read. Fluency (Chapter 14) is addressed under the overarching goal of meaning construction because meaning construction requires that the reader be able to devote most of his or her cognitive resources to understanding the text, and this is only possible when most of the words in the text can be identified effortlessly and automatically. It also makes sense to include it under the meaning construction heading because fluent reading, which by definition includes appropriate phrasing and intonation, is also a signal of comprehension—at least at the sentence level, as it would not be possible to apply proper intonation and phrasing without understanding the meaning of the sentence.

The division between the latter two chapters is somewhat arbitrary. Language and knowledge are, obviously, intricately interconnected, and comprehension is heavily dependent on both.

Meaning Construction and Early Intervention

The existing research on RTI has placed heavy emphasis on aspects of fluency (i.e., fast and accurate word recognition) but has generally not attended to the role that limitations in language skills and background knowledge may play in the evolution of reading difficulties. We think this is unfortunate, because we suspect that both persistent and "late-emerging" reading difficulties are often attributable to limitations in these areas. Further, we fear that because of the common emphasis on oral reading skills, children who need support in developing language skills and world knowledge may be largely ignored until they begin to encounter texts that make heavier demands on these skills (in the middle elementary grades and beyond). Therefore, we encourage attention to the development of language and general knowledge of young learners in hopes of preventing later reading comprehension difficulties.

As is discussed in some detail in Chapters 15 and 16, language and knowledge develop incrementally over extended periods of time. The goal of increasing vocabulary and knowledge development needs to be at the forefront of teachers' thinking as they plan and deliver instruction for children who have had limited opportunity to develop in these areas. Teachers should be constantly asking themselves whether their students understand the language (both vocabulary and syntax) and the concepts that they encounter in instructional interactions, and teachers need to be prepared to take steps to intervene for children who do not have the requisite knowledge. Knowledge and vocabulary development can be promoted by engaging children in reading and listening to informational books, watching information-rich videos, providing experiential learning opportunities, and the like. All such instructional opportunities are more productive for children when they have extensive opportunities to discuss what they are reading and learning.

Of course, even children with well-developed knowledge and language skills sometimes have difficulty comprehending the texts that they "read" with relative ease. For at least some of these children, the comprehension difficulties may be attributable to failure to attend to the meaning of the text as it is being read. Virtually every reader has had the experience of reading something and then having no idea what was just read. When this happens on occasion, it is due to the fact that the reader had his or her mind on something else while reading. When this happens routinely, it can be a signal that the reader does not fully understand that the purpose of reading is to make sense of the text and to integrate the knowledge gained with already existing knowledge. This lack of understanding can arise for a variety of reasons; for struggling readers, it is apt to be due to the type of guidance and feedback they receive while reading. Thus, for example, if the feedback primarily focuses on word-reading accuracy and speed, the child is likely to focus on accuracy and speed and attend little to the meaning of the text. Over time, such an approach may become habitual and, once established, will require explicit intervention to help the child overcome this inclination and to actively attend to the meaning of the text. In the ISA, we strive to prevent children from ever adopting such an attitude toward reading by engaging them in active meaning construction in all interactions with texts.

CHAPTER 14

Fluency

> **MEANING CONSTRUCTION GOAL 1**
>
> The child will be able to read grade-appropriate text accurately with appropriate speed and with phrasing and intonation that convey the intended meaning.

In order to read fluently, the reader needs to be able to accurately and quickly identify the words in the text (Samuels, 2006) and, while doing so, group the words into meaningful phrases that serve to convey the author's intended meaning and use the correct intonation to communicate that meaning. The later components are often referred to as *prosody* (Kuhn & Levy, 2015). Thus fluency involves accuracy, automaticity, prosody, and comprehension, at least at the sentence level.

Because beginning readers do not have a large number of words that they can identify accurately and automatically, they generally do not read fluently unless they are reading a highly predictable or well-practiced text. They lack fluency because most of their cognitive resources are devoted to the process of puzzling through the words. They literally read one word at a time. In contrast, for proficient readers, word identification is so automatic that the readers' eyes are actually focused a word or two beyond the word they are articulating during oral reading (Inhoff, Solomon, Radach, & Seymour, 2011). This span between the reader's eyes and voice helps the reader to determine the intonation to apply to the word that is being articulated because, by having the eyes ahead of the voice, the reader knows what's coming next. This eye–voice span is only possible when word identification is automatic.

Of course, proper intonation is also determined by the larger context in which a given sentence occurs. Consider the sentence *This is my toy.* The sentence could be read as a simple statement. Alternatively, it could be read in a way that stresses ownership: *This is my toy.* It could also be read in a way that stresses the ownership of a particular toy relative to a larger group of toys: *This is my toy.* In the latter two instances, the stress placed on the words *my* and *this* subtly changes the meaning of the sentence. Thus the prosodic aspect of fluency is inextricably linked to comprehension of text in that it both conveys comprehension and facilitates it. For example, a reader will know which words require emphasis only if she or he has an adequate understanding of the text.

Assessing Fluency for Progress Monitoring

Measures of Accuracy and Rate

In our intervention studies, the last of which at the primary level was completed more than 10 years ago, we did not use the type of fluency measures that characterize many current screening and progress monitoring approaches in RTI contexts. However, because these approaches are so widespread, we feel that it is important to describe and comment on them. Common approaches to evaluating fluency typically involve the calculation of the number of words read correctly per minute (WCPM). The popular Dynamic Indicators of Basic Early Literacy Skills (DIBELS) is one such example. Using a measure of WCPM has become a popular tool for progress monitoring because the tool takes relatively little time to administer and because there is evidence of a moderate to strong relationship between measures of WCPM and measures of reading comprehension, with the relationships being stronger in earlier than in later grades (Kim, Petscher, Schatschneider, & Foorman, 2010; Silverman, Speece, Harring, & Ritchey, 2013). Thus, especially in the primary grades, children who obtain higher scores on a measure of WCPM tend to score higher on measures of reading comprehension.

To measure WCPM, the teacher gives a child an unfamiliar, on-grade-level text to read and, using a timer, listens to the child read the text while marking miscues/errors and omissions on a printed copy of the text. The teacher would mark the point in the text where the minute ends and then allow the child to read to a logical stopping point (rather than stopping the child mid-sentence). To compute WCPM, the teacher would count the total number of words up to the stopping point and then subtract the number of words on which a miscue or omission occurred. The result is the child's WCPM. Table 14.1 provides norms for WCPM for grades 1 and 2. These norms are drawn from widely referenced norms for grades 1 through 8 compiled on a broadly representative national sample by Hasbrouck and Tindal (2006). As perusal of the table will indicate, there are no fluency norms for fall of first grade because, at the time the norms were compiled,

TABLE 14.1. Oral Reading Fluency Norms

Grade	Percentile	Fall WCPM	Winter WCPM	Spring WCPM
1	90		81	111
	75		47	82
	50		23	53
	25		12	28
	10		6	15
2	90	106	125	142
	75	79	100	117
	50	51	72	89
	25	25	42	61
	10	11	18	31

Note. Data from Hasbrouck and Tindal (2006, p. 639).

most students were not expected to be able to engage in a "cold read" of a new text at the beginning of first grade.

Although WCPM is certainly an indicator of skill on measures of reading comprehension, it is far from infallible. For example, Schilling, Carlisle, Scott, and Zeng (2007) found that DIBELS oral reading fluency scores misidentified 32% of second graders and 37% of third graders as being at low risk for reading (comprehension) difficulties. That is, their reading rate was fast enough that they were predicted to comprehend on grade level, but they didn't. Further, Francis et al. (2008) found substantial differences in fluency performances between DIBELS passages that were, according to readability ratings, purportedly at the same level of challenge.

Anecdotally, we have encountered children who are really strategic about word solving and committed to solving the puzzling words they encounter, a process that makes them slower readers than their peers who are willing to skip unknown words and/or ignore mispronunciations and keep moving through a text. Children who are willing to skip words and/or ignore mispronunciations clearly have a different understanding of what reading is all about (i.e., reading quickly with little attention to meaning construction) as compared with those who are willing to slow down and puzzle over words so that they can construct meaning. We suspect that the latter group will, in the long term, become the stronger comprehenders.

Of course, the relationship between measures of rate and accuracy (such as WCPM) and reading comprehension will also be influenced by the instruction children receive. Given the emphasis on such measures of fluency that has emerged over the last decade or so, it is possible that, at least in some settings, children are learning that what's valued is reading the words as fast as they can, not understanding the text as best they can.

Measures of Prosody

Schwanenflugel and Kuhn (2016) argue that measures of WCPM are insufficient and that indices of prosody should be included in assessing fluency. Their summary of the research related to using measures of fluency to predict reading comprehension performance indicates that adding a measure of prosody to fluency evaluations improves the prediction of reading comprehension by as much as 20%. They argue that including measures of prosody is especially important because there is evidence that "children who read at acceptable rates but with poor expression comprehend less well" (Schwanenflugel & Kuhn, 2016, p. 109). Therefore, for teachers who choose to or who are required to formally assess oral reading fluency, we urge them to assess both words correct per minute *and* prosody. Further, in contexts in which teachers are required to assess all students' fluency on on-grade-level passages, we encourage them to also assess their students who are reading below grade level on passages that are in the range of their instructional/ independent reading levels (passages on which the student can accurately identify approximately 95% or more of the words) in order to get a sense of fluency in contexts when the text is not too challenging—as this will provide an indication of whether students are attempting to construct meaning as they read. (Of course, teachers who routinely make time to listen to individual children read and who are making note of their word identification strategies, as discussed in Chapter 12, and who are engaging their students in conversations about texts, as discussed in Chapters 15 and 16, will have little need of a measure of prosody in order to know whether the students perceive reading as being about meaning making. That will be evident in the interactions during instruction.)

Several qualitative scales for evaluating prosody during oral reading have been developed. For example, the scale published by Rasinski (2004) guides teachers to consider four dimensions of prosody:

- Expression and volume
- Phrasing
- Smoothness
- Pace

Teachers are to rate performance on each dimension using a 4-point scale. In contrast, the Oral Reading Fluency Scale used by the National Center for Education Statistics (2005) uses a single 4-point scale to evaluate prosody (see Figure 14.1). The scale essentially asks teachers to consider the multiple elements included in Rasinski's assessment of prosody. The latter scale strikes us as easier and more efficient for teachers to employ while still drawing teachers' attention to some of the most important elements of prosody.

Fluent	Level 4	Reads primarily in larger, meaningful phrase groups. Although some regressions, repetitions, and deviations from text may be present, these do not appear to detract from the overall structure of the story. Preservation of the author's syntax is consistent. Some or most of the story is read with expressive interpretation.
	Level 3	Reads primarily in three- or four-word phrase groups. Some small groupings may be present. However, the majority of phrasing seems appropriate and preserves the syntax of the author. Little or no expressive interpretation is present.
Nonfluent	Level 2	Reads primarily in two-word phrases with some three- or four-word groupings. Some word-by-word reading may be present. Word groupings may seem awkward and unrelated to larger context of sentence or passage.
	Level 1	Reads primarily word by word. Occasional two-word or three-word phrases may occur, but these are infrequent and/or they do not preserve meaningful syntax.

FIGURE 14.1. National Assessment of Educational Progress Oral Reading Fluency Scale. From National Center for Education Statistics (2005).

Attending to Fluency/Prosody during the Course of Instruction

Once children have moved beyond reading repetitive and predictable texts, we think it is important for teachers to attend to prosody whenever they listen to a child reading (which, at least for children who are struggling with literacy acquisition, should occur on a daily basis). In the ISA, we assess fluency in a qualitative rather than a quantitative way by attending to prosody as children read in the context of small-group or one-to-one lessons. For each book read, the teacher simply rates whether the child's reading was word-by-word (WBW), demonstrated some phrasing (PHR), or sounded fluent (FL). Our definition of fluent reading is that the child's reading is accurate, with appropriate phrasing and intonation, and at a smooth and reasonable pace, and that the teacher has a general sense that the child understands the meaning of the text. This rating is used in part to determine whether the book being read still presents enough learning opportunities for the child to benefit from reading the book again. If a book was not rated as having been read fluently and was not considered to be overly challenging, the book was a candidate for rereading in a subsequent lesson. For beginning readers, we believe that multiple readings of a book are useful, as they provide the opportunity for a child both to add words to his or her automatic sight vocabulary and to experience smooth, expressive reading. Of course, there is no reason why a rating scale such as the Oral Reading Fluency Scale described above couldn't be used instead of our 3-point scale.

Fluency and the CCSS

Fluency in reading "on-level" texts is included in the CCSS at every elementary-grade level except kindergarten. The fluency standard (RF.4) states that students should "read with sufficient accuracy and fluency to support comprehension" (NGA & CCSSO, 2010, pp. 16–17). Interestingly, the CCSS do not appear to expect fluent readings on the first reading of a text at any of the elementary-grade levels: "Read grade-level text orally with accuracy, appropriate rate, and expression on *successive readings*" (NGA & CCSSO, 2010, pp. 16–17, emphasis added). We find this interesting because it implies that texts need to be read multiple times in order to be comprehended, even as late as fifth grade. This is a rare instance in which it seems to us that the Standards have set the bar too low. We know that vocabulary, language skills, and the world knowledge upon which reading comprehension depend are built through broad reading. If students are expected to do a great deal of rereading, the breadth of their reading will likely be decreased, thereby affecting their opportunities to build language skills and world knowledge.

Fluency and ELs

For students who are learning English as an additional language, the relationship between reading fluency (as measured by WCPM) and reading comprehension is still apparent, but it is weaker than it is for native speakers of English (Crosson & Lesaux, 2010), and, not surprisingly, the strength of the relationship is dependent on the ELs' proficiency with the English language. Thus, for ELs with strong English language skills, an assessment of oral reading fluency is likely to be a better indicator of reading comprehension than it is for students with weaker English language skills. It is important to note that Quirk and Beem (2012) found that for many EL students there was a substantial gap between their status on a measure of reading fluency and their status on a measure of reading comprehension. Measures of WCPM are likely to overestimate text comprehension ability. That is, for example, students who appear to be reading at or above grade level on the fluency measure will likely perform more poorly on a measure of comprehension than would similarly fluent native English speakers. Thus it would seem that measures of fluency need to be interpreted with caution when considering the status of English language learners. Based on these findings, Schwanenflugel and Kuhn (2016) argue that the existing national norms for fluency are not valid for ELs.

Instruction to Promote the Prosodic Aspects of Fluency

The development of oral reading fluency depends on

- Having and using the ability to effectively puzzle through unfamiliar words encountered in context (the self-teaching mechanism we discussed in Chapter 12)
- Being able to automatically identify the most frequently occurring words (as discussed in Chapter 13)
- Knowing the meanings of most of the words encountered in given text (discussed in Chapter 15)
- Being familiar with the syntax and grammar of both spoken and written language (also discussed in Chapter 15), as such knowledge will influence the prosodic components of fluency
- Understanding that written language is supposed to make sense (discussed in Chapter 16).

There are multiple and widely accepted ways to support the development of reading fluency. The approaches basically entail a combination of modeling and practice with reading texts that present a limited amount of challenge.

Modeling

Reading aloud to children has multiple important benefits, many of which are discussed in Chapters 15 and 16. In this chapter we focus specifically on the role of reading aloud in promoting fluency. In order to understand what fluent reading should sound like, children need to hear text being read fluently. During a read-aloud, it is useful, on occasion, to draw the children's attention to the fluency of the reading. For example, at various times and depending on the book that is being read, the teacher might demonstrate how she or he notices and uses the ending punctuation or the difference between reading the text word by word versus in multiword phrases that make it easier to pay attention to the author's meaning.

When students are at a point in their own reading development at which the focus is shifting from a heavy emphasis on word identification and word learning to an emphasis on smooth, expressive reading, the teacher might, on occasion, have the children evaluate the teacher's fluency as she or he reads word by word or in multiword strings with pauses that are not aligned with the phrasal boundaries of the passage, or when she or he pays no attention to punctuation. The point of engaging in this type of activity is to draw the children's attention to the characteristics of appropriately expressive reading. Children generally think it is pretty funny when they get to evaluate whether or not their teacher is sounding like a storyteller and the experience may help them reflect on their own reading.

Choral Reading

In choral reading, the children are provided with both modeling and practice. This is a technique often used to support children in reading texts that are too challenging for them to read on their own. Often, the text is first read to the children by the teacher, sometimes more than once. Thereafter, the children are invited to read along with the teacher. Sometimes a single large-print version of a text is used. Examples of the kinds of texts often used include big books, poems, and language-experience stories that have been constructed by the class. When a single text is used, the print needs to be large enough for all students in the class to see. Smaller versions of texts can be enlarged using a document camera or interactive white board. The teacher points to the words as the class choral reads. These texts are often left available for the children to read with their friends during center or free-choice time.

Choral reading is also used when all of the students in the class or instructional group have their own copies of the text. Here, the teacher reads the text to the children one or more times before the children are invited to join in the reading. Then the children read the text, following along in their copies of it, generally pointing to the words as the group reads. The pointing is an important element here, especially for the students with more limited literacy skills. Without the pointing, the children can appear to be fully participating even if they are not attending to the printed words but just looking at their texts and echoing what they hear the other readers saying. The teacher monitors as the group reads to make sure that children are looking at the correct place in the text as they read and to redirect those children who are not doing so.

Repeated Reading versus Wide Reading

There was a time when it was believed that having children read texts repeatedly was the preferred way to build fluency, not only with the texts that were read repeatedly but with texts more generally (National Reading Panel, 2000). However, more recent reviews of the research literature suggest that it is the volume of reading that students do that is critical to fluency development, whether that volume is due to repeated readings or to wide reading. In our opinion, for beginning readers, there is value in engaging the children in some repeated reading, as noted above. However, as children develop their reading skills, we encourage wide reading because of its advantages to other aspects of literacy development, such as extending knowledge of word meanings and increasing world knowledge.

Supported Reading

Children learn to read by reading. The more reading they do, the more quickly they will become proficient. Pressley and Allington (2015) argue that the reading they do should consist primarily of texts in which their reading is highly accurate. However, to grow as readers, children must, of course, encounter texts in which they do not already know all of the words. High-accuracy reading for these students is the result of knowing many of the words in the texts they read and having the skills and strategies needed to figure out the not-yet-known words. In Part II of this text, we talked a lot about helping readers to develop skill with the alphabetic code that, in combination with the word identification strategies discussed in Chapter 12, will both enable this high-accuracy reading and help to extend children's sight vocabularies. Extending children's sight vocabularies, in turn, enables them to handle progressively more challenging texts.

Supported reading presents one of the main instructional contexts in which teachers have the opportunity to guide the application of developing skill with the alphabetic code and to encourage the development of the self-teaching mechanism. In Chapter 2, we suggested that in a classroom context the children with more limited literacy skills should spend more time in supported reading than their more skilled peers. The purpose is to provide the less skilled readers with greater opportunity to practice and receive guidance and feedback on the application of these skills and strategies—for the purpose of building their fluency.

Partner Practice/Buddy Reading

Teachers have limited time to spend with individual students and small groups. Therefore, to provide additional practice, children can be set to reading in pairs or small groups. When a child is in a context in which he or she needs to read aloud, he or she is more likely to attempt unfamiliar words. Further, a reader's partner may be able to provide assistance in the form of a suggested strategy that will lead to accurate word identification. In partner reading situations, children should be encouraged to first offer strategy support before providing the pronunciation of the unknown word. In such reading situations, children, in addition to taking turns reading the text to one another, should also be encouraged to react to and discuss the text. We must always strive to ensure that children perceive reading as a meaning-making enterprise.

Independent Practice

Beginning readers should have ready access to a collection of books and other texts (such as poems, brief articles from children's magazines, lyrics from songs, the chart texts that have been created) that they can read successfully. These would be books and texts that they have already read with guidance and support and/or books that are at or near their independent reading level. Reading should be a free-choice activity when the children have completed other work. Although some children may never opt for that choice, many will, especially if teachers are successful in portraying reading as an appealing activity rather than a job ("You *get* to read some of the books in our basket").

Reading for an Audience

Many students enjoy reading and rereading entertaining poems, nursery rhymes, plays, lyrics to popular music, and/or jump-rope rhymes for the purpose of performing for an audience. For example, for older struggling readers who are reluctant to read books that are at their instructional or independent level, and for students for whom fluency is a focal issue, we have found that, for the right purpose and audience, they are often willing to do so. Many second graders, for example, are happy to read and reread texts appropriate for beginning readers if their purpose is to record those texts to be used in the listening center in kindergarten. Many students are willing to engage in rereading if they know their reading will ultimately be recorded on an iPad or computer.

Evaluating and Documenting Children's Progress

Whenever a teacher listens to developing and maturing readers (as described in Chapter 2) read, attention should be paid to fluency using one of the 3 or 4 point scales described earlier in this chapter. In the teacher's lesson notes, she or he would record the name of the book and the fluency rating assigned along with information about whether it was a new read or a reread. When the rating assigned is something other than fluent, consideration should be given to whether lack of fluency was due to problems with accuracy, rate, phrasing, expression, or attention to punctuation. Figure 14.2 provides a snapshot for use in capturing aspects of the student's oral reading fluency. Ratings should be done based on reflection across the student's reading of at least a few texts read across a few lessons and should not be based on the reading of a single text. Also note that we are not suggesting that teachers do a count of WCPM when evaluating whether a student is reading at an appropriate rate. Rather, the point is for the teacher to determine whether, for the types of texts the students read, the rate was appropriate. Thus, for example, in reading an informational text about whales—which, for young children, would likely be packed with pictures and illustrations—it would be inappropriate for the child to read the text straight through without pausing to look at and learn from the pictures.

Group Snapshot—Oral Reading Fluency						
Student names						
Reads instructional level text with . . .	Acceptable accuracy					
	Appropriate pace					
	Appropriate phrasing					
	Appropriate expression					
Attends to punctuation						
Attends to author's signals for expression (e.g., all capital letters, italics, larger print)						

Key:

◻ *B—Beginning* indicates that instruction has addressed the objective but that the child has only a preliminary understanding or capability with regard to that particular objective.

⊠ *D—Developing* indicates that the child has some understanding of the objective but does not reliably demonstrate that understanding or capability or is not yet automatic (fluent) with the skill.

⊠ *P—Proficient* indicates that the child reliably and spontaneously demonstrates the understanding or capability.

FIGURE 14.2. Group snapshot for oral reading fluency.

CHAPTER 15

Vocabulary and Oral Language Development

> **MEANING CONSTRUCTION GOAL 2**
>
> The child will learn the meanings of new words encountered in instructional interactions and will be able to use the words conversationally. Further, the child's ability to understand and use complex grammatical structures will improve.

Reading is a language skill. Thus, to a great extent, this entire book is about language development. However, in this chapter we focus on the development of two aspects of language: knowledge of word meanings (vocabulary) and familiarity with sentence structure (syntax). We discuss both how these aspects of language develop during the primary grades and how they are related to reading development in the primary grades and beyond. Our major focus in this chapter is to help teachers to become attuned to the language challenges that children encounter while reading or listening to text and knowledgeable about methods of instruction that may help strengthen these critical language skills, particularly among children who struggle with literacy acquisition.

Language and Reading

There is a strong predictive relationship between language skills, especially vocabulary, measured in the preprimary and early primary grades and reading comprehension performance all the way through high school (Dickinson & Tabors,

2001; Cunningham & Stanovich, 1997; Gallagher, Frith, & Snowling, 2000; Sénéchal, Ouellette, & Rodney, 2006; for reviews, see Dickinson, McCabe, & Clark-Chiarelli, 2004, and Scarborough, 2001). That is, children who have relatively limited language skills when they are young are likely to have difficulty understanding the things that they read when they are older—even when they can identify all of the words effortlessly. The association between language skills and later reading comprehension is generally considered to be causal in nature and has led to calls for instituting efforts to improve early language skills in order to improve reading comprehension and academic performance more generally (e.g., Biemiller, 2006; Dickinson, McCabe, & Essex, 2006; Neuman, 2011).

Vocabulary knowledge and general language skills are strongly linked to children's home lives. Children arrive in kindergarten with very disparate experiences that, at least partially, account for their differing levels of vocabulary and language development. Children from low-income homes often have had more limited language experiences than children from more economically advantaged homes. In fact, Hart and Risley (1995) found that, on average, preschoolers from professional families experienced approximately 16 times more utterances per year than children from economically impoverished backgrounds. Further, Graves and Slater (1987) found that first graders from higher-income backgrounds knew the meanings of about twice as many words as those from lower-income backgrounds. Moreover, there is evidence that these early differences do not disappear. Low vocabulary knowledge relative to peers at the end of kindergarten typically means low vocabulary knowledge throughout schooling. This may, in part, be due to the fact that, at least until recently, there tends to be little emphasis on explicit vocabulary instruction in schools (Scott, Jamieson-Noel, & Asselin, 2003; Watts, 1995; Wright & Neuman, 2010). Further, research suggests that being in school does not seem to substantially affect vocabulary size. For example, one study found that January-born kindergartners (the oldest in their classes) had about the same size vocabulary as December-born first graders who were only a month older than the kindergartners but had been in school a year longer (Christian, Morrison, Frazier, & Massetti, 2000). Clearly, there is a need for teachers and schools to place greater emphasis on helping young children to develop greater breadth and depth of vocabulary knowledge.

Vocabulary and Language Development and the CCSS

The need to develop vocabulary and language skills is apparent throughout the CCSS. In order to be prepared for reading and understanding the complex texts that they will encounter as they move through the elementary grades and beyond, children need to have the language skills that comprehension of those texts require. The vocabulary acquisition and use standards for children in kindergarten through second grade call for attention to the development of language skills in three main categories:

1. "Determine or clarify the meaning of unknown and multiple-meaning words and phrases based on [grade-level] *reading and content*" (L.4; NGA & CCSSO, 2010, p. 27).
2. "Demonstrate understanding of word relationships and nuances in word meanings" ("with guidance and support from adults" in kindergarten and first grade) (L.5; NGA & CCSSO, 2010, p. 27).
3. "Use words and phrases acquired through conversations, reading and being read to, and responding to texts" (L.6; NGA & CCSSO, 2010, p. 27).

The inclusion of language standards in the CCSS will hopefully serve to make teachers more mindful of the important role that language plays in children's long-term learning and ultimate academic success and better able to plan how they go about providing instruction that supports language development, especially for children who enter school having had limited opportunities to acquire the vocabulary knowledge and language skills that are valued in academic settings. Thus, not only do we need to be concerned about expanding children's vocabulary in general, but we also need to be particularly mindful about helping them to develop academic vocabulary.

Vocabulary and Language Development and ELs

It is obviously beyond the scope of a single chapter in a text on early reading development to fully address the topic of vocabulary and language development for children who are learning English as an additional language. According to a 2011 U.S. Census Bureau report, the 10 most common languages other than English spoken in the United States, listed from most to least common, are Spanish, Chinese, Tagalog (the language of the Philippines), Vietnamese, French, German, Korean, Arabic, Russian, and Italian (Ryan, 2013). Taken together, the spoken forms of these languages vary from English in ways too numerous to address in the space available (to say nothing of the fact that we do not have the expertise to take on such a massive task!). Thankfully, Swan and Smith (2001), in their edited volume, have gathered, in one place, information on each of these languages that should help to inform teachers about the potential sources of confusion that ELs with given language backgrounds may encounter. We encourage teachers, especially those who teach concentrations of a given language group, to avail themselves of this resource.

Therefore, in this section we address what is known about how to support the development of English language proficiency among ELs. Claude Goldenberg, one of the most widely recognized experts on the education of ELs, offers three important principles that can help to guide instruction for ELs (Goldenberg, 2013, p. 5):

- Generally effective practices are likely to be effective with ELs.
- ELs require additional instructional supports.
- The home language can be used to promote academic development.

Beyond these general principles, Goldenberg (2013) reports that there is very little evidence that we know how to close the achievement gap that is typical in comparisons of ELs and their English-only peers. Given that there is a clear relationship between ELs' English proficiency and their academic achievement (Halle, Hair, Wandner, McNamara, & Chien, 2012), it is critical to support young ELs' development of proficiency with spoken English. This is a point highlighted in August and Shanahan's (2006) summary of the research on ELs: "Instruction in the key components of reading is necessary—but not sufficient—for teaching language-minority students to read and write proficiently in English. Oral proficiency in English is critical as well—but student performance suggests that it is often overlooked in instruction" (p. 4).

For the purpose of highlighting the need to attend to oral language development and usage among EL students as well as English-only students, the snapshot at the end of this chapter encourages teachers to consider multiple aspects of language development and usage. Further, in reflecting on students' language skills, teachers are encouraged to identify students who are in need of opportunities to extend their language skills and to provide opportunities for them to do so. These opportunities would include teacher–child and peer-to-peer engagements in extended conversations in various contexts, as described later in this chapter.

Vocabulary

Most of the words for which children know the meanings are learned in the context of conversations and/or through being read to and reading. The words are not learned through direct instruction provided by someone who has the specific intention of teaching their meanings. Although words certainly can be learned through purposeful instruction, children need to learn so many words that it would be virtually impossible for teachers (or anyone else) to specifically teach all of them. Therefore, teachers need to provide supportive contexts and strategies that will enable children to learn word meanings and that will generate enthusiasm for doing so. In addition, teachers can, and should, selectively teach and provide ongoing engagement with some words. Indeed, numerous studies demonstrate that direct and explicit teaching of word meanings has a positive impact on young children's vocabulary (e.g., Beck & McKeown, 2007; Coyne, McCoach, Loftus, Zipoli, & Kapp, 2009; Silverman, 2007a, 2007b). The basic premises of these instructional approaches are described later in this chapter.

Of course, knowing a word's meaning is not an "all-or-nothing" phenomenon. Gradations exist in knowledge of word meanings, with knowledge ranging from knowing nothing about a word to having elaborated knowledge of the word's meaning, how it relates to other words, being able to use it fluently and appropriately in conversation and in writing, and so forth. Ouellette (2006) suggests that deep knowledge of word meanings is the type of vocabulary knowledge that is most strongly related to reading comprehension. For most words, deep knowledge of meaning develops gradually through multiple encounters with the words in different contexts. In fact, Bloom (2000) suggests that children do not learn 10 words a day, as some estimates suggest (Nagy & Herman, 1987), but rather that they learn "one-hundredth of each of one thousand different words" (p. 25) each day. If Bloom's characterization is accurate, which we suspect it is, it becomes clear that vocabulary development is largely incidental and occurs through children's efforts to infer and refine the meanings of words as they participate in various language contexts. Teachers can assist in this incremental learning process by providing supportive language contexts for vocabulary acquisition and by being alert for occasions when children encounter words that are unfamiliar to them and providing explanations of those words. Of course, one of the most supportive contexts for vocabulary acquisition is engagement in making meaning of the texts that students read and that are read to them. Active meaning construction (discussed in Chapter 16) facilitates comprehension of the text, which, in turn, supports vocabulary development. For example, Cain and Oakhill (2011) report that students found to be poor comprehenders at age 8 experienced less growth in vocabulary knowledge by ages 11 and 14 than did students who were good comprehenders at age 8. This was true even though there were no differences between the poor and good comprehender groups in growth in sight vocabulary and word identification.

Syntax

Syntax is a component of grammar that involves knowledge of sentences and their structures (Fromkin, Rodman, & Hyams, 2003). For most people, syntactic knowledge is largely implicit. For example, people can generally identify when a sentence sounds right (e.g., *The boy found the dog*) and when a sentence does not sound right (e.g., *The boy found quickly*). However, explaining what's wrong with a sentence is often difficult (because knowledge of syntax is implicit rather than explicit). By the time children enter kindergarten, they generally have a fairly well-developed implicit grasp of the syntax of the language spoken in their homes. For example, the order of the words in their sentences and the types of words that follow one upon the other are likely to be quite like the sentence structures used by family members.

As children read, they rely heavily on their implicit syntactic knowledge to help them assemble the words they have read into the meaningful ideas that become the building blocks for their overall understanding of the text (see Chapters 1 and 16).

Vocabulary and Sight Vocabulary

In Part III, Word Learning, the focus was on the development of *sight vocabulary*—words that readers can identify automatically and in all contexts when they are seen in print. In this chapter, the focus is on *knowledge of word meanings*. When one knows the *meaning* of a word, it is considered to be in one's *vocabulary*. At early points in literacy development, the number of words in a child's vocabulary is much larger than the number of words in his or her *sight vocabulary*. That is, the child knows the meanings of many more words than he or she can read. For proficient readers, on the other hand, sight vocabulary and vocabulary are about the same size; these readers can read all of the words for which they know the meaning.

People sometimes confuse vocabulary and sight vocabulary when talking about developing readers. The distinction between the two is important, because it affects instructional decision making. Children's knowledge of word meanings (vocabulary), particularly if it is very limited, has the potential to influence the development of their sight vocabularies. As discussed in Part III, most items in children's sight vocabularies are learned through successful word-solving efforts. An important step in word solving involves confirming that the hypothesized pronunciation of a word constitutes a real word that fits the context in which it is encountered. If the hypothesized pronunciation is a real word that is not in a child's vocabulary, that child, if he or she has learned to be strategic in word solving, is apt to reject the hypothesized pronunciation. For example, in reading the sentence *He wore a plaid shirt,* the word-solving efforts of a child who does not know the meaning of the word *plaid* are likely to yield a pronunciation with a long-*a* sound. Realizing that *played* does not fit the context, the child would reject that pronunciation and perhaps try the short-*a* sound (being flexible with the vowels). This would yield the correct pronunciation, but the child would be unable to confirm it because the word is not in his or her vocabulary. The child might try a few more pronunciations, perhaps trying both the long and short sounds of the *i*, still to no avail. At this point it would be reasonable for the child to settle on one of the pronunciations and move on. However, this encounter with the unknown word will have served to disrupt the child's reading of the text and to undermine his or her confidence in his or her word-solving skills. Further, the child will have made no progress in adding the word to his or her sight vocabulary. This is just one of the many ways in which vocabulary development and reading development are reciprocally related—development in one influences development in the other. At least in the primary grades, teachers are encouraged to preview texts that children will be reading to identify words for which the children may not know the meaning. These words should be introduced and discussed with the children before they are asked to read the text.

Syntax also plays a role in the development of sight vocabulary. Thus, when children are "testing the fit" of a word's hypothesized pronunciation, one factor that would signal a poor fit is whether or not the sentence sounds right. If it does, the word's identity would be confirmed, and the word would be a step closer to being part of the student's sight vocabulary.

As with vocabulary, children vary in their syntactic competence, and that variation is at least partially related to their language experiences. The syntax in books is often quite different from, and more complex than, the syntax of everyday spoken language. Therefore, if children have had limited experience with being read to, they are likely to find book syntax challenging. Teachers and proficient readers are so familiar with book syntax that they may not recognize the challenge it poses for some children. Consider this excerpt from *The Turkey Girl* (Pollock, 1996) below:

> "Hear me, hear me, children of the Sun Father and Earth Mother, in four days time, before the harvest moon, the dance of the Sacred Bird will be held. It is fitting that you all attend."
> Murmurs of plans for the festival rippled throughout the crowd. (no page)

This book is a Zuni folktale that bears resemblance to the European folktale known as Cinderella, and young children are the intended audience. Children who have been read to widely and frequently and who have discussed such books with their reading partners will have encountered the types of syntactic structures (e.g., multiple embedded clauses and phrases) and gained experience in interpreting those structures. For children without such experience, the syntactic challenges provided by this portion of the text will be difficult or impossible to negotiate without assistance.

Even books written to be read by emergent and developing readers sometimes include challenging syntax that could interfere with word-solving attempts. For example, a book titled *Where Is the Queen?* (Minkoff, 1996) includes the following as part of the description of a queen's preparation for giving a ball: "First, she set the table for eating in the green room" (p. 4). The phrase *set the table for _eating_* is at odds with the more typical phrase *set the table for _dinner_* and may well confuse children and lead them to reject even an accurate decoding of the word. The more unfamiliar children are with the types of syntax encountered in books, the more likely they are to experience difficulty with such structures.

Much more is known about the role of vocabulary development in reading than is known about the role of syntactic knowledge. Therefore, this chapter focuses more on vocabulary than on syntax. However, this imbalance should not be taken as an indication that syntax is somehow less important than vocabulary. Further, because language skills are tightly interrelated, it is likely that whatever teachers do in the name of enabling children to expand their vocabularies is likely to promote children's syntactic development as well.

Instruction to Support Vocabulary Development

In working with the teachers who participated in the research on the effectiveness of the ISA, we addressed vocabulary development in three basic ways. First, we encouraged teachers to be generally attentive to the need to support vocabulary development among their students and to "think vocabulary" across the school day. Second, we encouraged them to explicitly teach and provide practice with a few "generally useful" words from each book they read during interactive read-alouds and to rely on instructional recommendations provided by Beck, McKeown, and Kucan (2002) in doing so. Third, we encouraged teachers to develop content-area concepts and vocabulary by immersing students in thematically organized units of study for the purpose of building the knowledge base upon which reading comprehension depends. Currently, while we certainly still stand by these instructional recommendations, we add our voices to the call for paying greater attention to the development of academic vocabulary, that is, the vocabulary encountered most

---

Academic Word List

The Academic Word List (AWL; Coxhead, 2000, 2011) was developed primarily for the purpose of supporting the vocabulary development of high school and college ELs in order to prepare them for successful college careers. The list consists of words that are used widely across multiple content areas in academically oriented texts. There are 570 word families on the list (a word family here is the root word and its various forms resulting from the addition of affixes [e.g., *approach, approachable, approached, approaches, approaching, unapproachable*]). The list is further broken down into 10 sublists, with the first sublist of 60 words containing the most frequently occurring of the word families. Words on this list include words such as *analyze, assume, benefit, distribute, create, indicate, proceed,* and *respond.* These and many other words on the list can certainly be meaningfully worked into both instructional and informal interactions with primary-grade children for the purpose of expanding their vocabularies. Over time, drawing on higher numbered lists as the children move through the elementary grades and beyond can serve to support the college and career readiness goals of the CCSS. (Even some of the words on the highest numbered sublist can be used in conversation with young children [e.g., *assemble, collapse, enormous, persist*]). These words are also likely to be found in many of the sophisticated texts that are used for read-aloud in the primary grades and can be targeted for explicit instructional focus following the read-aloud. The suggestion here is that, if the teacher uses more sophisticated vocabulary in routine interactions and instruction with children, the children are likely to acquire more sophisticated vocabulary and thus be more likely to accomplish the college and career readiness goals set by the CCSS.

(Note that the Coxhead Academic Word List is readily available at various sites on the Internet that can be found via a Google search.)

often in the academic content areas (such words as *identify, define,* and *analyze,* to name a few of the most frequent). In the remainder of this chapter, we discuss instruction to develop knowledge of words that have broad utility and other more general language skills.

Attention to Vocabulary All Day, Everyday

The goal of reducing the vocabulary gap that exists between more and less economically advantaged children and between ELs and their non-EL peers is unlikely to be accomplished if vocabulary instruction is relegated to a few minutes in the day during which it is explicitly delivered. Therefore, we encourage teachers to be mindful throughout the school day of the vocabulary challenges that children encounter (especially those children with the weakest language skills) and to be alert for opportunities to enhance children's development. This mindful approach entails engaging children in conversation as much as possible, providing multiple opportunities for children to engage in conversations with their peers, recognizing (and anticipating) when limitations in vocabulary might interfere with word solving, using vocabulary that has been explicitly taught while engaging in genuine conversations, and so on.

Television, Video, and Digital Resources to Support Vocabulary Development

As educational television, video, and other digital resources have become more widely available, researchers have been investigating the impact of the use of those resources on children's vocabulary development. There is substantial evidence that viewing educational television shows and videos can enhance vocabulary development, and this seems to be especially true for children who are learning English as an additional language (Silverman and Hines, 2009). Of course, this is not really a surprising finding, as actually seeing the undulating movements of a sea creature as it moves through the water will make the meaning of the word much more memorable than would an attempt by a teacher to explain undulation with hand gestures. It is important to point out here that, although the evidence to date supports video viewing as a supportive context for vocabulary learning, it does not suggest that, comparatively, it is more supportive than being read to (Silverman, 2013).

Research on the use of digital books to support vocabulary development has also yielded positive results, although teachers are cautioned to be selective in their use of digital texts, as some of the games and activities that accompany these texts have too much play value. This can result in children spending too much time engaged with the games and activities and too little time focused on the meaning of the text (Shamir, 2009). Thus, while the evidence base with regard to the use of television, video, and digital resources continues to expand, we encourage teachers to view these resources as important components of a multifaceted approach to vocabulary and language instruction that also includes discussion of texts read and listened to, explicit instruction focused on specific words, and, as children develop as readers, encouragement of broad reading across genres.

Explicit Vocabulary Instruction

Which Words Should Be Taught?

Unfortunately for teachers, vocabulary researchers are not in agreement about how to go about selecting words for vocabulary instruction. Beck and her colleagues (2002, 2013) suggested selecting words for instruction based on such characteristics as their utility and interest value. Biemiller (2006), on the other hand, argued that words tend to be acquired in a rough sequence and that instruction should respect this sequence. Thus, for children with limited vocabularies, from Biemiller's perspective, the words that are taught should be words that most children at that age already know. Neuman, Dwyer, Koh, and Wright (2007) suggest focusing on words that would help children access the knowledge in content areas (e.g., science, social studies, math). Consistent with this latter view and the emerging concern for developing academic vocabulary, Silverman and Hartranft (2015) suggest that teachers focus vocabulary instruction on words that are useful, that are not yet known by the children, that occur frequently in academic texts, and that are related to the content and/or other vocabulary words that the children are learning. A further consideration in choosing words to teach is the importance of understanding the meanings of particular words relative to the text or texts that the children will hear or read in the near future. If understanding a particular word is crucial to understanding the text, obviously that word should be taught either before the text is read or at the point where it is encountered in the text.

Research on vocabulary instruction is ongoing and may provide clearer guidance on how to select words for specific instruction. We think it is important for teachers to be aware of the differing views on the matter of word selection, as they may want to make different choices for different groups of children at different points in time. For example, in whole-class read-aloud contexts, if the text being read is intended to support a particular topic or theme that the class is learning about, some of the words selected for vocabulary instruction should be words that are related to the theme. On the other hand, if the text being read is part of an author study, it may make more sense to select words that are useful and interesting, following Beck et al.'s (2002, 2013) suggestions. For children with very limited vocabularies, additional vocabulary instruction in a small-group context is called for, and for these children it would make sense to draw on Biemiller's guidance. Of course, in addition to planned vocabulary instruction, teachers should be mindful of the need to promote vocabulary and language development throughout the course of the day. In fact, Pressley and Allington (2015) conclude that highly effective teachers teach vocabulary opportunistically; that is, they are aware of when children may not know the meanings of words, and they teach the meanings of the words as they come up.

Below we share the guidance we provided to teachers in the most recent ISA study (Scanlon et al., 2008, based on the work of Beck et al., 2002[1]). Beck and her colleagues (2002) divide words into three large groups, which they refer to as *tiers*.[2]

- *Tier One* consists of the most basic words (e.g., *house, boy, hand*) that rarely require instruction in school, at least for children who are native speakers of English.
- *Tier Two* consists of words that are relatively high in their frequency of usage by mature language users and that are useful in a variety of contexts (e.g., *remarkable, extraordinary, hesitant, pursue*). Beck et al. recommend explicitly teaching Tier Two words.
- *Tier Three* consists of words that are low in frequency of usage and whose application is typically limited to a specific domain (e.g., *stamen, voltage*). Instruction of these words, Beck et al. (2002) argue, is best left to occur in the content area when they are needed.

According to Beck et al. (2002), instructional emphasis should be placed on Tier Two words, because they are most likely to be useful to children in a variety of contexts and because children are likely to encounter them often enough that their meanings can be learned well.

Finally, Beck and her colleagues (2002) argue that children will learn new words more readily if they already have ways of expressing the concepts to which the new words refer. Thus, in learning these words, they are not learning entirely new concepts but more precise ways to refer to concepts that they already understand. Below is a list of Tier Two words and the expressions that children would be likely to use to refer to the concepts.

Tier Two words	Students' likely expressions
merchant	salesperson or clerk
required	have to
tend	take care of
	(Beck et al., 2002, p. 17)

---

[1] Note that there is a more recent edition of this book (Beck, McKeown, & Kucan, 2013) that elaborates on the approaches recommended in the first edition.

[2] Use of the word *tier* in this context has nothing to do with the use of the word *tier* in discussions of RTI.

Beck et al.'s Criteria for Tier Two Words

Teachers are encouraged to review reading materials prior to reading the texts with their students and to select a few words that will be used for focused instruction. The words should meet all three of the following criteria:

1. *Importance and utility*: Words that are characteristic of mature language users and appear frequently across a variety of domains.
2. *Instructional potential*: Words that can be worked with in a variety of ways so that students can build rich representations of them and of their connections to other words and concepts.
3. *Conceptual understanding*: Words for which students understand the general concept but which provide precision and specificity in describing the concept. (Beck et al., 2002, p. 19)

General Principles for Helping Children Learn Word Meanings

Beck et al. (2002), Graves (2006), and Silverman and Hartranft (2015) suggest a variety of ways that teachers can help children build their vocabularies and language skills. A listing of their combined recommendations is provided below, along with our commentary.

• *Provide a language-rich environment.* Children should have many opportunities throughout the course of the school day to talk and listen for both social and academic reasons. Further, they should be read to on a daily basis and provided with the opportunity to discuss things that are read.

• *Develop a fascination with learning and using more sophisticated words.* Young children tend to value what their teachers value (at least, if they like their teachers). If teachers express an interest in and a love of words, the children are likely to catch the excitement. In classrooms that focus on vocabulary development, we often hear teachers exclaiming "Isn't that a great word!" or "Oh! I love that word—let's put it in our Great Word Box!" or "Did you hear that word that Sara just used? It's one of our sparkle words!" In these same classrooms we also notice children asking about the meanings of words and being motivated to use more sophisticated words when speaking and writing.

• *Teach words by providing both definitional and contextual information.* Dictionary definitions are generally weak sources of information for children, particularly those with limited word knowledge and limited reading skill. Such definitions are often vague, circular, and cryptic (Beck et al., 2002). For example, the definition of the word *coax* is "to persuade or try to persuade by gentle urging or flattery" (*American Heritage Children's Dictionary*, 2003). Children who do not know the meaning of *coax* may also not know the meaning of the words *persuade, gentle, urging*, and/or *flattery*. Using a context in which the word occurs, such as the sentence in the book in which the word was first encountered, as the initial point of departure for teaching the word's meaning will help children to more readily understand the meaning. For example, if the word *coax* occurred in a book about a poorly behaved dog, in a sentence such as "Mom tried to *coax* the dog into the house," by the time the children encounter this word they are likely to already have a sense of what the mother and the dog are like and so will have both the broader context of the passage and the more immediate context of the sentence to help them learn the meaning of the word.

Promoting an Interest in Words

In my (JMS) reading groups, when we encounter a Tier Two word in our reading, we put the word on a sticky note (each group has its own section around the small room and a different colored sticky note). This simple act encourages students to become more word conscious, and it helps me be more mindful when planning my lessons to revisit specific vocabulary. Occasionally, if there are a few minutes left at the end of a lesson, we'll play a game in which a student selects a word from the wall and, by using pantomime, tries to get the other students to identify the word. These activities have generated enthusiasm about learning new vocabulary.

- *Explain the new words using words and concepts that the children already understand.* Children definitely know about *coaxing*, although they are unlikely to know the word.

- *Use "child-friendly" language.* For example, "To *coax* means to, in a nice way, get somebody to do something that he or she doesn't really want to do."

- *Provide multiple examples of how the new word might be used and use the word in a variety of contexts.* For example, after children encounter the word *coax* in a book, the teacher might say "This week I am going to try to *coax* you into keeping the cubby area neat" or "Salad is on the lunch menu today. I know some of you don't eat salad. Today I plan to try to *coax* you into trying it because it is tasty and good for you."

- *Teach groups of words that are related in meaningful ways.* In order to have a deep understanding of the meaning of a word, students need to know how the word relates and compares to other words. So, teaching multiple words relating to the same general meaning can provide opportunities to analyze word meanings more fully. Thus, for example, synonyms (words that mean the same or similar thing) and antonyms (words with opposite meanings) might be taught together. Synonyms for *coax* include *cajole, persuade,* and *entice.* Antonyms for *coax* include *command, demand*, and *force.* Children will learn the meanings of these words well if they use them in describing how they interact with their parents and friends and how characters in books interact.

• *Keep using new words so that they become a stable part of children's vocabularies.* Words whose meanings have been specifically taught will be retained better if they are revisited periodically. Teachers and students should use the words in their everyday interactions and in their writing. Many teachers who have instituted vocabulary instruction of this type have developed some method for reminding themselves of the words that have been taught. For example, some teachers keep a list of the words so that they can quickly refer to it. Others keep a word box or a word can with the individual words written on strips of paper, and they periodically draw out a few of the words and discuss their meanings with the students. In one school with which we have worked, a schoolwide effort to enhance vocabulary development was instituted. Each week there is a schoolwide word of the week, which the principal announces on Monday and then uses in his morning announcements for the rest of the week. Teachers have lists of the words of the week, and the words have been stenciled on the walls in the hallways. Everyone in the school is encouraged to incorporate these more sophisticated words in their interactions both during the week when they are introduced and thereafter.

"Isn't That Dreadful?"

One of the kindergarten intervention teachers (P. Connors) who was responsible for instigating the greater focus on vocabulary in the school mentioned above, which is a school that serves a high-needs population, tells the following story. One of her students reported to her on an incident that he had heard about on the television news. An elderly woman had been attacked and beaten for her pocketbook. Having conveyed the story to his teacher, the child concluded with "Isn't that dreadful?" *Dreadful* was a Tier Two word in his classroom. Clearly, the child owned it!

Interactive Read-Alouds and Conversations to Promote the Development of Vocabulary and Oral Language

Two basic techniques have been cited widely and consistently recommended by child language researchers (e.g., Biemiller & Boote, 2006; Dickinson et al., 2006; Dickinson & Smith, 1994; Whitehurst et al., 1994) as powerful ways to promote vocabulary knowledge and syntactic skills:

• Reading to children and engaging them in conversations about what is read.
• Engaging children in lots of conversations throughout the day.

Interactive Read-Alouds

Reading aloud to children and engaging them in conversations about what is read is a powerful tool for promoting vocabulary and literacy development more generally

---

A Great Read-Aloud Website

www.storylineonline.net is an online streaming video program featuring well-known actors reading children's books aloud. Accompanying activities and lesson ideas are included. Teachers who elect to use this resource are cautioned against simply turning the video on and leaving the children to view passively. These read-alouds can be made interactive by pausing the video periodically and engaging the children in discussion.

(e.g., Lennox, 2013; McGee & Schickedanz, 2007; Morrow & Gambrell, 2000). In fact, nearly all of the studies on ways to enhance vocabulary development in the primary grades have utilized read-alouds as a central component of the intervention (Biemiller & Boote, 2006). Graves (2006) reports that the most successful attempts at bolstering vocabulary come from interactive read-alouds. In this section we focus on the role of interactive read-alouds in enhancing vocabulary and oral language development. Read-alouds are, of course, useful in many other ways, including for the purpose of modeling and engaging children in the active construction of the meaning of text, for developing the background knowledge upon which comprehension depends (discussed in Chapter 16), and for providing a context in which children can—and often do—become captivated by books and thus develop and sustain their motivation to learn to read.

The major difference between an *interactive* read-aloud and a read-aloud is the expectation that, while reading the book, there will be extensive interaction between and among the teacher and the students and that the interaction will not all be directed and controlled by the teacher. Both the children and the teacher should have opportunities to ask and answer questions, to share their reactions and expectations, to revisit parts of the book, and so on.

Overactive Interactive Read-Alouds

In order to avoid total chaos during read-alouds, teachers need to have well-established routines and signals that let the children know when they need to quiet down so that individuals can be heard or that they need to stay on topics directly related to the book with which they are engaging. To quiet down the class, one teacher we know simply sits up a little straighter and folds her hands in her lap (i.e., she models silence). To ensure that an individual child is heard, she simply says, "Let's listen to what Alex is saying"—which is a much more collaborative and inviting statement than something like "Shh! Alex is talking!" When a child's comments venture too far from the topic at hand, she might say something like, "I see that this reminded you of your visit to the dentist, but right now that's not what we're talking about. Can you tell me (or a friend) more about going to the dentist during snack time?"

Selecting Books for Read-Alouds

A number of factors need to be considered in selecting books to read aloud to children in a classroom or small-group context. While sometimes a book might be read just for the pure enjoyment of it, virtually every book lends itself to helping teachers address some of the many curricular goals that they have for their students. In order to most effectively address those goals, some planning is required. At the very least, the teacher needs to be thoroughly familiar with a book before she reads it to students. Previewing a book for the purpose of determining how it might be used to enhance students' language development (only one of the goals that a teacher might have for a book), the teacher needs to think about the following considerations:

- The students
  o Will the text be interesting and engaging for the children in the instructional group?
  o What do they already know?
  o What are they ready to learn?
  o What are their interests?
- The classroom curriculum
  o How does the book fit with the topics and themes that have been and will be covered in language arts, science, social studies, and/or math?
  o How does the vocabulary in the book fit with other vocabulary words that have already been taught?
- The book
  o What kinds of language challenges does the book present?
  o What words and/or syntactic structures will need explanation or clarification?
  o How will those words and structures be explained?
  o Is the language so advanced relative to students' current language skills that they will feel overwhelmed?

Conducting Interactive Read-Alouds

Once a book has been selected for use, the teacher needs to plan how to use it. As part of this planning, the teacher needs to think about engaging the students in discussions of the book before, during, and after reading in order to take full advantage of all instructional opportunities that a read-aloud provides. Much of the discussion will revolve around the events and the information presented in the book (see the section on interactive read-alouds in Chapter 16). During these discussions, however, teachers have the opportunity to address vocabulary encountered in the book and some of the more complex syntactic structures. They also have the opportunity to encourage children to use more complete and ultimately more complex sentence structures and more sophisticated vocabulary in their conversations.

Instruction to Enhance Syntactic and Grammatical Skills

Clarification of potentially confusing syntactic structures generally takes the form of reading the segment of text, as stated by the author, and then restating that segment using a more familiar syntactic structure. For example, in the book *The Turkey Girl,* one of the pages starts with the following sentence: "The Turkey Girl caught the excitement, imagining herself dancing with the others" (Pollock, 1996, n.p.). Both phrases in this sentence use syntax that is different from the syntax that is likely to be used in everyday conversation, wherein we might say "The Turkey Girl got excited too and started to think about dancing with the others." The teacher might choose to simply restate the sentence, or she might read to the end of the page and then engage the children in a conversation about how the Turkey Girl was thinking and feeling and, at this point, explain the meaning of "caught the excitement." On a second or subsequent reading of this book, it probably would not be necessary to explain this particular syntactic structure again, but when the children hear it again, their syntactic competence will be slightly extended. When they hear other, similar structures such as "caught the spirit," they are more likely to understand them, too.

Instruction to Enhance Knowledge of Word Meanings during Interactive Read-Alouds

In any given book, there are likely to be a number of words for which the children do not know the meanings. These words cannot all be taught thoroughly. Rather, several might be explained incidentally while reading, with a few selected for more thorough instruction and discussion. Before meeting with students, the teacher should identify the words that will need explanation and plan child-friendly

---

Ambiguous Words

Many words in the English language carry more than one meaning. Examples include *can* (the container and the ability to do something) and *bank* (the side of a river or the place where money is stored). Further, if spelling is disregarded, as it must be in the context of read-alouds (since children cannot see the words), there are many more ambiguous word pairs. Examples include *herd/heard, higher/hire, flower/flour,* and so on. It is important to be mindful that ambiguous words may be responsible for creating confusion in young learners. Proficient readers generally access context-appropriate word meanings effortlessly. However, young children often don't, and confusion may be the result. If such a word occurs in a context that doesn't provide clarity regarding the intended meaning of the word, the teacher should be prepared to clarify things.

explanations for them. Words that will be the focus of more detailed discussion should be selected and instructional activities planned before the book is read to the group.

BEFORE READING

- Discuss critical vocabulary before beginning to read the text (e.g., "This book is about volcanoes. A volcano is a kind of mountain. It is a mountain that grows!").
- Ensure that children can pronounce the new word acceptably (e.g., "Let's all say that word, *volcano*"). This will help them store a phonological representation of the word in memory.

Why Not to Ask Children about the Meaning of a Word

In our observations of teachers conducting read-alouds, we have been surprised by how often they start by asking the children to provide the meaning for a word that they intend to teach about. For example, in preparing to read a book about octopi, they might ask: "Does anyone know what an octopus is?" The problem with starting out with a question like this is that, often, children will not know what the word is—which the teacher has apparently anticipated. However, many times in situations such as this, a child will offer a definition that is wide of the mark, thereby providing incorrect information to the other children in the group. Interestingly, often in these situations, the teacher will not come right out and indicate that the definition is incorrect. Instead, a teacher might say "Could be _____? Does anyone else have some ideas?" We view this type of instructional interaction as problematic because it allows the other children in the group to believe that what the first child offered is at least partially correct. As a result, the children who originally had no information about the concept now have faulty information, which may lead to confusion going forward. Our advice to teachers is that, if you think many of the children in the group will not know the meaning, provide the definition/explanation right from the start of the conversation (e.g., "Today in our new book we are going to be learning about an octopus. An octopus is . . . ").

DURING READING

- Encourage thoughtfulness about knowledge of word meanings. For example, the teacher might say, "Last year when I read this book to my first graders they didn't know what the word *extremely* meant in the sentence 'It was extremely hot.' It helps me be a better teacher when children tell me about words that they don't know. I hope you will tell me when you hear a word and you are not sure what it means."
- Stop and briefly explain or discuss the meanings of words that are novel for children but that they are likely to encounter in other contexts.

- On occasion, reread the portion of the text that includes the novel vocabulary item, but substitute a word that the children already know.
- When a child comments on or asks a question about an aspect of the text to which the new word could reasonably be applied or incorporated, encourage him or her to use the newly introduced word (or the teacher can use it in responding to the inquiry).
- Notice when children use the new words and celebrate. ("Ah! You are already using that new word we learned! Great!")

AFTER READING

- Review the meanings of new words that were explicitly taught either before or during the reading of the text. Children need multiple exposures to words in order for them to become part of their useable vocabulary.
- After the words have been introduced, the teacher should look for multiple opportunities both to use them in her or his own speech and to encourage children to use them in speaking and writing.
- Some texts introduce enough new words that it is reasonable to compare and contrast the new words after reading the text.
- Have children think of other words they may know that mean the same thing, or almost the same thing, as the new words encountered in the text.
- Continue to notice and celebrate the use of newly acquired words.

Beck et al. (2002, 2013) provide specific recommendations for helping children establish new vocabulary after a text has been read. These recommendations follow.

- Present the word in the context in which it occurs in the story.
- Ask the children to repeat the word to help them establish a phonological representation of it.
- Explain the meaning of the word.
- Provide examples of the word's usage other than the one used in the story.
- Have the children interact with the examples or provide their own examples.
- Have the children say the word again to reinforce its phonological representation.

The guidance provided is very similar to more recent guidance offered by Silverman and Hartranft (2015), with the exception that they suggest that the words that are being taught be presented in printed form. The logic is that doing so may help the children to remember the word better. They suggest that, even in kindergarten, many children will be able to attend to some of the letters and sounds, thus making the printed word somewhat more familiar and perhaps helping to extend and reinforce the knowledge of the alphabetic code.

Sample Instructional Dialogue
for Teaching the Meaning of the Word *Fierce*

Following is a sample instructional dialogue taken from video of D. Rutnik, one of the teachers who participated in the Scanlon et al. (2008) study. Using the procedure described by Beck et al. (2002), she was implementing explicit vocabulary instruction following a read-aloud of the book *Swimmy* (Lionni, 1963). The focus of this vignette is on the word *fierce*, which occurred in the context of the book.

TEACHER: In the story it said, "One bad day, a tuna fish, swift, *fierce*, and very hungry, came darting through the waves." The word I want to talk about is *fierce*. Say the word with me—*fierce*.

STUDENTS: (*Say the word.*)

TEACHER: When something is *fierce*, it is very powerful and strong. We have had some really bad weather lately, with lots of very hard rain and very *fierce* winds. The winds were very, very strong. Show me how they were blowing.

TEACHER AND STUDENTS: (*Move arms to demonstrate strong, powerful, indeed, fierce winds.*)

TEACHER: Tell me something you know that might be *fierce*. Try to use the word *fierce* when you tell about it.

STUDENT: A fierce shark!!!

TEACHER: Yes, a fierce shark. *Fierce* means strong and powerful, in a mean kind of a way. (*Several children were given the opportunity to use the word, and the teacher commented on and clarified usage for each one.*) You might want to use the word *fierce* today when you are talking or writing.

TEACHER: Let's say the word *fierce* again.

STUDENTS: (*Say the word.*)

Helping Children to Effectively Learn Words from Context

Clearly, children will not always have a supportive adult available to help them learn the meanings of new words. As noted previously, most words are learned from context. For this reason it is helpful to provide children with guidance on how to try to figure out the meanings of words encountered in context. Graves (2006) offers some suggestions with regard to helping students at least get an approximate idea of a word's meaning. He suggests that teachers start by helping students understand that context *may* provide hints or clues about a word's meaning. If the reader does some thinking, he or she may be able to generate a hypothesis about what the word means. A better understanding of the word's meaning may come if the reader is persistent and continues to look for clues about the word in other contexts. Graves (2006, p. 99) suggests that it is useful for readers to do the following:

- Monitor whether what they are reading makes sense.
- Slow down when they don't know the meaning of a word.
- Reread the sentence that is causing confusion and the previous sentence, looking for clues to word meaning.
- Make their best guess at the meaning of the unknown word, substitute the hypothesized word meaning, and then read the sentence to see if it makes sense.

Teachers can model the process of using context to infer word meanings during the course of interactive read-alouds. For example, we observed a teacher reading the Beatrix Potter book *The Tale of Peter Rabbit* (Potter, 2002) to her class. One line of text read "Now run along, and don't get into any mischief." One of the children piped up and asked "What does *mischief* mean?" (a sure sign that this teacher had successfully developed an interest in words among her students). Rather than explaining the word to the children, the teacher said, "Let's see if we can figure it out." She then went back to the beginning of the paragraph and reread. After reviewing what had happened up to that point, children hypothesized that the word *mischief* might mean *trouble*. The teacher then reread the sentence, substituting the word *trouble* so that the children could decide whether *trouble* made sense in the sentence. They concluded that it did, and therefore decided that *mischief* probably meant something like *trouble*.

In this example, it was possible for the children to effectively infer the meaning of the word. However, there are many instances in which context is not helpful or may be downright misleading. It is important to be clear with children that context is not always helpful. Beck et al. (2002) describe a continuum of contexts from directive to misdirective. They offer the following as an example of a context that might actually serve to move children toward an incorrect meaning of the word *grudgingly*:

> Sandra had won the dance contest, and the audience's cheers brought her to the stage for an encore. "Every step she takes is so perfect and graceful," Ginny said *grudgingly* as she watched Sandra dance. (p. 4)

If students make hypotheses about word meanings in contexts that are not supportive, the result may be an inaccurate or confused understanding of the words. Future encounters with the same words may, however, serve to correct and refine their meaning. This again supports the notion that students need to encounter words in a wide variety of contexts in order to develop rich and accurate understandings of their meanings. Learning word meanings without explicit instruction is very much an incremental process.

Additional Suggestions for Learning Word Meanings

WORD PARTS

As described in Chapter 11, many words consist of a root word and one or more affixes (prefixes and suffixes). In that chapter the focus was on helping children to learn how to puzzle through and infer the meaning of printed words composed of more than one meaningful part. But, of course, children encounter words with prefixes and suffixes in read-aloud contexts and in everyday spoken language. Therefore, teachers can begin to develop children's sensitivity to morphology even before they can read any words independently. For example, with all of the tying, untying, and retying of shoes that goes on in kindergarten, why not take the opportunity to focus on the prefixes *un* and *re* and help the children to become aware of their use in other contexts, such as buttoning, zipping, and doing?

DICTIONARIES

As children gain proficiency in reading, dictionaries can sometimes be useful to them in learning about the meanings of words they encounter while reading. Children should be encouraged to look up words and then consider the definitions they find in light of the contexts in which the words were first encountered. Children's dictionaries should be made available for this purpose. A particularly useful dictionary is the *Collins COBUILD Student's Dictionary Plus Grammar* (2005). This dictionary focuses on words that occur over and over again in spoken and written English; detailed entries provide multiple examples and include the use of the words within the context of a complete sentence.

Children who have access to the proper technologies can be encouraged to use one of several online dictionaries intended for children. Examples include:

The Word Central Student Dictionary—*www.wordcentral.com/*
Kids' Wordsmyth—*http://kids.wordsmyth.net/we/*

Such dictionaries have the added advantage of providing pronunciations of the words.

GLOSSARIES AND OTHER TEXT CONVENTIONS

Nonfiction books often provide explicit definitions of important words introduced in their texts. The important words are often signaled by boldface font in the text. Children need to be alert to this convention for signaling importance and to look for the definitions that may be provided either in the same section of text where the word is first encountered, in a text box or illustration on the same page, or in a glossary at the end of a text.

Conversations

Discussions between teachers and students and among students provide important opportunities for language development. Some children have had few experiences with conversing and so may need some explicit modeling and coaching relating to how to engage in conversations. In the primary grades, snack time can provide a useful opportunity to model and engage children in conversations because the teacher can focus on a small number of children and engage them in more extended conversations than would be possible or appropriate if the entire class were expected to participate.

Promoting Conversation during Snack Time

In my school (JMS), one of the kindergarten teachers (G. Mahan) has an independent center for snack, which works out well and lends itself to authentic conversations and problem-solving opportunities. In the beginning of the year, before centers start, there is extensive modeling of what conversation should look and sound like: turn taking and practice with possible problem-solving scenarios like spilled milk, opening containers, and so forth.

The accumulated research on classroom supports for language development (see Dickinson et al., 2004, for a review) suggests that conversations across instructional contexts are especially helpful when:

- *The children are given the opportunity to do a lot of the talking.*

- *There are several conversational turns between the children and their conversation partners.* Some researchers have observed that it is rare for children in classroom settings to engage in true conversations in which the participants have more than one or two turns each (see Snow et al., 1998). In classrooms in which more extended conversations occur, children's language develops at a faster rate.

- *The child's responses are more than single-word utterances.* Teachers encourage the use of longer and more complex sentences by asking open-ended questions. These are questions that call for more than a one-word response. Thus, instead of asking "Did you like the movie?" which calls for a "yes" or "no" response, the teacher might say "Tell me about the movie" or "Tell me what you liked about the movie."

- *Teachers restate answers or comments made by children that do not represent well-formed sentences,* especially when well-formed sentences are called for. This can be especially helpful for ELs. Restatements should be made in the form of elaborations and comments on what students say and should *not* come across as corrections of students' language. For example, if the student says "He a big one!" the teacher might say "Yes, he *is* a big one!", with the emphasis on the word *is* suggesting agreement rather than correction. The hope is that providing students with opportunities to hear their thoughts expressed using standard syntax will help them develop skill with that syntax.

- *Teachers elaborate on a student's statement* by using a somewhat more complex syntactic structure than the structure used by the student. For example, if the student says "The dog is sad," the teacher might agree by saying "Yes, the dog does seem to be sad" and extend the conversation by asking "Why do you think that he's feeling sad?"

- *Teachers occasionally notice and comment on children's use of using well-formed sentences* (e.g., "What a nice sentence that was!").

- *Teachers do not talk down to children.* When adults use mature vocabulary and more sophisticated syntax (within reason), children have more opportunities to advance their language skills. For example, in noting what a child is eating at snack time, the teacher might say "My! That looks absolutely scrumptious!" rather than "That looks good!"

- *Conversations often focus on nonpresent topics and pretend play* (e.g., what the child did yesterday, what the child saw on a field trip, who is going to play what role in the housekeeping area). Such conversations call for more explicit language because the child cannot rely on shared knowledge in the same way as is possible when talking about an immediate experience in which both conversation partners are involved. Experience and support with such decontextualized language helps to prepare children for the world of print, which requires them to think beyond the here and now.

There are, of course, many ways to encourage conversations among students. A few are described next.

"Describe and Guess"

"Describe and guess" is a group-sharing activity in which one child describes an item that is kept out of sight. The other students ask questions about the item and try to guess what it is, based on the description. When children (and adults) are describing things that are not visible, they have to use more sophisticated language. They cannot just point, and they cannot assume that others know what they are talking about. As compared with the more traditional show and tell, describe and guess promotes more complex language on the part of the child doing the describing and on the part of the children doing the guessing as they refine their questions in attempts to solicit the information needed to make an accurate guess.

Sociodramatic Play

Research summarized by Snow et al. (1998) indicates that participation in socio-dramatic play increases oral language use because such play typically requires a good deal of negotiation among the children as they determine who will play what role, how the storyline will unfold, whether events are unfolding as planned, and so on. Research has also found that, for the purpose of promoting the development of reading and writing skills, play settings are more attractive and engaging to children when they represent authentic literacy contexts in the children's real-world environment. In other words, children seem to play best at what they know. Their play will be more complex and involved in, for example, a housekeeping or grocery store setting than in a bank or post office setting because, for most children, the latter two are comparatively unfamiliar contexts. (See Morrow and Schickedanz, 2006, for a review of the relationship between sociodramatic play and literacy development in early childhood.)

There is also evidence that, in settings in which there are more literacy arti-facts, children engage in more literacy acts, and the acts tend to become more com-plex over time (Neuman & Roskos, 1993). Thus pretend play settings should be well supplied with literacy props such as notepads, pencils, markers, cookbooks, recipe cards, magazines, newspapers, labeled food packages, message boards, envelopes, stamps, tape, and, if possible, a computer—or even a nonfunctioning computer keyboard.

Many children who enter school with limited language skills will have had limited verbal interactions and/or limited experiences with these kinds of props and/or with sociodramatic play prior to entering school. Therefore, for them, it will be important for the teacher to model and provide guidance and feedback across these contexts.

Cooperative Projects

When children work together to accomplish a common goal, they generally need to do a good deal of conversing in order to clarify aspects of what needs to be done, to negotiate roles and responsibilities, to evaluate progress toward the intended goal, and so on. Cooperative projects might include conducting and documenting the results of science experiments, gathering information about the local community and preparing and sharing what was learned, writing a book on a topic of mutual interest, and so forth. Cooperative projects are especially useful for encouraging language development among children who are past the point of engaging in socio-dramatic play in the classroom.

Share Your Thinking

This is a form of "every student response." During whole-class and small-group instruction, only one child gets to talk at a time if the teacher leads every discussion. If teachers frequently ask children to turn to their neighbors or to partners at their tables and talk about whatever the topic is, all of the children will have more opportunity to engage in conversation. This approach is becoming more and more common in the context of interactive read-alouds and is often referred to as "think, pair, share" (Lyman, 1981). However, virtually any context that might lend itself to a classroom conversation can incorporate opportunities for children to share their thinking with one another.

Evaluating and Documenting Children's Progress

Figure 15.1 provides a record form for documenting teachers' observations of children's status with regard to knowledge and acquisition of word meanings, children's interest in and use of language, and their status related to the sentence structure. Children who rarely or only sometimes appear to demonstrate the language behaviors described will likely benefit from having increased opportunities to work in small-group and one-on-one situations wherein they are exposed to extended opportunities to engage in conversations focused on books read or heard and in planned and supported activities intended to promote the development of expressive and receptive language skills.

Group Snapshot—Observation of Vocabulary (Word Meaning) and Language Development					
Student names					
Seems to understand the meanings of words at an age-appropriate level.					
Uses newly taught/learned words conversationally.					
Is eager to use spoken language to communicate.					
Asks to have word meanings explained.					
Asks for clarification when confused by a statement.					
Uses complete sentences.					
Uses standard sentence structures.					
Uses standard inflectional endings for plurals, first-person singular verbs, and past-tense verbs.					
Engages in sustained conversations.					

Key:

R = Rarely   S = Sometimes   F = Frequently   A = Always or almost always

FIGURE 15.1. Group snapshot for vocabulary and language development.

CHAPTER 16

Comprehension and General Knowledge

MEANING CONSTRUCTION GOAL 3

The child will develop the foundational knowledge and comprehension skills and strategies that will enhance his/her ability to construct the meaning of, and learn from, texts heard or read.

The Process of Comprehension

Comprehension occurs as the reader builds a mental representation of the text (Perfetti et al., 2005). Comprehension is an active, constructive process in which the ultimate understanding of the text is determined by the integration of what is stated directly in the text and the reader's preexisting knowledge related to the topic of the text (Kintsch, 1998). That understanding is reflected in the wording of the meaning construction goal above. The instructional goal is to help children to both develop the knowledge upon which comprehension depends and to become self-regulated learners who are motivated to understand the texts they read and hear and who, therefore, notice when things are not making sense to them and take action to resolve the confusion that arises. Thus instruction to foster comprehension goes beyond helping children comprehend a particular text at a particular point in time to helping them develop productive ways of thinking about texts that will enhance their comprehension of texts they encounter in the future.

Active Meaning Construction

In the following example, we provide the reader with the opportunity to become conscious of the type of active meaning construction in which proficient readers engage. The example is three sentences long. After reading each sentence, the reader should stop and think about the main character a bit.

Sentence 1: Sam walked slowly on the way to school.

(Stop and think.)

Sentence 2: She was worried about today's math test.

(Stop and think.)

Sentence 3: While walking, she wondered how she could be more effective in helping her students understand place value.

Most readers who participate in this exercise find that their thinking changes quite radically from one sentence to the next. Many think *Sam* is a young boy in the first sentence and make attributions about the reasons for his slow pace—some think he doesn't like school, others suggest that he does most things slowly. Often people have an image of Sam and the setting in which he is walking. Upon reading the second sentence, many readers immediately alter their interpretation of the first sentence: Sam is now an older girl. The gender change is due to the pronoun *she*, and the age change is due to the fact that young children are less likely to be worried about math tests. Readers now attribute the slow pace to anxiety about the test or the desire to avoid it. After reading the third sentence, readers' perceptions of Sam again change radically—Sam is now a teacher rather than a student, and she takes on an entirely different set of characteristics in readers' minds.

This illustration demonstrates that active and engaged readers integrate information directly stated in the text with their existing knowledge to "fill in the gaps" left by the author and then to go well beyond the information directly stated in the text. Further, they shift their thinking about a text as they encounter new information that doesn't fit with their unfolding interpretation of it. Essentially, proficient readers expect the texts they encounter to be coherent, and they interact with those texts in efforts to make them so. Thus, when things don't make sense, proficient readers change their thinking or reread the text to seek clarification—or, more commonly, do both in an iterative fashion until the confusion is resolved. Often, proficient readers take all of these steps without being conscious of them. Mostly they are just thinking about the text, not their approach to comprehending it, unless, of course, the process has been purposefully slowed (as we have done in the example above).

Constructing and Reconstructing Meaning

The active, fluent construction and revision of the meaning of the text that proficient readers experience when reading the example of Sam represent the kind of comprehension processing that we would ultimately like to see all readers achieve. Such an achievement requires that they (1) know something about the topic of the passage they are reading, (2) access that information, (3) recognize when things don't make sense, and (4) be willing to exert the cognitive effort it takes to revise their thinking about the text.

Levels of Comprehension

In constructing the meaning of a text, readers may engage in different types or *levels* of thinking. Three levels of comprehension are typically identified: literal, inferential, and critical.

- *Literal comprehension* involves the understanding of information stated directly in the text. Examples of literal comprehension from the Sam example include knowing that:
  - Sam walked slowly.
  - Sam was worried.
  - There is a math test today.

- *Inferential comprehension* involves making inferences that bridge the information directly stated in the text with information that the reader already possesses. Effective readers draw on their knowledge to make inferences that fill in the gaps left by the author; ineffective readers fail to do so (Yuill & Oakhill, 1991). Early in the Sam example, the reader is left to make inferences about:
  - Sam's age.
  - Sam's gender.
  - Sam's reasons for walking slowly and for worrying.

- *Critical comprehension* involves evaluating the information in the text relative to what it means to the reader and relative to the intentions, expertise, and/or perspective of the author. In the Sam text, the reader is likely to conclude that the author developed the text with the intention of misleading the reader and might read additional text by the same author with this in mind.

Research suggests that children who struggle with comprehension, but not with decoding, differ from their abler peers primarily in their ability to engage in inferential thinking (see Perfetti et al., 2005, for a review). The reasons for this difficulty are still being researched. However, Yuill and Oakhill (1991) suggest several possibilities, including that less skilled comprehenders (1) do not have the knowledge needed to make the necessary inferences, (2) do not know when it is appropriate to make inferences, and/or (3) have processing limitations that interfere with their ability to integrate text information with prior knowledge. Cain and Oakhill (1999) also suggest that failure to make inferences may be attributable to a focus on reading the words in the text rather than on deriving a coherent understanding of the text. Clearly, all of these possibilities could play a role in limiting comprehension, and most of them are at least partially amenable to instructional interventions. In what follows, we describe the types of knowledge sources that need to be developed and describe how interactions with texts, particularly in the context of interactive read-alouds, can help to promote the type of active thinking about text that needs to be established in order to enable the inferential thinking that is so critical to comprehension.

Knowledge and Comprehension

World knowledge is an essential component of reading comprehension, because every text takes for granted the readers' familiarity with a whole range of unspoken and unwritten facts about the cultural and natural world. (Hirsch, 2003, p. 28).

When an individual listens to or reads a text, a complex interaction takes place between what the individual already knows and what is presented in the text. Thus differences between individuals in the amount of text-relevant knowledge they bring to a reading task will have a substantial influence on their ability to make the required inferences and to comprehend the text (e.g., Kendeou & O'Brien, 2016). For example, someone who has taken a college chemistry class will learn more from reading an article about some aspect of biochemical engineering than will someone who has no background in chemistry. In fact, if someone with no background knowledge persists with the reading at all, he or she is likely to read the text quite passively and with little expectation of understanding. If, on the other hand, a biochemical engineer were to read the article, he or she is likely to learn much more than the individual with only college chemistry, because he or she is more thoroughly versed in the terminology and concepts and in how various biochemical processes work. Before even beginning to read the article, though, the biochemical engineer is likely to consider the quality of the journal in which it was published and the credentials of the author(s) in order to determine whether the article is likely to provide trustworthy information and therefore warrant the time to read it. If the engineer does decide to read it, he or she is likely to read very actively and to begin forming hypotheses and questions about what will be learned even before he or she has finished reading the title (Anderson & Pearson, 1984). While reading, the engineer is likely to think actively about the content and to compare it to what he or she already knows about the topic. If there are discrepancies between his or her knowledge and the information presented in the text, the engineer may change his or her thinking on the topic, reject the new information, and/or decide that there is a need to seek out further information so that he or she can be more confident in the interpretation of the topic of the text.

Types of Knowledge that Influence Comprehension

As illustrated above, how one interprets a text and what one learns from a text depends, to a great extent, on what one already knows. Several types of knowledge play a part in comprehension, including general world knowledge, topic-specific knowledge, schematic knowledge, and genre knowledge. Although the various types of knowledge clearly overlap, it is useful to consider them individually, because they carry somewhat different instructional implications. Each of the knowledge types is discussed next.

General Knowledge

General knowledge is sometimes referred to as *world knowledge, background knowledge,* or *prior knowledge.* This is an overarching term that encompasses the other types of knowledge described here. General knowledge incorporates the facts and concepts that an individual "knows" and includes the interrelations among more isolated bits of knowledge. General knowledge accumulates over time, often in small increments. This type of knowledge would include the knowledge that readers draw on when they infer, in the Sam example, that Sam is a boy because most people named *Sam* are male; this type of knowledge is not explicitly taught. General knowledge would also include the knowledge that the engineer drew upon in evaluating the credentials of the author and the quality of the journal in which the article appears. This kind of knowledge might or might not be taught explicitly.

In working with young children, teachers should try to be alert for general knowledge gaps that may interfere with children's ability to understand instructional interactions. Knowledge of word meanings is one general area in which this will be an issue. However, there are a myriad of other points of confusion that can arise because children lack specific bits of information that the teacher assumes they have.

Topic-Specific Knowledge

Topic-specific knowledge refers to knowledge that relates directly to topics covered in a text. Thus, for example, the engineer had a good deal of topic-specific knowledge that would give him or her an advantage in reading a research article that addresses a problem in biochemical engineering. The individual who had never even taken a chemistry course, on the other hand, would probably have very little topic-specific knowledge to assist in reading the article. The individual with just one course in chemistry is somewhere in between. As this example illus-trates, having topic-specific knowledge is generally not an all-or-nothing matter. For any given topic, individuals vary along a continuum ranging from little or no knowledge to a level of expertise that requires a substantial investment of time and energy to acquire. Individuals can also possess incorrect knowledge and, when this is the case, that knowledge can seriously interfere with one's ability to gain new, correct knowledge (Kendeou & O'Brien, 2016).

During the course of the elementary years and beyond, children are expected to become knowledgeable about many social studies and science topics. In the early primary grades, engaging children in read-alouds of informational books on topics that will be revisited in later grades will help to prepare them for content they will be expected to master.

Schematic Knowledge

Schematic knowledge refers to knowledge that is structured and organized. Because individuals encounter so many, many bits of information in a typical day, it would be impossible to store and retrieve much of the information unless it were orga-nized in some way. An individual's *schemas* affect how one perceives, notices, and interprets information (Anderson, 1984). For example, most of us have a school schema that was probably activated in reading the Sam example. Although each individual's school schema is likely to be somewhat unique, there are likely to be some commonalities for those who have experienced typical American educational settings—such as a school having multiple classrooms with each classroom having children of similar ages, a teacher, work surfaces and chairs, books, and so forth. Incorporated in the school schema are likely to be schemas for student and teacher, which were also activated in the Sam example.

Having a schema related to the topic plays a big role in facilitating one's under-standing of a text. For example, understanding the following text is challenging for most people:

> The procedure is actually quite simple. First, you arrange things into different groups. Of course, one pile may be sufficient depending on how much there is to do. If you have to go somewhere else due to lack of facilities, that is the next step; otherwise, you are pretty well set. It is important not to overdo things. That is, it is better to do too few things at once than too many. In the short run this may not seem important but complications can easily arise. A mistake can be expensive as well. At first, the whole procedure will seem complicated. Soon, however, it will become just another fact of life. It is difficult to foresee any end to the necessity for this task in the immediate future, but then one can never tell. After the pro-cedure is completed one arranges the materials into different groups again. Then they can be put into their appropriate places. Eventually they will be used once more and the whole cycle will then have to be repeated. However, that is a part of life. (Bransford & Johnson, 1972, p. 722)

The authors of the passage intended it to be ambiguous and challenging to understand in order to evaluate the extent to which schemas influence comprehension. And, indeed, most proficient readers find it difficult to retell or summarize the passage after reading it. However, readers who were given the title of the text, "Washing Clothes," activated the proper schema and found it much easier to comprehend. Thus, without any changes in the text, the reader who knew the title would know that the *things* and *materials* were items of clothing, and that *facilities* referred to washers and dryers. The expensive mistake is also perfectly comprehensible. Clearly, having an appropriate schema relevant to the text and activating that schema are both important to the comprehension process. Book introductions can help children to activate relevant schemas and thus facilitate richer comprehension of a text. In fact, as noted in the example above, even just providing a descriptive title for a book can make a big difference in the reader's ability to integrate the information in the text and make the necessary inferences.

Genre Knowledge

Genre knowledge is a specific type of schematic knowledge that involves understanding the characteristics of different categories of text. *Fiction* and *nonfiction* represent major subdivisions relative to text structures, and each type carries different expectations for the reader. For example, fiction is meant to entertain and not to be factual, whereas nonfiction is meant to be believed and may or may not have entertainment as a purpose. Within each of these major subdivisions are several genres that have characteristic features that, if understood, may help the reader more readily comprehend a text. For example, narrative stories tend to follow the structure of a story grammar in which the author provides information about the setting, the characters, one or more problems, the characters' attempts to solve the problems, and the resolutions. Children who are familiar with this genre and its characteristics are likely to read or listen to the text with an expectation that these story elements will be provided by the author, and they are therefore apt to read the text in a more active way. Knowing the characteristics of informational text, on the other hand, would lead to a different set of expectations.

Comprehension and Knowledge and the CCSS

The CCSS document has the clearly articulated purpose of systematically building knowledge to facilitate comprehension:

> Building knowledge systematically in English language arts is like giving children various pieces of a puzzle in each grade that, over time, will form one big picture. . . . texts—within and across grade levels—need to be selected around topics or themes that systematically develop the knowledge base of students. . . .

children in the early grades (particularly K–2) should participate in rich, structured conversations with an adult in response to the written texts that are read aloud, orally comparing and contrasting as well as analyzing and synthesizing, in the manner called for by the Standards. . . .

Having students listen to informational read-alouds in the early grades helps lay the necessary foundation for students' reading and understanding of increasingly complex texts on their own in subsequent grades. (NGA & CCSSO, 2010, p. 33)

The commitment to build knowledge is also evident in the expectation that children in the primary grades will be exposed to much more informational text than was the tradition prior to the adoption of the Standards. In addition, the speaking and listening standards emphasize that comprehension and knowledge building is not an individual and isolated undertaking but rather a social practice that involves conversation with teachers, peers, and others and active processing and sharing of newly encountered information, including seeking clarification when comprehension is uncertain.

In this chapter we address aspects of the reading standards for both literature and informational texts through our focus on having children be actively engaged in thinking and talking about the texts that they hear and read. We also address many of the speaking and listening standards for K–2 in describing the types of discussions that should be occurring concerning the books they encounter.

Comprehension and Knowledge and ELs

In a review of the studies that evaluated approaches to improving EL students' reading comprehension, August et al. (2014) report that approaches that work for students who speak English only also improve outcomes for ELs. These approaches included such things as increasing the availability of books in the classroom, coupled with rereading books at home with audio recordings as models (Koskinen et al., 2000) and increasing the emphasis placed on discussion of texts (Saunders & Goldenberg, 1999). Gersten et al. (2007) also report that there is strong evidence in support of providing peer-assisted learning opportunities in which ELs are paired or grouped with native English-speaking or more English-proficient peers to work together on academic tasks several times a week. It is presumed that the benefits of such arrangements accrue through opportunities for the students to engage in the use of academic language for the purpose of accomplishing a shared academic goal. Goldenberg (2013) also points to the potential advantages of using the EL students' home language to support instruction. For example, the home language might be used to introduce key concepts and/or build background knowledge related to the content of texts that will be read. Alternatively, if they are available, texts can be read in the home language (by a parent or the child, depending on the child's level of literacy in the home language) and then read again in English. The International Children's Digital Library (*www.childrenslibrary.org*) provides several such texts. Unite for Literacy (*www.uniteforliteracy.com*) offers free online books in English print but provides the option of having them read in multiple languages.

Instruction and Knowledge Development

Because knowledge is so critical to comprehension and because the vehicles for knowledge development are so unevenly distributed in American society, teachers need to consider whether or not children have the various types of knowledge that a particular text takes for granted. Taking this into consideration may mean that, in planning to read a book in which the setting is a farm, one teacher may need to explicitly tell children who are urban dwellers about farms and what they are for, whereas a teacher using the same book in a rural farming community can reasonably assume that the children have a schema that allows them to analyze and interpret the text. Similarly, teachers of children who have recently moved to a country may need to carefully support the children's understanding and knowledge of cultural traditions and expectations relating to holidays, national heroes, and the like, and, if possible, help the children draw parallels between and among traditions in their former country and in their adopted country.

Knowledge discrepancies also characterize children who come from homes of differing socioeconomic status. There is a widely recognized "knowledge gap" between economically advantaged and less advantaged children, at least when it comes to the knowledge that children are expected to have to facilitate school learning. In fact, the development of the CCSS was driven in part by the concern that too little attention was being devoted to knowledge development in school, at least in the primary grades (Hirsch, 2006; Neuman, 2006). As a result of the knowledge gap, children who begin school knowing the least are at a particular disadvantage and are, essentially, being asked to learn much more than their more advantaged peers (because they have to learn what their peers already know *plus* what their peers are learning). Without additional instructional attention and support for this level of knowledge development, it seems likely that many economically disadvantaged children would be unable to accomplish this daunting task.

Although we certainly do not have a ready solution for addressing this knowledge gap (although experientially and academically rich summer programs would likely help), we encourage teachers to think carefully about the extent to which the gap affects their students and to consider how they might begin to address it. For example, technological advancements have made many vehicles for knowledge development much more readily available than in the past. Most children have access to television and cable or satellite programming options. A wealth of educational programming can be accessed and thus used to help expand children's knowledge. Teachers are encouraged to consider compiling a list of appropriate educational programs and encouraging children to view them at home, preferably with family members who will engage them in conversation about what they are learning during and after the viewing. Many children also have access to the Internet, which is an important resource for knowledge building. Here again, teachers are encouraged to investigate appropriate websites for students to explore and to communicate their recommendations to the children's families.

Sample Websites for Knowledge Enhancement

Listed below are several websites that teachers find useful in the classroom or recommend to families for exploration and online learning at home. Please note that although all of these websites are considered to be highly reputable, in many cases not-so-reputable websites are only a click away. For this reason, and because the content on Internet sites can change so quickly, adult supervision of Internet use is always recommended.

www.ala.org/greatsites	*www.kids.gov*
http://kids.nationalgeographic.com	*www.pbskids.org*
www.smithsonianeducation.org/students	*www.Kidsclick.org*

Teachers also, of course, need to take responsibility for addressing the knowledge gap in their classrooms. Neuman (2006) is a staunch advocate of the need to address the knowledge gap and has provided five research-based principles for improving the knowledge base of young children (pp. 35–36). These principles are very consistent with the advice we provided to teachers in an earlier iteration of the ISA professional development handbook. Below we list Neuman's principles (in *italic*) and elaborate a bit on each.

- *Children's learning benefits through integrated instruction* (p. 35). By this Neuman means that instruction should be organized around themes or projects that have coherence and depth and therefore provide children with the opportunity to develop concepts and apply them in new learning situations. Reading and discussing several books on the same or related topics will help children develop a depth of understanding that is not likely to occur when reading selections are not organized topically or thematically.

- *Learning requires children's minds (not just their bodies) to be active* (p. 35). This principle relates back to a principle discussed in Chapter 1: Engagement leads to learning. We need to try to ensure that children's minds are engaged in the thinking that is intended. Instruction should be goal oriented, not activity oriented.

- *High levels of teacher interaction optimize children's learning* (p. 35). One of a teacher's major roles is to guide children's thinking by modeling ways of thinking about and analyzing situations and then supporting children as they begin to grow as strategic learners. Effective teachers interact with their students almost constantly—at times in whole-class contexts, at other times in small groups or one to one.

- *Play supports children's learning* (p. 35). As long as the adults around them don't make it seem like work, much of what children are asked to do in the primary grades can be fun, even if it is not play per se. Thus, for example, children can be given props related to a book they just read and be allowed to "play" at reenacting the story. Such an activity has the advantage of engaging the children in thinking about the elements of narrative texts. Another option would be to "play" teacher and read a book to a couple of their friends, lead a book discussion, respond to their writing, or explain and demonstrate the steps in a science experiment.

- *Developing competence enhances motivation and self-esteem* (p. 36). Successful learning experiences breed more successful learning experiences and the good feelings that go along with them. Unfortunately, for children who suffer from a knowledge gap, success in school learning endeavors is less certain. Repeated failures have the potential to reduce a student's willingness to engage in learning activities, thereby increasing the likelihood of repeated failure.

Comprehension Instruction

In the last several years, a great deal of research has focused on what "good" comprehenders do. We put the word *good* in quotation marks to signal our discomfort with it in this context: *Good* often serves as the opposite of *bad*, and certainly we don't want anyone who is not yet a *good* comprehender to be considered *bad*. Therefore, in what follows, we substitute the word *proficient*. In 2011 Duke, Pearson, Strachan, and Billman (2011) provided a summary of what "good" (proficient) readers do. Much of the summary was based on research in which competent adult readers were asked to *think aloud* as they read; that is, people were asked to describe their thinking as they read. There was a good deal of commonality in the reports that the participants made. They tended to be very active as they read, used a large number of strategies, and were routinely monitoring their understanding. Figure 16.1 reproduces an adapted summary of what proficient readers do. We share this listing to emphasize how active and thoughtful proficient readers are and what the targeted endpoint for reading development looks like.

When Proficient Readers Read . . .

- They are active readers.
- From the outset, they have clear *goals* in mind for their reading. They constantly *evaluate* whether the text, and their reading of it, is meeting their goals.
- They typically *look over* the text before they read, noting such things as the *structure* of the text and text sections that might be most relevant to their reading goals.
- As they read, they frequently *make predictions* about what is to come.
- They read *selectively*, continually making decisions about their reading—what to read carefully, what to read quickly, what not to read, what to reread, and so forth.
- They *construct, revise,* and *question* the meanings they make as they read.
- They try to determine the meanings of *unfamiliar words and concepts* in the text, and they deal with inconsistencies or gaps as needed.
- They draw from, compare, and *integrate their prior knowledge* with material in the text.
- They think about the *authors* of the text, their style, beliefs, intentions, historical milieu, and so forth.
- They *monitor their understanding* of the text, making adjustments in their reading as necessary.
- They *evaluate the text's quality and value* and react to the text in a range of ways, both intellectually and emotionally.
- They *read different kinds of text differently*.
- When reading narrative, they attend closely to the setting and characters.
- When reading expository text, they frequently construct and revise summaries of what they have read.
- They process not only during "reading," but also during short breaks taken during reading and even after the reading has ceased.
- Comprehension is a consuming, continuous, and complex activity, but one that is both *satisfying and productive.*

FIGURE 16.1. Characteristics of proficient readers. Adapted from Duke, Pearson, Strachan, and Billman (2011). Copyright by the International Literacy Association. Adapted by permission.

Comprehension Strategies

As the strategies used by proficient readers came to be understood, researchers began exploring whether it was possible to teach these strategies to people, including children, who were not using them and, if so, whether such strategy instruction would help to improve comprehension. The results of these studies indicated that a variety of approaches to comprehension strategy instruction are effective in helping children to learn and use the strategies and thereby improve their reading comprehension (e.g., Brown, Pressley, Van Meter, & Schuder, 1996; Fuchs, Fuchs, & Burish, 2000; Guthrie et al., 2004; Klingner, Vaughn, & Schumm, 1998). However, most research on comprehension strategies instruction has focused on children beyond the early primary grades, and, as pointed out by Paris and Paris (2007), when children in the early primary grades are included, the effects of comprehension strategy instruction can be confounded by differences in decoding skills. In a recent confirmation of the point made by Paris and Paris (2007), Müller, Richter, Križan, Hecht, and Ennemoser (2015) found that, when comprehension strategies were explicitly taught to second-grade poor comprehenders with either weak or adequate decoding skills, those with adequate decoding skills benefited, whereas those with weak decoding skills did not. In fact, the latter group performed somewhat more poorly than the control group that did not receive strategy instruction.

The Müller et al. (2015) study is the only study we know of that has looked at the impact of teaching comprehension strategies to struggling readers with different patterns of strength and weakness. However, it is consistent with the approach we have taken to comprehension strategy instruction in the ISA, as discussed below. In developing the ISA, we were mindful of the studies of comprehension strategy instruction but leery of emulating their procedures with the young children who were our primary focus because we place considerable emphasis on strategic word solving (see Chapter 12), which, like using comprehension strategies, is a cognitively demanding enterprise. We did not want to overwhelm beginning and struggling readers by asking them to be consciously strategic about both word solving and meaning construction. However, certainly we did want them to be involved in the process of meaning construction and to have meaning making as their primary purpose for reading and for listening to text.

Therefore, rather than specifically teaching and practicing comprehension strategies, we opted to engage children in meaning construction by engaging them in conversations about the texts they read or heard, and, in the context of these conversations, teachers modeled some of the most commonly taught comprehension strategies without labeling them as strategies per se. Because some comprehension strategies are widely accepted as being useful to share with elementary-age children, we identified those strategies and encouraged teachers to become familiar with them and to use them to prompt and structure their conversations with students during read-alouds and shared and supported reading. The strategies we encouraged teachers to consider are listed and briefly described in Table 16.1. We have provided a brief commentary on what each strategy entails and why it is thought to be useful.

Too Much of a Good Thing?

Having spent a good deal of time observing in primary grade classrooms, we have often been concerned that comprehension strategy instruction is overdone or even misguided. Teachers need to be mindful of the fact that the primary purpose of strategy instruction is to ensure that children are active thinkers as they read (and listen). When too much emphasis is placed on the strategies and too little on the material being read, children may come to believe that it is the application of the strategies that is valued and important rather than comprehension of the text. Indeed, we have noticed that, for some students, the explanation of the strategy they have used becomes their end goal when strategies are emphasized heavily. The challenge for teachers is to model active engagement in meaning construction in a way that allows students to generalize this mind-set when reading new texts.

TABLE 16.1. Comprehension Strategies Discussed in the ISA

Strategy	What it involves	Why it is useful
Activating prior knowledge	Thinking about what one already knows about a topic or concept	New information from the text will be easier to interpret if readers think about what they already know about a topic. That way, when something is read that doesn't fit with the existing schema or knowledge base, readers will be alert to that fact and will be more likely to take steps to clear up the discrepancies (e.g., by rereading, reading on for more information, altering the existing schema). Connecting information encountered in a text with existing knowledge is the essence of meaning construction.
Prediction	Anticipating what will occur in the text and then checking to see whether the prediction matches the events in the text	Readers need to integrate prior knowledge and information from the text in order to make predictions. Generally, when readers have made a prediction, they become invested in determining whether their prediction is validated. This serves to sustain their interest in, and engagement with, the text.
Visualization	Imagining what events in the text would look like if illustrated or made into a movie	In order to construct a visual image, readers must attend to the text in an active way, modifying their images as the text unfolds.
Summarization	Retelling the events from the text, typically using some sort of organizational structure, such as sequencing (*first, then, finally*) or story grammar (setting, characters, problem, resolution) for narrative texts and, for informational texts, using the organizational structure of the text (e.g., compare and contrast, sequence, problem–solution).	When, after reading a text, readers reflect on it in such a way as to be able to summarize it, it is likely that they will retain more of the information. Perhaps more importantly, over time, it is assumed that the practice of summarization will lead to more active engagement during the reading of the text because readers will use the summarization structures to guide their thinking as they read. In fact, in support of this, Almasi (2003) encourages teachers to have children complete graphic organizers such as story maps *while* they are reading rather than after reading.
Questioning	A very broad strategy that entails asking questions related to the content of the text and/or directed to the author of the text (e.g., "I wonder why . . . ," "Why didn't he . . . ,?" "How come . . . ?")	When readers frequently generate questions they would like to ask the characters or author, they are likely to read upcoming text with an eye toward answering those questions. Further, the questions that they generate often lead them back into previously read text to look for clarification. Pressley et al. (1992) report that teaching children to ask "why" questions is especially effective, because children often have the necessary knowledge to understand a text, but they do not apply it.
Comprehension monitoring	Throughout the reading of a text, noticing whether it makes sense and, if not, taking steps to clarify the areas of confusion	To an extent, this strategy involves all of the others discussed above and can be considered a *metacognitive* strategy, in that it involves individuals in thinking about their own thinking (Weinstein & Mayer, 1986). This strategy is particularly important to develop because it emphasizes the need for readers to take responsibility for determining whether the text makes sense to them and to take steps to clarify when comprehension breaks down.

Conversations about Text

While our decision not to encourage explicit comprehension strategy instruction in the early primary grades was partly driven by the concern that teaching both word identification strategies and comprehension strategies would overextend the cognitive capacities of young children, it was also driven by the conviction that there are multiple less formalized ways of engaging children in meaning construction while reading or listening to books. And we suspected that these less formal forms of engagement could be more enjoyable and motivating for the children. Enjoyment and motivation struck us as particularly important elements for children who begin school with limited early literacy skills and limited literacy experiences more generally. The type of conversation-focused approach that we endorsed has been dubbed a "content" approach by McKeown, Beck, and Blake (2009) because it entails focusing most of the interaction with a text on constructing its meaning rather than on strategies that might be used to enable that construction. Although there has not been a great deal of research on the role of discussion in promoting comprehension in the primary grades, the research that exists indicates that discussion about text can promote problem solving, comprehension, and learning (Anderson, Chinn, Waggoner, & Nguyen, 1998; Nystrand, 1997; Taylor et al., 2000; Wegerif, Mercer, & Dawes, 1999). Roberts and Duke (2009) suggest that discussion of texts likely fosters comprehension owing to the "accountability inherent in saying something oneself and the opportunity to hear the interpretations of others" (p. 37).

Using Interactive Read-Alouds to Enhance Knowledge and Promote Engagement

Because many of the books that primary-grade children are able to read provide limited comprehension challenges and few opportunities to build knowledge about the world, a good deal of the comprehension-focused instruction in the ISA occurs in the context of interactive read-alouds in the classroom. In addition, classroom teachers are encouraged to use classroom volunteers and other available personnel to address knowledge and comprehension needs of the children about whom they have concerns.

Research evaluating the effects of reading frequently to children has demonstrated its value (McKeown & Beck, 2006). In fact, Marriott (1995) argued that "it is almost impossible to overemphasize the value of this activity for children of any age or reading level" (p. 65). Morrow and Gambrell (2000) and Snow et al. (1998) summarized the results of several studies that compared children from classrooms in which there were daily read-alouds with children from classrooms in which read-alouds occurred only occasionally. In general, these studies found that children who were read to often demonstrated greater motivation to read, greater gains in vocabulary, better comprehension of new stories they heard, greater familiarity with literary language, and better decoding skills.

KEEP IN MIND Although this section focuses on read-alouds, many of the same types of interactions concerning the meanings of texts can occur in the context of a shared reading experience. In a shared reading activity, however, the teacher generally addresses several additional goals, including talking about the purposes and conventions of print and how the writing system is related to spoken language.

Similarly, as children begin to engage in reading texts themselves, both in supported reading groups and independently, the teacher needs to establish a specific focus on the meaning of the text. The events and/or information in the text should be discussed before, during, and after the reading of the text.

Implementing Interactive Read-Alouds

The effectiveness of read-alouds in supporting the development of active thinking during reading depends on the qualities of the interactions between the teacher and the children (see McKeown & Beck, 2006). As discussed briefly in Chapter 3, the teacher's level of enthusiasm for the books read and the reading activity in general are important. So too is the level of freedom children feel they have to initiate conversations about the book. If reactions and questions have to wait until the end of the book or until the teacher initiates a discussion, then the children might well react less and comprehend less altogether.

Virtually everyone has had the experience of missing a point midway through a passage while reading and then having difficulty understanding everything that comes later. When children encounter a confusing part of a text, it would be ideal if they could clear up their confusion almost immediately by asking questions of the teacher or perhaps the other children in the group. We certainly expect older students to attempt some sort of "fix-up" when they realize that they are not comprehending what they are reading. Such active monitoring of one's understanding has been found to be vitally important to comprehension (Cain, Oakhill, & Bryant, 2004; see Baker & Beall, 2009, for a review). In the context of a read-aloud, the only option children have for addressing a breakdown of comprehension is to rely on someone else—they cannot go back and reread. So, teachers are strongly encouraged to make read-alouds as interactive as possible.

KEEP IN MIND One of the major purposes of interactive read-alouds is to develop the belief that text should make sense and that, when it doesn't, readers or listeners should do something to clear up their confusion. If, in the context of read-aloud, children aren't allowed to seek clarification, they may come to believe that it is all right not to understand what is going on in a text, and the development of that belief has the clear potential to carry over into the students' engagement in meaning construction when they are reading on their own.

In addition to answering questions as they arise, teachers can also be proactive, anticipating potential points of confusion and addressing them before a comprehension problem arises. In a study of exemplary literacy teachers at the kindergarten level, Block and Mangieri (2003) found that, when a portion of a book was likely to be unfamiliar to their students, exemplary teachers were likely to stop and rephrase the confusing aspect of the text or to create an example from students' life experiences.

Studies of the influences of reading aloud to children suggest that the greatest benefits accrue when the children are actively engaged during the course of the read-aloud (Beck & McKeown, 2001; Fisher, Flood, Lapp, & Frey, 2004; Hickman, Pollard-Durodola, & Vaughn, 2004; Santoro, Chard, Howard, & Baker, 2008). Participation can occur before, during, and after reading.

BEFORE READING

Participation *before reading* might include:

- Previewing the text through discussions of the title and the cover illustration.
- Discussions of the author and/or illustrator, particularly if the group is familiar with other texts by the author and/or illustrator.
- Making predictions about the text's content.
- Encouraging the children to think about the elements of genre and text structure in anticipating the book's content.
- Setting a purpose for listening, perhaps by relating it to a classroom theme or area of inquiry that the group is exploring.

DURING READING

Participation *during reading* should include spontaneous discussions of the text. Ideally, the discussions would be initiated by both the students and the teacher. Further, when the teacher initiates discussion, she or he needs to encourage thinking beyond the literal level and model and prompt inferential and critical analysis of the text. This kind of guidance might include:

- Encouraging children to ask questions and make comments as the book unfolds. Welcoming questions and comments in a conversational way will send the clear message that spontaneous reactions to the book are appropriate.
  - "Ah, good question! Does anyone have any ideas about that?"
  - "Interesting question! I'm not sure. Let's read to find out."
  - "Don't forget, if you are confused about something, listen a little longer to see if you can figure out what's going on. If not, you may want to ask a question."
  - "I agree. . . ."

- Noticing and discussing elements of story grammar.
  - "So, it looks like this story is set in the winter. Look at how they are all bundled up."
  - "What's the problem between our characters?"
  - "That is a solution I never would have guessed!"
  - "So, now we know what the problem is. Any ideas on how it will be resolved [solved]?"
- Comparing predictions to the events in the texts. Note that it is important to avoid talking about predictions as being either right or wrong, as some children really don't like to be wrong—and a prediction cannot really be wrong if it follows logically from what was known at the time it was made.
  - "That's just what Jared thought would happen."
  - "What did the author do that was different from what we expected [predicted]?"
- Making further predictions based on what has already happened in the text.
  - "Before I thought that. . . . But now I think. . . ."
- Generating questions or comments relating to the text and/or the characters.
  - "I wonder why he didn't. . . ."
  - "Did you notice the look on his face? I bet he's. . . ."
  - "I wonder why the author. . . ."
  - "How do you think _____ is feeling right now?"
  - "Why do you think . . . ?"
  - "What do you notice . . . ?"
  - "If you could talk to the author right now, what would you ask?"
  - "Why . . . ?"
  - "Why . . . ?"
  - "Why . . . ?" (As noted previously, research suggests that teaching children to ask *why* questions is particularly helpful in getting them to apply their knowledge in interpreting text; Pressley et al., 1992.)
- Asking open-ended questions.
  - "Who has something they would like to say about this page?"
- Seeking clarifications.
  - "What do you think the author meant by. . . ."
- Offering personal reactions and connections.
  - "I just love the way he keeps. . . ."
  - "I really don't like the way. . . ."
  - "How would you feel if . . . ?"
  - "How would you handle this situation?"
  - "Does this book remind you of . . . ?"
  - "Did you ever . . . ?"

- Visualizing
  - ○ "Just listen to this page as I read it to you and make a picture of what's happening in your head."
  - ○ "The illustrator didn't make a picture for that part. What do you think it would look like?"
- Comparing information in the current text with other texts with which the children are familiar.
  - ○ "This is sort of like the [book] we read."
  - ○ "This is the second book we've read where the. . . ."
  - ○ "Is this reminding you of another book we've read?"
    - ■ "In what way?"
- Restating (perhaps using simpler vocabulary and/or sentence structures) any confusing portions of the text when they are encountered.

AFTER READING

Participation *after reading* might include:

- Discussions of how predictions compared to the events in the text.
- Discussions of whether the purposes that were set were accomplished.
- Discussions of parts that may have been a bit confusing and then returning to those parts to reread for the purpose of clarification.
- Discussing or writing alternative endings (e.g., "What would have happened if . . . ?").
- Rereading the entire text either with the specific purpose of clearing up points of confusion or simply for the sake of enjoying it.
- Encouraging children to draw a scene from the text as they envisioned it.
- Reflecting on what was learned and talking or writing about it.
- Reflecting on why the author might have written the book.
- Reenacting the story with the aid of story-related props.
- Retelling the stories for authentic purposes (e.g., retelling into an audio recorder for the benefit of a child who was absent).
- Reconstructing stories using pictures (for very beginning readers).

The comments and questions that teachers use to foster conversations serve to help children develop ways of thinking about and reacting to texts. The hope is that the ways of thinking encouraged through these conversations will ultimately be internalized by children and thus be useful to them when they are reading independently. In conducting these conversations, however, the teacher also needs to be mindful of the fact that too much talk can disrupt the flow of the text. As in all aspects of instruction, striking the right balance is important.

Using Informational (Nonfiction) Texts to Promote the Development of General World Knowledge

Although much can be learned from interactive read-alouds of storybooks, the wealth of knowledge that prepares children for later academic pursuits is most readily addressed via nonfiction books and other types of information-rich books, such as historical fiction and fantastical science books such as the *Magic School Bus* series (published by Scholastic). Children generally encounter greater amounts of new information with these types of text than with storybooks. As a result, children will likely need more teacher support to integrate the new information. This extra support might include:

- Reading simpler texts on a given topic before reading more challenging ones.
- Careful planning by the teacher, with the goal of anticipating the portions of the text that might confuse children and preparation of explanations that will help to clarify points or prevent the confusion altogether.
- Lengthier discussions before, during, and after reading the text.
- Frequent think-alouds in which the teacher models her or his thinking while reading.
- Extended discussions focused on specific concepts or causal relationships encountered in the text—often connecting new concepts to ideas that are familiar to children.
- Discussion of text structure (e.g., compare–contrast, cause–effect, sequence)
- Periodic encouragement to summarize what has already been learned in the text; early on, children will typically need assistance with such summaries, including encouragement to organize summaries based on text structure.
- Rereading the entire book, perhaps more than once; each time children listen to a book, they are likely to understand the content at a deeper level and are therefore more likely to integrate the knowledge more effectively.

Useful Resources

Duke, N. K. (2014). *Inside information: Developing powerful readers and writers of informational text through project-based instruction.* Newark, DE: International Literacy Association.

Duke, N. K., & Bennett-Armistead, V. S. (2003). *Reading and writing informational text in the primary grades: Research-based practices.* New York: Scholastic.

Both of these books are great resources for teachers working to effectively incorporate information-rich texts into their literacy and content area instruction.

Comprehension Instruction/Focus during Shared and Supported Reading

This discussion of the development of active comprehenders has largely focused on read-aloud interactions because there are richer opportunities to focus on content in the types of books that are read aloud to primary-grade children than there are in the types of texts that most children are able to read. However, this focus on read-alouds should certainly not be taken to suggest that comprehension should be ignored during shared and supported reading. To the contrary, a major reason for encouraging active thinking during a read-aloud is so that the children will be more inclined to be active thinkers when they themselves read.

Virtually all of the suggestions made relative to read-aloud situations can be applied to shared and supported reading situations. Texts should be discussed *before, during,* and *after* reading. The discussion should involve open-ended questions and reactions that prompt inferential and critical thinking. Discussions should give children the opportunity to think through what they are reading and integrate it with what they already know. (See the discussion of supported reading in Chapter 17.)

High-Volume Reading

The amount of reading that children do is a strong predictor of their reading success (Taylor, Pearson, Clark, & Walpole, 2000). Although this may seem like a bit of a chicken–egg problem (Does reading more lead to reading success? or Does being a successful reader lead one to read more?), Allington et al. (2010) have shown that simply increasing the availability of books over the summer break leads to significant increases in the reading achievement of children living in high-poverty areas. This suggests that the volume of reading readers do has a causal impact on reading outcomes. Although this is certainly no surprise, we hope that it prompts teachers to consider how much reading their students do in the course of a typical school day and what their home reading assignments and options entail. Allington and McGill-Franzen (2013), for example, suggest that in some settings the children read for as little as 10 minutes in a typical 90-minute classroom reading block. Such limited reading is unlikely to help the children build the needed knowledge of words and of the world upon which reading comprehension depends.

Further, several studies have demonstrated that the reading achievement gap between children from low- versus higher-income backgrounds is largely attributable to losses in reading skills that occur over the summer for children living in poverty (see Allington & McGill-Franzen, 2013, and Kim & Quinn, 2013, for reviews). Based on the findings of the Allington et al. (2010) study cited above, this would seem to be largely due to lack of access to reading materials. This strikes us as a very fixable problem for anyone with a bit of grant writing experience!

There are, of course, other issues that influence the volume of reading that students do. One important factor is the difficulty level of the text. Children will read more (in terms of total words read and content covered) in a given period of time if the text is not too challenging. Plus, they will be more motivated to read when they can focus on the content of what they are reading rather than having to devote a great deal of their cognitive resources to the process of word solving. This is an issue that we have touched on in some of the early chapters, and we repeat it here because we feel we can't stress it enough.

Writing to Enhance Comprehension and Knowledge Development

As the children's literacy skills evolve, their comprehension can be supported through writing. For example, during independent reading, the children might:

• Use sticky notes to record their questions and thoughts and apply them to the appropriate pages. Later, when it is time to discuss the text, the children will have these reminders to help them participate in the discussion.

• Keep a reading journal wherein they record their reactions to, and learning from, the texts that they read. For example, they might draw a picture of how they envision a scene, write one or two of their predictions and whether the text matched them, or write questions they wish they could ask the author or main character and read on to see if their questions are answered.

• Write book reviews to post as a way to encourage others to read particular books.

• Describe texts using structural formats such as story grammar (setting, characters, problem, and resolution of the story) or sequencing (*first, then, next, finally*).

• Keep a learning log in which they record information gleaned from nonfiction readings—perhaps using a *know–w*ant to know–*l*earned (K-W-L) format (Ogle, 1986).

• Write their own texts (e.g., nonfiction books, short stories) modeled after the book they've read and/or drawing on what they have learned through their reading.

Evaluating and Documenting Children's Progress

Figures 16.2 and 16.3 provide vehicles for teachers to systematically record their observations of children's level of, and strategic approach to, comprehension in the context of read-alouds (Figure 16.2) and reading (Figure 16.3). Teachers would use W to document that ability or characteristic was *well developed*—meaning above expectation for the student's age/grade level, A to indicate appropriate development for the age/grade level, and N to indicate that the student is not meeting expectations. Figure 16.4 provides a vehicle for teachers to record their observations of children's relative standing in the area of knowledge acquisition. To document the rate of knowledge acquisition teachers would use E (easily), S (slowly), or V (very slowly). In order to document potential growth and change over time for each characteristic, space is provided for the teacher to record observations up to 10 times across the school year. The purpose of these forms is, primarily, to help teachers notice aspects of children's development that may need extra instructional attention in order to prevent future academic difficulties.

Group Snapshot—Listening Comprehension						
Student names						
Ability to understand texts: **W**ell developed **A**ppropriately developed **N**eeds development	Date					
	Date					
	Date					
	Date					
	Date					
	Date					
	Date					
	Date					
	Date					
	Date					
Actively engages in discussion of texts (e.g., makes predictions, offers reactions, asks questions): **W**ell developed **A**ppropriately developed **N**eeds development	Date					
	Date					
	Date					
	Date					
	Date					
	Date					
	Date					
	Date					
	Date					
	Date					
Ability to retell/summarize text in authentic situations (i.e., for the purpose of communicating with someone unfamiliar with the text): **W**ell developed **A**ppropriately developed **N**eeds development	Date					
	Date					
	Date					
	Date					
	Date					
	Date					
	Date					
	Date					
	Date					
	Date					
Connects information in text to own life, other texts, broader contexts: **W**ell developed **A**ppropriately developed **N**eeds development	Date					
	Date					
	Date					
	Date					
	Date					
	Date					
	Date					
	Date					
	Date					

FIGURE 16.2. Group snapshot for listening comprehension.

Group Snapshot—Reading Comprehension						
Student names						
Ability to understand texts: **W**ell developed **A**ppropriately developed **N**eeds development	Date					
	Date					
	Date					
	Date					
	Date					
	Date					
	Date					
	Date					
	Date					
	Date					
Actively engages in discussion of texts (e.g., makes predictions, offers reactions, asks questions): **W**ell developed **A**ppropriately developed **N**eeds development	Date					
	Date					
	Date					
	Date					
	Date					
	Date					
	Date					
	Date					
	Date					
Ability to retell/summarize text in authentic situations (i.e., for the purpose of communicating with someone unfamiliar with the text): **W**ell developed **A**ppropriately developed **N**eeds development	Date					
	Date					
	Date					
	Date					
	Date					
	Date					
	Date					
	Date					
	Date					
Connects information in text to own life, other texts, broader contexts: **W**ell developed **A**ppropriately developed **N**eeds development	Date					
	Date					
	Date					
	Date					
	Date					
	Date					
	Date					
	Date					
	Date					

FIGURE 16.3. Group snapshot for reading comprehension.

Group Snapshot—Knowledge Acquisition and Background Knowledge						
Student names						
Knowledge acquisition—Learns and uses new information **E**asily **S**lowly **V**ery slowly	Date					
	Date					
	Date					
	Date					
	Date					
	Date					
	Date					
	Date					
	Date					
	Date					
Background knowledge relative to grade-level peers **W**ell developed **A**ppropriately developed **N**eeds development	Date					
	Date					
	Date					
	Date					
	Date					
	Date					
	Date					
	Date					
	Date					
	Date					

FIGURE 16.4. Group snapshot for knowledge acquisition and background knowledge.

PART V

Integration of the Goals

Introduction

In the foregoing chapters, we discussed the complexity of the reading process and how difficulties with any of the components could lead to long-term reading difficulties. The major emphasis in this book is on the provision of effective instruction to help alleviate early difficulties and limitations in foundational literacy skills and to support the accelerated growth in literacy skills that must occur if children who are at risk are to close the gap with their higher-achieving peers.

For children who struggle at the early stages of literacy acquisition, we believe that instruction is the most important determiner of their ultimate success. Therefore, it is important that teachers have the knowledge and skills needed to identify and respond to the instructional needs of early literacy learners, especially those who experience difficulty with the literacy acquisition process. The development of teacher knowledge related to each of the instructional goals discussed in the previous chapters has been a major focus of the book. In the two remaining chapters, we integrate the various goals into a cohesive plan for small-group and one-to-one instruction for early literacy learners, particularly those who have been identified as being at risk for experiencing literacy learning difficulties (Chapter 17). In Chapter 18, by way of summarizing the text and further demonstrating the integration of the goals, we revisit the complexity of the reading process and graphically represent the interrelatedness of the various instructional goals that were addressed throughout the text.

In order to close the gap with their better prepared peers, children who begin school with limited early literacy skills need to learn more in a given period of time than do their peers. In order to accomplish this accelerated learning, the children need intensified, high-quality instructional interventions. In Chapter 17, we discuss small-group and one-to-one instruction that is designed to be both responsive to the children's needs and comprehensive. Throughout we have argued that instruction needs to emphasize the aspects of the process that children find particularly challenging and needs to be comprehensive enough that the children fully understand how to apply what they are learning to the reading and writing of texts. To illustrate this dual goal, we describe lesson planning in some detail, as well as the type of thinking in which teachers might engage as they plan, deliver, and reflect upon instruction for children who are at various points along the con-tinuum of early literacy development. In doing so, we demonstrate how the vari-ous instructional goals discussed in the preceding chapters can be integrated into coherent and comprehensive small-group and one-to-one lessons. Themes that were addressed earlier in the text reemerge in this chapter, including (1) the need for instruction to be targeted just beyond students' current capabilities (i.e., the zone of proximal development; Vygotsky, 1978); (2) the need for children to be actively engaged in the thinking that enables learning; (3) the need to help children develop a *self-teaching mechanism* (Share, 1995) so that they become more effec-tive readers with each encounter with text; (4) the need for children to learn the alphabetic code well enough that they can be both flexible and efficient in apply-ing their knowledge in the context of both word solving and writing; (5) the need for instruction to keep the construction of meaning at the forefront so that the children understand, from early on, that the purpose of reading and writing (and reading and writing instruction) is to enable communication; and (6) the need to enhance the development of world knowledge and language skills, because such knowledge sources are central to the meaning-construction process.

We have focused almost exclusively in this text on the instruction and inter-vention that children should receive in an RTI process rather than on some of the important decision making that must go on in terms of which children are served and at what degree of intensity and for how long. Although these are important decisions with which schools must grapple, we provide only minimal guidance on how these decisions should be made because, at this point in time, there is no widely agreed-upon approach to such decision making. In fact, it appears that a fairly major shift is occurring in the thinking about how RTI should be imple-mented.

Thus, when RTI was first introduced as a process for preventing long-term literacy learning difficulties and for determining which children might be consid-ered for special education services, there was a fairly widespread consensus that children who were identified as being at risk should spend some amount of time in Tier 1 (classroom level) intervention and would only be considered for additional services at Tier 2 if they made limited or no progress. Children placed in Tier 2 would again spend some amount of time at that level of support and, again, would be considered for more intensive supports at Tier 3 only if they demonstrated limited or no progress with the combination of Tier 1 and Tier 2 supports. The idea behind this process was partly to conserve intervention resources but also to try to ensure that classroom instruction was as effective as possible in that the expectation was set that classroom instruction alone should enable 80% or more of the students to meet grade-level expectations. The higher-numbered tiers then should be able to accelerate the progress of the 20% of children who received those supports, enabling all or nearly all of them to meet expectations. While, in general, these are desirable goals, with this approach, the 20% of children who need more intensive support may spend a considerable amount of time without receiving it. As a result, once they do qualify for more intensive intervention, it may be harder to catch them up, as the gap may be wider than it was at the beginning of the school year. Based on concerns such as these, recent research has investigated alternative approaches, most especially providing higher tiers of intervention earlier in the school year, with assignment to tiers being based on the severity of the students' need. At this point in time, the few studies that have been done suggest that such an approach is more likely to yield better outcomes for students (e.g., Al Otaiba et al., 2014; McAlenney & Coyne, 2015), consistent with Vaughn, Denton, and Fletcher's (2010) proposal that "schools should consider placing students with the lowest overall initial scores in the most intensive interventions" (p. 442).

Based on these concerns and the recent evidence, we currently recommend that children who, at the beginning of the school year, appear to be at risk of not meeting grade-level expectations, be provided with Tier 1 and Tier 2 intervention services if they have no prior history of receiving such services (e.g., children entering kindergarten or children who may be suffering from having done too little reading over a summer break). Several weeks into the school year, children should be reevaluated to determine whether they have made sufficient gains to warrant discontinuing their Tier 2 services, should continue with Tier 1 and Tier 2 support, or are in need of more intensive Tier 3 support in place of their Tier 2 services.[1] Children for whom Tier 2 services are discontinued should continue with the supports offered at Tier 1 (daily small-group instruction provided by the classroom teacher) until (1) it is clear that they are working at the level of students who are not considered to be at risk and so can be best served in a group of students with similar, at least, grade-level skills or (2) they are not making as much progress as they did when receiving both Tier 1 and Tier 2 supports and so should once again be provided with that additional support.

Children who at the beginning of the year appear to be at risk of not meeting grade-level expectations and who have a history of being involved in an RTI process would receive Tier 1 and Tier 2 or Tier 3 support depending on their

---

[1] In our conceptualization of an RTI model, Tier 3 involves very intensive intervention and would precede consideration of special education placement.

performance in the previous year and their current status on the screening measure. The children with the lowest performance levels and the slowest growth in the previous year would ideally be provided with Tier 3 supports right from the start. From our perspective, Tier 3 support services should be offered on a daily basis for 30 minutes or more if possible and should be provided by someone with particular expertise in early literacy intervention.

There are some important general trends that should be observed when an effective RTI model is implemented. First, there should be substantial coordination between and among the tiers of intervention so that children are not faced with attempting to integrate fragmented and contradictory information related to literacy. In fact, the intervention lessons offered at each of the tiers should look quite similar to one another, with the major differences involving group size (the higher the tier number, the lower the number of children in the group) and individualization (more intensive forms of intervention allow instruction to be planned for the specific needs of the children in the group) and, perhaps, the expertise of the teacher who delivers the lessons. A second general trend that should be evident is that, at each tier of intervention, many children should show accelerated growth and no longer need intensified intervention. As a result of this general trend, the number of children who are served at each successive tier should be smaller and smaller, with only a very small number eventually considered to be in need of special education services. If the RTI process instituted in a given school does not follow this second general pattern, the quality and characteristics of the instruction offered at each of the tiers need to be reconsidered.

CHAPTER 17

Small-Group and One-to-One Intervention

This chapter focuses primarily on the small-group and one-to-one instruction that might be offered to children who are considered to be at risk for experiencing reading difficulties. The small-group instruction offered in the classroom as part of Tier 1 intervention and the small-group instruction provided at Tiers 2 and 3 should look very much alike, with the major differences being that, at Tiers 2 and 3, the instruction would typically involve:

- Smaller groups (three or four children at Tier 2 and one or two children at Tier 3)
- More focused teacher attention, which can occur because the teacher is not simultaneously overseeing the rest of the class. This intensity of instruction, in turn, allows:
  - More careful and thorough documentation of children's skills and abilities, and as a result
  - Instruction planned to more specifically address the needs of the individual children
  - More opportunities for the children to respond and receive guidance and feedback.

Given the instructional needs of children at Tier 3, *daily* intervention, in addition to Tier 1 instruction in the classroom, is strongly recommended.

The implementation of additional instructional opportunities for children with limited skills should begin as early in their schooling as possible. For children in the early primary grades, the additional support might be offered only at the classroom level (Tier 1) for a period of time, as initial limitations may be due primarily to limitations in their literacy experiences either at home or in preschool settings. Children whose difficulties are primarily attributable to limitations in experience are apt to show a strong response (e.g., rapid growth) to comprehensive classroom language arts instruction that includes intensified small-group (Tier 1) experience, if the instruction is appropriately differentiated and targeted and competently delivered. These children may not need support beyond Tier 1. However, other early primary-grade children may need additional tiers of intervention in order to meet grade-level expectations. Decisions about instituting these additional tiers of intervention should be made as soon as possible and certainly not later than 6–8 weeks into the school year.

Small-group and one-to-one instruction for all young children, but particularly for children who struggle at the early stages of learning to read, should take account of what the children already know and are able to do and should reflect continuation of skills development, as described in the previous chapters. Moreover, instruction should focus on helping children to develop a *self-teaching mechanism* (see Chapter 12) and on keeping them involved in the meaning-construction process that is central to literacy development.

Coordination across Instructional Settings

Given that one important goal of intervention is to increase children's ability to profit from classroom instruction, it is essential that intervention teachers be knowledgeable regarding instruction occurring in the classroom. This does not mean that intervention teachers simply reteach or preteach classroom content. Rather, it means that intervention teachers should adjust their instruction to ensure that what the children are learning in Tier 2 or Tier 3 intervention is as congruent and as coordinated as possible with what the children are doing in the classroom.

To this end, ideally, teachers within a given school will share a common philosophy and approach to early literacy instruction, use common instructional language, provide common resources for their students, and have common expectations as to what should be accomplished by the end of the school year. However, even if teachers are using a highly scripted, rigidly paced program (which, from our perspective, is far from ideal), instruction is likely to vary between classrooms. Intervention teachers should, therefore, begin by meeting with each child's classroom teacher in order to learn about the classroom language arts program and how differentiation for the at-risk students is being accomplished. Figure 17.1 lists aspects of literacy instruction that should be coordinated across instructional settings in the primary grades. Figure 17.2 lists aspects of classroom language arts instruction that intervention teachers should keep abreast of as they work with children from particular classrooms. To facilitate communication, it is useful for

- Expectations for literacy competencies at the end of each grade level.
- Approaches to teaching about the alphabet and decoding skills more generally.
- Strategies to be taught to promote word solving.
- Terminology teachers use for important concepts such as:
  - Upper case (*capital, big*)
  - Lower case (*small, little*)
  - Word families (*chunks, phonograms, keys*)
  - Silent-*e* (*magic-*e, *bossy-*e)
- Comprehension strategies taught.
- Approaches to assessing and documenting progress.

FIGURE 17.1. Target areas for consistency and congruency across instructional settings.

- The books and other instructional materials that are available in the classroom.
- The themes or instructional units that are to be covered.
- The foundational skills that are currently being worked on in the classroom and have been covered in the past. For example:
  - High-frequency words
  - Spelling words
  - Decoding skills
  - Strategies
- The extent to which the classroom and intervention teachers have a shared vision of what individual children are able to do.
- The group snapshots.

FIGURE 17.2. Important areas of ongoing communication between classroom and intervention teachers.

classroom teachers to keep file folders in which they put both notes for the intervention teacher and communications that are sent home with the children. Intervention teachers can pick up their folders when they pick up the children.

Goals of Instruction

Table 17.1 lists the goals for intervention and the components of intervention lessons during which the goals might be addressed. All of the goals can be addressed in more than one of the intervention components, with several being addressed across most of the components. Our purpose in including this chart is to make the point that small-group and one-to-one interventions, like classroom instruction more generally, should be goal oriented. Teachers are encouraged to think about their instructional goals as they plan, deliver, and reflect upon each component of a lesson.

TABLE 17.1. The Intersection of the Goals of Instruction and the Components of ISA Lessons

Lesson components	Motivation	Alphabetics			Word learning		Fluency	Meaning construction	
	Motivation	Print concepts	Phonological analysis	Alphabetic coding skills (letter names, sounds, alphabetic principle, etc.)	Strategic word identification	High-frequency sight words	Fluency	Language and vocabulary development	Knowledge and comprehension
Read-aloud/shared reading/rereading	✓	✓	✓	✓	✓	✓	✓	✓	✓
Phonological awareness	✓		✓	✓	✓			✓	
Decoding and encoding	✓	✓	✓	✓	✓	✓	✓		
Reading new book(s)	✓	✓	✓	✓	✓	✓	✓	✓	✓
Writing	✓	✓	✓	✓	✓	✓	✓	✓	✓
High-frequency words	✓	✓	✓	✓		✓	✓	✓	

Note. Adapted from Scanlon and Anderson (2010). Copyright by the International Reading Association. Adapted by permission.

In the ISA, intervention lessons at Tiers 2 and 3 are typically 30 minutes long. In the classroom, small-group lessons may need to be a bit shorter, given scheduling constraints. The time devoted to different components of a lesson is not fixed but rather varies based on students' instructional needs. In general, however, we would expect children to be engaged in reading and writing as part of every lesson and that, as children progress as readers, the allocation of time would shift from more time spent on the development of foundational skills (alphabetics and high-frequency words) to more time spent on authentic reading and writing.

Intervention Lessons: General Overview

Ideally, small-group instruction in classroom and intervention settings and in one-to-one intervention lessons should look quite similar, as teachers in all three contexts are working toward the same instructional goals. Of course, classroom teachers may be working with larger groups than intervention teachers and will also be responsible for simultaneously overseeing the rest of the class. Therefore, the level of individualized planning, instruction, and record keeping that a classroom teacher can manage will be different from what an intervention teacher can do.

In Chapter 2 we identified the major components of an ISA lesson and illustrated how a lesson might differ as the children progress as readers and writers (Table 2.3, pp. 51–53). In this chapter we describe each component of the lesson (read-aloud, shared reading, rereading; phonological awareness; decoding and encoding;

reading new books; writing; and high-frequency word practice) in greater detail and attempt to provide glimpses of a teacher's thoughts and reflections before, during, and after she or he teaches a small-group lesson. Figure 17.3 provides a modified version of the lesson sheet that was used in small-group intervention lessons in our most recent primary-grade study (Scanlon et al., 2008). We refer to this tool as a lesson *sheet* rather than as a lesson *plan* because teachers used it in planning the lesson, during the lesson to make note of what the children were able to do and what the teacher wanted to do in upcoming lessons, and after the lesson to aid in planning future lessons and to provide information for updating the group snapshots. Although teachers working with larger groups might find this form cumbersome to use during lessons, they may find it helpful to use as a guide for thinking about both the general structure and the specific plan for their small-group lessons. For teachers working one-to-one with children, we provide, at a later point, a lesson sheet that allows for more detailed documentation of individual lessons.

When first encountering the lesson sheet, teachers often comment that they feel a bit overwhelmed by the level of detail. However, after using the sheet for a while, teachers generally acknowledge that the detail serves to remind them of the multiple aspects of literacy teaching and learning that might be addressed in any given lesson and that should be addressed at various points during the course of instruction. In fact, one teacher indicated that, for her, the lesson sheet served as a quick review of the ISA professional development program.

As a general overview to the lesson sheet, note that it is set up to be used with groups of three children. Children's names are listed at the top of each column, and room is provided for teachers to make notes pertaining to individual children in the appropriate section of the lesson sheet either in preparation for the lesson or as the lesson unfolds. This is explained more fully below as we discuss each segment of a small-group lesson. Such a lesson generally follows the order depicted on the lesson sheet. However, some lessons include some elements but not others. For example, early in kindergarten, the high-frequency word segment would not be included for children identified as at risk because they would not yet be prepared to profitably focus on high-frequency words in small-group lessons.

In the following pages we provide a general description of each of the lesson segments and, for each segment, one or two more detailed examples of how a teacher might plan, deliver, and reflect on that lesson for a particular group of children. We have tried to avoid becoming mired in the details while still providing enough information about what the lesson components might look like and how they fit together. For some lesson components we discuss "Using the Lesson Sheet" and "After the Lesson." To limit redundancy, we do not discuss these for all segments. However, teachers are encouraged to use the lesson sheet in similar ways for all segments and to routinely reflect across the group snapshots and the lesson sheets to identify instructional priorities.

(text resumes on page 378)

Lesson Sheet

Date _____   Session # _____

Child 1 _____   Child 2 _____   Child 3 _____

1. Read-Aloud/Shared Reading or Rereading		
Title (and Level):		
Text Comprehension: GU, AE, RET, PC, CON		
Word Identification Strategy: Code (TS [F, L, M], LP, DS, BW), Meaning (CP, MS, RP, SA), Interactive and Confirmatory (IC)		
Fluency		
Letter/Sound: REC, NAM, LS		
Print Concepts: LR, TB, CW, CL, COM, PUN, 1-1		
High-Frequency Words: REC, ID		
Phonological Awareness: CR, IR, IA		
Vocabulary—Words to focus on:		
Comments/Notes for Next Session:		

FIGURE 17.3. Lesson sheet for small-group instruction. From Anderson (2010). Copyright by the International Literacy Association. Reprinted by permission. *(page 1 of 4)*

Child 1 _____ Child 2 _____ Child 3 _____

2. Phonological Awareness		
Sound Sorting RH, BEG, END, MID		STRETCH??
Sound Blending Onset–Rime, Single Phonemes; w/Pics, w/o Pics		STRETCH??
Sound Counting/Segmentation 2 Phonemes, 3 Phonemes		STRETCH??
Comments/Notes for Next Session:		

3. Decoding and Encoding		
Letter Names: RE, NAM, PR Letter Sounds: LS, CS-B, CS-E Other Decoding Elements: SV, VCe, D, Bl		
Word Building		
Word Reading		
Written Spelling		
Comments/Notes for Next Session:		

FIGURE 17.3. *(page 2 of 4)*

Child 1 _____ Child 2 _____ Child 3 _____

4. Reading		
Title (and Level):		
Text Comprehension: GU, AE, RET, PC, CON		
Word Identification Strategy: Code (TS [F, L, M], LP, DS, BW), Meaning (PIC, MS, RP, SA), Interactive and Confirmatory (IC)		
Fluency: WBW, PHR, FL		
Letter/Sound: REC, NAM, LS		
Print Concepts: LR, TB, CW, CL, COM, PUN, 1-1		
High-Frequency Words: REC, ID		
Phonological Awareness: CR, IR, IA		
Vocabulary—Words to focus on:		
Comments/Notes for Next Session:		

FIGURE 17.3. *(page 3 of 4)*

Child 1 _____ Child 2 _____ Child 3 _____

5. Writing
Writing Prompt or Dictated Sentence:

Letters/Sounds: PR, LS, BS, ES Other Elements: SV, VCe, DI, BI		

Print Concepts: LR, TB, CW, CL, COM, PUN		

High-Frequency Words: CP, CS		

Comments/Notes for Next Session:

6. High-Frequency Words
Practice Plan:

FIGURE 17.3. *(page 4 of 4)*

In what follows, we draw examples from children who are at a variety of developmental points to provide a sense of how teachers would think about, and plan for, different children. Following this overview, we describe a complete lesson for one group of children who are receiving Tier 2 intervention. We do this to provide a sense of the flow of a lesson and to illustrate that the components are interrelated and mutually supportive. Finally, we illustrate the shift in intensity that occurs when intervention is provided in a one-to-one context.

Segment 1: Read-Aloud/Shared Reading or Rereading

Depending on the children's point in development, the first segment might involve the teacher in reading to or with the children, or it might involve the children rereading one or more books that were read in previous lessons. For children with very limited literacy experience and/or for children with little or no understanding of the writing system, read-alouds and shared reading are commonly used in this first segment. For children who are further along, rereading of emergent-level (and eventually more challenging) texts is routine for this segment. Below we describe what the teacher might do before, during, and after a lesson in which she or he uses one or the other of these activities during the first segment of a lesson.

Small-Group Read-Aloud: Before the Lesson

CONSIDER THE CHILDREN

For children who have very limited early literacy skills (e.g., those who are identified as at risk at kindergarten entry), small-group read-alouds provide important opportunities to help children learn about the pleasure that books can bring and to begin to familiarize them with foundational literacy skills. In planning, the teacher might review the snapshots for purposes and conventions of print, phonological skills, and alphabetic knowledge for the group. For these children (we'll call them TeRoy, Maria, and Sam), the teacher notes that they are just beginning to learn about the left-to-right directionality of print, that they are learning to attend to the sounds in words, and that each knows a couple of the letters in his or her name. The need to move the children forward with these skills influences the teacher's choice of the book for the read-aloud. Of course, motivation, comprehension, and knowledge building are goals addressed in every read-aloud.

SELECTING THE BOOK

The teacher chooses *Dr. Seuss's ABC* (Seuss, 1963) because it is a playful introduction of the entire alphabet and because the alliteration in the book will help to draw the children's attention to the sounds in spoken words. The teacher realizes that the font used for the focal letters on each page is fairly fancy and is not ideal for teaching about the alphabet, but she also realizes that if she were to limit her choices to alphabet books that utilized a clean font, she wouldn't have many alphabet books to read! Given the phonemic analysis and motivational opportunities that the book offers, she decides to go ahead and use the book.

Preparing the Lesson Sheet

The teacher prepares for the lesson by listing the names of the children at the top of the lesson sheet and the name of the book to be read in the title line and by making brief notations regarding which instructional goals and objectives she will address during the course of the read-aloud. In examining the listing of goals and objectives that might be addressed during the read-aloud, the teacher might plan as follows:

- *Text comprehension.* Draw the children's attention to some of the pictures and discuss how the pictures help to clarify the text. This might be noted on the lesson sheet by simply circling or highlighting the *PC*, which stands for *picture cues*, on the Text Comprehension line. (The codes for the small-group lesson sheet are presented in Figure 17.4.)

- *Word identification strategy.* This book does not lend itself to supporting this goal for children at this early stage of development. Therefore, no notations would be made here.

- *Fluency.* The book does not lend itself to supporting this goal. Further, for the children in the group under discussion, this is not an appropriate goal at this point.

- *Letter/sound.* For children who know little about the alphabet, becoming familiar with the names of the letters is a preliminary step, even if the children are not yet connecting those names with the printed letters. Reading this book and pointing to the individual letters will help children begin to recognize the letters and become familiar with their names. The teacher would indicate that objective by circling or highlighting the *REC* (for *recognize*) in the Letter/Sound section.

- *Print concepts.* The teacher plans to point to the words and perhaps draw the children's attention to print concepts by occasionally talking about where on the page she starts reading, where she goes once she gets to the last word on a line, and so on. This will help the children begin to understand some of the most basic conventions of print. The teacher would note this plan by circling or highlighting *LR* (for *left-to-right*) and *TB* (for *top-to-bottom*) directions of print. (Note that, in a small-group lesson, with the children grouped by similar instructional needs, it is appropriate to address print concepts in a read-aloud. However, teachers would typically not do much print referencing in a whole-class read-aloud.)

- *High-frequency words.* The book does not lend itself to supporting this goal. Further, for the children in the group under discussion, this is not an appropriate goal at this point.

READ-ALOUD/READ (Segments 1 and 4)

Text Comprehension
GU—general understanding
AE—active engagement
RET—retell
PC—picture cues
CON—connect to existing knowledge

Word Identification Strategy
TS-F—Think sounds—first
TS-L—Think sounds—last
TS-M—Think sounds—middle
BW—break word
DS—different sounds
LP—look for parts
CP—check pictures
MS—make sense
RP—read past
SA—start again
IC—Interactive and confirmatory use

Fluency
WBW—word by word
PHR—phrasing
FL—fluent

Letter/Sound
REC—recognize
NAM—name
LS—letter sound

Print Concepts
LR—left-to-right directionality
TB—top-to-bottom directionality
CW—concept of a word
CL—concept of a letter
COM—print as communication
PUN—punctuation
1-1—voice–print match

High-Frequency Words
REC—recognize
ID—identify

Phonological Awareness
CR—completes rhyme
IR—identifies rhyming words
IA—identifies alliterative words

PHONOLOGICAL AWARENESS (Segment 2)

Sort by Sound
RH—rhyme
BEG—beginning
END—ending
MID—middle vowel

Sound Blending
w/Pics—with pictures
w/o Pics—without pictures

DECODING AND ENCODING (Segment 3)
REC—recognize
NAM—name
PR—print or produce
LS—letter–sound association
CS-B—consonant substitution, *begin*
CS-E—consonant substitution, *end*
SV—short vowel
VCe–vowel consonant e
DI—digraph
BL—blend

WRITING (Segment 5)

Letters and Sounds
PR—print or produce
LS—letter–sound association
BS—beginning sound
ES—ending sound
SV—short vowel
VCe—long vowel
DI—digraph
BL—blend

Print Concepts
LR—left-to-right directionality
TB—top-to-bottom directionality
CW—concept of word
CL—concept of letter
COM—print as communication
PUN—punctuation

High-Frequency Sight Words
CP—copy from resource
CS—correct spelling without model

HIGH-FREQUENCY WORDS (Segment 6)
(no codes needed)

FIGURE 17.4. Codes for lesson objectives. From Anderson (2010). Copyright by the International Literacy Association. Reprinted by permission.

- *Phonological awareness.* Although the alliteration in this book will help to heighten children's sensitivity to the beginning sounds in words, the teacher chooses not to explicitly address this area because the book's primary utility is its usefulness in helping children learn the names of the letters of the alphabet. There would be no notation in the Phonological Awareness row nor in the corresponding columns for the children.

- *Vocabulary.* The teacher does not plan to teach the meanings of any particular words. There would be no notation in this row.

This illustration of the planning phase is intended to underscore the points that multiple goals should be addressed with a given book and that not all goals need to be addressed with each book.

Small-Group Read-Aloud: During the Lesson

READING THE BOOK

As the teacher reads the book, she holds it so that the children can see the words and pictures, and she points to the letters as they are named. Once every couple of pages, she points to each word on the page as she reads it. At least once, she explicitly explains how reading proceeds—for example, "When we read, we usually start at the top of the page and over on this side." Once or twice, she might ask the children to point to the place on the page where she should start reading. As she comes to letters that have particular meaning for the children, she might lead a brief discussion of the letter (e.g., "Oh, look! There's the letter *S*! Sam, you have an *S* at the beginning of your name! Does anyone else have an *S* in their name?"). Throughout this discussion, the teacher would keep her finger under the letter *S* in the book or point to another *S* in the teaching space (perhaps on Sam's name card). To help the children better connect the name of the letter *S* with its visual representation, the teacher might also invite children to find and name the *S*'s on the *S* page and to say the letter name each time.

Also while reading, the teacher and children would enjoy the silliness of the book, such as the duck-dog that David Donald Doo dreamed about (pp. 12–13). To develop comprehension and advance general knowledge, the teacher might ask why the dog is called a duck-dog (because it has duck feet) and discuss why ducks have feet of that sort.

USING THE LESSON SHEET

As the group enjoys the book, the teacher might use the lesson sheet to jog her memory for the things she was planning to do with the book. The sheet would also be used to capture brief notes concerning the responses of the individual children. In particular, the teacher would note children's progress toward accomplishing listed objectives and/or other observations she makes about individuals, using the *beginning* (B), *developing* (D), and *proficient* (P) designations discussed in Chapter 1. For example, if TeRoy seems confident in directing the teacher to the uppermost and leftmost word on the page when asked where to start, the teacher might record a *D* or a *P* (depending upon her previous observations of TeRoy) in TeRoy's box under Print Concepts on the lesson sheet. The teacher might also use the Comments/Notes for Next Session space at the bottom of the page for additional note taking. The lesson sheet would be used in similar ways across subsequent components.

Small-Group Read-Aloud: After the Lesson

At some point after the lesson, the teacher would take a few minutes to reflect on the focus and pace of the lesson and the children's responses to it and add any additional notes and comments that may help with planning upcoming lessons and that may be important for capturing on the group snapshots. In planning future lessons, the teacher would, once again, review the snapshots and look through the last couple of lessons for a particular group.

Rereading: Before the Lesson

CONSIDER THE CHILDREN

For children who are a bit further along, the first segment of the lesson would involve rereading one or more books that had been read in previous lessons. The purposes of rereading are to:

- Enable the children to read the text more fluently, which will, in turn, enable them to better comprehend it.
- Build children's confidence and sense of competence as readers.
- Reinforce children's ability to identify newly encountered high-frequency words.
- Provide children with practice in using decoding elements that occur in the text.
- Give children the opportunity to employ their developing word identification strategies with greater fluency and ease.

To reap the maximum benefit from the rereading segment, the teacher would give children some choice about which books they read; choice in reading materials is an important contributor to motivation. Also, ideally, each child would read a different book during this segment, or, if two children chose the same book, they would not read in unison. The point is to allow each child the opportunity to read an entire book and to do the thinking and problem solving that this entails.

If children read a book in unison, some children may simply shadow their friends, saying each word just a split second after the other children. As a result, these children will not extend their word-solving skills or build their sight vocabulary as effectively.

SELECTING THE BOOKS

Although book selection for rereading is limited to books previously read, the teacher would offer books that will help to reinforce particular skills or strategies that the children are learning. In general, books offered for rereading in the context of an intervention lesson should engage children in some strategic processing, as these books will provide more opportunity to guide the children's application of word-solving strategies. Books that the children read quite fluently are best utilized for free choice and/or take-home reading.

PREPARING THE LESSON SHEET

The names of the books to be offered for rereading would be listed in the Title (and Level) box on the lesson sheet. The teacher may plan to review particular skills or strategies that are appropriate for the children in relation to each book that will be offered. For example, for children who are just beginning to read emergent-level texts, the teacher might plan to remind them of the *check-the-pictures* strategy and the *think about the sounds* strategy. For children at this point in development the *think about the sounds* strategy would be qualified (e.g., "Think about the sound of the first letter"). The teacher would note that plan on her record sheet by circling or highlighting *TS* (for "think about the sounds") and *F* (for "first sound") and *CP* (for "check pictures") on the Word Identification Strategy line. For a more advanced group of children, the teacher might plan to remind them of a word family that was previously taught and that appears in a given book. She would record that plan by writing in the phonogram in the Letter/Sound section in Segment 1 (Read-Aloud/Shared Reading or Rereading) of the lesson sheet.

Rereading: During the Lesson

READING THE BOOK(S)

Listening to children read provides the opportunity to observe their individual approaches to word solving and to guide the development of their strategic approach to reading. In a small-group context, the teacher can listen to one child read while the other children either read independently or take turns reading to one another. Alternatively, all (in our example, three) of the children in the group can be asked to read, but in a quiet voice or whisper, so that the teacher can "tune in" to each child on an as-needed basis (this usually means that the teacher is out of her chair and at the side of different children as they read). As the children read, the teacher should note such areas as the word identification strategies and decoding skills they use effectively and which skills and strategies need to be revisited. As always, there should be some brief discussion of the story or information encountered in the book before, during, and after the children read.

Rereading: After the Lesson

Once the lesson is completed, the teacher would make a determination about whether the book(s) used would be useful for another rereading in the small-group context. The teacher would also reflect on, and make note of, instructional priorities for future lessons for the group.

Segment 2: Phonological Awareness

In this segment the instruction is designed to help children become attuned to the phonemes in spoken language. The development of sensitivity to, and awareness of, the individual sound components in spoken words tends to follow a predictable pattern. As discussed in Chapter 5, familiarity with this progression enables teachers to identify where children are in the process of becoming phonemically aware and what they are ready to learn next. In early lessons with beginning kindergartners who have been identified as being at risk for early reading difficulties, we suggest that teachers begin by focusing on the easiest phonological analysis skills and advancing through those skills as quickly as the children are able. For older and/or more advanced children, the teacher might consider using a dictated spelling assessment (e.g., the Primary Spelling Inventory provided by Bear et al. in all of the editions of their text) to gain initial insight into the parts of spoken words that the children are noticing and representing. Children who, in their attempted spellings, represent many of the sounds in spoken words probably do not need to receive instruction on isolated phonological analysis skills. For them, ongoing instruction about the alphabetic code will serve to further their ability to analyze spoken words at the level of the phoneme. For such children, the second segment (phonological awareness) of the lesson might be utilized only as an introductory step in teaching about some aspects of decoding. For example, in teaching about the long and the short sound of a vowel, the teacher might begin by having the children listen for the vowel sounds in spoken words and decide whether the targeted vowel sound comes at the beginning, in the middle, or at the end of spoken words.

The group snapshot for phonological skills provided in Chapter 5 (p. 123) is intended to help teachers keep the progression of skills in mind and to provide a way of documenting observations of students' skills. The first section of this snapshot would be used to record observations of the children's sensitivity to rhyme and alliteration in the context of read-alouds. The remainder is intended to be used during more isolated instructional activities, which are the focus of this second segment of the lesson.

Before the Lesson

CONSIDER THE CHILDREN

During the lesson planning phase, the teacher would review the group snapshot for phonological skills and her notes from prior lessons to determine the appropriate next steps for the children in the group.

- *Instruction for children at the earliest points in the development of phonological skills* would begin with activities that involve them in analyzing words at the level of onsets and rimes. The teacher might start with sound-sorting activities focused on either rhyming words or words with the same beginning sounds. When first introducing a particular sorting principle, the teacher would start with an odd-one-out procedure (e.g., choosing the one word in a set of three or four that doesn't rhyme with the rest of the words in the set). When children seem to understand the sorting principle, the teacher might use sorting boards (see Figure 5.5, p. 112). For sound-blending instruction, the teacher would begin with blending onsets and rimes and have the children select the picture that represents the blended word from a small set of pictures. For both beginning sound sorting and initial blending instruction, the teacher would use words with "stretchable" sounds in the onset (e.g., *net, fan, soup*) because it is easier to draw children's attention to sounds that can be elongated without distortion.

Children who are just beginning to attend to the sounds in words will not benefit from phoneme counting activities, so that type of instruction would be reserved for when they have made some progress in sound-sorting and -blending skills.

- *For children who are able to sort by beginning sound and rhyme and who can blend onsets and rimes,* instruction would focus their attention on all of the sounds in single-syllable words. The teacher might, for example, engage the children in sound blending with single phonemes by using a puppet. The first time this activity is initiated, the puppet would pronounce each phoneme in a word, and the children would identify the word by choosing it from a small group of pictures. Words in which all of the consonant sounds are stretchable would be used in the earliest lesson(s). As the children progress, such restrictions are relaxed. When the children demonstrate the ability to easily select the correct picture, the level of challenge is adjusted by removing the pictures from view while the teacher articulates the sounds. Later still, the teacher would engage the children in doing the segmenting. Some children will pick up these skills quite readily. This segment of the lesson can be eliminated when the children are proficient with all of the skills listed in sections II through IV of the group snapshot for phonological awareness (see Figure 5.11, p. 123).

PREPARING THE LESSON SHEET

In any given lesson, the teacher would typically engage the children in only one or two phonological awareness activities. Three types of phonological awareness activities are listed on the lesson sheet: sound sorting, sound blending, and sound counting/segmentation. For each type of activity, teachers choose different kinds of words and provide different supports, depending upon children's needs. In preparing the lesson sheet for the children at the earliest point in development, for example, the teacher might plan to teach them how to sort pictures by commonality in beginning sounds. This would be noted on the lesson sheet by circling or highlighting *BEG* in the Sound Sorting line. For at least the first sorting lesson, the teacher would use only words with stretchable beginning sounds. This would be noted by circling or highlighting the word *stretch*. The teacher would also note whether odd-one-out or sorting board activities will be used. For the group with more advanced phonological skills described above, the teacher would circle Single Phonemes and w/Pics (with pictures) on the Sound Blending line on the lesson sheet.

During the Lesson

Instruction for the two groups of children under discussion would begin with explicit instruction on the relevant skills, including demonstration and modeling if the activity is new. For the first several items that the children sort or blend, the teacher would emphasize the portion of the words to which the children are to attend. For example, the word *sun* would be pronounced *sssssssun* for a beginning sound sort and *sunnnnnn* for an ending sound sort. However, as the children begin to demonstrate the ability to sort or blend, the teacher should gradually reduce the amount of stretching she does to the point where the words are articulated in a normal way. When children are able to analyze (i.e., sort, blend, segment) words that are articulated normally, they are ready to move on to the next skill in the sequence, which involves the same task but with words that do not have stretchable sounds.

In the context of small-group lessons, children will inevitably make gains at different rates. Therefore, the teacher will need to modify instruction during the lesson, based on the skills of individual children. For example, the teacher might do more word stretching for some children than for others. Or, in a blending activity, she might leave less time between word segments for some children and leave more time between segments for others.

Segment 3: Decoding and Encoding

As noted in Chapters 6–10, children learn about individual letters in the alphabet in a predictable sequence. First they learn to recognize a letter, then to name it, then its most common sound; ultimately, they learn to use it in decoding (or sounding out) words. Most children who qualify for intervention in kindergarten need to learn the names of the letters (recognition and naming). Once they have learned a letter's name, they are ready to learn its sound and how to use it in reading and writing. As children begin to learn about the sounds of letters, the phonemic analysis and letter-sound segments of the lessons should be brought together so that they can more readily understand the purposes of both phonemic analysis and letter-sound instruction. As children progress in learning about the alphabetic code, they need to learn to process larger orthographic units (word families, prefixes, suffixes, etc.) to effectively and efficiently identify new words in text. Throughout this process the children need to learn to be flexible in their use of the code, because many words in written English are only partially decodable. In this segment of the lesson, the focus is on helping the children (1) learn about the elements of the alphabetic code and how the code works, and (2) become automatic (fluent) in the use of a variety of phonologically and morphologically based reading and spelling strategies.

Chapters 6–11 provide substantial detail on the development of skill with the alphabetic code. The chapters also provide group snapshots, which are designed to help teachers think about the various components that comprise skill with the code and to document the skills of individual children. For children who are just beginning to learn about the alphabet, the group snapshots for Alphabet Knowledge and for Alphabetic Code—Early Development will be most useful. For more advanced students, the snapshots for Alphabetic Code—Later Development and for Morphology and Multisyllabic Words will be most helpful.

As noted in Part II, instruction on new alphabetic skills should generally occur in preparation for reading a book in which a particular skill or skills can be applied. Once a skill has been taught, it should be revisited in subsequent lessons until children seem fairly secure in their ability to utilize the skill in isolation and, most important, in their ability to rely on the skill when attempting to identify unfamiliar words encountered while reading.

Before the Lesson

CONSIDER THE CHILDREN AND THE BOOK THAT THEY WILL READ

The order in which given elements of the alphabetic code are taught is partly dependent on the instructional materials (i.e., the books in both intervention and classroom settings) that are available for the children to read and partly dependent on what the children are ready to learn. We address book selection a bit in discussing

Segment 4 (Reading a New Book) of the lesson. Further discussion of that topic is presented in the Introduction to Part III, Word Learning (see pp. 231–235). Here it is important to point out that in our more recent primary-grade intervention study, we used a series of books that were designed to build decoding skills and sight vocabulary in a systematic way. In this series, the first book in which a particular element is addressed provides the children with multiple opportunities to practice decoding that element. In the next several books, that decoding element appears again, although not as frequently. These additional practice opportunities are intended to reinforce children's developing skills. While using such a series simplifies book selection a bit, for the children who struggled the most, it was often necessary for teachers to search for additional books to help reinforce particular decoding skills or books that focused more on other kinds of skills (e.g., high-frequency words). Clearly, no single set of instructional materials will meet the needs of all of the children all of the time.

Once the teacher has considered the skills of the students and has selected a book, instructional planning for this segment is fairly straightforward. For children who know little about the alphabet, developing letter-name knowledge would be the focus. Usually one or two letters would be introduced for specific attention, but whole-alphabet activities would be used as well (see Chapter 6). In the next segment of the lesson, the children would read one or more emergent-level books in which the targeted letter(s) occurs frequently. After reading the book with the children, the teacher would focus his or her attention on the new letter(s) through letter hunts and similar playful activities.

For children who have learned some letter sounds and who are ready to learn more, the teacher might plan to specifically teach a letter–sound correspondence and the appropriate key word. Word building, word reading, and written spelling would be used to practice and reinforce the newly taught and previously taught correspondences. Children who know most letter–sound correspondences for consonants and who can successfully engage in word-building, word-reading, and written-spelling exercises that require them to make changes at the beginnings and ends of words are ready to learn the vowel sounds and to engage in practice activities that involve switching between the long and short sounds of each vowel (Chapter 10). These children are also ready to learn to use phonograms and word families in their decoding and spelling attempts (Chapter 9) and, because they will also be encountering multisyllabic words in their reading, they will need guidance on how to puzzle through such words (Chapter 11).

PREPARING THE LESSON SHEET

The teacher would note the skill(s) she is planning to work on with the children by circling or highlighting the type of activity and writing in the specific elements for Segment 3. For example, for a group that is going to be learning the name of the letter *M* and doing a whole-alphabet activity (e.g., singing an alphabet song and pointing to the letters as it is sung), on the Letter Names line the teacher would write in the *M* and might write "Alphabet Song." She would also circle or highlight REC (for *Recognize*), or NAM (for *Name*), or PR (for *Print*), depending on the purpose of the instruction. For children learning to be flexible with the long- and short-*a* sounds, the teacher would write in "*a* sounds" on the "Other Decoding Elements" line. If the teacher plans to use word-building, word-reading, and/or written-spelling activities, she would write in the words that she will use on the appropriate lines and be sure to have the moveable letters needed to engage the children in these activities.

During the Lesson

The teacher would introduce and teach new skills explicitly, as detailed in Chapters 6–11. As the children engage in the practice activities, the teacher should carefully observe individual children and provide guidance and feedback as appropriate. The activities should allow each child in the group to engage in the intended thinking. Thus each child would have his or her own set of letters to use for word-building activities and his or her own writing materials during written spelling.

Segment 4: Reading a New Book

As discussed in some detail in Chapter 1, reading really is a complicated process. Indeed, we've devoted pages and pages to detailing the multiple attitudes, subprocesses, knowledge sources, strategies, and skills that a proficient reader ultimately develops. The complexity of reading development becomes even more evident when one considers that the reader has to coordinate all of these components and, for the most part, do most of it in an automatic and unconscious way while attending primarily or exclusively to the information or story that the text conveys. Despite this complexity, there is one rather simple rule regarding reading development: The more reading a child does, the better reader he or she becomes (see, for example, Allington & McGill-Franzen, 2013). Of course, it has to be engaged reading, meaning that the child needs to be thinking about what he or she is reading while reading. It also needs to be fairly accurate reading, meaning that the child needs to read the words that are on the page, not just supply words that fit the context fairly well but don't match the printed letters. Disengaged and inaccurate reading are common occurrences among young readers and older struggling readers. This occurs, in part, because the children do not really understand what they are supposed to be doing when they read. In ISA small-group and one-to-one reading lessons, the new-book segment provides the opportunity to clarify what reading entails and to guide the children's thinking about the process.

In most lessons, the children should read at least one new book that is some-what, but not too, challenging for them. Books that present some challenge give children the opportunity to apply what they are learning about the reading pro-cess and provide the teacher with the opportunity to coach the children in word-solving strategies. Because the teaching opportunities and the potential points of confusion vary considerably from one book to the next, all of the children should be reading the same book the first time a book is read in a small-group con-text. The book should be discussed before, during, and after reading to maintain a focus on reading for meaning rather than simply for the purpose of accurate decoding.

The children should be explicitly prepared to read the new book through the teaching of one or more high-frequency words and/or through instruction on new decoding elements that will be encountered in the book. Instruction relating to the decoding elements was discussed in Segment 3 above. The high-frequency words selected for explicit teaching would be those that the children are unlikely to be able to read given their current decoding skills and the strength of the context in which the word appears. These words would be taught before the children begin to read. For each book, the teacher plans to focus on particular instructional objectives that are appropriate for the children. Furthermore, in each lesson the teacher might plan to pay particular attention to one child as the children read so that she can document that child's effectiveness in using word identification strat-egies either when specifically prompted or spontaneously while reading. As was discussed briefly for Segment 1, a variety of goals and specific objectives might be pursued in the context of preparing for and reading the new book. Greater emphasis is placed on strategic word solving in this segment, as there is generally more opportunity to be strategic on the first reading of a book than in a reread-ing.

One of the most important goals we hope to achieve in the course of reading instruction is to teach children to help themselves learn to read. By providing them with a variety of strategies to use in figuring out words and encouraging them to take responsibility for ensuring that their reading makes sense, we increase the likelihood that the children will become successful, independent readers (see Chapter 12).

Before the Lesson

CONSIDER THE CHILDREN AND SELECT THE BOOK

Choosing an appropriate book for the children to read is an important first step. Books should be chosen that allow children to build upon what they already know and are able to do. Thus, if children are just beginning to learn the names of some of the letters, then predictable books with a repetitive pattern and strong picture support would be used. These books will help children learn about important print concepts and provide a vehicle for letter-recognition and letter-naming activities. For children who know several letter–sound correspondences and who have some basic print concepts established, the easiest strategy-promoting books would be a better match (see Part III, pp. 234–235). The use of such books might be interspersed with the use of books that focus on the development of high-frequency sight vocabulary (e.g., early sight word books, pp. 232–233).

As children grow as readers, they need increasingly challenging books. There is widespread agreement that, in supported reading settings, children should read books that are at their *instructional level*. This is sometimes defined as texts in which the child can accurately identify 90–94% of the words (e.g., Clay, 1993; Fountas & Pinnell, 1996). However, in intervention settings in which children are provided with close support and in which the goal is to help them learn effective word-solving strategies, we tend to be less concerned about such a precise match, as exactly how challenging a book will be for a given child or group of children will depend partially on the preparation they have for reading the book. Further, for beginning readers, the difficulty of a particular text will depend, to a great extent, on the children's instructional experiences prior to encountering the text. For example, young children who are in a program that emphasizes decoding are likely to find decodable texts easier to read than will children in programs that make heavy use of predictable texts and place comparatively little emphasis on teaching decoding strategies. Therefore, although teachers will certainly want to consider the designated level of difficulty for the books that their students read, it is most important to consider the challenges posed by the book for their students at their point of development and relative to the instructional experiences that the children have had. A review of the group's snapshots for listening and reading comprehension, as well as for strategic word solving, is particularly important when selecting the book and planning the instruction.[1]

PREPARING THE LESSON SHEET

The name of the book and the book's level (if it has one) should be recorded at the top of the reading segment of the lesson sheet. Prior to meeting with students, the teacher would consider the various goals and objectives listed on the lesson sheet for Segment 4. There should be a specific plan for addressing several of the major goals listed before, during, and/or after reading the book with the children. The Comprehension goal would be addressed every time children read a book. Therefore, it is at the top of the list. The teacher would circle the particular objectives

---

[1]There are multiple leveling systems available (e.g., Chall & Dale, 1995; Fountas & Pinnell, 1996; Fry, 2002) and ongoing concern about the reliability and validity of such systems (Benjamin, 2012; Pitcher & Zhihui, 2007; Glasswell & Ford, 2010).

she plans to address and (may) make brief notes about how this will be done. For example, the teacher would think about the comprehension challenges and opportunities posed by the text and what she might need to do to prepare the children to make sense of the text by, perhaps, explaining the structure of the text (see the example for the book *Look Closer* [Logan, 1997], described below), identifying an appropriate schema for the text, or engaging the children in anticipating what will happen in the text based on the title and the picture on the cover. Sometimes, for books with particular challenges, a teacher would plan a more thorough book introduction. Similarly, for word identification strategies, the teacher might plan to teach a new strategy before the children read or to review all of the strategies that have already been taught. Also during this phase, the teacher would determine whether the children will encounter any new concepts or words for which they may not know the meaning. If so, she would prepare a brief, child-friendly explanation of the word and note it in the vocabulary section of the lesson sheet. The teacher would print words that may need explanation on a word card.

During the Lesson

The teacher would start by introducing the book and generating enthusiasm for reading it (e.g., "I think you are really going to like this book," or "We are going to learn a lot about whales in this book," or "I picked this book because I know how much you like cats"). She might then show the high-frequency words, name each one, and have children practice reading them a few times. To draw the children's attention to the internal structure of the words, the teacher might have the children name the letters in the words or write the words. Before moving into the book, the teacher might also teach a new word identification strategy and/or remind the children of strategies that have already been discussed and practiced. Or, for children who are further along in the development of skill with the word identification strategies, the teacher might ask the children to name the strategies they can use when puzzling through unfamiliar words. She or he would then briefly discuss the content of the book. All of these introductory activities would take only a few minutes and might occur in any order.

Following the introductory activities, the children begin to read. Each would read the entire book individually and simultaneously—although not in unison. As the children read, the teacher would observe and provide guidance and support on the application of word-solving strategies and the use of resources (e.g., the word wall, the key-word chart, the word family display, and the strategies list) as scaffolding for independence. The teacher might move from child to child, or focus on an individual child, providing guidance and engaging in brief conversations to maintain a focus on the meaning of the text. The teacher would be attentive to the children's strategic word solving, making note of observable strategy use on the lesson sheet.

For the purpose of supporting strategic processing, the teacher will need to make multiple, on-the-spot decisions about how to respond to individual children's word-solving attempts. In doing so, the teacher would try to:

- Provide the child with enough time to think about the puzzling words—it takes time to be strategic.

- Consider whether or not to interrupt (or prompt) for minor miscues (errors) that do not disrupt the meaning of the text. If a miscue occurs on a high-frequency word that has been taught but that the child does not yet have in his or her sight vocabulary, the miscue may be important to address. If, however, a miscue occurs on a word that the child knows well, does not change the meaning of the text, and simply reflects the child's focus on the meaning of the text, then there is no benefit in bringing the child's attention to the miscue.

- Encourage the child to look carefully at the words on the page when a highly repetitive text leads the child to overgeneralize or overpredict the contents. Although errors of this type may not seriously disrupt the meaning of the text, overreliance on the repetitive refrain is a habit that is sometimes difficult for children to overcome. In these situations, it is helpful to remind children to be sure that their spoken words "match the words on the page."

- Avoid responding too quickly to meaning-disruptive miscues. The goal is for the child to realize that meaning has been disrupted and to self-correct. Therefore, the teacher needs to wait until the child has read far enough along to realize that an error has occurred. (This often means allowing the child to read to the end of the sentence or perhaps further.) If, at this point, the child doesn't notice and/or attempt to correct the error, the teacher would ask whether what was read made sense or sounded right and provide him or her with some suggestions for fixing the error, if need be. (The teacher should sometimes ask "Did that make sense?" when what the child read did, in fact, make sense, because the goal is to help children learn to monitor their own reading.)

- Provide low-utility and low-frequency words, such as unusual proper names or other words that the child is unlikely to encounter often in other contexts, if he or she hesitates over them at early points in development. As his or her reading skills develop, the child should be expected to at least make an attempt at such words.

When children are finished reading, there should be a brief group discussion of reactions to the book.

USING THE LESSON SHEET

As the children read, the teacher would use the lesson sheet to record observations regarding individual children. For example, in the comprehension section, the teacher might note whether the child draws the needed inferences to make sense of the text or whether he or she uses the picture cues (PC) to enhance understanding. Similarly, the teacher might use the letter codes for the word identification strategies to note the strategies that the child uses spontaneously (noting RP = Spon when she observes a child spontaneously reading past a puzzling word in an effort to identify it) or the strategies that the teacher needed to prompt (noting RP = Prom when she or he needed to prompt a child to read past a puzzling word). The lesson sheet can also be used to note high-frequency words that children might need additional practice on, print concepts that do not appear to be firmly established, and so forth. At the bottom of the lesson sheet for Segment 4, the teacher would make more extensive notes to help her plan upcoming lessons.

Support for Lesson Planning

Teachers have often commented that there are a lot of things to consider when engaging children in reading new books. There is thinking and decision making to be done before, during, and after the book is read. To remind teachers of all of the things that we would like them to consider, we have composed the reflection form presented in Figure 17.5. While the reflection form allows room for teachers to actually write in their thoughts, we find that, after a few uses, most teachers simply use the form as a reminder of the many things they should be considering as they work through new books with children. Several teachers have reported that they made a double-sided copy of the form, laminated it, and keep it handy in the space where they do their instructional planning.

Segment 5: Writing

In the context of a small-group-supported literacy lesson, writing is used to provide opportunities for children to learn to apply their developing alphabetic skills, including print concepts and phonemic analysis, and to emphasize the need to spell known high-frequency words conventionally. Because of this focus, the writing that the children do is often fairly contrived and/or determined and dictated by the teacher. Although the objectives addressed in the writing component are generally focused on the mechanical aspects of writing rather than on the development of composition skills and story/text elements, this particular lens should not suggest that composition skills are unimportant for beginning and struggling readers. Rather, there is simply too little time in an intervention lesson to allow for a focus on composition. In whole-class contexts children should, of course, be given the opportunity to compose text for authentic purposes.

(text resumes on page 399)

Before Reading	
Questions to Consider	**Thoughts and Plans**
Did I set a purpose (or help the students set a purpose) for reading and promote enthusiasm for reading?	
Did I choose a book that was at an appropriate level of challenge for the students in the group?	
Did I introduce and provide practice on one or two decoding elements that would be encountered in the text?	
Did I introduce and provide practice with a few high-frequency words that would be encountered in the text and that the students would be unlikely to be able to figure out given their current skills and strategies?	
Did I provide a book introduction that made the text accessible to the students but still allowed opportunities for problem solving?	
Did I teach or review word identification strategies that were appropriate for the children in the group?	
Did I discuss the meanings of important words for which the students might not know the meaning?	

FIGURE 17.5. ISA-supported reading of a new book—reflection form. From Scanlon, Anderson, and the ISA Professional Development Project (2012). Copyright by the authors. Reprinted by permission. *(page 1 of 4)*

During Reading	
Questions to Consider	**Thoughts and Plans**
Were the resources students might use during reading readily available (e.g., word wall or Words We Know chart, Bb/Dd chart, strategies list, phonogram/word family list)?	
Did the students approach reading as a meaning-making enterprise?	
Did the students rely too heavily on me when they encountered words they could not immediately identify?	
Did students use both meaning-based and code-based strategies in mutually supportive ways?	
Was the support that I provided on puzzling words appropriate for these students at this point in time?	
When a student puzzled over a word, did I allow sufficient time before intervening?	
When students misidentified a word, did I wait for them to read far enough along to recognize that an error had occurred before I intervened?	
Am I careful to avoid confirming accurate word identification when the student could do so him- or herself?	

FIGURE 17.5. *(page 2 of 4)*

Questions to Consider	Thoughts and Plans
Am I working toward encouraging independence in word solving?	
Do the students seem to construe word solving as "doable"?	
Was I careful not to take all of the responsibility for noticing word identification errors?	
Did the students monitor their own comprehension?	
Was there sufficient conversation about the text to support and enhance the development of comprehension?	
Was meaning-focused discussion of the text collaborative and nonevaluative?	
Did the children enjoy their reading?	

FIGURE 17.5. *(page 3 of 4)*

After Reading	
Questions to Consider	**Thoughts and Plans**
Did the follow-up discussion initially focus on the meaning and enjoyment of the text?	
Did I help the children reflect on their word-solving strategies, and/or did the students do so spontaneously?	
Were the children able to articulate their word-solving strategies?	
What do I need to learn more about concerning the reading skills of these children?	
What knowledge or concepts do I see as needing attention?	

FIGURE 17.5. *(page 4 of 4)*

Before the Lesson

CONSIDER THE CHILDREN

As for reading, writing requires the orchestration of various types of knowledge and skill. To identify reasonable next steps for children in the writing segment of the lesson, the teacher might review the group snapshots for purposes and conventions of print, phonological skills, alphabet knowledge, early and/or later development of the alphabetic code, morphological units and multisyllabic words, and the group's "Words We Know" chart (see Segment 6 on p. 400). For children who are just beginning to learn about print, the writing segment often involves shared writing (as discussed in Chapter 2), wherein the teacher emphasizes concepts and processes that are appropriate for the children with whom she is working. For more advanced children, less time would be spent on shared writing and more time would be devoted to having the children write. Thus, for example, the teacher might model a sentence she'd like the children to write and then ask them to write their own similar sentence. For children who are even further along, the writing in an intervention lesson would often be done in response to the book they read in the previous segment. For the sake of efficiency, the teacher might give the children a specific writing prompt related to the book so that most of the writing time can be devoted to guiding the children's thinking related to how to apply their developing knowledge of the writing system and how to use resources such as word walls and key-word charts. In writing a response to a book, the children would be encouraged to use the book as a resource to support conventional spelling of words from the book.

PREPARING THE LESSON SHEET

The sentence or writing prompt that will be used during the writing segment should be noted on the lesson sheet prior to the lesson. The sentence or prompt should be constructed to elicit the skills that the children have been learning. Thus the prompt would lead the children to include recently taught high-frequency words and elements of the code (letters, word families, digraphs, etc.). In addition, the teacher should plan to observe how successfully the children handle various aspects of the process. For example, for the Letters/Sounds line of the writing segment, the teacher might circle ES (for ending sound) to remind herself to notice whether the children are using acceptable letters to represent the ending sounds in the words they write.

During the Lesson

As in other segments of the lesson, instruction should be as explicit as necessary to help children understand the processes and to learn to use the resources. Shared writing should be used to introduce new skills and concepts (e.g., leaving spaces between words, adding a silent *e* on long vowel words, checking the word chart for the spelling of a high-frequency word). The teacher should model the thinking that she'd ultimately like the children to do by thinking aloud (e.g., "I need to leave a space before I start to write the next word").

When the children write, the teacher should move from one child to the next, offering assistance and guidance as needed, while being mindful of the goal of building independence. Thus, for example, when a child is puzzling over how to write a particular word, the teacher would need to decide whether to stretch the word for the child or to help him or her do the stretching. The latter approach contributes to the development of the child's ultimate independence as a writer.

After the Lesson

As for other segments, the teacher would reflect on what occurred in the lesson and make note of what should be addressed in upcoming lessons. Periodically she should update the group snapshots in order to document the children's progress relative to print concepts and skill with the various aspects of the alphabetic code.

Segment 6: High-Frequency Words

This segment of the lesson is used primarily for practice activities with high-frequency words and to evaluate growth in sight vocabulary; it does not include initial explicit teaching (high-frequency words are taught in preparation for reading a book). Therefore, we do not discuss the before, during, and after phases of lesson planning for high-frequency words as we did for previous segments.

Recently taught high-frequency words and/or words that the children continue to confuse can be used in game-like activities during this segment. Words that are particularly troublesome for children should be practiced by writing them several times, as writing a word helps children attend to its internal features. Because there are several productive games that can be used to provide practice on high-frequency words, a teacher can periodically find time to assess individual children's knowledge in this area by having some of the children play sight word games (e.g., tic-tac-toe, parking lot) while she assesses one child. As an alternative to an explicit assessment, the teacher might engage one child in a Your Pile/My Pile game while other children in the group play sight word games. Periodically this segment of the lesson should be used to review all of the words on the group's "Words We Know" chart by reading the entire chart or sections of it and/or by administering spelling "tests" in which the children *get* to refer to the chart for conventional spellings.

A Complete Small-Group Lesson

The preceding discussion of the segments of a small-group lesson was intended to cover various aspects of the thinking, planning, decision making, and record keeping that go into delivering effective and responsive small-group early literacy instruction. Because we attempted to represent children at various points along the developmental continuum, the discussion does not provide a sense of the flow and pacing of an actual lesson. Therefore, in this section we provide a description of an entire lesson provided by an intervention teacher for a group of kindergartners toward the end of the school year. Two of the children (Michaela and Jaquan) have been in the group since October. The third (Max) joined the group more recently, having moved to the school in March. All three have the same classroom teacher. Figure 17.6 presents the lesson sheet for the lesson described here. Cursive font is used to show what was written on the lesson sheet before the lesson began; things that the teacher wrote during and after the lesson appear in manuscript font. (The codes provided in Figure 17.4 will aid in the interpretation of this lesson sheet. Also, note that the teacher uses the codes B, D, and P to indicate whether she perceives each child to be at a beginning, developing, or proficient level of performance.)

Segment 1: Read-Aloud/Shared Reading or Rereading

Early in the school year, Mrs. D used the first part of the lesson as a time for read-aloud or shared reading, often choosing an alphabet book or a book that featured rhyme or alliteration. More recently, she has begun to use this time for rereading emergent-level books from earlier lessons. Today she has chosen two emergent-level (EM on Figure 17.6) books, *My Bear* (Beech, 2003) and *Go to* (Short, 1999), because they provide important opportunities for the children to practice a number of high-frequency words that have already been taught, and because the pictures, while supportive, are sometimes ambiguous and require the children to attend to the print in addition to being guided by context. For example, in *Go to*, the children must attend to at least the first letter in the final word on the page to know if the sentence should read "I go to *bed*" or "I go to *sleep*."

As she prepares them for rereading, Mrs. D reminds the children to point carefully to the words as they read, and she reviews what they have learned to do when they come to a word they don't know: "You really have to look at the letters, think about the sounds, and match the pictures." She lets each child decide which book to read first, and then she moves about the group, listening to each student read. Her interactions with the children focus on enjoying and understanding the stories, as well as reading the words correctly. Because later in the lesson she plans to teach the children how to use the ending sounds as well as the beginning sounds when puzzling through words, she uses this opportunity to begin to focus their attention on the letters at the end of words. For example, when Michaela reads the sentence, "My bear can read," Mrs. D asks her how she knows the word is *read*. Mrs. D extends Michaela's response of "because it says *r-e-a-d*" by commenting, "Great, and you heard the /d/ at the end, rea*d*, and the picture shows him reading!" She uses a similar approach with each of the students, guiding them to attend to the ending sound in a word they have just read as they confirm that the pictures and the letter sounds do indeed match.

(text resumes on page 406)

Lesson Sheet

Child 1 _Jaquan_ _____   Child 2 _Michaela_ _____   Child 3 _Max_ _____

1. Read-Aloud/Shared Reading or Rereading		
Title (and Level): _My Bear (EM), go to (EM)_		
Text Comprehension: (GU,) AE, RET (PC,) CON		
D	P	D
Word Identification Strategy: _IS-L (notice final letter sound)_ Code (TS) [F,(L,)M], LP, DS, BW), Meaning (CP,) MS, RP, SA), interactive and confirmatory (IC)		
D	D	B
Fluency: WBW, PHR, FL		
Letter/Sound: REC, NAM, LS		
Print Concepts: _Track print while reading_ _point while reading_ LR, TB, CW, CL, COM, PUN (1-1)		
P	P	D
High-Frequency Words: _review: my, can, go_ REC, ID		
P	P	P—my, can D—go
Phonological Awareness: CR, IR, IA		
Vocabulary		
Comments/Notes for Next Session: **Max occasionally used picture and first letter in confirmatory way.** **Jaquan and Michaela—consistent in doing so.**		

FIGURE 17.6. Completed lesson sheet for small-group instruction. Adapted from Anderson (2010). Copyright by the International Literacy Association. Adapted by permission. _(page 1 of 4)_

Child 1 *Jaquan* _____ Child 2 *Michaela* _____ Child 3 *Max* _____

2. Phonological Awareness		
Sound Sorting RH, BEG, (END) MID		STRETCH??
Sound Blending Onset–Rime, Single Phonemes w/Pics, w/o Pics		STRETCH??
Sound Counting/Segmentation 2 Phonemes, 3 Phonemes		STRETCH??
P	P	B
Comments/Notes for Next Session:		
Very difficult for Max—have Jaquan and Michaela work to complete an ending sound sort with letters for column headers. Work w/ Max on ending sound sort with stretchables.		

3. Decoding and Encoding		
Letter Names: BE, NAM, PR Letter Sounds (LS,) CS-B, CS-E *Review LS for L* Other Decoding Elements		
Word Building		
Word Reading		
Written Spelling		
Comments/Notes for Next Session:		
Consonant substitution for beginning and ending sounds—have Max focus mostly on beginning sound.		

FIGURE 17.6. *(page 2 of 4)*

Child 1 *Jaquan*   Child 2 *Michaela*   Child 3 *Max*

4. Reading		
Title (and Level): *Look Closer (EM)*		
Text Comprehension: GU, AE, RET, PC, CON *Text Structure—opposing pages Concepts of photography and magnifying glass*		
Word Identification Strategy: *TS-L, I see the leaf demo* Code ((TS)[F,(L)M], LP, DS, BW), Meaning (PIC, MS, RP, SA), interactive and confirmatory (IC)		
TS-*L* & Pic-Spon	**TS-*L*-Prom**	**Pic and TS-B Spon** **Pic and TS-*L*-Prom**
Fluency: WBW, PHR, FL		
Letter/Sound: REC, NAM, LS		
Print Concepts: *Exclamation point—Look, look, look!* LR, TB, CW, CL, COM, (PUN) 1-1		
D	**D Surprised by last page:** **"They're all the same!"**	**B**
High-Frequency Words: *New: look Review: at* REC (ID)		
look—**D** *at*—**P**	*Look*—**D** *at*—**P**	*look*—**B** *at*—**D**
Phonological Awareness: CR, IR, IA		
Vocabulary *photograph, magnify, vein* *log*—no one knew		
D	**D**	**D**
Comments/Notes for Next Session: Review meaning of log on reread. Excited about photographs—include more nonfiction. Max needs more modeling re use of key-word chart. Jaquan can't wait to get to the books! Independently checked ending sound.		

FIGURE 17.6. *(page 3 of 4)*

Child 1 *Jaquan* _____   Child 2 *Michaela* _____   Child 3 *Max* _____

5. Writing		
Writing Prompt or Dictated Sentence: *Look at the . . . —Model writing and then remove before the children write.*		
Letters/Sounds: *Sound spell word from book that starts with L* PR, LS, BS, ES, SV, L, VCe, DI, BL		
LEF	LDBG	LXO
Print Concepts: (LR)(TB,)CW, CL, COM, PUN		
LR, TB-P	LR, TB-P	LR, TB-?
High-Frequency Words: *Remind re WWK chart ("Words We Know")* CP, CS		
used chart for MY		
Comments/Notes for Next Session: Jaquan and Michaela noticing beginning, middle, and end sounds—using key-word chart independently. Max attending to beginning sounds only: needs more work on Phonemic Analysis.		

6. High-Frequency Words		
Practice Plan: *Parking lot with HF words*		
Fast and accurate at finding words.	Loves this game; promised one for take home.	Needs to look at model to find words.

FIGURE 17.6. *(page 4 of 4)*

Segment 2: Phonological Analysis

Jaquan, Michaela, and Max have already spent time sorting pictures that rhyme and that have the same beginning sounds and have done quite well with those activities. They are also able to use beginning sounds when figuring out printed words and when they attempt to write. At this point, Mrs. D's goal is to help them use the sounds at both the beginning and the end of words for these purposes. Today, she uses a quick picture-sorting activity as a way to help them attend to the ending sounds in words without having to also think about the letter that goes with that sound. She gives the children a purpose for what they are learning: "This is going to help us when we read. We've been looking at the beginning letters and thinking about their sounds and matching sounds with the pictures, but sometimes we need to look all the way through to the end of the word to make sure that we know what the word is." Because these children already know most of the consonant sounds, Mrs. D will make the connection to letters in the next segment.

Segment 3: Decoding and Encoding

The picture sort done in the phonemic analysis segment of the lesson is followed by a brief review of the sound for the letter *L*, with Mrs. D modeling the use of the key-word chart to remind them that, if they need to, they can use the picture of the lamp to remember the sound for *L*. (Note that the intervention teacher uses the key words that are in use in the children's classroom rather than the key words provided in Chapter 7.) Mrs. D then tells the group: "When we read our new book today, there'll be a lot of words that start with *L*. So you'll need to use your *L* sound, /lllll/, and check your picture, but you'll need to check your ending sound, too."

Because Mrs. D plans to focus more on letters and sounds, as well as phonemic analysis, in the writing portion of the day's lesson, she uses the time prior to reading a new book to introduce a new decoding strategy. Therefore, this portion of the lesson is abbreviated to allow time for strategy discussion in preparation for the new book.

Segment 4: Reading a New Book

At this point, Jaquan and Michaela are consistently able to use the first letter in an unfamiliar word to help in word identification; Max is somewhat less consistent with this but is showing progress. All three children are able to use pictures and contextual cues, and they have been learning to use these various cues in conjunction with one another (i.e., interactive and confirmatory strategy use). An important next step for them is to use both beginning and ending sounds for decoding, in conjunction with picture and contextual cues in order to confirm the identity of words.

Before introducing a text in which she will assist the children in applying this new strategy, Mrs. D first teaches the strategy. She begins by reminding the children of what they already know how to do when they encounter a puzzling word ("You know you can look at the pictures, think about the beginning sound, and think of what would make sense"). She then explains: "Sometimes, you could try all of those things and you still won't be sure what the word is. So today we are going to learn another thing we can try. We're going to try looking at the ending sound in the puzzling word. Let me show you." The teacher displays a sentence strip with the sentence "I see the leaf." She knows that the first three words are part of the children's sight vocabularies. *Leaf* is the word that they will need to puzzle over. The group reads the sentence up to the word *leaf*, and while pointing to the word *leaf*, the teacher says: "There are a lot of words that begin with *L*. So, to figure out a word, sometimes we need to think about the beginning sound *and* the ending sound. I have four pictures here: lamp, leaf, lion, and lamb. They all start with that /l/ sound. We need to decide which word comes at the end of this sentence. Could it be *lamp*? . . . *Leaf*? . . . *Lion*? . . . *Lamb*?" When the children decide that the puzzling word must be *leaf*, the teacher confirms and reflects with them on how paying attention to the ending sound "comes in handy" when they are figuring out words. This brief activity allows the teacher to keep the children's attention focused on the extension of the *think about the sounds* strategy that, until now, only applied to the first sound for these children. Mrs. D uses these isolated activities, as needed, for introducing and extending word identification strategies, but her goal is to have the children apply what they learn about strategies within the context of books. She reminds the children that when they think about the sounds in words, they now know how to use the beginning sound and the ending sound and that they will get to do it in their new book today.

Mrs. D introduces the new book, *Look Closer* (Logan, 1997). This book features many words that begin with the letter *L* and will provide extra practice with this letter–sound association. Because so many of the words begin with the same letter, it also provides an opportunity for the children to begin using ending sounds as well as beginning sounds for figuring out words.

As part of her book introduction, Mrs. D introduces two new vocabulary words: *photograph* and *magnifying glass*. These words are not in the book, but they are useful in helping the children to understand how the book is designed. (Each set of opposing pages features a photograph of an object in nature, such as a leaf, and then a close-up view of the same object, as seen through a magnifying glass.) She also introduces the new high-frequency word *look* and reviews the words *at* and *the* on the word wall. Because there are only a few unfamiliar words in this book and because she thinks the pictures are sufficiently supportive, Mrs. D chooses not to do a picture walk; she wants to provide the children with the opportunity to use the strategies they are learning for figuring out the new words as they occur.

After the book introduction, Mrs. D gives each child a book and reminds them all to "use your finger" to point to the words as they read. All three children stop at the word *log* on the first page after reading "Look at the. . . ." The teacher asks them, "What are you going to do to figure that word out?" and then prompts with a specific strategy, "Why don't you make your beginning sound first."

When Jaquan says the word *land* instead of *log*, Mrs. D responds by first pointing out all the things he did right: "Does *land* begin with *l*?" and "Is the picture showing land?" Then she suggests that it might not be the right word, saying "What does *land* end with?" as she emphasizes the /d/ sound. "So, that was a good thought, but we want a word that ends with *g*. What sound does *g* make?" The children readily respond with the hard *g* sound (as in *goat*). After a bit of time, it becomes clear that the children do not have the word *log* in their spoken vocabulary, so she tells them the word and then gives a child-friendly explanation of what a log is, being sure to have them repeat the word after her. Having established the label for the picture, she returns to her systematic means of having them think about the sounds in the word: "Does *log* begin with *l*? Does *log* end with *g*? And this is a picture of a *log*. . . ."

This back-and-forth between meaning and print is seen on several occasions, as Mrs. D explains how the magnifying camera works and compares the veins in the leaf to the veins in the children's own wrists. Importantly, she draws their attention to the sounds in the word even when they are correct, reinforcing the problem solving they have done. "Could that word be *ladybug*? How do you know?" When the children respond that *ladybug* "starts with *l* and ends with *g*," she encourages them to also think about the picture by asking, "And does that look like a ladybug?"

On the last page of the book, Mrs. D draws the children's attention to the exclamation mark at the end of the sentence and models reading "like you're excited." She also takes the opportunity provided by the photographs on the last page to remind the children of the meaning of the word *log*. As they find the picture of the log on the page, she describes it again: "It's that big piece of a tree that's fallen down in the woods."

Segment 5: Writing

Mrs. D has planned two separate but related writing activities for today. First she asks each of the children in the group to think of one thing that was photographed in the book they just read that begins with the letter *L* (using the word *photographed* purposefully to reinforce its meaning for the children). She asks the children to keep the word they are thinking a secret, and she gives each of them a sticky note on which to write their word, using sound spelling. She encourages them to think about beginning, middle, and ending sounds and tells them that she will use the clues from their sound spelling to figure out which word from the story they have written.

After figuring out the word each child wrote—LEF, *leaf*; LDBG, *ladybug*; and LXO, *leaf*—Mrs. D shows each of the children the "book spelling" for their words. As she writes the book spelling on the sticky notes underneath the words the children have written, she is careful to point out the places where the two spellings match. It is important to note here that, on many occasions, Mrs. D would have figured out the children's words and complimented them on their sound spelling but would not have shown them the book spellings. However, she shows the book spelling on this occasion because she is going to have the children write the words in their personal alphabet books, and she wants these permanent representations of the words to be spelled conventionally.

Finally, Mrs. D models the sentence that they are going to write in their alphabet books, explicitly engaging the children in conversation about important print concepts (e.g., "I am going to start writing up in this corner of the paper"; "I don't have room to finish my sentence here—what should I do?"; "I need to be sure to put a period at the end of my sentence") and the use of instructional resources (e.g., "If I can't remember how to spell the word *the*, what can I do?"). Each sentence will begin the same—"Look at the . . ."—and end with the child's own word from the sticky note. Mrs. D then gives each of the children their personal alphabet book that they have been working on throughout the year. When they finish writing, each child chooses a picture that matches their *L* word and glues it on the page with the sentence. They will take this alphabet book home at the end of the school year and will be encouraged to share it with their families and to continue to add to it over the summer.

Segment 6: High-Frequency Words

In the last few minutes of the lesson, the children play a parking lot game that includes some of the high-frequency words they have learned so far. Most of the words are those that have recently been introduced, including the day's new word, *look*.

Reflection on the Group

As is evident in Figure 17.6, Max is at a different point in development than the other two children in the group. The intervention teacher and the classroom teacher are both concerned that he has not made the kind of accelerated progress needed to close the gap between himself and his classmates. Jaquan and Michaela, on the other hand, are beginning to demonstrate the skills and strategies that are expected of kindergartners in their school at the end of the year. Because the group is not currently well matched in terms of the instructional needs of the children, the teachers and administrators involved in the school's early intervention program plan to meet in the near future to consider the most reasonable course of action. Given that there are 6 weeks of school remaining, they will consider several possibilities. The first consideration will be to regroup the children, putting Jaquan and Michaela in a group with one or more children who have similar skills and Max in a different group with one or two other children who are at similar points in development. Ideally this group would have more sessions than the two per week currently offered, as there is a clear need to intensify instruction if Max and similar children are going to begin to approach end-of-the-year expectations.

An alternative might be to discontinue Jaquan's and Michaela's involvement in Tier 2, thereby allowing the intervention teacher to provide Max with one-to-one intervention for the remainder of the year. The teachers will also work with Max's family to ensure that he will attend the district's summer literacy program. Unless dramatic changes are noted during the rest of the school year or during the summer, Max will likely qualify for Tier 3 intervention in the fall.

Intensifying Instruction: One-to-One Intervention

The goals and procedures described for small-group instruction are very similar to the goals and procedures utilized in a one-to-one instructional situation. The major difference between small-group and one-to-one is the intensity of the instruction and the degree to which the lesson can be responsive to the individual child. For ongoing record keeping the teacher might utilize the group snapshot forms, tracking only one child on that form or use the individual snapshot forms available on the companion website. The Daily Lesson Sheet used in the ISA, however, is a bit more detailed than the small-group lesson sheet. Figure 17.7 provides a slightly revised version of the lesson sheet used for one-to-one instruction in our most recent primary-grade intervention study. The segment numbers align with the segments as discussed for the small-group lesson described above. The major differences between small-group and one-to-one instruction related to lesson planning and documentation are described below. The most important difference for the child is, of course, that he or she has vastly increased opportunities to respond and to receive explicit guidance and feedback.

Segment 1: Rereading

The lesson sheet provides room for the teacher to plan and record observations for two books in both Segments 1 and 4. Although it is not always the case that two books would be read in each segment, it is often possible to do so, especially when the child is still reading emergent-level books that tend to be quite short. In the rereading segment, for each book there is space for the teacher to record what, if anything, she plans to review with the child before he or she rereads a book. The review could focus on one or more strategies, high-frequency words, decoding elements, aspects of text structure, and so forth. The strategies section in both Segments 1 and 4 provides space for the teacher to record her observations of the child's strategy use while reading. The codes for noting strategies are provided in the text box at the bottom of both Segments 1 and 4. Teachers are encouraged to note the strategies that the child uses spontaneously (e.g., DS-Spon) and the strategies that the teacher prompts (e.g., BW-Prom). Teachers are not expected to note strategies that the child routinely employs (as would be evident on the child's

(text resumes on page 413)

Lesson Sheet

Name _____ Date _____ Session # _____

<table>
<tr><td colspan="2" align="center">**1. Rereading**</td></tr>
<tr><td>Text/Level:</td><td>Text/Level:</td></tr>
<tr><td>Review:</td><td>Review:</td></tr>
<tr><td>Strategies:
Spontaneous (Spon)/Prompted (Prom)</td><td>Strategies:
Spontaneous (Spon)/Prompted (Prom)</td></tr>
<tr><td>Important words missed:</td><td>Important words missed:</td></tr>
<tr><td>Fluency:
WBW—word by word
Phr—Phrasing   Fl—fluent</td><td>Fluency:
WBW—word by word
Phr—Phrasing   Fl—fluent</td></tr>
<tr><td colspan="2">Comments/Notes for Next Session:</td></tr>
</table>

<table>
<tr>
<td>TS—think sounds
DS—different sounds</td>
<td>LP—look for parts
BW—break word</td>
<td>CP—check pictures
MS—make sense</td>
<td>SA—start again
RP—read past</td>
</tr>
</table>

<table>
<tr><td colspan="2" align="center">**2. Phonological Awareness**</td></tr>
<tr><td>Sound Sorting RH, BEG, END, MID</td><td align="right">STRETCH??</td></tr>
<tr><td>Sound Blending Onset–Rime, Single Phonemes w/Pics, w/o Pics</td><td align="right">STRETCH??</td></tr>
<tr><td>Sound Counting/Segmentation 2 Phonemes, 3 Phonemes</td><td align="right">STRETCH??</td></tr>
<tr><td align="right" colspan="2">Level of success:</td></tr>
</table>

<table>
<tr><td colspan="2" align="center">**3. Decoding and Encoding**</td></tr>
<tr><td colspan="2">Letter Names: REC, NAM, PR
Letter Sounds: CS-B, CS-E
Other Decoding Elements

                    Level of success:</td></tr>
<tr><td colspan="2">Alphabetic Mapping: Units/Decoding Principles</td></tr>
<tr><td>Word Building:</td><td>Level of Success:</td></tr>
<tr><td>Word Reading:</td><td>Level of Success:</td></tr>
<tr><td>Writing:</td><td>Level of Success:</td></tr>
<tr><td colspan="2">Comments/Notes for Next Session:</td></tr>
<tr><td colspan="2">**Level of Success:**   **B—beginning**   **D—developing**   **P—proficient**</td></tr>
</table>

FIGURE 17.7. One-to-one daily lesson sheet. *(page 1 of 2)*

4. Reading					
Text/Level:			Text/Level:		
Prereading activities:			Prereading activities:		
High-Frequency Words:			High-Frequency Words:		
Word Identification Strategies	Comprehension		Word Identification Strategies	Comprehension	
Planned focus:			Planned focus:		
Observed use:			Observed use:		
Important words missed:			Important words missed:		
Fluency: WBW—word by word Phr—Phrasing Fl—fluent			Fluency: WBW—word by word Phr—Phrasing Fl—fluent		
Reading Log Entry:			Reading Log Entry:		
Comments/Notes for Next Session:					

TS—think sounds	LP—looking for parts	CP—check pictures	SA—start again
DS—different sounds	BW—break word	MS—make sense	RP—read past

5. Writing
Writing Prompt or Dictated Sentence(s)
Notes/Comments for Next Session:

6. High-Frequency Words
Practice Activity:
Words **added** to "Words I Know" chart:
Words **missed** on "Words I Know" chart:
Comments/Notes for Next Session:

FIGURE 17.7. *(page 2 of 2)*

snapshot for Word Identification Strategies). Rather, the teacher notes emerging and developing strategies. There is also a place for the teacher to note important words that the child misreads, so that she can consider addressing those words in either Segment 5 of the current lesson or in upcoming lessons. In this context an important word is a high-frequency word that the teacher thought was part of the child's sight vocabulary. There is also a section for noting the degree of fluency for each book. Fluency determinations are based primarily on consideration of prosody, which includes phrasing and intonation. Books that a child reads accurately and fluently (i.e., sounding like a storyteller) would not typically be offered for rereading in upcoming lessons because they offer no opportunity for teaching or supporting the child's developing skills and strategies. Few, if any, books should be read in a word-by-word fashion in the context of a one-to-one lesson, so this code is rarely used. However, it is left on the lesson sheet as a reminder to teachers that, if they use the code often, they need to make adjustments to the books they are offering and/or to the preparation they are doing for those books.

Segment 2: Phonological Awareness

Instruction and record keeping for this segment of the lesson are similar to what was described for the small group. The major difference, of course, is that what is done in this segment should fit the child's current skills fairly precisely.

Segment 3: Decoding and Encoding

For Segment 3, instruction and record keeping are quite similar to what was described for Segment 3 of the group lesson. New skills taught in this segment are skills that can be applied in the book(s) that will be read in the next segment. The new skills are practiced in combination with previously taught skills. Further, to provide more individualized support, a word family chart is developed for each child. Based on earlier instruction and practice, the chart contains the word families that the teacher expects the child to know and to be able to use effectively in his or her reading and writing (see Chapter 9).

Segment 4: Reading

This segment of the lesson sheet looks quite different from the parallel segment for the small-group lesson. The different look is due primarily to an effort to save paper rather than to any shift in focus. For the reading segment, the teacher would note plans for introducing and preparing the child to read each book. The pre-reading activities section would include notations concerning the book introduction and any words for which the child may not know the meaning. The High-Frequency Words section is used to record words that are taught in preparation for reading the book. The next section provides space for the teacher to note the word identification strategies she plans to teach. Just below the Planned Focus area is a space for the teacher to record her observations related to strategy use. To the right of the Word Identification Strategy section, there is room for the teacher to indicate what she or he plans to do to support comprehension. The Important Words Missed and Fluency sections were described in Segment 1. The Reading Log Entry section is an optional component that is used if the child seems motivated to keep a list of books that he or she has read and to make comments on those books. If this approach appeals to the child, the reading log entry is often used to fulfill the writing component of the lesson.

Segment 5: Writing

The writing segment has the same purposes in the one-to-one context as it does in the small-group context. However, because the teacher is focused exclusively on one child, she can more effectively identify and address the child's needs and interests. In particular, the teacher can be flexible with regard to the type of writing that the child does, based on his or her preferences. For example, some chatty children are eager to share out-of-school experiences with the teacher; the teacher might channel that energy by asking the child to write about the experience. Alternatively, the teacher might prompt the child to write about something that was discussed while reading the new book for the day. Because this segment typically follows directly after reading, the discussion of the text can serve as an important scaffold for writing, providing the child the opportunity to articulate his or her understanding and responses before attempting to express them in writing. In order to ensure that what the child writes provides the desired opportunities to apply developing skills and strategies, the teacher should always be prepared with a writing prompt or a sentence to dictate. If a better and more motivating alternative emerges during the course of a lesson, teachers are free to utilize it.

Segment 6: High-Frequency Words

This segment of a one-to-one lesson is used both to provide practice on high-frequency words that were previously introduced and to document the child's progress. Important words missed during the course of reading the day's books might be incorporated into practice activities. Various games are used to practice previously taught high-frequency words. The Your Pile/My Pile game (see Chapter 13, pp. 289–291) is used to practice and assess the child's knowledge of high-frequency words and to make a determination of which words should be placed on the individual's "Words I Know" chart. Words on this chart are expected to be identified automatically when encountered in context and to be spelled conventionally when the child writes. Conventional spelling should be supported by reference to the chart.

CHAPTER 18

Revisiting and Concluding

In this chapter we revisit the instructional goals that have been discussed throughout the text for the purpose of demonstrating the multiple ways in which the skills, abilities, and attitudes and beliefs that we hope to develop in young children are interconnected and mutually supportive. We also revisit the instructional principles introduced at the beginning of the book and take the opportunity to emphasize once again the critical role that teachers, teachers' knowledge, and teachers' ability to utilize that knowledge play in preventing long-term reading difficulties.

Reading Is a Complex Process

We began Chapter 1 with a discussion of the complexity of the reading process and made the argument that, in order to effectively support the literacy development of beginning and struggling readers, teachers need to be thoughtful about this complexity so as to be better able to identify and address potential sources of challenge for developing readers. In concluding this text, we revisit the notion of complexity by way of summarizing much of what we have discussed throughout the book. We use a graphic representation of the complexity of the reading process that we have found useful in our work with teachers (see Figure 18.1).

Comprehension and Knowledge are located at the center of Figure 18.1, as comprehension and knowledge development are the central reason for reading and the two are inextricably linked. Comprehending a text allows the reader to build knowledge, and the reader's knowledge influences his or her ability to comprehend

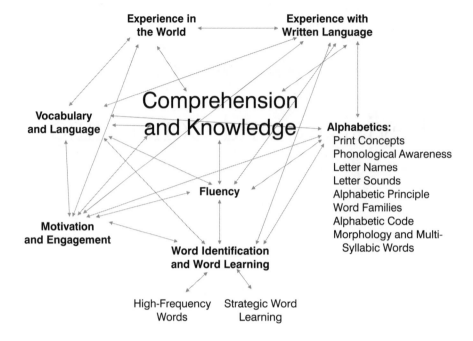

FIGURE 18.1. The complexity of the reading process.

text. The more someone knows about something, the more readily he or she can learn more about that particular thing through reading and/or listening to text. Comprehension and knowledge are influenced by and influence all of the factors to which they are connected in the model, and many of the factors are reciprocally related to one another, as illustrated by the double-headed arrows. Here we discuss prominent interconnections but leave the reader of this book to ponder the full complexity of the model and the process. We discuss each aspect of the model in turn, beginning with Vocabulary and Language and moving around the model in a clockwise direction.

Obviously, in order to understand a text, a reader needs to understand the meaning of the vast majority of the words in the text and have sufficient skill with syntax and grammar to be able to interpret the meanings of the sentences in the text. Thus, **Vocabulary and Language** skills influence comprehension and knowledge development. And the relationship is reciprocal. A reader's existing knowledge base and success in comprehending a text have the potential to build the reader's vocabulary and general language skills, as, generally, one encounters more sophisticated vocabulary and more sophisticated grammatical structures in text than in everyday spoken language. Indeed, the research suggests that, once children are literate, most new words that become part of their vocabularies are learned through reading.

Experience in the World, obviously, builds knowledge. The experiences one has had will influence how one comprehends a text. For example, a child who has visited an aquarium and seen penguins will comprehend a text about penguins differently than a child who has never seen penguins. Reciprocally, a child who has read or listened to books about penguins prior to first seeing them in the flesh will have a different experience than a child who has no relevant prior knowledge. Further, as illustrated by the double-headed arrow connecting to Vocabulary and Language, experience in the world influences and is influenced by one's vocabulary and language skills. To continue with the penguin example, a child who has read about and/or visited an aquarium with penguins has the potential to acquire vocabulary (and knowledge) related to penguins (e.g., flippers, insulation, icebergs, camouflage, Antarctica), and a child who has more advanced language skills is likely to be able to more effectively formulate questions (to be asked of adults accompanying them on a visit to an aquarium) that will elicit the desired information. They are also more likely to be able to comprehend the oral explanations that an aquarium guide might offer and the explanatory texts that may be read to them by the accompanying adult.

There are many, many interconnections and reciprocal relationships related to **Experience with Written Language**. We have already touched on the role of experience with written language as it relates to comprehension and knowledge, experience in the world, and vocabulary and language skills. Such experience also, again obviously, influences and is influenced by skill with **Alphabetics.** When young children engage with written language, through reading and writing, their understanding of the workings of the alphabetic code expand. Reciprocally, readers and writers who have greater understanding of the workings of the alphabetic code will have different experiences with written language than will those with more limited understanding. For example, a child who is at an early point in development may represent only the beginning sound of a word with a letter when he or she is writing, whereas a child with greater knowledge of the code (and greater sensitivity to the sounds in spoken words) is likely to more fully represent the sounds in words he or she attempts to write. These two children are apt to have a different sense of the utility of print as a result of the reactions of their readers, who will either mostly understand what the writer has written or be fairly clueless about the message.

Unlike the other aspects that are illustrated in the complex model, we do not view Alphabetics as having a direct and reciprocal relationship with Comprehension and Knowledge. Rather, while it is clearly critical for readers and writers to develop skill with the alphabetic code, the impact on comprehension and knowledge is indirect—through the process of **Word Identification and Word Learning.** Thus, for example, knowledge of the workings of the alphabetic code enables the reader to more effectively solve unfamiliar words encountered while reading, and this more effective word solving enables Comprehension and Knowledge development. Reciprocally, **Strategic Word Learning**, which for beginning readers generally requires that they use both alphabetic and contextual information (Vocabulary and Language skills) to confirm that they have identified a real word that fits the context (Share, 2008), has the potential to help the student learn more about the alphabetic code. For example, upon having effectively puzzled through such words as *pizza* and *piano*, and across a variety of contexts, the child might learn, at least implicitly, that the letter *i* is sometimes pronounced like a long-*e*.

Knowledge of **High-Frequency Words** is also reciprocally related to Word Identification and Word Learning. Knowing some of the most frequently occurring words enables the reader to more effectively draw on context to help to identify unfamiliar words, and some high-frequency words may be added to a reader's sight vocabulary through effective word solving while reading.

The relationship between **Fluency** and Comprehension and Knowledge is also reciprocal in nature. In order to impose the proper intonation and phrasing during oral reading, the reader must be comprehending the text at least at the level of the sentence. At the same time, being able to quickly and accurately identify words, the skill that contributes to the rate aspect of fluency, enables comprehension by freeing up cognitive resources that can instead be devoted to the process of meaning making.

The last factor in the model, **Motivation and Engagement,** has a pervasive and reciprocal relationship with all of the other factors; note that there are arrows depicting reciprocal relationships with all of the other aspects of the complex process. Indeed, we view Motivation and Engagement as so important that we identify it as our number one goal, and in working with teachers we find ourselves frequently reminding them of the power they have over children's attitudes toward reading and their beliefs about themselves as readers. Learners who believe that reading and writing are enjoyable, informative, and "doable" are more likely to be motivated by and engaged in learning opportunities and are more likely to profit from them. For example, they are more likely to ask questions and seek answers, and they are more likely to persist in the face of learning challenges.

We encourage teachers to keep the complexity of the reading process and the process of becoming literate in mind as they work with their young learners, as considering this complexity may help the teacher "zero in on" the source of a child's difficulties. For example, when a child doesn't understand the meaning of a passage, the reason could be that the child wasn't motivated or sufficiently engaged. Alternatively, the reason could be that the child doesn't know the meanings of some of the key words in the passage or that the syntax was too unfamiliar; or it could be that the child doesn't have the requisite background knowledge and/or experience in the world that the author of the text has taken for granted. Further, if the child is reading rather than listening to the text, difficulties with comprehension could be due to the fact that the child doesn't have the experience with written language and/or skill with the alphabetic code to enable him or her to effectively puzzle through the unfamiliar words encountered. And, even if the child does possess those skills, the unknown word may not be part of his or her vocabulary, and/or the child may not have the language skills that would enable him or her to use sentence context to confirm that the word(s) have been accurately identified. It is complex! In order to effectively guide a young reader, the teacher needs to be mindful of all of these possibilities (and more) so as to determine how to respond to difficulties.

General Principles for Preventing Reading Difficulties

Following is a list of the principles for preventing reading difficulties that we discussed in some detail in Chapter 1. Here our goal is to remind readers of these principles and to discuss how the principles relate to one another and to the instructional goals more generally.

- Teach children to be effective and independent problem solvers.
- Ensure that students are actively engaged in learning.
- Set high expectations for all children.
- Integrate support services with the classroom program.
- Plan for success.
- Track student progress.

For purpose of illustration, we consider how these principles apply in relation to Comprehension and Knowledge Development, the central goal of reading and reading instruction. Teaching children to be effective and independent problem solvers involves helping children to realize when their comprehension has broken down; to understand that, when this happens, they must do something to try to resolve the problem; and to learn about and practice the kinds of things they might do to resolve their confusion. In the context of listening to text read aloud, this would involve asking a question. In the context of reading, this would involve such things as rereading and reading ahead in search of additional information, considering whether the words have been accurately identified, perhaps trying some alternative pronunciations, and so forth. *Ensuring that children are active and engaged learners* is obviously highly related to the principle just discussed. For children to realize that their comprehension has broken down, they need to be really thinking about the text they are listening to or reading. Teachers communicate their high expectations in the texts they offer the children and in how they respond when students encounter difficulties. In the context of comprehension, if the teacher asks a question about a text that a child is unable to answer satisfactorily, a teacher who has high expectations for the child would explore the reasoning behind the child's response and perhaps spend some time guiding his or her thinking regarding the comprehension challenge posed. In contrast, a teacher with low expectations might simply move on to another child with the same question. To *integrate support services with the classroom program*, classroom and intervention teachers would, ideally, share common language in talking about certain comprehension processes (e.g., they might agree on talking about "visualizing" rather than "making a picture in your mind," or vice versa). *Planning for success*, in the context of Comprehension and Knowledge Development, is largely about being thoughtful about the comprehension (and other types of) challenges a text will present, determining what needs to be done in advance of reading the text to increase the likelihood that children will be successful while not doing so much preparation for the text that the students have little opportunity to exercise their developing problem-solving skills. The last of the principles listed, *track student progress*, is obviously related to a number of the other principles; it is critical, for example, in determining what aspects of comprehension need more thorough guidance (e.g., focusing on inference making, comprehension monitoring, etc.).

There are numerous other ways in which abiding by the principles becomes mutually supportive toward the overarching goal of preventing reading difficulties. For example, by *teaching children to be effective, independent problem solvers* we are essentially giving them the tools they need to grow as readers and writers; thereby, they become more likely to be able to meet *high expectations* we set for them and to be *active and engaged learners.* As another example, it is more likely that we will be able to teach children to be *active and independent problem solvers* if the *support services are integrated with the classroom program.* For instance, if teachers in support and intervention settings provide different guidance as to word solving and/or use different key words to remind students of letter–sound correspondences, children are less likely to become independent problem solvers, as they are receiving conflicting guidance.

Of course, it is entirely possible for instruction to be guided by some of these principles and not others. For example, in conversations with teachers in our professional development offerings, we have frequently found that *support services are not integrated with the classroom program,* resulting in children receiving very different and uncoordinated instruction in classroom and intervention settings. When this happens, the research suggests, it will limit children's growth in literacy (e.g., Wonder-McDowell et al., 2011). It is also possible to be guided by a principle but in a less than productive way. For example, many schools have elected to *track student progress* in RTI implementation through frequent administrations of measures of low-level skills (Scanlon, Anderson, & Goatley, 2015) (using instruments such as the DIBELS), which provide no useful information to guide instruction. As a result, teachers and children have lost time to assessment with no instructional benefit. Thus, this is a net loss for children. In contrast, in the ISA, we encourage teachers to *track progress* using the snapshots provided, which provide detailed information about what students know and are able to do and thereby provide information about what children are ready to learn next. This, in turn, enables teachers to *plan for success.* And when that planning is successful and the children therefore experience a sense of success in their learning, this is likely to lead them to be *more engaged and active learners.*

Concluding Thoughts

Our goal in writing this book has been to share what has been learned about how to support beginning and struggling readers in the development of literacy skills. The book is focused around a particular approach to early literacy instruction and intervention that we have found to be effective when implemented in intervention and classroom settings (Vellutino et al., 1996; Scanlon et al., 2005; Scanlon et al., 2008). In our studies, we focused on the critically important role of the teacher in identifying what children are ready to learn and in planning and delivering early literacy instruction that will serve to move each individual forward. Because of the complexity of the reading process, and because each child brings a different mix of prior experiences and underlying aptitudes to the literacy learning context, teachers need a good deal of expertise in order to help all children meet with success. In support of this perspective, our mantra across the last many years has become "Every child is ready to learn something, but they are not all ready to learn the same thing." Our job as educators is to figure out *what* the child is ready to learn, not *whether* the child is ready to learn.

References

Adams, M. J. (1990). *Beginning to read: Thinking and learning about print.* Cambridge, MA: MIT Press.

Adams, M. J., Foorman, B. R., Lundberg, I., & Beeler, T. (1998). *Phonemic awareness in young children.* Baltimore: Brookes.

Al Otaiba, S., Connor, C. M., Folsom, J. S., Wanzek, J., Greulich, L., & Wagner, R. K. (2014). To wait in Tier 1 or intervene immediately: A randomized experiment examining first-grade Response to Intervention in reading. *Exceptional Children, 81*(1), 11–27.

Allington, R. L., & Johnston, P. (1989). Coordination, collaboration, and consistency: The redesign of compensatory and special education interventions. In R. Slavin, N. Karweit, & N. Madden (Eds.), *Effective programs for students at risk* (pp. 220–263). Boston: Allyn & Bacon.

Allington, R. L., & McGill-Franzen, A. (2013). Summer reading loss. In R. L. Allington & A. McGill-Franzen (Eds.), *Summer reading: Closing the rich/poor reading achievement gap* (pp. 1–19). New York: Teachers College Press.

Allington, R. L., McGill-Franzen, A., Camilli, G., Williams, L., Graff, J., Zeig, J., . . . Nowak, R. (2010). Addressing summer reading setback among economically disadvantaged elementary students. *Reading Psychology, 31*(5), 411–427.

Almasi, J. F. (2003). *Teaching strategic processes in reading.* New York: Guilford Press.

American Heritage Children's Dictionary. (2003). New York: Houghton Mifflin.

Anderson, K. L. (2009). *The effects of professional development on early reading skills: A comparison of two approaches* (doctoral dissertation). Retrieved from ProQuest (ATT 3365837).

Anderson, K. L. (2010). Spotlight on the Interactive Strategies Approach: The case of

Roosevelt Elementary School. In M. Y. Lipson & K. K. Wixson (Eds.), *Successful approaches to RTI: Collaborative practices for improving K–12 literacy* (pp. 66–87). Newark, DE: International Reading Association.

Anderson, R. C. (1984). The role of readers' schema in comprehension, learning, and memory. In R. C. Anderson, J. Osborn, & R. Tierney (Eds.), *Learning to read in American schools: Basal readers and content texts* (pp. 243–257). Hillsdale, NJ: Erlbaum.

Anderson, R. C., Chinn, C., Waggoner, M., & Nguyen, K. (1998). Intellectually stimulating story discussions. In J. Osborn & F. Lehr (Eds.), *Literacy for all: Issues in teaching and learning* (pp. 170–186). New York: Guilford Press.

Anderson, R. C., & Pearson, P. D. (1984). A schema-theoretic view of basic processes in reading. In P. D. Pearson (Ed.), *Handbook of reading research* (pp. 255–291). New York: Longman.

August, D., McCardle, P., & Shanahan, T. (2014). Developing literacy in English language learners: Findings from a review of experimental research. *School Psychology Review, 43*(4), 490–498.

August, D., & Shanahan, T. (Eds.). (2006). *Developing literacy in second-language learners: Report of the national literacy panel on language minority children and youth.* Mahwah, NJ: Erlbaum.

Baker, L., & Beall, L. C. (2009). Metacognitive processes and reading comprehension. In S. E. D. Israel (Ed.), *Handbook of research on reading comprehension* (pp. 373–388). New York: Routledge.

Ball, E., & Blachman, B. (1991). Does phoneme awareness training in kindergarten make a difference in early word recognition and developmental spelling? *Reading Research Quarterly, 26*(1), 49–66.

Bandura, A. (1997). *Self-efficacy: The exercise of control.* New York: Freeman.

Bear, D. R., Invernizzi, M., Templeton, S., & Johnston, F. (2015). *Words their way: Word study for phonics, vocabulary, and spelling instruction* (6th ed.). Upper Saddle River, NJ: Prentice-Hall.

Beck, I. L., & McKeown, M. G. (2001). Text talk: Capturing the benefits of read-aloud experiences for young children. *The Reading Teacher, 55,* 10–20.

Beck, I. L., & McKeown, M. G. (2007). Increasing young low-income children's oral vocabulary repertoires through rich and focused instruction. *Elementary School Journal, 107*(3), 251–271.

Beck, I. L., McKeown, M. G., & Kucan, L. (2002). *Bringing words to life: Robust vocabulary instruction.* New York: Guilford Press.

Beck, I. L., McKeown, M. G., & Kucan, L. (2013). *Bringing words to life: Robust vocabulary instruction* (2nd ed.). New York: Guilford Press.

Benjamin, R. G. (2012). Reconstructing readability: Recent developments and recommendations in the analysis of text difficulty. *Educational Psychology Review, 24,* 63–88.

Berko, J. (1958). The child's learning of English morphology. *Word, 14,* 150–217.

Berninger, V. W., Abbott, R. D., Nagy, W., & Carlisle, J. (2010). Growth in phonological, orthographic, and morphological awareness in grades 1 to 6. *Journal of Psycholinguistic Research, 39,* 141–163.

Biemiller, A. (2006). Vocabulary development and instruction: A prerequisite for school learning. In S. B. Neuman & D. K. Dickenson (Eds.), *Handbook of early literacy research* (Vol. 2, pp. 29–40). New York: Guilford Press.

Biemiller, A., & Boote, C. (2006). An effective method for building meaning vocabulary in primary grades. *Journal of Educational Psychology, 98*(1), 44–62.

Blachman, B. A. (1991). Early intervention for children's reading problems: Clinical applications of the research in phonological awareness. *Topics in Language Disorders, 12,* 51–65.

Blachman, B. A., Ball, E. W., Black, R., & Tangel, D. M. (1994). Kindergarten teachers develop phoneme awareness in low-income, inner-city classrooms: Does it make a difference? *Reading and Writing: An Interdisciplinary Journal, 6,* 1–18.

Block, C. C., & Mangieri, J. N. (2003). *Exemplary literacy teachers: Promoting success for all children in grades K–5.* New York: Guilford Press.

Bloom, P. (2000). *How children learn the meanings of words.* Cambridge, MA: MIT Press.

Borman, G. D., Wong, K. K., Hedges, L. V., & D'Agostino, J. V. (2001). Coordinating categorical and regular programs: Effects on Title I students' educational opportunities and outcomes. In G. D. Borman, S. C. Stringfield, & R. E. Slavin (Eds.), *Title I: Compensatory education at the crossroads* (pp. 79–116). Mahwah, NJ: Erlbaum.

Bowers, P. N., Kirby, J. R., & Deacon, S. H. (2010). The effects of morphological instruction on literacy skills: A systematic review of the literature. *Review of Educational Research, 80,* 144–179.

Bradley, L., & Bryant, P. (1991). Phonological skills before and after learning to read. In S. A. Brady & D. P. Shankweiler (Eds.), *Phonological processes in literacy: A tribute to Isabelle Y. Liberman* (pp. 37–45). Hillsdale, NJ: Erlbaum.

Brady, S. A., Shankweiler, D., & Mann, V. (1983). Speech perception and memory coding in relation to reading ability. *Journal of Experimental Child Psychology, 35,* 346–367.

Bransford, J. D., & Johnson, M. (1972). Contextual prerequisites for understanding: Some investigations of comprehension and recall. *Journal of Verbal Learning and Behavior, 11*(6), 717–726.

Branum-Martin, L., Sha, T., & Gamaat, S. (2015). Bilingual phonological awareness: Reexamining the evidence for relations within and across languages. *Journal of Educational Psychology, 107*(1), 111–125.

Brown, K. J. (2003). What do I say when they get stuck on a word?: Aligning teachers' prompts with students' development. *The Reading Teacher, 56*(8), 720–733.

Brown, R., Pressley, M., Van Meter, P., & Schuder, T. (1996). A quasi-experimental validation of transactional strategies instruction with low-achieving second graders. *Journal of Educational Psychology, 88,* 18–37.

Brown, W., Denton, E., Kelly, L., Outhred, L., & McNaught, M. (1999). RRs effectiveness: A five-year success story in San Louis Coastal Unified School District. *ERS Spectrum, 11,* 3–10.

Brown-Chidsey, R., & Steege, M. W. (2005). *Response to intervention: Principles and strategies for effective practice.* New York: Guilford Press.

Bryant, P. E., MacLean, M., Bradley, L. L., & Crossland, J. (1990). Rhyme and alliteration, phoneme detection, and learning to read. *Developmental Psychology, 26,* 429–438.

Burgess, S. R. (2006). The development of phonological sensitivity. In D. K. Dickinson & S. B. Neuman (Eds.), *Handbook of early literacy research* (Vol. 2, pp. 90–100). New York: Guilford Press.

Cain, K., & Oakhill, J. (1999). Inference ability and its relation to comprehension failure in young children. *Reading and Writing, 11,* 489–503.

Cain, K., & Oakhill, J. (2011). Matthew effects in young readers: Reading comprehension and reading experience aid vocabulary development. *Journal of Learning Disabilities, 44*(5), 431–443.

Cain, K., Oakhill, J., Barnes, M., & Bryant, P. (2001). Comprehension skill, inference making ability, and their relation to knowledge. *Memory and Cognition, 29*(6), 850–860.

Cain, K., Oakhill, J., & Bryant, P. (2004). Children's reading comprehension ability: Concurrent prediction by working memory, verbal ability, and component skills. *Journal of Educational Psychology, 96,* 31–42.

Carlisle, J. F., & Goodwin, A. P. (2014). Morphemes matter: How morphological knowledge contributes to reading and writing. In C. A. Stone, E. R. Silliman, B. J. Ehren, & G. P. Wallach (Eds.), *Handbook of language and literacy: Development and disorders* (2nd ed., pp. 265–282). New York: Guilford Press.

Carlson-Paige, N., McLaughlin, G. B., & Almon, J. W. (2015). *Reading instruction in kindergarten: Little to gain and much to lose.* A report of the Alliance for Childhood and Defending the Early Years.

Center, Y., Wheldall, K., Freeman, L., Outhred, L., & McNaught, M. (1995). An evaluation of Reading Recovery. *Reading Research Quarterly, 30,* 240–263.

Cervetti, G., & Hiebert, E. H. (2015). Knowledge, literacy, and the Common Core. *Language Arts, 92*(4), 256–269.

Chall, J. S. (1967). *Learning to read: The great debate.* New York: McGraw-Hill.

Chall, J. S., & Dale, E. (1995). *Readability revisited: The new Dale–Chall readability formula.* Cambridge, MA: Brookline Books.

Chapman, J. W., & Tunmer, W. E. (1995). Development of young children's reading self-concepts: An examination of emerging subcomponents. *Journal of Educational Psychology, 87*(1), 154.

Chorzempa, B. F., & Graham, S. (2006). Primary-grade teachers' use of within-class ability grouping in reading. *Journal of Educational Psychology, 98*(3), 529–541.

Christian, K., Morrison, F. J., Frazier, J. A., & Massetti, G. (2000). Specificity in the nature and timing of cognitive growth in kindergarten and first grade. *Journal of Cognition and Development, 1*(4), 429–448.

Clay, M. M. (1985). *The early detection of reading difficulties.* Exeter, NH: Heinemann.

Clay, M. M. (1991). *Becoming literate: The construction of inner control.* Portsmouth, NH: Heinemann.

Clay, M. M. (1993). *An observation survey of early literacy achievement.* Portsmouth, NH: Heinemann.

Clymer, T. (1963). The utility of phonic generalizations in the primary grades. *The Reading Teacher, 16,* 252–258.

Collins COBUILD student's dictionary plus grammar (3rd ed.). (2005). Glasgow, UK: HarperCollins.

Connor, C. M., Morrison, F. J., & Katch, L. E. (2004). Beyond the reading wars: Exploring the effect of child-instruction interactions on growth in early reading. *Scientific Studies of Reading, 8*(4), 305–336.

Connor, C. M., Morrison, F. J., Schatschneider, C., Toste, J. R., Lundblom, E., Crowe, E. C., & Fishman, B. (2011). Effective classroom instruction: Implications of child characteristics by reading instruction interactions on first graders' word reading achievement. *Journal of Research on Educational Effectiveness, 4*(3), 173–207.

Coxhead, A. (2000). A new academic word list. *TESOL Quarterly, 34*(2), 213–238.

Coxhead, A. (2011). The academic word list 10 years on: Research and teaching implications. *TESOL Quarterly, 45*(2), 355–362.

Coyne, M. D., McCoach, D. B., Loftus, S., Zipoli, R., & Kapp, K. (2009). Direct vocabulary instruction in kindergarten: Teaching for breadth versus depth. *Elementary School Journal, 110*(1), 1–18.

Coyne, M. D., Simmons, D. C., Hagan-Burke, S., Simmons, L. E., Kwok, O.-M., Kim, M., . . . Rawlinson, D. A. M. (2013). Adjusting beginning reading intervention based on student performance: An experimental evaluation. *Exceptional Children, 80*(1), 25–44.

Crosson, A. C., & Lesaux, N. K. (2010). Revisiting assumptions about the relationship of fluent reading to comprehension: Spanish-speakers' text-reading fluency in English. *Reading and Writing, 23,* 475–494.

Cunningham, A. E., & Stanovich, K. E. (1997). Early reading acquisition and its relation to reading experience and ability 10 years later. *Developmental Psychology, 33*(6), 934–945.

Dickinson, D. K. (2001). Book reading in preschool classrooms: Is recommended practice common? In D. K. Dickinson & P. O. Tabors (Eds.), *Beginning literacy with language: Young children learning at home and school* (pp. 175–203). Baltimore: Brookes.

Dickinson, D. K., McCabe, A., & Clark-Chiarelli, N. (2004). Preschool-based prevention of reading disability: Realities versus possibilities. In C. A. Stone, E. R. Silliman, B. J. Ehren, & K. Apel (Eds.), *Handbook of literacy and language: Development and disorders* (pp. 209–227). New York: Guilford Press.

Dickinson, D. K., McCabe, A., & Essex, M. J. (2006). A window of opportunity we must open to all: The case for preschool with high-quality language and literacy. In D. K. Dickinson & S. B. Neuman (Eds.), *Handbook of early literacy research* (Vol. 2, pp. 11–28). New York: Guilford Press.

Dickinson, D. K., & Smith, M. W. (1994). Long-term effects of preschool teachers' book readings on low-income children's vocabulary and story comprehension. *Reading Research Quarterly, 29,* 104–122.

Dickinson, D. K., & Tabors, P. O. (Eds.). (2001). *Beginning with language: Young children learning at home and school.* Baltimore: Brookes.

Dole, J. A., Nokes, J. D., & Drits, D. (2009). Cognitive strategy instruction. In S. E. Isreal & G. G. Duffy (Eds.), *Handbook of research on reading comprehension* (pp. 347–372). New York: Routledge.

Duffy, G. G. (2003). *Explaining reading: A resource for teaching concepts, skills, and strategies.* New York: Guilford Press.

Duffy, G. G., & Hoffman, J. V. (1999). In pursuit of an illusion: The flawed search for a perfect method. *The Reading Teacher, 53*(1), 10.

Duke, N. K. (2014). *Inside information: Developing powerful readers and writers of informational text through project-based instruction.* Newark, DE: International Reading Association.

Duke, N. K., & Bennett-Armistead, V. S. (2003). *Reading and writing informational text in the primary grades: Research-based practices.* New York: Scholastic.

Duke, N. K., & Martin, N. M. (2011). 10 things every literacy educator should know about research. *The Reading Teacher, 65*(1), 9–22.

Duke, N. K., & Pearson, P. D. (2002). Effective practices for developing reading comprehension. In A. E. Farstrup & S. J. Samuels (Eds.), *What research has to say about reading instruction* (3rd ed., pp. 205–242). Newark, DE: International Reading Association.

Duke, N. K., Pearson, P. D., Strachan, S. L., & Billman, A. K. (2011). Essential elements of fostering and teaching reading comprehension. In S. J. Samuels & A. E. Farstrup (Eds.), *What research has to say about reading instruction* (4th ed., pp. 51–93). Newark, DE: International Reading Association.

Durrell, D. D. (1963). *Phonograms in primary grade words.* Boston: Boston University Press.

Dweck, C. S., & Molden, D. C. (2005). Self-theories: Their impact on competence, motivation, and acquisition. In A. J. Elliot & C. S. Dweck (Eds.), *Handbook of competence and motivation* (pp. 122–140). New York: Guilford Press.

Dweck, C. S., Walton, G. M., & Cohen, G. L. (2014). Academic tenacity: Mindsets and skills that promote long-term learning. Retrieved from *www.edutopia.org/resource/mindset-research.*

Ehri, L. C. (1998). Grapheme–phoneme knowledge is essential for learning to read words in English. In J. Metsala & L. C. Ehri (Eds.), *Word recognition in beginning literacy* (pp. 3–40). Mahwah, NJ: Erlbaum.

Ehri, L. C. (2005). Learning to read words: Theory, findings, and issues. *Scientific Studies of Reading, 9*(2), 167–188.

Ehri, L. C., Deffner, N. D., & Wilce, L. S. (1984). Pictorial mnemonics for phonics. *Journal of Educational Psychology, 76,* 880–893.

Ehri, L. C., Dreyer, L. G., Flugman, B., & Gross, A. (2007). Reading Rescue: An effective tutoring intervention model for language minority students who are struggling readers in first grade. *American Educational Research Journal, 44*(2), 414–448.

Ehri, L. C., Satlow, E., & Gaskins, I. (2009). Grapho-phonemic enrichment strengthens keyword analogy instruction for struggling young readers. *Reading and Writing Quarterly, 25,* 162–191.

Elkonin, D. B. (1973). U.S.S.R. In J. Downing (Ed.), *Comparative reading* (pp. 551–579). New York: Macmillan.

Ellefson, M. R., Treiman, R., & Kessler, B. (2009). Learning to label letters by sounds or names: A comparison of England and the United States. *Journal of Experimental Child Psychology, 102*(3), 323–341.

Fisher, D., Flood, J., Lapp, D., & Frey, N. (2004). Interactive read alouds: Is there a common set of implementation practices? *The Reading Teacher, 58,* 8–17.

Flannigan, K. (2007). A concept of word in text: A pivotal event in early reading acquisition. *Journal of Literacy Research, 39*(1), 37–70.

Fletcher, J. M., Shaywitz, S. E., Shankweiler, D., Katz, I., Liberman, I., Steubing, K. K., . . . Shaywitz, B. A. (1994). Cognitive profiles of reading disability: Comparisons of discrepancy and low achievement definitions. *Journal of Educational Psychology, 86,* 6–23.

Fountas, I. C., & Pinnell, G. S. (1996). *Guided reading: Good first teaching for all children.* Portsmouth, NH: Heinemann.

Fox, B., & Routh, D. K. (1975). Analyzing spoken language into words, syllables, and phonemes: A developmental study. *Journal of Psycholinguist Research, 4,* 331–342.

Francis, D. J., Santi, K. L., Barr, C., Fletcher, J. M., Varisco, A., & Foorman, B. R. (2008). Form effects on the estimation of students' oral reading fluency using DIBELS. *Journal of School Psychology, 46,* 315–342.

Francis, D. J., Shaywitz, S., & Steubing, K. (1996). Developmental lag versus deficit models of reading disability: A longitudinal, individual growth curves analysis. *Journal of Educational Psychology, 88,* 3–17.

Fromkin, V., Rodman, R., & Hyams, N. (2003). *An introduction to language* (7th ed.). Boston: Wadsworth.

Fry, E. (1999–2000). *1000 instant words.* Westminster, CA: Teacher Created Resources.

Fry, E. B. (2002). Readability versus leveling. *The Reading Teacher, 56,* 272–286.

Fuchs, D., & Fuchs, L. S. (2006). Introduction to response to intervention: What, why, and how valid is it? *Reading Research Quarterly, 41*(1), 93–98.

Fuchs, D., Fuchs, L. S., & Burish, P. (2000). Peer-assisted learning strategies: An evidence-based practice to promote reading achievement. *Learning Disabilities Research and Practice, 15,* 85–91.

Fuchs, L. S., & Vaughn, S. (2012). Responsiveness-to-intervention: A decade later. *Journal of Learning Disabilities, 45,* 195–203.

Gallagher, A., Frith, U., & Snowling, M. J. (2000). Precursors of literacy delay among children at genetic risk of dyslexia. *Journal of Child Psychology and Psychiatry, 41,* 203–213.

Garcia, G. E. (2000). Bilingual children's reading. In M. Kamil, P. Mosenthal, P. D. Pearson, & R. Barr (Eds.), *Handbook of reading research* (Vol. 3, pp. 813–834). Mahwah, NJ: Erlbaum.

Gelzheiser, L. M., Scanlon, D. M., Vellutino, F. R., Hallgren-Flynn, L., & Schatschneider, C. (2011). Effects of the Interactive Strategies Approach—Extended: A responsive and comprehensive intervention for intermediate grade struggling readers. *Elementary School Journal, 112*(2), 280–306.

Gersten, R., Baker, S. K., Shanahan, T., Linan-Thompson, S., Collins, P., & Scarcella, R. (2007). *Effective literacy and English language instruction for English learners in the elementary grades: A practice guide* (NCEE 2007-4011). Washington, DC: U.S. Department of Education, Institute of Education Sciences, National Center for Education Evaluation and Regional Assistance. Retrieved from *http://ies.ed.gov/ncee/wwc/publications/practiceguides.*

Gersten, R., Compton, D., Connor, C. M., Dimino, J., Santoro, L., Linan-Thompson, S., & Tilly, W. D. (2008). *Assisting students struggling with reading: Response to intervention and multi-tier intervention for reading in the primary grades: A practice guide* (NCEE 2009–4045). Washington, DC: U.S. Department of Education, Institute of Education Sciences, National Center for Education Evaluation and Regional Assistance. Retrieved from *http://ies.ed.gov/ncee/wwc/publications/practiceguides.*

Gibson, E. J., & Levin, H. (1975). *The psychology of reading.* Cambridge, MA: MIT Press.

Glasswell, K., & Ford, M. P. (2010). Teaching flexibly with leveled texts: More power for your reading block. *The Reading Teacher, 64*(1), 57–60.

Goldenberg, C. (2013). Unlocking the research on English learners. *American Educator, 37*(2), 4–38.

Gomez-Bellenge, F. X., Rogers, E., & Fullerton, S. K. (2003). *Reading Recovery and Descubriendo la Lectura national report 2001–2002*. Columbus: Ohio State University Reading Recovery National Data Evaluation Center.

Goodman, K. S. (1967). Reading: A psycholinguistic guessing game. *Journal of the Reading Specialist, 6,* 126–135.

Gough, P., Juel, C., & Griffith, P. (1992). Reading, spelling, and the orthographic cipher. In P. Gough, L. C. Ehri, & R. Treiman (Eds.), *Reading acquisition* (pp. 35–48). Hillsdale, NJ: Erlbaum.

Graham, S., Harris, K. R., & Fink, B. (2000). Is handwriting causally related to learning to write? Treatment of handwriting problems in beginning writers. *Journal of Educational Psychology, 92,* 620–633.

Graves, M. F. (2006). *The vocabulary book: Learning and instruction*. New York: Teachers College Press.

Graves, M. F., & Slater, W. (1987, April). *The development of reading vocabularies in rural disadvantaged students, inner-city disadvantaged students, and middle-class suburban students*. Paper presented at the annual meeting of the American Educational Research Association, Washington, DC.

Guthrie, J. T., & Humenick, N. M. (2004). Motivating students to read: Evidence for classroom practices that increase reading motivation and achievement. In P. McCardle & V. Chhabra (Eds.), *The voice of evidence in reading research* (pp. 329–354). Baltimore: Brookes.

Guthrie, J. T., & Wigfield, A. (2000). Effects of integrated instruction on motivation and strategy use in reading. *Journal of Educational Psychology, 92*(2), 331–341.

Guthrie, J. T., Wigfield, A., Barbosa, P., Perencevich, K. C., Taboada, A., Davis, M. H., . . . Tonks, S. (2004). Increasing reading comprehension and engagement through concept-oriented reading instruction. *Journal of Educational Psychology, 96*(3), 403–423.

Halle, T., Hair, E., Wandner, L., McNamara, M., & Chien, N. (2012). Predictors and outcomes of early versus later English language proficiency among English language learners. *Early Childhood Research Quarterly, 27*(1), 1–20.

Hart, B., & Risley, T. R. (1995). *Meaningful differences in the everyday experience of young American children*. Baltimore: Brookes.

Hasbrouck, J., & Tindal, G. A. (2006). Oral reading fluency norms: A valuable assessment tool for reading teachers. *The Reading Teacher, 59*(7), 636–644.

Hickman, P., Pollard-Durodola, S., & Vaughn, S. (2004). Storybook reading: Improving vocabulary and comprehension for English-language learners. *The Reading Teacher, 57,* 720–730.

Hirsch, E. D. (2006). *The knowledge deficit: Closing the shocking educational gap for American children*. Boston: Houghton Mifflin.

Hirsch, E. D. J. (2003). Reading comprehension requires knowledge of words and the world: Scientific insights into the fourth grade slump and the nation's stagnant comprehension scores. *American Educator, 27*(1), 10–48.

Inhoff, A. W., Solomon, M., Radach, R., & Seymour, B. A. (2011). Temporal dynamics of the eye–voice span and eye movement control during oral reading. *Journal of Cognitive Psychology, 33,* 543–558.

Johnston, P. H. (1997). *Knowing literacy: Constructive literacy assessment.* York, ME: Stenhouse.

Johnston, P. H. (2004). *Choice words: How our language affects children's learning.* Portland, ME: Stenhouse.

Juel, C. (1988). Learning to read and write: A longitudinal study of 54 children from first through fourth grades. *Journal of Educational Psychology, 80,* 437–447.

Justice, L. M., & Piasta, S. B. (2011). Developing children's print knowledge through adult–child storybook reading interactions: Print referencing as an instructional practice. In S. B. Neuman & D. K. Dickinson (Eds.), *Handbook of early literacy research* (Vol. 3, pp. 200–213). New York: Guilford Press.

Kena, G., Aud, S., Johnson, F., Wang, X., Zhang, J., Rathbun, A., . . . Kristapobich, P. (2014). *The condition of education 2014* (NCES 2014-083). Washington, DC: U.S. Department of Education, National Center for Education Statistics. Retrieved June 15, 2016, from *http://nces.ed.gov/pubsearch.*

Kendeou, P., & O'Brien, E. J. (2016). Prior knowledge acquisition and revision. In P. Afflerbach (Ed.), *Handbook of individual differences in reading* (pp. 151–163). New York: Routledge.

Kessler, B., & Treiman, R. (2003). Is English spelling chaotic?: Misconceptions concerning its irregularity. *Reading Psychology, 24,* 267–289.

Kim, J. S., & Quinn, D. M. (2013). The effects of summer reading on low-income children's literacy achievement from kindergarten to grade 8: A meta-analysis of classroom and home interventions. *Review of Educational Research, 83,* 386–431.

Kim, Y.-S., Petscher, Y., Schatschneider, C., & Foorman, B. (2010). Does growth rate in oral reading fluency matter in predicting reading comprehension achievement? *Journal of Educational Psychology, 102,* 652–667.

Kintsch, W. (1998). *Comprehension: A paradigm for cognition.* Cambridge, UK: Cambridge University Press.

Klingner, J., Vaughn, S., & Schumm, J. S. (1998). Collaborative strategic reading during social studies in heterogeneous fourth-grade classrooms. *Elementary School Journal, 99,* 3–22.

Konstantopoulos, S., & Sun, M. (2012). Is the persistence of teacher effects in early grades larger for lower-performing students? *American Journal of Education, 188,* 309–339.

Koskinen, P. S., Blum, I. H., Bisson, S. A., Phillips, S. M., Creamer, T. S., & Baker, T. K. (2000). Book access, shared reading, and audio models: The effects of supporting the literacy learning of linguistically diverse students in school and at home. *Journal of Educational Psychology, 92,* 23–36.

Kuhn, M. R., & Levy, L. (2015). *Developing fluent readers: Teaching fluency as a foundational skill.* New York: Guilford Press.

Lennox, S. (2013). Interactive read-alouds: An avenue for enhancing children's language for thinking and understanding: A review of recent research. *Early Childhood Education Journal, 41*(5), 381–389.

Lesaux, N. K., & Siegel, L. (2003). The development of reading in children who speak English as a second language. *Developmental Psychology, 39*(6), 1005–1019.

Lou, Y., Abrami, P. C., & Spence, J. C. (2000). Effects of within-class ability grouping on student achievement: An exploratory model. *Journal of Educational Research, 94,* 101–112.

Lyman, F. T. (1981). The responsive classroom discussion: The inclusion of all students. In A. Anderson (Ed.), *Mainstreaming digest* (pp. 109–113). College Park: University of Maryland Press.

Marinak, B. A., Malloy, F. B., Gambrell, L. B., & Mazzoni, S. A. (2015). Me and my reading profile. *The Reading Teacher, 69*(1), 51–62.

Marriott, S. (1995). *Read on: Using fiction in the primary school.* London: Paul Chapman.

Mathes, P. G., Denton, C. A., Fletcher, J. M., Anthony, J. L., Francis, D. J., & Schatschneider, C. (2005). The effects of theoretically different instruction and student characteristics on the skills of struggling readers. *Reading Research Quarterly, 40*(2), 148–182.

McAlenney, A. L., & Coyne, M. D. (2015). Addressing false positives in early reading assessment using intervention response data. *Learning Disability Quarterly, 38*(1), 53–65.

McCoach, D. B., O'Connell, A. A., & Levitt, H. (2006). Ability grouping across kindergarten using an early childhood longitudinal study. *Journal of Educational Research, 99*(6), 339–346.

McGee, L. M., & Schickedanz, J. A. (2007). Repeated interactive read-alouds in preschool and kindergarten. *The Reading Teacher, 60*(8), 742–751.

McKay, R., & Teale, W. H. (2015). *No more teaching a letter a week.* Portsmouth, NH: Heinemann.

McKenna, M. C., Kear, D. J., & Ellsworth, R. A. (1995). Children's attitude towards reading: A national survey. *Reading Research Quarterly, 30,* 934–956.

McKeown, M. G., & Beck, I. L. (2006). Encouraging young children's language interactions with stories. In D. K. Dickinson & S. B. Neuman (Eds.), *Handbook of early literacy research* (Vol. 2, pp. 281–294). New York: Guilford Press.

McKeown, M. G., Beck, I. L., & Blake, R. G. K. (2009). Rethinking reading comprehension instruction: A comparison of instruction for strategies and content approaches. *Reading Research Quarterly, 44*(3), 218–253.

Mellard, D. F., & Johnson, E. (2008). *RTI: A practitioner's guide to implementing response to intervention.* Thousand Oaks, CA: Corwin Press.

Mesmer, H. A. (2008). *Tools for matching readers to texts.* New York: Guilford Press.

Mesmer, H. A., & Williams, T. O. (2015). Examining the role of syllable awareness in a model of concept of word: Findings from preschoolers. *Reading Research Quarterly, 50*(4), 483–497.

Metsala, J. L. (2011). Lexical reorganization and the emergence of phonological awareness. In S. B. Neuman & D. K. Dickinson (Eds.), *Handbook of early literacy research* (Vol. 3, pp. 66–82). New York: Guilford Press.

Morgan, P. L., Fuchs, D., Compton, D. L., Cordray, D. S., & Fuchs, L. S. (2008). Does early reading failure decrease children's reading motivation? *Journal of Learning Disabilities, 41*(5), 387–404.

Morris, D., Bloodgood, J., Lomax, R. G., & Perney, J. (2003). Developmental steps in learning to read: A longitudinal study in kindergarten and first grade. *Reading Research Quarterly, 38,* 302–328.

Morrow, L. M., & Gambrell, L. B. (2000). Literature-based reading instruction. In

M. L. Kamil, P. B. Mosenthal, P. D. Pearson, & R. Barr (Eds.), *Handbook of reading research* (Vol. 3, pp. 563–586). Mahwah, NJ: Erlbaum.

Morrow, L. M., & Schickedanz, J. A. (2006). The relationships between sociodramatic play and literacy development. In D. K. Dickinson & S. B. Neuman (Eds.), *Handbook of early literacy research* (Vol. 2, pp. 269–280). New York: Guilford Press.

Mosenthal, J., Lipson, M., Torncello, S., Russ, B., & Mekkelsen, J. (2004). Contexts and practices of six schools successful in obtaining reading achievement. *Elementary School Journal, 104*(5), 343–367.

Müller, B., Richter, T., Križan, A., Hecht, T., & Ennemoser, M. (2015). Word recognition skills moderate the effectiveness of reading strategy training in Grade 2. *Learning and Individual Differences, 40,* 55–62.

Nagy, W. E., & Anderson, R. C. (1984). How many words are there in printed school English? *Reading Research Quarterly, 19,* 357–366.

Nagy, W. E., & Herman, P. A. (1987). Breadth and depth of vocabulary knowledge: Implications for acquisition and instruction. In M. G. McKeown & M. E. Curtis (Eds.), *The nature of vocabulary acquisition* (pp. 19–36). Hillside, NJ: Erlbaum.

National Association of State Directors of Special Education. (2005). *Response to intervention: Policy Considerations and Implementation.* Alexandria, VA: Author.

National Center for Education Statistics. (2005). *The nation's report card: Fourth-grade students reading aloud: NAEP 2002 Special Study of Oral Reading* (NCES 2006-469). Washington, DC: U. S. Department of Education. Retrieved March 29, 2016, from *http://nces.gov/nationsreportcard/pdf/studies/2006469.pdf.*

National Center for Education Statistics. (2015). *The condition of education: English language learners.* Washington, DC: U.S. Department of Education. Retrieved February 26, 2016, from *http://nces.ed.gov/programs/coe/indicator_cgf.asp.*

National Early Literacy Panel. (2008). *Developing early literacy.* Washington, DC: National Institute for Literacy.

National Governors Association Center for Best Practices & Council of Chief State School Officers. (2010). *Common Core State Standards for English language arts and literacy, history/social studies, science, and technical subjects.* Washington, DC: Author.

National Reading Panel. (2000). *Teaching children to read: An evidence-based assessment of the scientific research literature on reading and its implications for reading instruction: Reports of subgroups.* Washington, DC: National Institute of Child Health and Human Development.

Neuman, S. B. (2006). The knowledge gap: Implications for early education. In S. B. Neuman & D. K. Dickenson (Eds.), *Handbook of early literacy research* (Vol. 2, pp. 29–40). New York: Guilford Press.

Neuman, S. B. (2011). The challenge of teaching vocabulary in early education. In S. B. Neuman & D. K. Dickinson (Eds.), *Handbook of early literacy research* (Vol. 3, pp. 358–372). New York: Guilford Press.

Neuman, S. B., Dwyer, J., Koh, S., & Wright, T. (2007). *The world of words: A vocabulary intervention for preschool children.* Ann Arbor: University of Michigan.

Neuman, S. B., & Roskos, K. (1993). Access to print for children of poverty: Differential effects of adult mediation and literacy-enriched play settings on environmental and functional print tasks. *American Educational Research Journal, 30,* 95–122.

Nicholls, J. G. (1978). The development of the concepts of effort and ability, perception of academic attainment, and the understanding that difficult tasks require more than ability. *Child Development, 49,* 800–814.

Nicholls, J. G. (1990). What is ability and why are we mindful of it?: A developmental perspective. In R. Sternberg & J. Kolligian (Eds.), *Competence considered* (pp. 11–40). New Haven, CT: Yale University Press.

Niiya, Y., Crocker, J., & Bartmess, E. N. (2004). From vulnerability to resilience: Learning orientations buffer contingent self-esteem from failure. *Psychological Science, 15,* 801–805.

Nolen, S. B. (2001). Constructing literacy in the kindergarten: Task structure, collaboration, and motivation. *Cognition and Instruction, 19,* 95–142.

Nunes, T., & Bryant, P. (2006). *Improving literacy through teaching morphemes.* London: Routledge.

Nye, B., Konstantopolous, S., & Hedges, L. V. (2004). How large are teacher effects? *Educational Evaluation and Policy Analysis, 26*(3), 237–257.

Nystrand, M. (with Gamoran, A., Kachur, R., & Prendergast, C.). (1997). *Opening dialogue: Understanding the dynamics of language and learning in the English classroom.* New York: Teachers College Press.

O'Connor, R. E. (2000). Increasing the intensity of intervention in kindergarten and first grade. *Learning Disabilities Research and Practice, 15*(1), 43–54.

O'Connor, R. E., Harty, K. R., & Fulmer, D. (2005). Tiers of intervention in kindergarten through third grade. *Journal of Learning Disabilities, 38*(6), 532–538.

Ogle, D. (1986). K-W-L: A teaching model that develops action reading of expository text. *The Reading Teacher, 40,* 564–570.

Ouellette, G. P. (2006). What's meaning got to do with it?: The role of vocabulary in word reading and reading comprehension. *Journal of Educational Psychology, 98*(3), 554–566.

Ouellette, G. (2010). Orthographic learning in learning to spell: The roles of semantics and type of practice. *Journal of Experimental Child Psychology, 107*(1), 50–58.

Paris, A. H., & Paris, S. G. (2007). Teaching narrative comprehension strategies to first graders. *Cognition and Instruction, 25*(1), 1–44.

Paris, S. G. (2005). Reinterpreting the development of reading skills. *Reading Research Quarterly, 40*(2), 184–202.

Paris, S. G., Lipson, M., & Wixson, K. K. (1983). Becoming a strategic reader. *Contemporary Educational Psychology, 8,* 293–316.

Pearson, P. D., & Gallagher, M. (1983). The instruction of reading comprehension. *Contemporary Educational Psychology, 8,* 317–344.

Perfetti, C., & Stafura, J. (2014). Word knowledge in a theory of reading comprehension. *Scientific Studies of Reading, 18,* 22–37.

Perfetti, C. A., Landi, N., & Oakhill, J. (2005). The acquisition of reading comprehension skill. In M. J. Snowling & C. Hulme (Eds.), *The science of reading: A handbook* (pp. 227–247). Malden, MA: Blackwell.

Phillips, L. M., Norris, S. P., Osmond, W. C., & Maynard, A. M. (2002). Relative reading achievement: A longitudinal study of 187 children from first through sixth grades. *Journal of Educational Psychology, 94*(1), 3–13.

Piasta, S. B., Petscher, Y., & Justice, L. M. (2012). How many letters should preschoolers in public programs know?: The diagnostic efficiency of various preschool letter-naming benchmarks for predicting first-grade literacy achievement. *Journal of Educational Psychology, 104*(4), 945–958.

Pitcher, B., & Zhihui, F. (2007). Can we trust levelled texts?: An examination of their reliability and quality from a linguistic perspective. *Literacy, 41*(1), 43–51.

Prawat, R. S. (1989). Promoting access to knowledge, strategy, and disposition in students: A research synthesis. *Review of Educational Research, 59*(1), 1–41.

Pressley, M. (2006). *Reading instruction that works: The case for balanced teaching* (3rd ed.). New York: Guilford Press.

Pressley, M., & Allington, R. L. (2015). *Reading instruction that works: The case for balanced teaching* (4th ed.). New York: Guilford Press.

Pressley, M., Wood, E., Woloshyn, V. E., Martin, V., King, A., & Menke, D. (1992). Encouraging mindful use of prior knowledge: Attempting to construct explanatory answers facilitates learning. *Educational Psychologist, 27,* 91–110.

Prochnow, J. E., Tunmer, W. E., & Chapman, J. W. (2013). A longitudinal investigation of the influence of literacy-related skills, reading self-perceptions, and inattentive behaviours on the development of literacy learning difficulties. *International Journal of Disability, Development and Education, 60*(3), 185–207.

Quinn, J. M., Spencer, M., & Wagner, R. K. (2015). Individual differences in phonological awareness and their role in learning to read. In P. Afflerbach (Ed.), *Handbook of individual differences in reading: Reader, text, and context* (pp. 80–92). New York: Routledge.

Quinn, J. M., Wagner, R. K., Petscher, Y., & Lopez, D. (2015). Developmental relations between vocabulary knowledge and reading comprehension: A latent change score modeling study. *Child Development, 86*(1), 159–175.

Quirk, M., & Beem, S. (2012). Examining the relations between reading fluency and reading comprehension for English Language learners. *Psychology in the Schools, 49*(6), 539–553.

Rasinski, T. V. (2004). Creating fluent readers. *Educational Leadership, 61*(6), 46–51.

Rayner, K., Foorman, B. R., Perfetti, C. A., Pesetsky, D., & Seidenberg, M. S. (2002). How should reading be taught? *Scientific American, 286,* 84–91.

Read, C. (1971). Preschool children's knowledge of English phonology. *Harvard Educational Review, 41,* 1–34.

Read, C., Zhang, Y. F., Nie, H. Y., & Ding, B. Q. (1986). The ability to manipulate speech sounds depends on knowing alphabetic writing. *Cognition, 24,* 270–292.

Roberts, K. L., & Duke, N. K. (2009). Comprehension in the primary grades. In K. Ganske & D. Fisher (Eds.), *Comprehension across the curriculum: Perspectives and practices K–12* (pp. 23–45). New York: Guilford Press.

Roehler, I. R., & Duffy, G. G. (1984). Direct explanation of comprehension processes. In G. G. Duffy, I. R. Roehler, & J. Mason (Eds.), *Comprehension instruction: Perspectives and suggestions* (pp. 265–280). New York: Longman.

Ryan, C. (2013). *Language use in the United States: 2011.* Washington, DC: U.S. Census Bureau. Retrieved June 18, 2016, from *www.census.gov/prod/2013pubs/acs-22.pdf.*

Samuels, S. J. (2006). Reading fluency: Its past, present, and future. In T. Rasinski, C. Blachowicz, & K. Lems (Eds.), *Fluency instruction: Research-based best practices* (pp. 7–20). New York: Guilford Press.

Santoro, L. E., Chard, D. J., Howard, L., & Baker, S. (2008). Making the very most of classroom read-alouds to promote comprehension and vocabulary. *The Reading Teacher, 61*(5), 396–408.

Saunders, W. M., & Goldenberg, C. (1999). Effects of instructional conversations and literature logs on limited and fluent English proficient students' story comprehension and thematic understanding. *Elementary School Journal, 99*, 277–301.

Saunders-Smith, G. (2003). *The ultimate guided reading how-to book: Building literacy through small-group instruction.* Tucson, AZ: Zephyr Press.

Scanlon, D. M. (2011). Response to intervention as an assessment approach. In A. McGill-Franzen & R. L. Allington (Eds.), *Handbook of reading disability research* (pp. 139–148). New York: Routledge.

Scanlon, D. M., & Anderson, K. L. (2010). Using the interactive strategies approach to preventing reading difficulties in an RTI context. In M. Y. Lipson & K. K. Wixson (Eds.), *Successful approaches to RTI: Collaborative practices for improving K–12 literacy* (pp. 20–65). Newark, DE: International Reading Association.

Scanlon, D. M., Anderson, K. L., & Gelzheiser, L. M. (2010, December). *Impact of professional development for teachers on children's early literacy development.* Paper presented at the annual convention of the Literacy Research Association, Fort Worth, TX.

Scanlon, D. M., Anderson, K. L., & Goatley, V. (2015, December). *National RTI Survey.* Presented at the annual convention of the Literacy Research Association, Carlsbad, CA.

Scanlon, D. M., Anderson, K. L., & the ISA Professional Development Project. (2012). Unpublished teacher resource (*www.isaprofessionaldevelopment.org*).

Scanlon, D. M., Anderson, K. L., Morse, M., & Yurkewecz, T. (2012). *Helping your child become a reader.* Retrieved from *http://www.albany.edu/crsc/parents.shtml.*

Scanlon, D. M., Gelzheiser, L. M., Vellutino, F. R., Schatschneider, C., & Sweeney, J. M. (2008). Reducing the incidence of early reading difficulties: Professional development for classroom teachers versus direct interventions for children. *Learning and Individual Differences, 18*(3), 346–359.

Scanlon, D. M., & Vellutino, F. R. (1996). Prerequisite skills, early instruction, and success in first-grade reading: Selected results from a longitudinal study. *Mental Retardation and Developmental Disabilities Research Reviews, 2*, 54–63.

Scanlon, D. M., & Vellutino, F. R. (1997). A comparison of the instructional backgrounds and cognitive profiles of poor, average, and good readers who were initially identified as at risk for reading failure. *Scientific Studies of Reading, 1*(3), 191–215.

Scanlon, D. M., Vellutino, F. R., Small, S. G., Fanuele, D. P., & Sweeney, J. M. (2005). Severe reading difficulties—can they be prevented?: A comparison of prevention and intervention approaches. *Exceptionality, 13*(4), 209–227.

Scarborough, H. S. (2001). Connecting early language and literacy to later reading (dis)abilities: Evidence, theory, and practice. In S. B. Neuman & D. K. Dickinson (Eds.), *Handbook of early literacy research* (Vol. 1, pp. 97–110). New York: Guilford Press.

Scarborough, H. S., & Dobrich, W. (1994). On the efficacy of reading to preschoolers. *Developmental Review, 14*, 245–302.

Scarborough, H. S., & Parker, J. D. (2003). Matthew effects in children with learning disabilities: Development of reading, IQ, and psychosocial problems from grade 2 to grade 8. *Annals of Dyslexia, 53,* 47–71.

Schilling, S. G., Carlisle, J. F., Scott, S. E., & Zeng, J. (2007). Are fluency measures accurate predictors of reading achievement? *Elementary School Journal, 107*(5), 429–448.

Schneider, W., Roth, E., & Ennemoser, M. (2000). Training phonological skills and letter knowledge in children at risk for dyslexia: A comparison of three kindergarten intervention programs. *Journal of Educational Psychology, 92,* 284–295.

Schultheiss, O. C., & Brunstein, J. C. (2005). An implicit motive perspective on competence. In A. J. Elliot & C. S. Dweck (Eds.), *Handbook of competence and motivation* (pp. 31–51). New York: Guilford Press.

Schunk, D. H., Pintrich, P. R., & Meece, J. L. (2008). *Motivation in education: Theory, research, and applications* (3rd ed.). Upper Saddle River, NJ: Pearson.

Schwanenflugel, P. J., & Kuhn, M. R. (2016). Reading fluency. In P. Afflerbach (Ed.), *Handbook of individual differences in reading: Text and context* (pp. 107–120). New York: Routledge.

Scott, J. A., Jamieson-Noel, D., & Asselin, M. (2003). Vocabulary instruction throughout the day in twenty-three Canadian upper-elementary classrooms. *Elementary School Journal, 103*(3), 269–286.

Sénéchal, M., Ouellette, G., & Rodney, D. (2006). The misunderstood giant: On the predictive role of early vocabulary to future reading. In S. B. Neuman & D. K. Dickinson (Eds.), *Handbook of early literacy research* (Vol. 2, pp. 173–184). New York: Guilford Press.

Shahar-Yames, D., & Share, D. L. (2008). Spelling as a self-teaching mechanism in orthographic learning. *Journal of Research in Reading, 31*(1), 22–39.

Shamir, A. (2009). Processes and outcomes of joint activity with e-books for promoting kindergarteners' emergent literacy. *Educational Media International, 46*(1), 81–96.

Share, D. L. (1995). Phonological recoding and self-teaching: Sine qua non of reading acquisition. *Cognition, 55,* 151–218.

Share, D. L. (2008). Orthographic learning, phonology and the self-teaching hypothesis. *Advances in Child Development and Behavior, 36,* 31–82.

Silverman, R. (2007a). A comparison of three methods of vocabulary instruction during read-alouds in kindergarten. *Elementary School Journal, 108*(2), 97–113.

Silverman, R. (2007b). Vocabulary development of English-language and English-only learners in kindergarten. *Elementary School Journal, 107,* 365–383.

Silverman, R. (2013). Investigating video as a means to promote vocabulary for at-risk children. *Contemporary Educational Psychology, 38,* 170–179.

Silverman, R., & Hines, S. (2009). The effects of multimedia-enhanced instruction on the vocabulary of English-language learners and non-English-language learners in pre-kindergarten through second grade. *Journal of Educational Psychology, 101*(2), 305–314.

Silverman, R. D., & Hartranft, A. M. (2015). *Developing vocabulary and oral language in young children.* New York: Guilford Press.

Silverman, R. D., Speece, D. L., Harring, J. R., & Ritchey, C. D. (2013). Fluency has a role in the simple view of reading. *Scientific Studies of Reading, 17,* 108–133.

Simmons, D. (2015). Instructional engineering principles to frame the future of reading intervention research and practice. *Remedial and Special Education, 36*(1), 45–51.

Smith, A. E., Jussim, L., & Eccles, J. (1999). Do self-fulfilling prophecies accumulate, dissipate, or remain stable over time? *Journal of Personality and Social Psychology, 77,* 548–565.

Smolkin, L. B., Yaden, D. B., Jr., Brown, L., & Hofius, B. (1992). The effects of genre, visual design choices, and discourse structure on preschoolers' responses to picture books during parent–child read-alouds. In C. K. Kinzer & D. J. Leu (Eds.), *Literacy research, theory, and practice: Views from many perspectives* (41st yearbook of the National Reading Conference, pp. 291–301). Chicago: National Reading Conference.

Snow, C. E., Burns, M. S., & Griffin, P. (1998). *Preventing reading difficulties in young children.* Washington, DC: National Academy Press.

Stage, S., Sheppard, J., Davidson, M. M., & Browning, M. M. (2001). Prediction of first graders' growth in oral reading fluency using kindergarten letter fluency. *Journal of School Psychology, 29*(3), 225–237.

Stanovich, K. E. (1986). Matthew effects in reading: Some consequences of individual differences in the acquisition of literacy. *Reading Research Quarterly, 21,* 360–407.

Storch, S. A., & Whitehurst, G. J. (2002). Oral language and code-related precursors to reading: Evidence from a longitudinal structural model. *Developmental Psychology, 38,* 934–947.

Swan, M., & Smith, B. (Eds.). (2001). *Learner English: A teacher's guide to interference and other problems* (2nd ed.). Cambridge, UK: Cambridge University Press.

Tangel, D. M., & Blachman, B. A. (1992). Effect of phoneme awareness instruction on kindergarten children's invented spelling. *Journal of Reading Behavior, 24*(2), 233–261.

Tangel, D. M., & Blachman, B. A. (1995). Effect of phoneme awareness instruction on the invented spelling of first-grade children. *Journal of Reading Behavior, 27*(2), 153–186.

Taylor, B. M., Pearson, P. D., Clark, K. M., & Walpole, S. (2000). Effective schools and accomplished teachers: Lessons about primary-grade reading instruction in low-income schools. *Elementary School Journal, 101,* 121–165.

Taylor, L., & Adelman, H. S. (1999). Personalizing classroom instruction to account for motivational and developmental differences. *Reading and Writing Quarterly, 15,* 255–276.

Tivnan, T., & Hemphill, L. (2005). Comparing four literacy reform models in high-poverty schools: Patterns of first-grade achievement. *Elementary School Journal, 105*(5), 419–441.

Torgesen, J. K., Alexander, A. W., Wagner, R. K., Rashotte, C. A., Voeller, K., & Conway, T. (2001). Intensive remedial instruction for students with severe reading disabilities: Immediate and long-term outcomes from two instructional approaches. *Journal of Learning Disabilities, 34,* 33–58.

Torgesen, J. K., & Burgess, S. R. (1998). Consistency of reading-related phonological processes throughout early childhood: Evidence from longitudinal-correlational and instructional studies. In J. L. Metsala & L. C. Ehri (Eds.), *Word recognition in beginning literacy* (pp. 161–188). Mahwah, NJ: Erlbaum.

Torgesen, J. K., Wagner, R. K., & Rashotte, C. (1994). Longitudinal studies of phonological processing and reading. *Journal of Learning Disabilities, 27,* 276–286.

Treiman, R., Sotak, L., & Bowman, M. (2001). The role of letter names and letter sounds in connecting print to speech. *Memory and Cognition, 29,* 860–873.

Treiman, R., & Zukowski, A. (1996). Children's sensitivity to syllables, onsets, rimes, and phonemes. *Journal of Experimental Child Psychology, 61,* 193–215.

Tunmer, W. E., & Chapman, J. W. (1998). Language prediction skill, phonological recoding ability, and reading. In C. Hulme & R. M. Joshi (Eds.), *Reading and spelling: Development and disorders* (pp. 33–68). Mahwah, NJ: Erlbaum.

Tunmer, W. E., & Nicholson, T. (2011). The development and teaching of word recognition skill. In M. L. Kamil, P. D. Pearson, E. B. Moje, & P. P. Afflerbach (Eds.), *Handbook of reading research* (Vol. 4, pp. 405–431). New York: Routledge.

Turnbull, K. L. P., Bowles, R. P., Skibbe, L. E., Justice, L. M., & Wiggins, A. K. (2010). Theoretical explanations for preschoolers' lowercase alphabet knowledge. *Journal of Speech, Language, and Hearing Research, 53(6),* 1757–1768.

Valiandes, S. (2015). Evaluating the impact of differentiated instruction on literacy and reading in mixed ability classrooms: Quality and equity dimensions of education effectiveness. *Studies in Educational Evaluation, 45,* 17–26.

Vaughn, S., Denton, C. A., & Fletcher, J. M. (2010). Why intensive interventions are necessary for students with severe reading difficulties. *Psychology in the Schools, 47,* 432–444.

Vaughn, S., Linan-Thompson, S., & Hickman, P. (2003). Response to treatment as a means of identifying students with reading/learning disabilities. *Exceptional Children, 69(4),* 391–409.

Vellutino, F. R. (1979). *Dyslexia: Theory and research.* Cambridge, MA: MIT Press.

Vellutino, F. R., Fletcher, J. M., Snowling, M. J., & Scanlon, D. M. (2004). Specific reading disability (dyslexia): What have we learned in the past four decades? *Journal of Child Psychology and Psychiatry, 45(1),* 2–40.

Vellutino, F. R., & Scanlon, D. M. (2002). The interactive strategies approach to reading intervention. *Contemporary Educational Psychology, 27(4),* 573–635.

Vellutino, F. R., Scanlon, D. M., Sipay, E. R., Small, S. G., Pratt, A., Chen, R., & Denckla, M. B. (1996). Cognitive profiles of difficult-to-remediate and readily remediated poor readers: Early intervention as a vehicle for distinguishing between cognitive and experiential deficits as basic causes of specific reading disability. *Journal of Educational Psychology, 88(4),* 601–638.

Venezky, R. L. (1998). An alternative perspective on Success for All. *Advances in Educational Policy, 4,* 145–165.

Vygotsky, L. S. (1978). *Mind in society: The development of higher psychological processes.* Cambridge, MA: Harvard University Press.

Wagner, R. K., Torgesen, J. K., & Rashotte, C. (1994). The development of reading related phonological processing abilities: New evidence of bidirectional causality from a latent variable longitudinal study. *Developmental Psychology, 30,* 73–78.

Wanzek, J., Roberts, G., Al Otaiba, S., & Kent, S. C. (2014). The relationship of print reading in Tier I instruction and reading achievement for kindergarten students at risk of reading difficulties. *Learning Disability Quarterly, 37(3),* 148–160.

Wanzek, J., & Vaughn, S. (2008). Response to varying amounts of time in reading intervention for students with low response to intervention. *Journal of Learning Disabilities, 42*(2), 126–142.

Watts, S. (1995). Vocabulary instruction during reading lessons in six classrooms. *Journal of Reading Behavior, 27*(3), 399–424.

Wegerif, R., Mercer, N., & Dawes, L. (1999). From social interaction to individual reasoning: An empirical investigation of a possible socio-cultural model of cognitive development. *Learning and Instruction, 9*(6), 493–516.

Weinstein, C. F., & Mayer, R. F. (1986). The teaching of learning strategies. In M. C. Wittrock (Ed.), *Handbook of research on teaching* (pp. 315–327). New York: Macmillan.

Welsch, J. G. (2008). Playing within and beyond the story: Encouraging book-related pretend play. *The Reading Teacher, 62*(2), 138–147.

Whitehurst, G. J., Arnold, D. S., Epstein, J. N., Angell, A. L., Smith, M., & Fischel, J. E. (1994). A picture book reading intervention in day care and home for children from low-income families. *Developmental Psychology, 30*, 679–689.

Whitehurst, G. J., & Lonigan, C. J. (1998). Child development and emergent literacy. *Child Development, 68*, 848–872.

Wonder-McDowell, C., Reutzel, D. R., & Smith, J. A. (2011). Does instructional alignment matter?: Effects on struggling second graders' reading achievement. *Elementary School Journal, 112*(2), 259–279.

Wood, D., Bruner, J. S., & Ross, G. (1976). The role of tutoring in problem solving. *Journal of Child Psychology and Child Psychiatry, 17*(2), 89–100.

Wright, T. S., & Neuman, S. B. (2010). *Opportunities to learn vocabulary at school: The contribution of teachers.* Paper presented at the annual meeting of the National Reading Conference, Fort Worth, TX.

Yell, M. L., Shriner, J. G., & Katsiyannis, A. (2006). Individuals with Disabilities Education Improvement Act of 2004 and IDEA Regulations of 2006: Implications for educators, administrators, and teacher trainers. *Focus on Exceptional Children, 39*(1), 1–24.

Yopp, H. K. (1988). The validity and reliability of phonemic awareness tests. *Reading Research Quarterly, 23*, 159–199.

Yopp, H. K. (1995). Read-aloud books for developing phonemic awareness: An annotated bibliography. *The Reading Teacher, 48*(6), 538–542.

Yopp, H. K., & Yopp, R. H. (2009). Phonological awareness is child's play. *Young Children, 64*(1), 12–18.

Yuill, N., & Oakhill, J. (1991). *Children's problems in text comprehension.* Cambridge, UK: Cambridge University Press.

Ziegler, J. C., & Goswami, U. (2005). Reading acquisition, developmental dyslexia and skilled reading across languages: A psycholinguistic grain size theory. *Psychological Bulletin, 131*(1), 3–29.

Children's Books

Beech, L. W. (2003). *My bear.* New York: Scholastic.

Cameron, P. (1961). *"I can't," said the ant.* New York: Scholastic.

Carle, E. (1974). *All about Arthur (an absolutely absurd ape).* New York: Franklin-Watts.

Day, E. (1997). *Good dog Carl.* New York: Aladdin Paperbacks.

Dobeck, M. (1996). *Six fine fish* (Celebration Press Ready Readers). Parsippany, NJ: Modern Curriculum Press.

Dowd, N. (1996). *One bee got on the bus.* Parsippany, NJ: Modern Curriculum Press.

Gordon, J. (1991). *Six sleepy sheep.* New York: Puffin Books.

Hague, K. (1984). *Alphabears.* New York: Holt.

Hillert, M. (1963). *The three little pigs* (Modern Curriculum Press Beginning to Read Series). Upper Saddle River, NJ: Pearson Education.

Lauber, P. (1990). *An octopus is amazing.* New York: HarperCollins.

Lionni, L. (1963). *Swimmy.* New York: Knopf.

Logan, C. (1997). *Look closer.* Parsippany, NJ: Pearson Education.

Mark, A. (1997). *Monster mop* (Celebration Press Ready Readers). Parsippany, NJ: Modern Curriculum Press.

Minkoff, M. (1996). *Where is the Queen?* (Celebration Press Ready Readers). Parsippany, NJ: Modern Curriculum Press.

Pollock, P. (1996). *The turkey girl.* New York: Little, Brown.

Potter, B. (2002). *The tale of Peter Rabbit.* London: Penguin. (Original work published 1902)

Robinson, F. R. (1997). *Eggs!* (Celebration Press Ready Readers). Parsippany, NJ: Modern Curriculum Press.

Seuss, Dr. (1963). *Dr. Seuss's ABC.* New York: Random House.

Seuss, Dr. (1974). *There's a wocket in my pocket.* New York: Random House.

Shaw, N. E. (1986). *Sheep in a jeep.* New York: Houghton Mifflin.

Short, L. (1999). *Go to.* Jenison, MI: Short Books.

Spevack, J. (1997). *My room* (Celebration Press Ready Readers). Parsippany, NJ: Modern Curriculum Press.

Thomas, J. (2009). *Rhyming dust bunnies.* New York: Beach Lane Books.

Williams, M. (1922). *The velveteen rabbit.* New York: Knopf.

Index